To Fight the Mahrattas

SIEGE OF SASNI
DECEMBER 11TH, 1802 TO FEBRUARY 6TH, 1803

To Fight the Mahrattas
The Journal of an Officer of the
2nd Bengal Native Infantry
1802-1806

John Pester

To Fight the Mahrattas
The Journal of an officer of the
2nd Bengal Native Infantry
1802-1806
by John Pester

First published under the titles
War and Sport in India
1802-1806

Leonaur is an imprint
of Oakpast Ltd

Copyright in this form © 2009 Oakpast Ltd

ISBN: 978-1-84677-716-5 (hardcover)
ISBN: 978-1-84677-715-8 (softcover)

http://www.leonaur.com

Publisher's Notes

In the interests of authenticity, the spellings, grammar and place names used have been retained from the original editions.

The opinions of the authors represent a view of events in which he was a participant related from his own perspective, as such the text is relevant as an historical document.

The views expressed in this book are not necessarily those of the publisher.

Contents

Introduction	7
Attack and Capture of Camney (Khamni)	14
March from Shikoabad to Attack Sarssney	21
The Siege, Assault and Capture of Sarssney (Sasni)	27
In the Fort at Sarssney	52
Storm and Capture of Cachoura (Kachoura)	58
From Teteeah to Bareilly with the 3rd Native Cavalry	67
On Leave at Bareilly	76
Tiger Shooting near Bareilly	91
Social and Sporting Life at Bareilly	103
Bareilly to Futty Ghur, Mynpoorie, and Shikoabad	110
Assault and Capture of Buddown (Budaon)	115
In Cantonments at Shikoabad	119
March to Ali Ghur from Shikoabad	130
The Storming of Ali Ghur	139
Battle of Delhi (Putper Gunge)	152
Siege and Occupation of Agra	167
March from Agra to Gwalior	199
Siege of Gwalior	221
In Garrison, Fortress of Gwalior	251
From Gwalior to Bareilly	274
From Bareilly to Agra	289

With the Grand Army from Agra to Muttrah and Delhi	300
Siege and Capture of Dieg Fort	315
The Siege of Bhirtpore	345
In Pursuit of Scindiah	365
On Sick Leave	381
Journey from Bareilly to Calcutta by River	392
Calcutta to Prince of Wales Island (Penang) on Board the *Althea*	411
At Prince of Wales' Island (Penang) Waiting for a Ship	417
On Board the *Cumberland* to St. Helena	426
Island of St. Helena and Voyage Home	433

Introduction

The writer of this *Diary*, Lieutenant John Pester, was one of my Mother's uncles, and the original manuscript is with my cousin, Captain P. P. Phelps, of Littleton, Winchester, who kindly allowed me to have it copied. I have claimed the privilege of editing it not only as a relative, but also because of my close acquaintance with that part of India in which the scene is laid, for it happened that I was for many years employed as the Engineer of the Bhurtpore State, in the vicinity of which most of the action related took place.

The gallant officer who wrote the *Diary* was born in 1778, and sailed from England in 1801 to join the forces of the Honourable East India Company.

A brief review of the political aspect of India at that period may serve to bring the events narrated into historical perspective.

The Mahrattas were then the most formidable of all the native powers with whom the Company had been in contact. During the two previous centuries they had gradually extended their inroads into the territories of the decaying Mogul Empire until they had possessed themselves of several large provinces, while their armies, though often defeated, returned as often to ravage the land and to extort tribute throughout the greater part of India.

The English, whose main object had been to guard their own trade and domains in Bengal, Madras, and Bombay, had sometimes combined with other native states to repel them, but more frequently had been associated with them or with sections of their tribe in order to maintain a balance of power between the various conflicting parties in the turbulent arena of the interior.

The Directors of the Company were, however, unwilling to be drawn into responsibilities that seemed to be beyond their resources, and although as the result of Clive's success in arms the Emperor at Delhi in 1765 became subject to their control, yet when the Court and person of his successor had fallen into the hands of the Mahrattas the English had not been prepared to interfere, and the poor Emperor, whose eyes had been blinded when he had been taken captive by a Rohilla chief, was now dependent on the protection of Scindia, the great Mahratta prince of Gwalior, who, after rescuing him from the Rohilla, seated him again on the Imperial throne. The Mogul Viceroys still owned the suzerainty of the Emperor, but were virtually independent of the Delhi Court. One of the most important of these was the Vizier of Oudh, who since Clive's time had been subject to the political control of the Company, and whose province adjoining Bengal was protected by their troops at his expense.

At the beginning of the 18th century Lord Mornington had then finally crushed the aggressive power of Mysore in the Deccan (or South of India), and was able to turn his attention to the protection of Oudh, the security of which was threatened not only by an Afghan invasion but also by Mahratta intrigue, negotiations for an alliance with Scindia having failed.

It was resolved, therefore, to reorganize the corrupt administration of the Viceroyalty, and for that purpose the Governor-General insisted on the disbandment of the *vizier's* useless troops, and on the cession of the provinces of Corah, Allahabad, and Rohilkund, in order to provide from their revenues for the maintenance of an efficient force.

These were the "Ceded Provinces" referred to in the opening chapters of the *Diary*. They were annexed in lieu of the annual contribution hitherto levied, and the governor-general's brother, Lord Henry Wellesley, was appointed to govern them at Bareilly. Two of the provinces, Corah and Allahabad, had been an appanage of the Emperor, secured to him by Clive's treaty, but this assignment was revoked when the Emperor became dependent upon Scindia, who, moreover, had sequestered them, but had been prevented by our troops from occupying them. Rohilkund had been conquered by the English in Warren Hastings' time, and had been conveyed by treaty to the charge of the *vizier*. When the provinces were ceded the land was held in places by local chiefs, whose strong forts defied both the revenue collector and the plundering Mahratta hordes. The forts of Sarssney and Cachoura and others which, as described in the Diary, made a desperate resistance to our occupation, were probably held by Jâts, a martial tribe that had sometimes repulsed the Mahrattas, but were usually either allied to them or forced to pay them tribute.

The Jâts of Bhurtpore, united by feudal bonds under enterprising chiefs, had carved out a dominion from the Agra province, and had become a formidable military state, whose aid we accepted in the campaign against Scindia, which followed the occupation of the ceded provinces.

The Mahratta princes were often at war amongst themselves, as was the case in 1801 between Scindia of Gwalior and Holkar of Indore, and it was owing to their dissensions and to the instability of their policy that all the Mahratta leaders were in turn ultimately brought to terms.

The tactics by which the Mahrattas had best succeeded in war were those adapted to the use of immense numbers of mobile light horse, which, obtaining their supplies by plunder, attacked the communications of the enemy and retreated in face of a more compact force in order to draw it into an exposed position. But the superiority of well-equipped and disciplined troops in the decisive battles fought both by the English and by the French during the previous century had so impressed Scindia that he now maintained a large army highly trained by French instructors, together with most formidable artillery, while Holkar, jealous of Scindia's power, was not slow to follow his example. When, therefore, the governor-general found it necessary in 1803 to protect our territories and those of our allies against the growing Mahratta menace, the English were obliged to mobilize the largest armies that had ever been employed by them in India, the Company's seasoned native and European troops being supplemented by British infantry and cavalry, led by officers of the King.

Scindia having declined a peaceful settlement, General Wellesley conducted a campaign against him and his allies in the Deccan, and by a series of famous victories completely crushed their strength in that region, so that our feudatory, the Nizam of Hyderabad, was secured in his dominion, and the Mahratta sovereign, the Peshwah, whom we were supporting against the nominee of Scindia, was seated under our control on the throne of Poona. The great power of Scindia in Hindustan (or Upper India), however, remained until General Lake's brilliant campaign, which is described in the Diary, had resulted in the expulsion of the Mahrattas from the Mogul capitals of Delhi and Agra, and in the reduction of Gwalior, Scindia's almost impregnable stronghold.

Holkar meanwhile took no part against us, rejoicing in the discomfiture of his rival, but when peace with Scindia had been concluded Holkar at once took the offensive, and was greatly encouraged by the failure of a detachment despatched into his country under the command of the Honourable Colonel Monson. His disastrous retreat, occasioned by want of supplies and of anticipated support, made a profound impression throughout India, and was followed by the war of 1804, the events of which are fully described in the *Diary*.

The failure in this campaign to achieve decisive results after a heavy sacrifice of life and of dividends led to the recall of Lord Wellesley, and Lord Cornwallis was sent out for a second term as Governor-General, with instructions to restore to the Mahratta princes the provinces that had been set free from their yoke. Lord Cornwallis, however, died before this intention could be fully effected, and owing to the protests of Lord Lake the Union flag was not lowered from the walls of Delhi and Agra.

The motives which caused the Bhurtpore Rajah to break his treaty with us when Holkar claimed his support are not difficult to understand, nor were they entirely unjustified from his point of view by the sequel, particularly as our politicians at home withdrew our support from those who had been on our side, and as in the case of the Bûndi state, abandoned them to Holkar's vengeance.

The earthen ramparts of Bhurtpore, which stand almost perfect at the present day, are four and a quarter miles around, about fifty feet high, and nearly two hundred feet thick at the base, furnished with bastions and cunningly guarded gateways, the whole encircled by a deep outer ditch. The Jâts are expert irrigators, and were able to inundate the land surrounding the fortress and to fill the ditch with water. It was this method of defence that foiled the desperate assaults of Lord Lake's brave army. The reservoirs and sluices used for the purpose were in my charge when I was at Bhurtpore. The beautiful garden-palaces of Deeg were not much injured by the siege, and remain, perhaps, the finest examples of workmanship in stone to be found in India.

I have visited the battlefield of Laswari. The village, which is now called Naswâri, is in the Ulwar State. The mounds where the slain were buried are still to be seen, and a shot hole made by one of Lord Lake's guns in the wall of a mosque had just been repaired at the time of my visit. The fame of Lord Lake (*Leek Sahib*) survives in story, song, and picture throughout the land of his campaigns.

In editing the *Diary* I have been obliged, in order to reduce the bulk, to omit more than a third part of the original, and if it still appears too copious I may be excused because of the special local interest the detailed record will have to present and future residents in the places described. I have not altered the spelling of Indian words, which no doubt represents fairly the pronunciation of the time. This is often more correct than that obtained by transliteration from the vernacular, which method, moreover, leads to terrible distortion by those who do not know it.

A few words should be said about the water-colour picture,

a reduced photograph of which forms the frontispiece to this volume. This was very kindly presented to me by Miss Parsons, of Misterton, Crewkerne, to whom it had been bequeathed by a relative of mine. It is in perfect condition, and it affords an unique record, having been painted on the scene in 1803. The artillery in action are wearing blue coats with yellow facings, white cross-belts and breeches, and tall black hats with white plumes, and queues. Infantry in red coats, white breeches with dark overalls, hats with black badges in front. All officers in red sashes and with queues.

The diarist retired as a lieutenant-colonel in 1826, and in the record of his services it is stated that except for sick leave he was never absent from duty.

He married a Miss Phelips, of Montacute House, Somerset, who accompanied him to India in 1811. He died in 1856 at Millbrook, near Southampton. Amongst his friends in retirement were Sir Philip Blair, formerly the colonel of his regiment, who lived to be 83, and Sir Henry White, who left my great-uncle £500 in remembrance of his assistance in the siege of Gwalior. I have met an officer who well remembers that Lieutenant Pester saved the life of his father, who was left wounded on the field, and I hope that the publication of this *Diary* may interest many whose family names are represented amongst those mentioned, although the severity of the service was such that not many of those engaged could have left direct descendants. In the 1st Battalion of the 2nd Native Infantry out of eighteen officers only three were left fit for duty at the close of the 1804 campaign.

The sentiments confided to the *Diary*, some of which are omitted, reveal a heart fervent with patriotism but not proof against the more tender susceptibilities. It was an age when patriotism was a prevailing spirit, Great Britain being then an island kingdom prepared to stand at bay against invasion, while the foundations of an Empire were being laid by the enterprise and fortitude of her sons. Not only the military and naval commanders, but also the statesmen and civil governors were held in deep regard by all ranks, and the nobility of the veteran Lord

Cornwallis in accepting office a second time on a mission of peace evoked the admiration of the war-hardened subaltern no less than the glorious death of Nelson.

It is no longer an age of sentiment, but it is still the tradition of our race to press to the front in sport and in war, and respect will not be wanting for this glimpse at the life of the gallant Britons who shot and hunted in India in the early days of the last century, and who trained their brave native soldiers to follow them to death or victory.

J. A. Devenish,
Formerly Executive Engineer,
Public Works Department of India.

CHAPTER 1

Attack and Capture of Camney (Khamni)

August 28th.—In consequence of the refractory conduct of some *zemindars* who had been committing sad depredations and setting the laws of government at defiance, I was ordered to march with my grenadiers this evening. My friend Marsden expressed a wish to accompany me, and waited on Colonel Blair, who readily consented.

At four in the afternoon I paraded my men, and having examined their arms, flints, ammunition, bayonets, etc., and received my instructions from the commanding officer, we marched off before five o'clock. Owing to the very heavy fall of rain the country was completely inundated, and at many places the water was nearly up to the soldiers' waists. This rendered our moving very tedious, and it was pitch dark before we reached the village of Jellalabad. Most providentially no rain fell, so that our arms and ammunition were dry. It was so exceedingly dark that I was very apprehensive the guides would mistake the route. I was the more anxious on this account, being very desirous of attacking them if possible at daybreak.

We had thirty-two long miles to march, and not a moment's time was there to spare. The men were in the highest spirits, and waded through dirt, mire and water with the greatest cheerfulness. No track was visible, and our march was over an open plain without any other direction than now and then a solitary tree or a few bushes. But my guides were men of the country, and excellent fellows.

At four in the morning we arrived at Assnayder after incessant marching of twelve hours nearly; at this place I received information that Camney (where the rebels after whom I was marching were posted) was not more than two short miles distant from me. I was told that they were in force of at least five hundred men, and that they had received intimation of my approach. I halted there for about half-an-hour till day showed some symptoms of breaking, and during that time I was favoured with a most insulting message from the chief of the rebels, who had heard of my arrival. The purport of this communication was that "they had heard of my approach, and knew well the strength of my party; that if I would face about and march quietly back, they would not molest me, but that if I advanced a single step towards their post they would not allow a single man of us to live to tell the story!"

By way of completing the insult they told me that "we were fine looking fellows in our red clothes, but that our coats before sunset should be converted into shoes for them." Nothing could tend among the natives to convey more contempt than this last compliment. I addressed my men, told them the purport of the message from the enemy, and added that it remained with them to prove how far they merited such a reception. As I expected, they were all in great wrath, and promised to convince the enemy of his mistake. About five we came in sight of the village, and saw the flashes of musketry along the walls. I galloped on with one of my guides, and ascertained the situation of the two gates which led into the village; to do this, I went so near that they saw me, and fired on me.

August 29th.—A gun was what I wanted to assist in opening the gates, but I determined at once to commence the attack, and at least to make a vigorous effort before I asked any kind of reinforcements, for by doing so I should avoid comments which I knew many were always ready to pass on those occasions on any who were employed on them, and it also was the first command I had ever been placed in, and the opportunity was not to be lost. As soon as Marsden and the company came up, I pointed out the north gate to him, and, advancing the left division of the grenadiers, I ordered him to move on and attack the gateway, but not to fire a shot till he arrived at it.

At the same moment I placed myself at the head of the right grand division, and advanced to storm the principal gate. Ensign Marsden had a short detour to make, and I regulated the advance of my party, so as for us to arrive at our respective points of attack as nearly as possible at the same period. The moment we got within reach of their shot they commenced a very heavy and destructive fire of musketry, and Ensign Marsden, I observed, was received in a like manner. Many of my men dropped, and the shot flew very thick. My orders were strictly attended to, and the enemy's fire was not returned till we reached the sorties, when I ordered the rear division of my party to fire on the enemy, whilst with the other division I forced the gates, which with the greatest difficulty we happily effected. The instant we entered the village my men were like so many tigers let loose, and every man that opposed us was either shot or bayoneted.

The enemy now appeared absolutely panic struck; they gave way and began to fly in all quarters, some making their escape over the walls into the country, but I had not long been in the villages before I discovered a round tower pierced with loopholes, which commanded almost every street in the place; here a party of the most resolute had retired, and began to annoy us much by their fire. This was no season for delay, and I soon saw that unless we could possess ourselves of this tower the place could not be held without great loss to us. I collected about thirty men, and, with my *subadar* (black captain), I rushed on at their head to assault the post. In passing up the street we were completely exposed to their fire, and four of my grenadiers were shot at my heels.

We succeeded in getting so close under them that they could not fire upon us, but the tower gate was so strong that we were unable to force it. Marsden also succeeded in getting in to the village, and joined me here. I fixed on two good men, and told them if they could procure pickaxes and spades from the neighbouring village I would promote them—the enemy heard that we proposed digging them out, and instantly threw their muskets and swords from the loopholes, and, begging for mercy, declared they had surrendered.

Their conduct had been such, and so many of my men had fallen by them, that at first I was not inclined to listen to them, and had determined on making an example of them upon the spot, but as at the moment they were defenceless, I promised not then to take their lives, and we were instantly let in, and bound them all hand and foot. We now fired the village in every quarter, and many of the enemy who had secreted themselves were destroyed. By our best calculation nearly two hundred of them fell in this affair, and we had reason to conjecture that in future they would treat us with more respect. They knew us not, as this was the first time that a shot had been fired in the Ceded Provinces, and we taught them to know that they had a different description of troops to deal with from those which had often been employed against them by the *vizier* who ceded the country to us.

As soon as the place was completely in ashes, and we had collected our own wounded men, and secured the prisoners, we drew off again towards the village of Assnayder. We had not proceeded far when a countryman came running up and assured me that all the villages in the neighbourhood had armed and were coming down with those who had escaped out of the place during the attack and after we got in, with a determination to rescue my prisoners or perish themselves in the attempt. I instantly ordered the sergeant of the Guard who had charge of the prisoners to put them immediately to death if we should be attacked, and then formed my men on an advantageous spot of ground to wait their arrival. Our fire had been very heavy in the morning, and on examining the pouches I found that the greater part of my ammunition expended. Some of the men had not more than two and three rounds each remaining.

I, therefore, resolved to charge them as soon as they should approach. In this situation we remained under arms for a full hour, but no enemy made his appearance! My men were much exhausted; it was now nearly eleven in the morning, and we had been positively marching and engaged full sixteen hours, and no troops under the heavens ever bore fatigue more patiently or executed their duty with more cheerful alacrity and gallantry than did the Grenadiers of the 2nd on this occasion.

As soon as we reached Assnayder I ordered a proportion of them to cook their dinner, and the inhabitants of this place supplied them with rice and everything else that their village afforded, more, I fancy, from dread of us than any good wishes towards us. To Marsden and myself they brought eggs, milk, and a very fine kid which we had for breakfast, and about three we took a kid chop and a bottle of claret each (which Major Collins had very kindly sent after us). This we enjoyed much, though Marsden fell asleep the moment we had swallowed our wine.

My servants had brought a camel and the upper fly of my tent, but we dined under a tree, and did not require it. I procured litters from the village, and sent off my wounded men for Shikoabad with a small guard. As many of our killed as we could collect we buried here, and at five in the evening we paraded again, and marched for Jellalabad, where we arrived about eleven at night, in such weather as I scarcely ever experienced.

About midway between Assnayder and Jellalabad it came on to rain in torrents, accompanied with the most awful claps of thunder and flashes of lightning. I took post in the ruins of an old fort, and made the best disposition I could to defend myself in case they should still entertain any idea of trying to release my prisoners, or of attacking us by means of a forced march in the night. We pitched the fly of my tent under the lee of an old bastion; in it Marsden, with a guard and the prisoners, took post. I was too anxious to sleep, notwithstanding I had been so many hours without it.

August 30th.—I went the rounds myself every hour, and sent patrols the intermediate half-hours, and in this way we passed the night, which continued throughout extremely boisterous and raining. At five we marched again for Shikoabad, and soon after daybreak met several of the officers riding out to meet us; they had heard of my letter to Colonel Blair of our affair and the result.

At seven we arrived in cantonments, beating the Grenadiers' March. All the men in wonderful spirits considering the extreme fatigue they had borne not a man of us had taken our clothes off since the 28th in the morning, nor had I closed my eyes since that time, and had I not experienced it I could not have supposed that it was in the power of men to bear up against such laborious exertions for such a length of time. I dismissed my men on their own parade, and waited immediately on Colonel Blair, who received me in a most flattering manner, and told me that we had done our duty in a manner very much to our credit, and that he should have great pleasure in forwarding my details to the commander-in-chief.

Marsden and myself breakfasted with the colonel, and afterwards retired to our own bungalows to get a little rest, of which we stood in much need. (Poor Marsden never recovered this fatigue, and died soon afterwards. He was shot through the jacket on this occasion).

In the evening I dined at Plumer's, when there was a large party, and as soon as the cloth was removed I fell asleep in my chair and slept undisturbed till nearly eleven o'clock, after which I took my bottle of claret and returned in my *palanquin*.

August 31st.—Slept till ten this morning, Weston and MacGregor *tiffed* with me. Two of my wounded men died this evening in the hospital, one had received a ball which carried away his under jaw completely, the other was wounded in the leg; it mortified and killed him.

A subscription was circulated this morning for the benefit of the widows and orphans of the men who fell in the attack at Camney with me, and it was very liberally filled. Every officer of the corps subscribed to it, and it was the means of affording them something handsome. I prevailed on Colonel Blair to put the son of one man upon the strength of the corps, which he most readily did, and soldier's full pay was drawn for him. The father of this poor boy was shot within a sword's length of me. I was firing a musket into a thatch that communicated with the tower in the village. To do this I was obliged to step out from under the loopholes, and expose myself to their fire within.

Whilst in the act of firing the piece, one of the enemy within was seen by my *subadar* to be levelling at me, and the *subadar* most gallantly stepped in and gave me a violent thrust against the wall (he had not time to speak to me) which saved me, and the soldier, whose son I petitioned to have put upon the strength of the corps, received the shot through his head which was intended for me. The poor fellow fell stone dead, and as his piece fell the bayonet tore my boot without cutting me at all.

We all dined with Colonel Blair this evening, and passed a very gay day; cards and singing, and the party did not break up till a very late hour. It was nearly one before I reached my bungalow.

CHAPTER 2

March from Shikoabad to Attack Sarssney

November 24th.—This forenoon orders were issued for us to march tomorrow morning, and in the course of the day Captain Drummond, with five companies of the 11th Regiment from Etawah, marched in to occupy the cantonments in our absence. Left my Mahratter mare in care of Lieutenant Heysham, to whom also I gave the use of my bungalow whilst I should remain in the field.

Prepared everything this evening for marching, and as we were in expectation of a tedious campaign, I carried with me a good stock of wines. Our 2nd Battalion, with battering cannon from Futty Ghur, joined us today, and we learnt that a further reinforcement would meet us at Khauss Gunge.

November 25th.—The battalion paraded this morning at daybreak, and we formed a junction with the 2nd Battalion and the train of artillery about one mile to the westward of our cantonments, and at seven moved off from the right, my grenadiers leading the column. Our line of march from Shikoabad was south-west, leaving the village of Mocanpore to our right. The country today which we marched over I was thoroughly acquainted with, having very often beat every inch of it for game.

We encamped about ten o'clock about eleven miles from the cantonments of Shikoabad, and in the course of the evening some messengers of Colonel Blair's came in with intelligence that the fort of Phurrah, against which we were immediately marching with our present forces, was preparing to defend it, and our orders were to attack it immediately if they showed the smallest disposition to be hostile. A large party of us dined with Colonel Blair this evening; among others we had the commanding officer of artillery, Captain Shipton, and Wood (of the Engineers).

November 26th.—We paraded this morning at half-past six, and just as the detachment was marching off a post came in, and by it I received a letter from my friend Welstead, full of England, dear England. I was on another kind of an excursion, and within a short distance of an enemy. About eight o'clock we arrived within sight of Phurrah, which appeared a strong and lofty place—with our glasses we plainly saw them on the works, cutting embrasures, and mounting fresh cannon the walls were crowded with soldiers, and everything wore the appearance of determined resistance.

We pitched our camp about gunshot distance from the eastern face, and a summons was immediately sent in requiring the surrender of the place at discretion, and giving them at the same time to understand the consequences of the slightest opposition. Two howitzers were at the same period run down to a garden in our front, ready to commence throwing shells into the tower if they made any opposition.

After some messengers from both parties, they at last agreed to surrender the garrison to the British; the troops were allowed to march out with their arms and private property, and at three in the evening Sinclair, Livesey, Parr and myself marched in with the four grenadier companies of our regiment, and took possession. Posted guards at the different gates, and reported to Colonel Blair our being in complete possession of all the gates and works. In the tower we found some few armed men, but these we soon dispersed, and ordered them into the country. Remained all night under arms in the garrison and town.

November 27th.—This morning a small party was ordered in to relieve the grenadiers, and we marched out and rejoined the detachment in camp. In the afternoon Cumberlege and myself took a ride into the country, which we found extremely rich and well cultivated, too much so for game, and there seemed to be very little in the neighbourhood of Phurrah.

I was on picquet this evening, Weston, Grant and MacGregor dined with me at the picquet, and did not leave my tent till nearly twelve.

November 28th.—At sunrise this morning the general beat, and the assembly soon after, when we moved off by the right. With my picquet and one six-pounder I formed the advance guard. In the course of our march we passed through some villages belonging to the Mahrattas, the inhabitants of which did not receive us with quite so much cordiality as those of villages immediately in our own Provinces. At ten o'clock we encamped about two miles to the southward of the village of Cumsaine, on the edge of a very fine jungle, which abounded with game.

After breakfasting Cumberlege and myself took out horses, spears and guns, and went into the cover. The grass was too strong to see a hog, though their traces were very visible in many places, and in every open spot we discovered where they had recently been rooting. We shot a great quantity of peacocks, black and grey partridges, quails and two brace of hares on the skirts of the cover. Returned late to dinner at Sinclair's, where we had a very jolly party, all in high spirits and good humour.

November 29th.—Camp near Kondroo. This morning we marched at the same hour, and in the same order as yesterday. The inhabitants showed us every respectful attention.

Encamped about ten o'clock in a very highly cultivated country on the borders of the ceded Province.

After taking our breakfast Cumberlege and myself rode to a cover in the vicinity of our camp, and killed a great quantity of game of various kinds. Colonel Blair and all the officers of our battalion and some of the 2nd dined with me this evening, and we did not break up till a late hour.

November 30th.—We marched off this morning at sunrise; the morning was quite sharp, and we began pretty seriously to find the cold weather setting in. Our march today was through some very strong forests, in which the track was barely wide enough to admit of our guns and tumbrils passing on them. We had quite a romantic march, and the drums and fifes were playing quick marches or lively dances nearly the whole way. At nine we came in sight of the town of Etah, under the walls of which we encamped.

The *rajah* of this place immediately came to our camp on a visit to Colonel Blair.

The town of Etah to the eastward is surrounded by a fine lake, and on it I was very happy to observe a great quantity of ducks, teal, and various kinds of wild fowls; after a hasty breakfast at my tent Cumberlege and self took our guns, and had a famous morning's sport. Snipe we found in great abundance upon the borders of the lake, and for them we left the ducks.

By four in the evening we had killed between us twenty-three brace of snipe, and this was one of the prettiest day's sport I had seen in India or in any other part of the world. On our return we killed four brace of teal and three ducks; of the latter we might have killed any quantity we chose.

This being the anniversary of Saint Andrew, a day always kept by Scotchmen, we dined at MacKaulay's, to whom we had sent all the game killed in the morning. We mustered very strong this evening, as nearly all the Scotch in our camp were invited, and also many of us.

We paid them the compliment of pushing the bottle handsomely, and the whole party was pretty high when we separated at one in the morning.

December 1st.—Camp near Zodaicnow. We took our departure from the town of Etah and the fine lake there at daybreak this morning; as we approached the banks of the Collah Nhuddy (Black River) we found the covers and jungles through which we moved swarming with game, and on the line of march the deer and hogs were perpetually crossing us. The peacocks were also extremely numerous. It was ten o'clock when we commenced pitching our camp on a delightful spot of ground, nearly surrounded by low jungles.

Cumberlege and myself swallowed our breakfast, and set off instantly to shoot. We had not far to go for game; close in the vicinity of the camp, and not three hundred yards from the picquets, we found a herd of hogs, but owing to the height of the grass we found it in vain to ride them. We penetrated the cover, and killed deer, *florikin, niel ghy* (blue wild cows), partridges, hares and quails in great abundance, with which we well loaded our servants before we returned to camp. Remained out till nearly sunset, and galloped furiously back, leaving our people with the guns and dogs, to find their way after us as well as they could.

December 2nd.—The detachment marched at six this morning, and soon after sunrise we reached the banks of the Collah Nhuddy and crossed over the bridge near the cantonment of Khauss Gunge, which we reached at nine o'clock. I had the rear guard today, and consequently did not arrive till nearly an hour after the line was up.

At Khauss Gunge we found Major Ball encamped with a battalion of the 8th National Infantry, a battalion of the 12th and four companies of the 2nd Battalion of ours.

The 3rd Regiment of Cavalry from Bareilly was also attached to us, and it was conjectured that with our whole force consisting of four battalions and a regiment of cavalry, we should march immediately against the strong fort of Sarssney; the *rajah* (or prince) of which had refused to accede to the established rules of our government, and had determined on disputing the point with us, and neither to surrender his forts or disband his troops. Colonel Blair, on our arrival here, received the command over from Major Ball, and assumed the direction of the whole.

December 7th.—Halted at Khauss Gunge since the 2nd, most of which time I passed in shooting with Cumberlege and Richardson of our 2nd Battalion. Near the cantonment of Khauss Gunge, a little to the westward, we found hares, peafowl, quail, black and grey partridges in great abundance, and never returned without filling our bags! We left Khauss Gunge at sunrise this morning.

We were in full expectation of falling in with some of the Sarssney Rajah's Cavalry during the march, but in this we were disappointed; there was a report that they had marched from Sarssney purposely to annoy us on the march. About ten o'clock we encamped at Secundra. I was on the rear guard this morning, and we got a pretty good grilling before we came up with the pack and magazine in the rear. The officers of our Battalion dined with me this evening.

December 9th.—The detachment halted a day, supposed to wait the result of a summons said to have been sent to the *rajah.*

Some of the enemy's spies were detected this forenoon in our camp, and instantly confined, Wemyss and Cunynghame joined us today; the latter as Collector of the District, and possessing full powers from the Governor General in Council, to treat and settle letters with all the *rajahs* in this part of the ceded provinces.

At three this afternoon Wemyss and self went out with our greyhounds, and found hares innumerable; our dogs were soon knocked up, and then sent into camp for our guns and shot a great number. Wemyss rode my grey horse this evening, and I an Arab of his.

We dined with Cunynghame (who married my friend and shipmate, Miss Grier) and did justice to his claret.

December 10th.—We marched off by the left at daylight this morning, and encamped without the smallest molestation on the march at ten o'clock, within sight of the Bidgie Ghur, one of the Sarssney *rajah's* forts.

Chapter 3

The Siege, Assault and Capture of Sarssney (Sasni)

December 11th.—This morning the general beat at five and the assembly at six o'clock. Soon after *reveillé* beating, we saw the fort of Sarssney and encamped before it, on the eastern face, about ten. The walls we could perceive were covered with fighting men, and with our glasses we could count a great number of heavy guns mounted on the ramparts.

A large body of cavalry and infantry were also encamped on the glacis of the fort, which appeared to be strong and very lofty. A messenger of the *rajah's* came into our camp this morning; the result we knew not. I dined with Cunynghame this evening, who told me that we should certainly have to fight this *rajah*.

December 23rd.—Ever since the day of our arrival the negotiation had been firmly carried on, in the meantime our pioneers and troops had been daily employed in collecting materials for our batteries.

It was now discovered that the delay had been caused by frivolous excuses on the part of the *rajah*, whose grand point was to collect supplies and troops from his other forts. At sunset this evening fourteen companies of infantry paraded in order to dislodge the enemy from two villages in front and there to establish ourselves as at a convenient distance to commence our approaches. I dined at Cunynghame's on cold beef at four o'clock, and then, as Cunynghame observed, "went down to be shot at." We gained the posts with a trifling loss. My Company and Captain W—— of our corps were pushed on to a grove in front and a party of pioneers under Lieutenant Bales with us to assist in covering us in. We instantly formed working parties of them and the soldiers, and at daybreak our trenches were completed after as hard a night's fagging as I ever knew.

December 24th.—We remained snug in our works till about the middle of the day, when very suddenly a smart fire of musketry commenced from a field of corn within musket shot distance of my post. In case of an attack we were ordered to defend the post to the last extremity and a party was ordered out from the village in our rear, which dislodged the enemy. It was evident by the numerous efforts they had made to reconnoitre us in the grove that they entertained a design to dislodge us, concluding from the confined space of our trench that our party must be small, and in this they were not mistaken, nor were we so in our expectations that they would attack us.

About two o'clock a tremendous fire of cannon suddenly opened upon our trench, and at the same moment about five hundred of the enemy rushed out sword in hand from a very high field of corn upon our flank. I saw that their intention was to attempt to carry the trench by assault, and instantly ordered my own company not to fire a shot without orders from me, at the same time I stepped out of the trench, and went to the officer commanding the other company, and entreated him to reserve his fire till the enemy should be close upon us, when every shot would tell. I am sorry to observe that I did not find this officer in a situation much to his credit.

The cannon shot, which came in showers about the trench, and the crashing of the trees over his head, torn by the shot, seemed to have scared him not a little, and he exclaimed that if "I did not come into the trench I should be killed," taking special care himself at the same time to keep very close to the bottom of it. I am convinced that from the time the guns opened on us he had not once looked over the parapet, nor did he at that moment seem to know that the enemy were within four hundred yards of us. I then gave his men the orders I had my own, and returned to my post.

Our soldiers received them with the greatest coolness and gallantry, and we repulsed them with great slaughter. The fire from the garrison, which had ceased when they saw their troops closing with us, to avoid destroying their own people, seemed, if possible, to redouble on seeing their failure. Numerous cannon shot came through the embankment and killed our men, and I had many very narrow escapes this day myself. Their fire from the fort was well directed, which, considering the small distance we were from them was not at all extraordinary.

I was much pleased to hear how coolly some of the old soldiers addressed and encouraged the less experienced.

My company of grenadiers on this, as on every other occasion in which I had been employed with them, behaved as well as men could do, and it was not without much difficulty that I could restrain them from quitting their trenches to follow the enemy, which it would have been highly improper to have allowed; for had they succeeded in drawing us upon the plain under the fire of the fort the slaughter must have been great, and without the possibility of effecting anything to our advantage.

The fire from the garrison commenced on the left post at the same period it did on us, but the nature of the ground would not admit of their making a sally then, and their whole efforts were, therefore, directed against our two companies!

To do the enemy justice, they behaved very gallantly, and came shouting on, sword in hand, in a most determined manner, but our well directed fire of musketry gave them a check which they could not recover, and their retreat was equally as precipitate as their advance. Their fire of cannon did not cease till five in the evening, and Major Ball, the field officer of the day, came to visit our post and to ascertain our loss, at the same time he gave us great credit and assured us that he should report the "meritorious conduct" of the two companies in the grove to the commanding officer.

Everything was now become perfectly silent, and about

half-an-hour after the evening had set in we were relieved after twenty-four hours' sharp service; trenching all the night, and engaged on skirmishing the greater part of the day.

I reached the lines, and got to my tent about eight o'clock; several random shots passed over us during the time of the relief, but we sustained no loss on our march back to camp.

The remaining companies of our battalion on duty at the different posts were relieved at the same time that I was, and we all met to dine at MacGregor's tent, where was passed a very jolly evening, and fought the day over again.

January 1st.—1803. Nothing particular occurred in camp since we broke ground on the 24th December. The trenches today were widened down to the first parallel, sufficiently to admit the battering guns. The approaches quite up to the spot intended for the battery were lined out, and strong working parties of soldiers employed during the nights. We had, daily, men killed and wounded.

The approaches having been completed and the battery erected, the eighteen-pounders were brought down from camp this evening.

The twelve-pounders and howitzers were also placed in the enfilading battery, and the guns sent into the six-pounder battery on the left of the Grand Battery. I was on duty in the trenches this evening, and we anxiously waited the break of day to witness the effect of our shot on the ramparts.

January 4th.—Morning came, and our eighteens immediately opened on a curtain between two bastions directly in our front. The twelve-pounder battery at the grove, which raked the enemy's works on the eastern face, opened its fire at the same time, and a smart fire from the three six-pounders was directed against some guns of the enemy on the upper ramparts. We continued battering with little cessation the whole of this day, and pretty clearly ascertained that the ramparts of the upper and lower forts were exceedingly well cemented and came down very sparingly. To me it appeared that our Grand Battery was at too great a distance from the object against which our fire was directed, and older and more experienced soldiers than myself were of the same opinion. The enemy returned a very brisk fire from every gun they could bring to bear upon us, and we lost some men in the batteries and trenches. We were relieved this evening an hour after sunset. All the officers of our battalion dined with me.

January 7th—Since the opening of our batteries on the 4th nothing material occurred. Our fire had been constant, and very heavy both on the upper and lower forts, and at the twelve and six pounder batteries our artillery had not been less active in endeavouring to dismount the enemy's guns and enfilading their works.

I was on duty this day at the right post in the grove; the branches of the trees there were now completely cut to pieces by the enemy's shot, and some of the trees destroyed entirely.

An unpleasant accident happened while Weston and myself were in the enfilading battery this day at noon. Lieutenant Bayles, commanding the guns, was endeavouring to dismount a fresh gun which the enemy had brought to annoy our post, and which had killed and wounded several of our men. Bayles was standing upon the parapet to see the effect of a gun which he had taken great pains to lay for that of the enemy; at this moment the soldier on the lookout called "Shot," poor Bayles leaped from the parapet into the battery, and by endeavouring to avoid the shot he unfortunately lost his life; one of the embrasures of the battery was masked with fascines immediately in front of which he jumped, and the shot at the same instant came directly through the embrasure and took away both his thighs.

It was a shocking sight, a fine young officer, possessing an uncommon degree of spirit and enterprise, so dreadfully wounded. We lost no time in putting him on a litter and sending him to camp, where he soon expired. Bayles had the direction of the pioneers employed with the working party the first night we broke ground at the grove, and although we had seldom met before, we got intimately acquainted on that occasion. Sergeant-

Major Lane, of the artillery, a man exceedingly lamented, and one of the finest fellows I ever saw, was killed by a cannon shot in the Grand Battery this morning. He was unfortunately sitting on the trails of a gun, and a shot came in at the embrasure and cut him asunder. We had daily many killed and wounded.

A battalion of the 12th Regiment relieved our post at eight this evening.

January 9th.—This evening our battalion went down for a four and twenty hours' spell in the trenches at the left post, and we had been regularly on that duty every other night, since the commencement of the siege.

The lower breach appeared much shattered, but there seemed a great deal yet to be done to render the upper breach practicable. Our fire was now principally directed against the upper rampart, which was uncommonly strong; something like a complete mound of earth, in which the shot seemed to bury themselves with little effect, and it came down very slowly.

January 10th.— During the night we had a heavy fall of rain, which made the water nearly knee deep in the trenches. Owing to the flat situation of the ground about us, it was impossible to hit upon any plan to draw it off, so that we stood up to our knees in mud and water all this day, with a scorching sun beating upon our heads, which made it not very pleasant, especially as we could get no rest, and we had been all night on our legs. It was impossible to sit down even, in the trenches, and a man could not step out of them, but with a certainty of being shot from the ramparts of the fort.

A redoubt was this day thrown up about one hundred and fifty yards from the first parallel, and two six-pounders put into it; it was named "Parker's Redoubt," as an officer of that name constructed it. The 2nd Battalion of our regiment relieved us at the usual hour of the relief this evening, and we got to camp at eight.

January 11th.—Being off duty this morning, Wemyss and myself injudiciously rode a couple of miles in the rear of our camp, with the greyhounds—this frolic was attended with the imminent risk of our lives, as the enemy had constantly strong parties of horse patrolling in the neighbourhood of our camp, with a view of cutting off supplies. We found plenty of hares among the young wheat, and were not long in killing two brace and a half, and a brace of jackals; the latter afforded us excellent sport before a brace of Persian greyhounds, which were very fierce and powerful, and exactly calculated for that game.

Our horses were completely knocked up, but we returned unmolested to camp—had an early dinner at Cunynghame's, and I marched down at seven o'clock with my battalion to the trench to relieve a battalion of the 12th at the left post. Several cannon shot passed very close over our column as we marched down, but providentially without doing mischief.

January 12th.—We longed for the dawn of day to see what effect our shot had on the breach since we were down on the 10th. The ramparts of the upper and lower forts appeared levelled a great deal with the two last days' firing, and the artillery officers began to talk of a practicable breach! Our fire from the batteries all this day was directed principally against the defences on each flank of the breach. The enemy kept up a sharp fire the whole day, and we had several men killed by their shot. At sunset I took post in the shoulder of the six-pounders battery with two companies. Murray commanded one of them under me.

From an artillery officer on duty in this battery I learnt that last evening some of the enemy were seen upon the flank of the post, and came so near as to fire into the trench—this induced me to post a double sentry about eighty yards in front; I carried the men to the post myself, and gave them orders to fire on anyone who may approach them from their front. I had scarcely reached the trenches with my escort when both the soldiers fired, but did not fall back. I returned with a *jemadar's* party to their support; the enemy commenced a straggling fire, but did not advance; the moment we commenced our musketry they perceived our direction by the flash of our pieces and opened three guns with grape upon us from the garrison. I judged it improper to allow a party of the enemy to remain so near our post, and therefore determined to dislodge them, which we speedily effected, for they knew not the strength of my party and retired.

I had two men killed and several wounded in this affair, and a grape shot grazed my side; it merely drew the blood, but gave me great pain all the following day. The same shot broke the barrel of a soldier's musket, at my heels, after striking me; it cut the piece completely asunder, although the metal appeared to be remarkably well tempered. The field officer of the day expressed himself much pleased at our having driven the enemy from the neighbourhood of our trenches, as on several occasions they had concealed themselves in the dark, and suddenly leaped among our men in the trenches with their swords and spears and killed several of them, and this appeared to have been the intention of the party I attacked.

They were the most desperate of the enemy who were employed on those excursions, and few of them ever returned from the trench who tried the experiment; they were generally bayoneted.

The report was that the *rajah* gave them large sums of money, and promised them promotion, if they would bring a European officer's head!

January 14th.—The breach this morning appeared as practicable as shot could make it. The upper breach the least so. We had no doubt in our minds but that the place would be stormed in the morning, nor were we disappointed. About four in the afternoon we saw the enemy bringing four heavy guns to flank the breach; nor could the artillery officers in either of our batteries bring a gun to bear on them, such was the situation in which the enemy had placed theirs. Major Ball was the field officer on duty in the trenches this day, and at sunset an orderly trooper came down to the battery with orders for him.

An officer of our corps met the dragoon in the trenches and imprudently looked at the orders which he carried, by which we ascertained that the assault would certainly take place at daybreak in the morning. The right Grenadiers of the 2nd (the Senior Corps) to lead, so that I was quite sure of being employed, and hoped to be the first in the breach. At seven this evening we were relieved, returned to camp, and I made some few arrangements in case an accident should happen to me; McGregor was not to be in the storm. I therefore gave him the keys of my trunks, and a note mentioning how I wished the contents to be disposed of.

Dined at MacGregor's, and at ten the orders for the storming party to parade at two in the morning were published.

The stormers to consist of all the grenadier companies of the detachment; my company (the right of the 2nd) to lead. The grenadiers to be supported by a proportion of battalion companies of the different corps.

Wemyss came down the moment the orders were issued to take a glass of wine with us and shake me by the hand. Loaded my pistols and put them under my pillow, and at eleven p.m. laid down with our clothes on.

January 15th.—At one o'clock Weston, who belonged to the left grenadiers of our regiment, came to my tent and awoke me by telling me it was drawing on to the time for parade. We stuck our pistols in our sashes, and went to the lines; it was a beautiful moonlight morning, and the storming party had begun to assemble. In order that the soldiers may be enabled to ascend the breach with the more facility, their *cumberbunds* (an ornamental but very incommodious part of their dress) were taken off, and left at the quarter guards of their respective corps, which, with the picquets, were ordered to stand fast, and be under arms during the assault.

A little before the battalion bells rung three we moved off the parade, and marched down to the trenches, where the storming party was drawn up between the third and the last parallel, and about eighty yards on the right of the Grand Battery. We primed and loaded, but it was at first intended that the flints should be taken from the men's pieces to prevent firing, and to teach them to confide in the bayonet, but this was not done, at the recommendation of the commanding officer. Captain Morrison, who commanded the rear division of the party, came to me at the head of the line, and from what passed between us I certainly thought he did not evince that steadiness which I had observed in him on some former occasions. He spoke as if he entertained a presentiment that he should fall, and repeatedly assured me that he believed from the strength of the garrison, and the determination with which they had hitherto fought, that we should have a very bloody morning's work.

I knew him intimately, and could not help expressing my surprise, and jokingly told him that I never before suspected him of croaking; we shook hands and parted, never to meet again! The instant that the day breaking was perceptible, Duncan of our corps was despatched on horseback across to the grove at the right post, to order the firing of the six-pounder, which was the signal for the attack! Major Hammond with three companies instantly began the false attack on the north gate, and his fire was uncommonly brisk; this succeeded completely in drawing the enemy to that quarter while we moved down to the breach under cover of the fire of our batteries and the dusk of the morning.

We had nearly reached the glacis before the enemy discovered us, and their own mistake. A galling fire now commenced upon us. Forty soldiers with the scaling ladders without their arms preceded my section, which led the column; the shot flew very thick, and they became a little staggered. Sinclair, who commanded the front division of the column, desired me to remain by him at the head, and to lead the men on if he should fall. Everything depended on our placing the scaling ladders with precision, and as I observed some little confusion among the men who carried them, I ran on and laid hold of the headmost ladder, desiring them if they were soldiers to follow me. They immediately cheered, and we were in a moment at the ditch outside the breach.

The first ladder I placed myself—our men were now dropping on every side of us. Sinclair and myself descended the two first ladders which we placed in the ditch, and instantly turned them and mounted on the fort side to scale the *fausse braye*, but how shall I describe my feelings when I found that our ladders would not reach the top by nearly ten feet! The whole of the ladders were placed and ascended with all possible gallantry by the soldiers, but, cruel to relate, they were all as much too short as that which I mounted.

A little to my right I observed the wall was somewhat shattered by some chance shot of ours which had lobbed over the glacis that defended it. I got across from the top of one ladder to another, and with every exertion, unencumbered as I was, I reached the top of the wall alone. The men were ineffectually struggling to follow me, but a soldier with his musket in his hand and forty rounds of ammunition is not capable of that exertion which an officer is. My sword was slung by the sword-knot round my wrist, and I had both hands to scramble for it.

My favourite *havildar*, who had thrown away his pike and drawn his sword, was endeavouring to ascend with me when he was shot, and his blood flew completely over me. My escape was certainly a miraculous one. I pistolled the man who was nearest me, and who was in the act of cutting at me with his sabre on the wall; several muskets were fired at me by men actually not fifteen paces from me! but I had scarcely got my footing on the wall when a musket shot grazed my arm just above the wrist, a spear at the same instant wounded me in the shoulder, and a grenade (which they were showering upon us) struck me a severe blow on the breast, and hurled me almost breathless backwards from the wall.

The men in the ladders caught me, but on seeing me fall exclaimed that I was shot. I soon recovered my breath. The fire upon us was extremely heavy, and it was a most fortunate circumstance our killing the few men who ascended the wall immediately over us from the inside, as it was the means of deterring others from taking possession of the top of the wall, which had they done, from our helpless situation in the ladders (under them entirely) not a man of us could have escaped. A tremendous fire from the bastions which flanked the breach was kept up on us in it, and our men dropped fast out of the ladders; in this mortifying predicament did we remain, struggling to ascend, for nearly a quarter of an hour, when Major Ball, who commanded, seeing that every endeavour was made to carry our point, and that it was impossible to effect it, ordered a retreat.

Sinclair and myself, being on the top of the ladders on the fort side, were the last to quit the ditch, and now our fate seemed inevitable, as the moment the enemy saw the column retreat, they got possession of the top of the wall immediately over our heads and we had to descend thirty feet on one side and to ascend the same height to reach the glacis, all which time they were firing and spearing at us at a distance not exceeding fifteen yards! Many of the soldiers mounting the ladders to clear the ditch over our heads were shot, and came falling down upon us, and numberless shot and spears came on every side as we ascended.

The ditch presented a sight which at other moments would have shocked the most flinty heart. In crossing it we had to walk over the killed and wounded soldiers, with which the bottom was strewed, and many of them were brave, unfortunate grenadiers of my own company. I had lost a considerable deal of blood, and felt weak, but Providence aided us, and we reached the sand side of the ditch (the glacis).

We had now to cross the plain, back to our trenches, under a most destructive fire from upwards of two thousand men on the walls and ramparts, and four heavy guns raking us with grape. As I returned from the fort towards our trenches, there appeared from the whistling of the shot and the dust they struck up in all directions literally a shower of ball, and the men retreating in my front were falling very thick. Providence, however, ordained that I should reach the trenches, and there I met Sinclair, who had expressed his doubts of my having fallen on my way back; from weakness and loss of blood I returned but very slowly.

Major Ball came instantly to us, and shaking us heartily by the hand, congratulated us upon our very extraordinary escape, and it was decreed by all that we were "never to be shot in action!" It is impossible to describe thoroughly the precarious situation we were in for a great length of time, and the chances against our ever returning were ten thousand to one. Sinclair had no less than ten shot holes in his hat! The wound in my shoulder was by no means deep, as the weapon ran up under the skin, and came out upon the top of the shoulder; a musket shot passed through the cuff of my jacket, and took a little of the skin of my arm with it.

As soon as I was able to collect the men, I paraded my company, and it made my heart ache to find that of eighty gallant fellows who marched down to the attack with me forty-three had fallen! With this remnant of my company I was carried back to the lines, and experienced many a hearty shake by the hand from my friends on my return. The report in the lines being that I was among the killed, and for which Forrest, of our corps, afterwards accounted. A very handsome, active grenadier of my company, who had often distinguished himself by my side in action, and was in every other respect, as far as I could judge, a good soldier; was consequently a great favourite of mine, and before we marched down to the assault, I directed him and the unfortunate havildar (corporal) who was shot near me in the breach to remain by my side, and to stay with me if I should be badly wounded, and I promised them both that if we survived the attack, and they behaved well, I would promote them immediately.

This man was one of the first back in the trenches when the check took place. Forrest, who was stationed as a battery guard during the attack, knew well that he belonged to my company, and also that he was a favourite of mine, and therefore eagerly enquired of him what was become of me, and he replied, without hesitation, that he saw me shot on the top of the wall, which account was instantly circulated, and I shall ever esteem Forrest to the longest day of my life for the feeling he evinced on seeing me returned alive to the trenches.

Wemyss, Peyron, and all my most intimate friends in camp had understood that I had fallen, and our surprise and pleasure at meeting again cannot be very easily described. It would naturally be asked, Why were our ladders not longer, or why throw the lives of men away, without a chance or possibility of success? And such actually was our case in the storming of Sarssney. The ditch had been sounded, at least such was the report of the engineer officers, but the mud into which the ladders instantly sunk had never been calculated on, nor any allowance made for the wall of the *fausse braye*, which stood at least six feet above the level of the glacis! Not one of these circumstances had ever been taken into consideration, to which alone could be attributed our failure.

This afternoon both Sinclair and myself, in a manner most gratifying to our feelings, received the thanks of the commanding officer, in consequence of the report made to him of our endeavour to carry the place, "in spite of the insurmountable and unforeseen obstacles which presented themselves at the breach." Major Ball, who commanded the party, and who stood the whole of the time of the assault upon the glacis, mentioned us most handsomely to the commanding officer as well as to His Excellency the commander-in-chief in his report of the affair to headquarters.

This evening we buried our dead, and my poor friend Morrison was among the slain; he was killed by a musket shot near the ditch. By the officers in camp the attack was represented to have been one of the most grand and awful sights imaginable. It was not quite daybreak when it commenced, and the ramparts and bastions of the garrison opened a fire upon us as soon as we were discovered, which completely illuminated the fort and continued until our retreat to the trenches in one entire blaze of cannon and musketry.

All our batteries at the same time directed their fires where it appeared it would have the best effect in checking that of the enemy, and in covering our retreat.

January 20th.—Nothing material occurred since the storm of the 15th till this day. The enemy continued a very brisk fire on our posts. Our relief was conducted exactly in the same manner it had been previous to the assault. Our battalion was in the trenches at the left post today.

I was stationed with the field officer of the day, with three companies at the village of Mindy, close in the rear of the trenches, from which we commenced our approaches. About three this afternoon a straggling fire of musketry opened from a grain field upon our post, and great numbers of the enemy at the same time were seen coming out at the eastern gate and moving round as if with an intention to attack our trenches.

A captain's party was immediately detached from the village with orders to dislodge the enemy from the jungle, the edge of which he reached, and a smart fire commenced. The guns of the fort also opened upon him. At this time I was ordered out to his support with a *jemadar* and sixty men, and the troop of cavalry at the post was mounted and directed to proceed to aid us. About half-way between the jungle and our post I observed the captain, whom I was going to enforce, coming with his party towards me; he had found his post too hot for him, and was retreating very precipitately. This was the identical officer with whom I was on duty the day we were attacked in the grove.

On meeting him, he assured me very earnestly that it was impossible to remain out, the fire from the guns in the fort was so heavy. I made him no reply, but pushed on to the jungle and took post at the spot he had quitted, where we entered the grain and fortunately succeeded in driving the enemy out of it under a very heavy fire from twelve pieces of cannon from the garrison. I then formed my men again upon the skirt of the jungle, when the enemy began to press on me in great numbers, and the cannon shot flew very thick from the garrison, but nothing could exceed the steadiness of my party.

Those who remained stood firm, although many of their comrades were every minute dropping about them. All this had been observed in the lines, and Major Ball came down with all possible expedition with a gun and three hundred men to support me. On observing this detachment coming to our aid, we instantly charged to the front, and the enemy ran through the grain in all directions before us, and when the reinforcements came up I fell in with my party on their right as I was directed to do by Major Ball. We instantly formed line and opened the six-pounder on a body of the enemy which still menaced the post. At this time the cannonade on us was very heavy, and their shot constantly passing through our ranks killed and wounded many of our men, whose firmness on this occasion was never surpassed. They remained at shouldered arms for nearly half-an-hour under as destructive a cannonade as was ever known on so small a party! Not a man flinched or offered to take his musket from his shoulder.

The oldest officers in camp, who saw plainly our situation and the perpetual obscurity we were in by the dust which the cannon shot threw up about us, declared they had never witnessed any occasion in which troops evinced more gallantry than our men did on this. I left the ranks, and pointed out to Major Ball a thin jungle in our front, in which I thought I could perceive several of the enemy, and he immediately requested me to lay the gun for them, which I did, and, fortunately, with effect.

The artillery sergeant who pointed the gun was killed, and this was an instance of the utility of all officers practising at the great guns, and to know how to point a gun in cases of emergency. I had often laid the breaching cannon, and made it a point to do it when any artillery officer commanded in the battery with whom I was at all acquainted.

The moment ours opened, the fire of three of the enemy's guns nearest to us seemed principally directed against it, with a view, no doubt, to dismount it. I had a very narrow escape of my life in this affair; while pointing the gun a shot from the garrison passed so close to my head that it actually stupefied me for a moment, and I felt a giddiness which soon passed off.

A grenadier of the 12th, a man much lamented by Major Ochterlony, was about thirty paces in my rear; the shot after passing me carried away this poor fellow's arm close to the shoulder joint, and he died a few minutes after he reached the post. Major Ball, seeing that the enemy were completely checked, and finding that we were losing men fast from the fire of the fort, and being aware at the same time that our remaining longer could answer nothing, he faced to the right and with our gun marched deliberately into the post, under cover of the village. We withdrew our gun by stationing some soldiers at the drag ropes, as most of the cattle which brought down the gun were killed or maimed by shot.

January 21st.—Honourable mention must be made of the troop of cavalry which was ordered out to support our infantry at the commencement of the affair. They were commanded by a cornet, and soon after I had moved out to support the first party detached, and long before I had reached the jungle these heroes went past my flank with uncommon rapidity to the front and towards the enemy; and apparently a little scared by the shot which were flying very plentifully about.

They had not gone two hundred yards in front of me before they wheeled about in the greatest confusion, and returned, pell-mell, at speed to the post, with their officer at their head, carrying a cocked pistol in his hand, looking cursedly frightened I must say. The field officer of the day, Major Hamilton, an easy quiet man, positively remarked to me the conduct of the cavalry on this occasion, and told me that the reason given by their officer to him for not advancing was that he saw the noble captain's party of infantry falling back.

The *jemadar*, a young lad of eighteen, who went out with my party, behaved most gallantly, and was wounded by my side. I immediately recommended him to the commanding officer, and he was promoted to a *subadar* (captain). A *jemadar* of Shairpe's company of grenadiers, belonging to the 12th, also distinguished himself, and I stated his conduct to Major Ochterloney, who promised me he would promote him the first vacancy.

After the affair was over Major Ball came up to me, shook me by the hand, and spoke to me in a manner which could not be otherwise than very gratifying, and I had also the satisfaction to receive some flattering proofs of approbation from the commanding officer, as well as from many officers whose eyes were upon my small party from the moment I went out till Major Ball joined me. The guns in Parker's redoubt were of great service during the affair in keeping a body of the enemy's cavalry in check; which threatened every moment to come down upon us.

We were relieved this evening by the 2nd Battalion of our regiment. I had a late dinner at Cunyinghame's, where we spent a very jolly evening, and did real justice to his claret.

January 28th.—About eleven o'clock his Excellency the commander-in-chief, with H.M.'s 27th Dragoons, arrived in our camp. Two regiments of native cavalry also accompanied General Lake, and General St. John, with the 76th Foot, expected to be also with us tomorrow. I met the commander-in-chief this evening at dinner, and His Excellency asked me a great number of questions respecting the place, and told me that my conduct in the storm on the fifteenth had been "reported to him in a manner much to my credit."

His Excellency did me the honour to speak to me in a manner which must be truly grateful to the feelings of every soldier, and assured me that he was anxious to reward me, and which he would do whenever an opportunity offered. I had been exceedingly fortunate in obtaining the commander-in-chief's notice and approbation in the storm of the village of Camney, and our affair here on the fifteenth in the assault and the repulse of the enemy in their attempt on our post on the twentieth were circumstances which promised to terminate fortunately for me; detailed reports of which had been transmitted to his Excellency, and everything had been minutely stated. The commander-in-chief was in high spirits, and we passed a very pleasant evening, during which there was kept up a smart fire from the fort, and from our Howitzer Battery in return.

I was much flattered by the attention which the general, as well as Captain Lake, showed me. His Excellency during dinner remarked to me that he hoped I should soon have an opportunity of trying the enemy again under more favourable circumstances, adding: "I will take care that the ladders shall be long enough the next time you are in the breach."

January 29th.—General Lake having determined on reconnoitring the fort himself, at daylight this morning I was ordered to parade the remaining men of my grenadiers, and with six grenadier companies from other corps and two regiments of cavalry we paraded on the left of the line, and the commander-in-chief soon joined us.

On approaching the *pettah* (an outwork) the enemy commenced a smart fire of musketry on us, and Captain Lake's horse was shot under him. The general halted the column and filed us (the artillery) through the dragoons which were before, between us and the *pettah*; we naturally concluded this manoeuvre was intended to put us in a situation to attack it, and at first it, no doubt, was the commander-in-chief's intention. Here the column remained halted some minutes. We at length moved on, and from the uncommon brisk fire kept up on us from the *pettah*, we concluded that General Lake was apprehensive that it required a larger force of Infantry to take it than that with us. The fire was not returned on our part, and as the morning was unusually foggy they could not discern us from the garrison for a considerable time, although they continued firing random shot at us, or rather in the direction where they supposed us to be.

The fog clearing up we were instantly exposed to a heavy cannonade. As mine were the Grenadiers of the senior corps (2nd) they were, of course, leading, and I was mounted at the head of the infantry column.

We were several hundred yards within the cavalry, and consequently as far nearer the fort. His Excellency in order to have as near a view of the works as possible was at the head of our column and not twenty paces in my front, when a cannon shot grazed close at his horse's forefeet; the animal was dreadfully alarmed, reared, and fell back with the general, but most providentially he received no other accident than a sprained foot and being otherwise a good deal bruised.

Within three minutes afterwards another shot came, and took my horse just behind the ribs, and close to the centre of the saddle, cutting him completely in two. This was a happy escape for me!

We at last drew off from the garrison, but lost many men before we got without reach of the guns. This was the first specimen we had of General Lake's intrepidity.

I could hardly keep my eyes from His Excellency the whole of the time, and in my life my anxiety was never greater than it was for the general's safety on this occasion. He continued making his remarks to his staff, and asking me several questions respecting the lower works, with as much composure as he would have done on a field day.

What must the man have been made of who would not have felt inspired in witnessing such undaunted conduct in his commander-in-chief! And who but the rankest of cowards could have felt nervous, when they saw so great a character exposed to the same danger as themselves? We went entirely round the fort, and they cannonaded us as long as a shot would reach us. We arrived in camp about ten o'clock, and the commander-in-chief had a pretty good specimen of the enemy, who, I believe, he found somewhat more active and formidable too than he expected; both himself and Captain Lake had very narrow escapes of their lives.

The cavalry were now ordered to take up different positions round the place, so as to prevent any intercourse between the garrison and the neighbouring *rajahs*.

February 4th.—Rajah Diaram of Hatrass was strongly suspected of aiding the Sarssney *rajah*.

During the last six days nothing particular occurred. The relief of the posts and trenches were carried on as usual, and Colonel Gordon, who now commanded the artillery, was employed in breaching the upper wall and destroying the defences of the enemy's lower ramparts. I was on duty in the trenches this morning, and at break of day we discovered the flash of guns near the *pettah* (an outwork) and could also discern a faint fire like that of distant musketry, and we rightly concluded that our troops were attacking the *pettah*, as it was talked of last evening on the parade before we marched off for the trenches.

The *pettah* was not much more than half-a-mile from our post, but so hazy and thick was the atmosphere that we could only see a continual flash of cannon and musketry, hardly once hearing any report.

At broad daylight the fire had completely ceased, and at sunrise we had the pleasure to recognise our soldiers on the ramparts of the *pettah*, and saw them throwing up works to strengthen the face next the fort, which continued a heavy cannonade on them till nearly eight o'clock, when all was quiet. We supposed that this silence portended something desperate on the part of the enemy, and accordingly about half-past eight two columns, consisting of at least fifteen hundred men, appeared moving out from the eastern gate, from which they had not more than five hundred yards to the *pettah*.

This was an anxious period to us who were calmly looking on from our trenches, as we instantly discerned the intention of the enemy to make an assault on the *pettah* to endeavour to retake it from our troops, who had not been idle the short time they had been in possession; they had thrown up temporary batteries for their field pieces on the side next the garrison, and had completely anticipated the designs of the enemy.

We saw their columns from the fort advancing sword in hand in a most gallant and determined manner; when they had approached within two hundred yards of the *pettah* our troops opened a most destructive fire of grape on them, which was followed by a tremendous peal of musketry all along the *pettah* walls. This greatly disordered the enemy, who we saw dropping in immense numbers; still the most resolute continued pressing on, and were shot, many of them, at the very gates, in the act of trying to force them.

There was nothing between the fort and the *pettah* to shelter them from our shot, and the fire kept up on them by our troops during the time of their advance and while they were retiring to the garrison was really awful (so it appeared to us, who were spectators only.) The plain was nearly covered with their killed and wounded, and we saw many fall in the act of bearing off their wounded companions. (The Indians are renowned for clearing the field of their wounded comrades whenever it is practicable.)

A heavy cannonade was all this time kept up from the fort, and it appeared by our return of killed and wounded that we sustained a considerable loss. They also kept their guns constantly playing upon our post, as if they suspected we should move out to the assistance of the party in the *pettah*, but they were soon convinced that those already there were too many for them.

A spy of ours was in the garrison during the whole of this affair, and in the evening he came to our post on his way to camp, and gave us the particulars; he assured us all the *sirdars* (commandants) employed in this bold enterprise swore with their turbans on the ground by the water of the Ganges never to return if they were not successful. Seven of these commandants were killed, and the havoc among their men was great in proportion. I never saw a body of troops so completely slaughtered.

A large reward was offered on this occasion by the *rajah* for every European's head they may return with, and this affair would not have been less sanguinary had the enemy but succeeded. Major Ochterloney commanded the assault on the *pettah*, and the arrangements were extremely well made for the reception of the enemy when they returned to retake it. They deferred it too long; had such a vigorous sally been made before our troops had placed their cannon and posted their men the chances of success would have been much greater; as it was it was best for us. We had every reason to conjecture that the severe loss sustained by the enemy on this occasion would have a serious effect on their nervous system!

February 4th.—Reports in camp this morning were that the enemy were so much disheartened at their loss yesterday, when some of their principal leaders fell, that it was imagined the *rajah* would not be able to prevail upon them to wait the result of another storm.

This evening, however, a large quantity of fascines, made up very short and small enough for a grenadier to carry under his arm, together with new scaling ladders of a proper length and some sandbags were sent down to the trenches. The fascines and sandbags intended as a foundation for the ladders, and to prevent their sinking in the mud. Just before we marched down to the relief of the trenches, the flank companies of the 76th, which were intended to lead the assault, were paraded, and each grenadier and light infantryman was provided from one of the dragoon regiments with a pistol to stick in his belt, and we marched down to the trenches with a full persuasion that we should storm the fort in the morning. In the course of the night it was said that the commander-in-chief received certain information that the enemy were preparing to evacuate the place, in consequence of their severe loss of officers and men In their desperate attempt to retake the *pettah*.

The general well knew that those who remained, if attacked, would make a serious resistance, and that much blood on our part, as well as on that of the enemy, would be spilt; the object was to gain possession of the place we were not seeking their blood! The *rajah* had fought gallantly, and his troops had proved themselves good soldiers, and these considerations, no doubt, were the cause of the storm being deferred.

February 6th.—The morning, therefore, instead of being ushered in with a scene of bloodshed and slaughter, which we were prepared to engage in and fully expected, came without any unusual occurrence. Colonel Gordon, who was in the Grand Battery the greater part of this day, seemed particularly desirous to dismount some guns of the enemy which bore directly into the breach, and which cut us up so much with grape shot in the storm on the morning of the fifteenth. From the garrison the fire was much slacker than usual. We were relieved at eight o'clock by a battalion of the 12th Regiment in the trenches, and the moment we reached camp, after swallowing a few mouthfuls for dinner, I was ordered to march with two companies to reinforce Major Nairne's post.

It had been reported that the enemy in the course of the

night intended to make a sally on it, with a view to draw off our attention to that quarter, whilst their *rajahs* with the main body of the garrisons purposed making off in the direction of Moorsaun. At Nairne's post I arrived before ten o'clock, and found there six companies of infantry and Major Nairne's own regiment of cavalry. We drew up immediately with the infantry in front of the village, with a battery of four six-pounders in our centre, all ready to give them a warm reception should they attack the post. The regiment of cavalry was posted in the rear of the village to shelter them from the enemy's shot, for during the day the fire had been heavy on the post.

About eleven o'clock we were suddenly alarmed by a great noise in front. We were all loaded, the men at their posts, the guns primed, and the artillerymen only waited the word to apply their matches. We were surprised at the instant when at the point of opening our battery we plainly distinguished the rattling of sword in steel scabbard (or rather the steel scabbards themselves.) We knew the enemy had no troops armed with European arms, and instantly concluded it must be a regiment of our own dragoons or native cavalry. The circumstances of the scabbards alone prevented our firing.

In the meantime the sound evidently left us, and seemed to go off in the direction of the fort; a straggling fire of musketry also commenced. All this time we were under arms, anxiously waiting information of what was going on. Presently one of our double sentries in front fired at a man passing him; the fellow was frightened and instantly surrendered himself. The soldier brought him into the post, and he informed us that they had evacuated the fort; he was himself one of the garrison, and stumbled upon our post in making off. We discerned flashes of musketry or pistols in all directions, and the cavalry, which we were on the point of opening our guns upon, was Nairne's regiment from our own post!

The major had placed his *videttes* close upon the glacis of the fort, in order to gain immediate information of the enemy moving, and he was consequently the first that knew they were leaving the place, and, of course, ought instantly to have made us acquainted with it, and his neglecting to do so had nearly cost him dear.

Nothing but the singular noise of his scabbards prevented a sad carnage, which must have taken place in his regiment from the fire of grape and musketry we should have favoured him with, for they passed down in front within half musket shot distance of us! Major Nairne pushed on, and with his regiment of cavalry took possession of an empty garrison, but his services would have been of much greater use in supporting some of our posts near which the enemy passed.

Nairne was renowned for his personal bravery, and had evinced it on numerous occasions, which gained him a friend in General Lake, who wished in some measure to suppress a most severe reprimand which Colonel Macan, commandant of all the cavalry, issued, censuring Nairne exceedingly for his conduct, the next morning. A party of the 76th Foot on duty in the *pettah* and some companies of *sepoys* under Major Macrae of the 76th, went down as soon as the alarm was given, but Nairne was already in the fort, the gates shut, and he would admit no one.

CHAPTER 4

In the Fort at Sarssney

February 7th.—It appeared this morning that great numbers of the enemy were killed and wounded in their attempt to escape last night. Many of these fanatics refused to surrender, and even fired upon our troops who offered them quarter, for which they were shot or cut to pieces.

Our guns were withdrawn from the different batteries, which, with the trenches, were immediately destroyed, and the platforms carried with the eighteens to camp. From our post we were ordered to proceed to camp, and to dismiss the men in our respective lines. Breakfasted with Colonel Blair, who informed me that our battalion was ordered in to garrison the place. We were fixed on for that duty on account of the serious losses we had experienced during the siege, great numbers of our men having been killed and wounded. A battalion and some cavalry marched this morning to block up Bidgie Ghur, a fort of the Sarssney *rajah's*, distant about five short miles from Sarssney.

At eleven o'clock we marched into the fort, and I instantly went to inspect the breach and to view the place from which our escape had been so truly miraculous. In a shed near the arsenal we found all the scaling ladders which we used on the morning of the fifteenth, and which the enemy had carefully drawn in after our retreat.

Sinclair and myself with Major Hammond and about a dozen other officers proceeded with the ladders instantly to the breach, to prove to those who were not employed how much too short they were to enable our men to reach the top of the *fausse braye* wall. The ladders were accordingly placed in the breach, and without making allowances for what they sunk in the mud, when filled with men, the longest of them would not reach the top by eight feet! The place at which I ascended we soon discovered, and even there it appeared extraordinary to everyone how it was effected. Had not the unfortunate circumstances of the ladders being so much too short occurred we should undoubtedly have succeeded in carrying the place, as we found the breaches in the upper and lower ramparts practicable, and that was all we should have required. I resolved on reporting the particulars relating to the ladders to Major Ball, who commanded the storming party, and immediately sat down to address him on that subject.

We found in the fort but very little property. Sinclair, Hammond, Livesey, Parr of our 2nd Battalion, and myself, after the guards were posted, proceeded round the ramparts, mounted on which and on the different bastions and works we found nearly forty pieces of cannon in good and serviceable condition, with ammunition sufficient for a seven years' siege! The calibre of the guns was from that of 6's to 80-pounders! A heavy gun on the eastern rampart, named by our artillerymen *Bidgili* (Moors for lightning) on account of its quickness in sending the shot, which was always with us the moment the flash was discernible, carried a shot of upwards of eighty pounds. I saw three men and several horses killed in Nairne's regiment, the day General Lake reconnoitred the fort, by a single shot from this gun. We all dined today in the *rajah's* palace, passed a very jolly evening, sung a great number of songs, and went quite happy to our quarters about one in the morning.

February 8th.—The commander-in-chief with the army excepting only our battalion and the 3rd Cavalry, marched this morning and took a position before Bidgie Ghur, which place, very inferior in point of strength and size to Sarssney, it was expected would immediately surrender on being surrounded.

From the ramparts of the upper fort we plainly saw the general's encampment at Bidgie Ghur. I received an answer this day to my letter to Major Ball respecting the scaling ladders; he thanked me very cordially for having ascertained so material a point and so accurately, and told me that he had carried my letter on that subject to the commander-in-chief, by whom it was "very well received."

We now proceeded to remove the powder from the different mines; the two nearest the breach were primed and in complete readiness to spring. They contained upwards of fifteen thousand pounds weight of powder, and were of uncommon extent.

The natives in this part of India are justly considered the finest miners in the world. Several mines of a much smaller construction we found charged at the different gateways, and their contents were immediately removed.

The whole of this day the fire from our breaching battery was very heavy at Bidgie Ghur; that from the fort was by no means spirited. The eastern gateway was the point of attack, and by accounts which I received from headquarters from Wemyss this evening, they expected speedily to effect a practicable breach. I relieved Livesey at the southern gate this evening at sunset, and ordered the rounds at nine, at twelve, and at three o'clock, with patrols the intermediate hours.

I found one of my sentries (a man of the 14th Regiment) sitting down at his post, his musket lying by him. I immediately relieved him, put him in the guardroom, brought him to a court martial, and he received seven hundred lashes. At eight a.m. one of my sentries challenged a man near the sortie, who said he had information of great consequence to communicate to the commanding officer. I was made acquainted with the arrival of the stranger, and admitted him, and sent him with a small guard to Colonel Blair's quarters. This man came from Moorsaun, and assured us that a near relation of the *rajah's* was coming with a strong force, prepared with ladders and every other requisite, to attempt to retake the fort by a *coup de main*.

The small force left in the garrison (only our battalion and two companies of the 14th) induced us to think it very probable, and the messenger assured Colonel Blair that when he left

Moorsaun they were actually preparing to march. No time was lost in reinforcing us at the different gates, and manning the most accessible parts of the lower fort and *fausse braye*. We stood to our arms all night, the artillerymen were at their guns, and everything in readiness for the reception of the enemy. The cavalry were encamped on the outside.

February 13th.—The morning came, but no signs of an enemy; about ten o'clock, however, we received positive information of a large body of troops having actually marched about one o'clock this morning from Moorsaun (eight miles only distant from us.) They continued their route about three miles on the Sarssney road, but were recalled, most probably on hearing that we were quite prepared for them. The fire was extremely heavy all this day at Bidgie Ghur, and by a letter from Shipton of the artillery to Hammond we were given to understand that the place would be stormed in the morning.

We had a tremendous hurricane this afternoon. It came on while we were relieving guard at the southern gate. Poor Pattle of the cavalry, with his groom, took shelter under a wall, which unfortunately was blown down upon them, and they were both killed with their horses on the spot.

February 14th.—At daybreak this morning a trooper arrived with accounts of the enemy having evacuated Bidgie Ghur in the night. They were just in time, as the fort would certainly have been stormed at daylight in the morning. At twelve Colonel Blair received orders for us to prepare to march immediately and rejoin the army, at which we were all much rejoiced, especially as the report was that we were going to attack some other forts in the ceded district. It was with some regret that we left Sarssney and our princely quarters in the garrison.

Livesey and myself had taken possession of the highest storey of the *rajah's* marble palace the moment we got possession of the place, and Colonel Blair himself inhabited the lower apartments, which were uncommonly superb and spacious. Ours was the *zenanah* part, and that allotted for the ladies, but, to our regret, they had all been carried off at the commencement of the siege! In the *zenanah*, however, we had a glorious party this evening. Colonel Blair, Major Hammond, Wilson, Arden, MacGregor, Grant, Weston, Murray, Macaulay, Major Middleton, Peyron, Ryder, Boileau and Stewart of the 3rd Regiment of Cavalry, dined with Livesey and myself. We each of us did our best to do justice to the guests.

It was the last night we were to pass in Sarssney, and I believe the first that ever fourteen honest gentlemen drank within its walls. Three dozen and a half of claret, and proportionable quantity of Madeira everyone sang his song, and this was as gay an evening and terminated as pleasantly as any I ever passed in my life. We concluded by breaking our candle-shades and glasses, pranks which too frequently finish drinking parties in this quarter of the globe. Every officer off duty dined with us (it was necessary to keep them at their posts to take care of the garrison!)

February 15th.—This morning at daybreak we packed our baggage, and sent it with our camp equipage out of the garrison, to remain on the glacis till we should move out. Livesey and myself took our breakfast in our own quarters for the last time; they were really princely apartments, and had it been for any other station, instead of joining the army, it would have vexed us much, being ordered away.

At seven Major Ball's Battalion was in sight from the ramparts, and our corps paraded. I was ordered down to make over the guard of the south gate to the officer who may come from Ball's battalion to relieve it.

Lieutenant Young arrived soon after, and I delivered over to him a detail of the sentries we usually furnished from the guard, and pointed out to him where they were posted by us.

Took leave of Young, and bade *adieu* to Sarssney, which really was one of the prettiest places and most fertile spots I ever saw in India. Sarssney had from time immemorial been the residence and pride of the *rajah's* family, and his dependents proved how firmly they were attached to him and his fortunes by the gallant defence they made, and during the siege many of his nearest relations lost their lives in his service.

About eleven o'clock we pitched our camp about two miles to the eastward of Bidgie Ghur. Livesey and I rode round the fort and examined the works very minutely. The place was strong, but not one-tenth part the size of Sarssney. The people were employed in the fort, digging out the remains of a great number of poor soldiers who were destroyed and buried by the explosion of a mine shortly after our troops got possession of the place. Colonel Gordon of the artillery was among the unfortunate men who lost their lives on this occasion. It was conjectured that on evacuating the garrison the enemy had left a slow match at the mine, which plan too well succeeded. We had not been a quarter of an hour in possession when the mine exploded.

On our return to camp we had as fine a course as I ever saw. The greyhounds met us at the gate of the garrison. We found a hare close to our picquets, and killed her in front of the line, after an uncommon severe run. In the evening Peyron of the 3rd Cavalry (a grandson of Sir George Colebrooke's) and myself took our guns, and walked about two miles on the left flank of our encampment. We shot a very large buck antelope, several brace of quail and partridge, and three hares. General Lake and the army had marched from this place in the morning; we had orders to follow.

We had a very pleasant party this evening at Major Middleton's, with whom we dined; did not break up till a late hour, with lots of Kilbey.

CHAPTER 5

Storm and Capture of Cachoura (Kachoura)

February 17th.—Our battalion and the 3rd Cavalry marched at daybreak this morning. At ten a.m. we saw the commander-in-chief's flag flying at Secundra, and soon after took up our old station in the line.

The fort of Cachoura, about six miles only in our front, reported to be the next place we are to attack, and we expected to march against it and take up our position in the morning. At noon, however, it was reported in our lines that the place had agreed to capitulate, and at sunset Muller with two companies of our 2nd Battalion marched to take possession; the cavalry also moved at ten at night towards Cachoura. This evening orders were issued for the different corps composing the army in the field to proceed to their respective destinations. Dined with General Lake this evening.

February 18th.—In conformity to yesterday's orders we took our respective routes this morning, and the camp completely broke up. The 76th Foot and our battalion marched off from Secundra together on the Cawnpore road. Shortly after we commenced our march and about daybreak we were surprised to hear a very sudden and smart cannonade, and we began to suspect that all was not right at Cachoura, in which direction the guns seemed to be firing. We slackened our pace, but continued to move on, and about eight commenced pitching our camp.

The cannonade still continued smart at times. Whilst we were preparing breakfast an *aide-de-camp* came up and brought orders from General Lake for us to face about and return immediately to Cachoura, where it appeared they had admitted Muller and his two companies within the lower fort last night, before promising him possession of all the works in the morning; the reason alleged by them for wishing to defer giving up the inner fort till the morning was that the women and families of the different commandants had not yet been removed, but would all leave the garrison in the course of the night. Muller suspected not their treachery, and remained under arms primed and loaded till morning.

When the day broke he was astonished to see the garrison all under arms, the gate of the upper fort fast, and several pieces of cannon pointing on his small party from the ramparts above him, and instead of admission he was desired in a most peremptory manner to leave the garrison instantly. They ordered him to march out by a wicket close to the spot on which he was then drawn up; to this Muller in a very spirited manner objected. He told them that it was true his life and those of his soldiers were in their hands, but that he would forfeit both sooner than disgrace the service to which he belonged by acting in a manner they pointed out, and by retreating through the wicket. He allowed that he had no alternative against the numbers opposed to him, in the situation he was placed, and would, if they insisted on his moving out, return by the same gate he entered the lower works. To this they at length assented, and no sooner had he got clear of the garrison than they opened their guns upon him and the cavalry, and this was the cannonade we heard early in the morning.

We immediately struck our camp, and marched for Cachoura, which place was not more than five miles from the ground we halted at. On passing up a road to the eastward of the fort we got within range of their shot, of which they soon convinced us, and several heavy shots passed over, and some grazed between our section, providentially without destroying any of us.

General Ware's *aide-de-camp*, Captain MacGregor, came to us and pointed out the ground allotted for the encampment of our battalion. We soon found that General Lake's intention was to surround the place, and we hoped with a determination to make an example of the garrison for their rascally conduct in turning our troops out, after they had actually signed an agreement to surrender. The commander-in-chief sent for Muller and learnt the particulars of the treatment he had experienced from them, at which his Excellency expressed himself highly incensed. The general gave Muller much praise for the masterly manner in which he conducted his party under circumstances so hazardous as those in which he was placed.

Muller was a captain in our regiment (2nd). He was a son of a Prussian general of that name. A battalion went down and took possession of the *pettah* without any serious opposition. At dusk Livesey and myself, with two companies from our battalion, were ordered down to take possession of a village close upon the glacis of the fort; this we effected under a galling fire, which killed and wounded several of our men and two native officers. During the night, as it was conjectured the post would not be tenable by day, we received orders to fire the village, and fall back upon one about three hundred yards in our rear. We soon had the place in a blaze and were at our new post. The garrison commenced peals of musketry and cannon on seeing the village in flames, but we had withdrawn without the line of fire. Livesey's company and mine alternately remained all night under arms, prepared to receive the enemy if they should attempt a sally on us.

February 19th.—In the course of the night the enemy brought several heavy guns to bear upon our post, and at daybreak the walls and houses began to fly about our ears. We succeeded in keeping our men pretty well under cover, and thereby saved the lives of many of them.

Livesey and myself had both many narrow escapes of cannon shot this day. At seven in the evening we were relieved by a party from the 76th Foot and three companies from the 2nd Battalion of our regiment. In camp we found they had commenced on cutting materials for fascines and gabions to erect our Batteries, which we hoped would be ready, at furthest, in two days. A party of troops came into camp this day from Khauss Gunge, and with them came a double-barrel Nock gun, which Colonel Glass purchased for me in Calcutta, and which I liked exceedingly.

February 20th.—The troops on duty yesterday remained all day in the lines today. I walked with Livesey to the cavalry camp, to see our friends of the 3rd. We dined early and at sunset paraded for the outposts; our battalion being for that duty this evening. On our arrival at the left post we were divided into different parties, as most convenient to watch the motions of the enemy during the night, and to act together in case we should be attacked.

Lieutenant Young, with fifty men of the 76th and myself with a company of our battalion, were advanced to within one hundred and fifty yards of one of the gateways. We took post in the road, the high banks on the fort side of which afforded us good shelter from the enemy's musketry. Young and myself proceeded to post our sentries, in doing which, as we were quite close upon the glacis, they discovered us from the works, and began firing on us. We were standing close together, looking about to ascertain the most advantageous post for our sentries, when a shot came and cut an oil stick completely asunder, without doing either of us the smallest injury; it was standing immediately between us, and not one foot from either of us.

We had a few men wounded in the night, and several of our own shot which were fired from the *pettah* on the opposite side of the fort, passed completely over, and grazed by us. A twelve-pounder of ours was picked up by a corporal of the 76th and brought into our post. These shot must have touched the glacis on the *pettah* side, which must have thrown them up so considerably as to send them over the garrison. A quarter of an hour before daybreak we were withdrawn to the village in our rear where Christie commanded; we had a six-pounder at the post, which Christie desired me to take charge of, and to fire it whenever I thought it could be done with effect. I commenced on two of the enemy's guns which bore immediately into our post, and in the course of an hour silenced them both, and not a man showed his face at the embrasures the whole day afterwards.

Our gun was a galloper from the 2nd Regiment of Cavalry, and actually carried a shot like a rifle, and I took great delight in pointing it. I completely emptied the tumbril of all the round shot before night, and the sergeant belonging to the gun gave me the credit of being a good artilleryman. Our battery of five 18-pounders opened this morning at daybreak and continued one incessant roar till sunset. The effect of it was astounding. The walls of both the inner and lower forts came down in immense flakes; they were completely torn and shattered to pieces by our shot, and in the evening the breach appeared to us to be in a fair way, and looked as if another day's battering would complete it.

The fire from our battery was unremitting this day; they had regular reliefs of men at the guns, and the fire was almost incessant.

February 21st.—Christie again advanced me with the party furnished as usual from the 76th, and, as I was senior to Campbell, desired me to take the command of the whole, and I received orders to be particularly vigilant during the night, as information had been received at headquarters that the enemy intended to evacuate the place in the night. I drew up in the road on the spot Young and myself had been posted before, and we had just finished posting our sentries and returned to our party when a straggling fire commenced on our left. At the same instant our sentinels fired, and we saw by the lighted matches of the enemy that they were leaving the garrison and making off in all directions.

After our sentries had given them their fire they came running in and assured us that a very large body of the enemy were advancing directly upon our post. We were all ready for their reception, and in a moment they were near enough for us to fire our fire with effect. I gave them a volley, and we instantly rushed on and took possession of the breach. It came out the following morning that my friend Livesey was the cause of saving, perhaps, the greater part of my party, as the moment the alarm was given that the enemy were evacuating the place, the artillery subaltern at that time on duty in the battery wished to have opened his guns (which at night were always kept loaded with grape) upon the breach. Livesey was on duty in the trenches, and prevented him. We were in the breach at the time! Many of the enemy were making their escape by it, and were consequently bayoneted by us.

At the foot of the breach I received a graze in my leg, but managed to ascend to the top of it, when I sent in Campbell and the Europeans to take possession of the gates, with orders to put all to death who opposed them. By this time the retreat of the enemy was generally discovered, and the whole neighbourhood of the fort was in a blaze, and the fire of grape and musketry from our posts in the rear, which formed a complete circle round the place, was exceedingly heavy. The enemy fought desperately to cut their way through us, and most of them perished in the attempt. Their conduct had been such that the commander-in-chief resolved to make a most severe example of them.

The cavalry were drawn up in the rear ready to cut to pieces such as escaped the fire and bayonets of our infantry. With my small party we kept possession of the breach and gateways. After everything was over, and the firing had completely ceased in all directions, I gave Campbell his orders, and in a *dooley* returned to camp, as I found my wound very painful, though, as I was able to stand, I was quite sure the bone of the leg could not be injured.

The surgeon assured me that with care and proper diet in one month I should be quite recovered. In this affair Major Nairne and Lieutenants Pollock and Cornish were killed, myself and several officers wounded. The daylight, I was told, discovered a very bloody scene. The enemy, who were extremely numerous, were almost to a man put to death. The ground in every direction near the fort was strewed with their dead, and they very dearly paid for their unaccountable conduct in turning out our troops.

Among their killed was the *rajah's* son, the man who, it was said, was the occasion of his father's resolve to fight us. Both himself and his horse were shot, and found lying close to each other. He was very richly dressed, and his horse was said to have been a beautiful animal. Hardly any of the garrison escaped the carnage, which by their own dishonourable conduct they entirely brought on themselves, and which they most richly merited. A party was ordered into garrison, and by the orders of the day we were to march in the morning. Major Lake and Wemyss came from headquarters this forenoon to see me. I felt as well as possible, considering all things, and thought myself fortunate in coming off without the loss of my leg.

February 22nd.—The order for the army to march today was countermanded, and we halted. I made the necessary arrangements for travelling in my *palanquin* until I should be able again to mount my horse. Poor Nairne and Pollock were buried last evening.

Nairne lost his life entirely owing to his rashness, in carrying down his regiment in front of our posts between them and the fort, when the firing began; he received a shot in his side, and not improbable but it came from one of our own muskets or six-pounders, which were keeping up a most destructive fire at the time on the enemy leaving the fort.

The night was very dark, and afforded no other light than that of the flashes of our pieces and those of the enemy. None dreamt of a regiment of cavalry being in front, and particularly as orders were given for no part of the troops to advance except a small party to take possession, and the cavalry were directed to remain fast at their respective posts till the enemy should pass on to them. Instead of which poor Nairne pushed on with his corps, and paid for it with his life. He was an uncommonly gallant fellow, and much lamented in the army.

Nairne was a great favourite of General Lake's, who once saw him spear a tiger on horseback, the only man most probably that ever was known to attempt so rash and desperate a thing. General Lake shot the tiger, which was a very large one, after Nairne had put his spear in him. The tiger tore it out, and instantly smashed it to shivers in his teeth. The tiger's skin and the broken spear were sent home by the commander-in-chief to the Prince of Wales, with an account of its having been speared by an officer of the Bengal Army, of which his Excellency mentioned his having been an eyewitness.

February 23rd.—This morning the general beat at four and the assembly at five o'clock, when we marched off by the left, the 76th Foot leading the line.

About nine we encamped near a village on the banks of Colla Nuddy (Black River.) I travelled in my *palanquin* this march; my leg was a little inflamed, and of considerable pain, though the surgeons assured me that nothing could look better than the appearance of the wound, and told me that the in a very short time I should be again on my legs. There was a great deal of game killed in the vicinity of our camp today. The jungle was swarming with hogs, deer, hares, partridges, peacocks and quails, and the river abounded with ducks and teal.

February 24th.—This morning we marched at the same hour and in the same order as yesterday. Arrived about nine at our new ground of encampment. I found myself considerably easier today, and came on very snugly in my *palanquin*. On the banks of the Esah, a small river, close to which we pitched our camp, there is fine shooting, and an amazing quantity of game was killed this day by different parties from our camp. An officer of our corps shot a hyena—the largest I ever saw; a great many were seen this morning. Teteeah, the place against which we were now marching, was reported to be but a short distance from us; and we expected to arrive near it tomorrow or at farthest the next day.

February 25th.—The army marched this morning, the general beat at four and the assembly at five o'clock. The commander-in-chief mentioned on the march that he believed everything to be finally settled for the present campaign, as the Teteeah *rajah* had "taken fright" at the manner in which his neighbours at Cachoura had been handled, and had in consequence come into our terms, and agreed to give his fort up to us without fighting. The general said, therefore, he hoped the army would be cantoned during the approaching hot months, a period so destructive to Europeans in this climate.

We pitched our camp before Teteeah about ten, and Worseley with the Grenadiers of the 15th marched in to take possession- the ditch of the fortress to be filled up, the covered way destroyed, the guns all to be dismounted and the fort dismantled, in which state it was again to be restored immediately to the *rajah*. The pioneers and public establishments all employed accordingly in demolishing the works.

March 19th.—We halted ever since the 25th of the last month, and I was astonishingly recovered, and was able to ride a little without any serious inconvenience.

CHAPTER 6

From Teteeah to Bareilly with the 3rd Native Cavalry

March 20th.—This day at noon orders were issued for the breaking up of the army, and the commander-in-chief gave me two months' leave of absence. I had promised Major Middleton and Peyron of the 3rd that when the campaign should be at an end, and the army break up, I would accompany them to Barielly, the station to which they belong, and one famous for shooting and hunting. Middleton and Peyron were both among the many friends I had made at Sarssney, the former in command of the regiment, and Peyron his staff.

The whole of the cavalry instead of marching with the infantry quite to Teteeah remained about ten miles encamped in our rear on account of forage, and at five this evening I got into my *palanquin*, took my pistols and one of my double-barrels with me, mounted two of my grooms, armed them, and gave them orders to keep close to my *palanquin*. This part of the country abounds with *banditti*, and at the most peaceable times the roads are constantly infested with robbers and murderers, and the precautions I took were very necessary ones; indeed it was much against the advice of my friends that I left the camp this evening, but I knew that the cavalry were to move also in the morning, and therefore it would only have made it worse to have delayed.

We therefore set forward, determined to make the best defence in our power should we be attacked. We passed several horsemen in the dark, some of them armed with spears and some with matchlocks, and swords; however, they did not molest us, and about nine we arrived safe in Middleton's camp; he had a large party at dinner, and I got there in good time for my bed.

I found some little pain from my wound, even the easy motion of the *palanquin*, at the rate I came, had a little inflamed it.

My friends of the 3rd gave me the kindest reception, and their being great sportsmen made my prospect a very pleasant one.

March 21st.—Camp at Merankasserie. Marched this morning at four, with the 3rd Regiment of Cavalry towards Bareilly. About eight o'clock we encamped in a fine mango grove, near which we found two excellent *puckah* wells.

The Grenadiers of the 8th, proceeding also to Bareilly to join their regiment, joined us this morning, and the Futty Ghur troops also encamped near us. Soon after breakfast we heard some firing and were apprehensive that they had been giving us a second edition of Cachoura; from this suspense we were soon relieved by the chaplain of the 76th Foot, MacKinnon, who came into our camp, and informed us that the firing we heard was Worseley's party scaling some guns in the covered way, previous to dismounting them.

We found that our road to Bareilly lay very near Teteeah, and we had passed within a few miles of it in the morning. Teteeah was strong, and well furnished with very good artillery, and would inevitably have cost us some officers and men had they not surrendered. The example made of his neighbour at Cachoura was the only thing that induced him to give the place up.

In the evening Peyron went on to secure boats at the Ganges, in readiness for the regiment to commence crossing tomorrow.

My leg was quite easy today, and a little before sunset Middleton, Stewart and Ryder on foot, and I in my *palanquin* went to the *serai* of the town close by us, to look at a string of horses which had just arrived from the North. They were Toorkies, and in general very good of their kind. The Toorkies are a very hardy, sure-footed cast of horse, but slow, and by no means active; their bottom, next to the Arabs, is supposed to be equal to any breed of horses in the East. Middleton offered 800 *rupees* (£100) for one of them, but it was refused. We all dined with Ryder this afternoon, and passed a very jolly evening, not forgetting to take a comfortable quantity of claret.

March 22nd.—This morning the regiment marched at daybreak. I got completely tired of travelling in my *palanquin*, and therefore mounted a very easy going horse of Peyron's, and rode with Middleton at the head of the corps.

About seven we arrived at the banks of the Ganges; Peyron had provided boats in great abundance, and the right squadron crossed this forenoon, without any kind of accident.

We bathed in the Ganges this evening, and amused ourselves firing ball at large birds on the banks of the river. Dined with Peyron, and passed a very cheerful pleasant evening.

March 23rd.—Camp, Mindy Ghaut. Close to our camp in the evening we discovered a very fine lake of water upon which Peyron, Martin and myself killed a great many ducks and teal; and the two former, who were better able to walk than I was, killed also several braces of snipe. It was now upwards of a month since I received my wound, and in which period I very seldom quitted my couch; at times I suffered great pain, but by rigidly attending to the advice of the surgeons, and living very moderately, I now found myself nearly well, and except a trifling lameness, I suffered but little inconvenience.

March 24th.—Halted today to cross our baggage. At daybreak we went again to the lake, on which we shot yesterday. Killed a great deal of wild fowl and several brace of snipe. After *tiffin* we carried our nets and dragged an arm of the lake, out of which we took upwards of two hundredweight of excellent fish.

In the evening we bathed in the Ganges, and dined today again with Stewart, who gave us an excellent dinner and lots of claret. The mornings and evenings we found very pleasant at this season, but the sun in the middle of the day was excessively hot.

March 25th.—Camp at Belgram. On our march this morning we crossed Catyney River; very little water in it at this season. The country through which we marched was an entire view of cultivation; thousands of acres of wheat, barley and grain just coming fit to cut. The crops appeared remarkably abundant, and a richer scene I never saw than this country in its present state afforded. After breakfast we commenced making plugs and double-headed shot for the tigers. In the evening Peyron, Middleton and myself went on the flank of our encampment with the greyhounds; found hares very plentiful, and had some very capital courses; knocked up all the dogs.

The hares at this place were running in all directions, and after we had done up our dogs, we sent for our guns, and shot several. It was long after sunset before we returned to our camp, and dinner was on Middleton's table before we got there.

At this place the *Nabob* of Lucknow has about thirty pieces of cannon, mostly very indifferent, and lying in the sheds in a very neglected, slovenly state.

March 26th.—Camp at Sataianpore. The trumpet sounded to boot and saddle at three this morning, and Peyron and myself, with his quarter-master-sergeant and an escort proceeded on in front to look out for ground for the encampment.

We pitched today on very pleasant spot, and close to a fine lake of water. After marking out the ground Peyron returned to meet the regiment, and I proceeded to reconnoitre the lake for a day's shooting; to my great joy I found it almost covered with duck and teal, and in walking my horse along the edge of it I sprung a great number of snipe. After breakfast Peyron and I went out for two hours only (I could not walk longer), and we killed sixteen brace and a half of snipe, and twenty-three ducks and teal; had we remained the whole day we might have killed more.

Our servants carried the fishing nets to the same lake, and caught more fish than they knew how to dispose of; this was perhaps the first time that the birds and fish of the lake were ever disturbed by Europeans. The natives hardly ever shoot, nor have they in general nets sufficiently large to fish such a piece of water as this was.

I rode a pony of Peyron's to the lake this morning; he ran off with me, and, getting entangled among the tent ropes, we came down together, but without doing any mischief. Doveton shot an immense quantity of *ortolans* this forenoon, on which and some snipe and *pufters* (a delicious dish) we had a sumptuous *tiffin*. In the evening we dressed, and walked in front of our camp. Most of the tents belonging to the men (and the horses also) were screened from the sun by the grove in which we pitched. The officers' tents were all on the *Mydawn* (plain).

Dined with Middleton at home this evening; the dinner table abounded with game we had killed in the morning, and on one dish were twelve brace of the largest snipe I ever saw. In claret we did justice to this excellent fare, and parted at a late hour.

March 28th.—Camp at Siroomanagur. The parts of the country through which we passed today that were at all cultivated, afforded excellent crops, principally wheat and barley. We encamped today on most delightful ground. Our tents stood in the centre of a mango grove, which was large enough to contain two regiments, men and horses. A brook ran round three sides of it, and contained fish in greater abundance than I ever witnessed. There were rather too many weeds for our nets, but we had excellent angling in the clear parts up the stream.

Peyron sent a soldier to the guard this morning for declaring that he would cut his wife's throat. They had been quarrelling, and the woman came to our tent to prefer her complaint. She was a very fine looking girl, and we were without much difficulty prevailed upon to take her part; she assured us that her husband frequently beat her unmercifully.

We heard a fire of cannon and musketry in the neighbourhood of our camp today, and at first supposed it was a day of rejoicing among the natives, but in the afternoon a *hircarah* of Middleton's informed us that some troops of his Highness the *Nawab* of Lucknow were laying close siege to a small fort, garrisoned by Rajpoots.

After *tiffin*, Peyron, Middleton and self went to a lake near our camp. We killed a remarkable coloured water snake, the skin of which exceeded in richness and variety of hues anything of the kind I ever saw, and strongly resembled the various colours of the dolphin, which we met with at sea in our voyage out from dear Old England. Near the lake were a great number of wells, into one of which my pony slipped with me. I saved myself at the side, and with great labour we drew her out without having received the smallest injury. At sunset we had some good angling. Dined today with Doveton, and the maxim of the 3rd, of pushing the bottle, was very strictly adhered to.

March 29th.—Camp half a mile west of Changoiny. The regiment marched this morning at three o'clock. The daylight discovered to us a country abounding in the finest crops of grain of various kinds. About six we passed the ruins of two spacious gateways, and which once, apparently, had been very superb buildings.

Passed close to the cantonment of Shahabad, commanded by Colonel Clarke. Five companies of his corps only were present, the other wing being detached on command. About eight we encamped in a grove, which rarely afforded shelter for the regiment. The River Gurrah ran close to our encampment, and this was altogether a delightful spot. After breakfast we amused ourselves with killing turtle with our rifles as they rose in the water. The Gurrah swarms with them, and many were caught by a party of officers, angling, though in general they made sad destruction with their fishing tackle, destroying many lines for them. After *tiffin* Middleton, Peyron and myself crossed the river to try a fine looking cover on the banks of it; it was too dry, and afforded but very little game.

A court martial was held this morning on one of the camp followers of the 3rd for insulting a trooper whilst doing his duty in protecting a sugar cane belonging to a village through which we marched, and which otherwise would have been destroyed by those vagabonds, hundreds of whom generally follow an Indian camp in pursuit of pillage. About sunset we went with our rods and lines to angle, caught in a little more than half-an-hour seven dozen of *batchwers*.

March 30th.—Camp at Aureze Gunge. We marched this morning soon after three o'clock. The country but thinly cultivated compared to that we had passed since we left the banks of the Ganges. At daybreak we entered the city of Shajahanpore; crossed the Gurrah again, and encamped in a mango grove on its southern banks. The grove held the whole of the regiment, and afforded excellent shelter to officers, men and horses.

Fish in great abundance, but the wind blew so strong in the early part of the day that it was impossible to angle, and the river at this place was too deep for our nets. Peyron and I had a long ride with our guns, and killed some partridges and three brace of hares. Fresh covered my shooting hat today with a pelican's skin, which repels the force of the sun more than anything. Took our mutton and claret with Ryder this evening, and as usual passed a very cheerful, pleasant day.

March 31st.—Camp near Talhar. Marched this morning at half-past two. The morning remarkably starlight.

Peyron and myself rode in front, and commenced marking out our ground at five o'clock. The regiment came up about an hour after; we rode back a mile to meet it, and to point out the nearest route to the ground of encampment. On our way back I rode Peyron's horse, Rajah, over an uncommonly strong leap, which he cleared admirably. Our camp today was in a delightful grove of mango trees, in the neighbourhood of which grew some of the finest *tamorin* trees in the world. In the part of the grove nearest the town of Talhar was a Musselman burial ground, and the remains of many ancient tombs gave us reason to suppose that natives of rank and consequence had formerly been interred there. Talhar (the town) appeared to us, as we passed on, to be in a ruinous state, but the remains of grandeur was still visible at many places.

The *gunge* attached to it formed two rows of neat huts. Peyron got a letter this morning from Bareilly, assuring us that the tigers were committing the most horrid depredations in that neighbourhood, destroying daily men and cattle, and obliging whole villages to decamp, and to carry off their stock with them. We felt rather keen to be at them, and made up an additional quantity of double-headed shot for our tiger guns. Walked in the evening with Peyron to a very fine *byer* garden, close to the right flank of our line, and from which we helped ourselves plentifully without any molestation from the owners. The only inconvenience I now felt from my wound was a stiffness at times in the leg. Dined with Ryder this evening; we had a dessert of the finest *byers* and mulberries I ever saw.

April 1st.—Camp at Futty Gunge. We marched at three this morning, and shortly after daylight we passed the town of Cuttorah; encamped near it at sunrise, on the spot of ground on which the memorable action was fought in 1774 between the English and Rohillahs. The Rohillah chieftain fell in the battle, and his army was routed with considerable slaughter.

Breakfasted and went with Middleton and Peyron to a jungle in sight from our camp; we had good shooting; killed a great many black partridges, hares and quail, and several teal. Our encampment today was very near the Boghool Nullah (a small river), over which there is a bridge, sadly in want of repair. We had good angling in the Boghool in the evening, and after crossing we amused ourselves shooting pigeons from the bridge, about which they swarmed. Dined with Mr. Turner, the surgeon of the 3rd, this evening, all in high spirits, and we drank a pretty good quantity of the doctor's claret. This worthy son of Esculapeus was a sad stingy fellow, and we did not spare his claret in the least on that account.

In consequence of the victory gained here, the ground was named Futty Gunge, which in Moors signifies the spot of victory.

April 2nd.—Camp at Fereedpore. The regiment marched this morning at three o'clock. The roads were remarkably fine, and the country tolerably cultivated. We came to our ground soon after six, and during breakfast an invitation from Colonel Powell's camp at Bareilly came to ask Middleton and all of us to breakfast and dine with him tomorrow. Our encampment today was not more than nine miles from the cantonments at Bareilly.

Peyron, Doveton and myself were out shooting this morning; killed a great many quail and two brace of hares. *Tiffed* at two, during which we agreed to mount our ponies, and gallop into Bareilly; in forty minutes we reached the cantonments, remained an hour with Lieutenant Anderdon, a friend and schoolfellow of Peyron's; drank two bottles of claret, in water, with him (for it was a dreadfully hot afternoon), got again on our cattle, and galloped every inch back to camp. We dined again with Doctor Turner this evening, and nearly finished his stock of claret before we left his tent.

Marched this morning at four, and the cantonments of Bareilly were in sight at sunrise.

CHAPTER 7

On Leave at Bareilly

April 3rd.—The two Grenadier Companies of the 8th, which had not marched with us since the first day we fell in with them, joined us, and followed us into cantonments. Breakfasted with Lieutenant Anderdon, and afterwards went to call on Colonel Powell. Settled ourselves very snugly in Middleton's and Peyron's bungalow this morning, sent off my tent and camp equipage to the magazine of the 3rd.

Placed my trunks and baggage in a veranda room next my bedroom, and we thoroughly enjoyed the bungalow, after having been so constantly and long exposed to the climate in tents. Put the locks on our tiger guns, and made the necessary preparations for attacking them, though we must be under the painful necessity of waiting a few days to rest our servants and elephants; many of the latter especially were quite tender-footed, with long and fatiguing marches. We had information of two tigers this very day, lying in a cover which we could plainly see from our bungalow.

We all dined with Colonel Powell this evening. The colonel gave us a sumptuous entertainment, plenty of excellent claret, and a very hearty reception. We drank a great deal of wine.

Colonel Powell did me the honour to speak of some occurrences which took place at Sarssney and Cachoura, in a manner that was very flattering to me.

April 4th.—Peyron and self got on our horses at daybreak this morning and rode to Mr. Thornhill's, a civilian who lived at a charming place called Asiff Bhang, built as a country residence by Mr. Wellesley when he was residing at Bareilly as lieutenant-governor of the ceded country, distant from the cantonment of Bareilly about five miles. Mr. Thornhill showed us his stud, and among them his beautiful English horse "Pepper Jacket," just sent him by his father.

Breakfasted with Thornhill, after which we went to a strong jungle in the neighbourhood, and killed two tigers; they were small, but exceedingly fierce, and showed good sport; we were not absent more than two hours. Peyron and self returned after *tiffin* to cantonments in Thornhill's buggy. On our way back I was introduced by Peyron to Mr. Seton, a gentleman almost at the head of the Civil Service, and as pleasant a man as I ever met with. We made arrangements this afternoon for a shooting excursion on the banks of the Rham Gungah.

Dined with Mr. Seton, who gave us a most splendid dinner, and the best of champagne, claret, etc. It was eight o'clock before we sat down, and very late before we parted.

April 5th.—Got up at dawn of day this morning, and went to reconnoitre a very strong jungle about six miles from the cantonments, and upon the banks of the Rham Gungah. The inhabitants of one of the villages near the cover's edge informed us that a few evenings since two of their bullocks were killed and carried off by the tigers; many of the poor unfortunate villagers themselves, it appeared, had also very lately been destroyed by those destructive savages of the woods.

April 6th.—Thornhill and self coursed this morning. We left his principality at daybreak, and had some capital sport; as usual, knocking up our dogs and horses. Hares close to Asiff Bhang were exceedingly numerous, and the country very favourable for greyhounds. One of the best courses I ever witnessed in my life was run this morning by Thornhill's Europe Bitch Trinket, and Smoaker, a powerful black half-Persian dog of mine. The dog had the foot, and frequently passed the bitch in the early part of the course, but the Europe Bitch had the best of it latterly, and the English bottom was very conspicuous. She killed the hare, which ran far stronger than any hare I had seen since my arrival in India. Owing to the pure air of the clear country near Bareilly, they are generally supposed to feed dryer and to be stouter than in almost any part of the country.

April 7th.—Peyron, Anderdon of the 8th, and myself left the bungalow this morning at three o'clock. Our elephants and servants went off at midnight, and after crossing the Rham Gungah River we found everything in complete readiness at a strong jungle on its banks. As soon as the day broke we entered a fine *jow* cover, and by nine o'clock we killed four fine deer, an antelope and two wild boars, and nearly twenty brace of partridges. The sun became exceedingly hot, and we mounted our ponies, and were back to the cantonments to breakfast soon after ten, having by that hour completed what I considered a glorious day's sport.

April 9th.—Rested our elephants and servants today, and in the course of the morning visited almost all Peyron's and Middleton's friends at Bareilly, a form which we had deferred till the last moment, and which, in part, we could have with pleasure dispensed with. At Middleton's this evening we had a large party at dinner, and our generous host pushed the bottle very handsomely; everyone had taken his full allowance of claret before we parted.

April 10th.—We had a glorious morning's shooting this morning across the Rham Gungah. Killed an enormous quantity of game deer, hogs, black partridges and hares. We were much disappointed to find that the tigers had changed their quarters, which they constantly do. Every likely spot of jungle we beat over and over again, but in vain. We could trace them, and in the deepest part of the cover we found skeletons, both of men and of the numerous cattle they had destroyed. Many also of deer and hogs, but it was evident that they had deserted their quarters, and gone most likely across the river, where we resolved shortly to try for them. We all felt somewhat inconvenienced by the heat of the sun, which was exceedingly powerful, and it took great part of the skin from our faces, and our noses were completely peeled. Our lips so much scored as to annoy us sadly, so acute was the pain.

April 11th.—Spent the day quietly in cantonments; made a great quantity of balls for our guns, and other arrangements for a fortnight's shooting in the jungles. In the evening we drove to Asiff Bhang and dined with Thornhill; our party was small and very pleasant. Ridge of the 4th Cavalry, a son of Mr. Ridge, who lately kept a pack of foxhounds in Hampshire, joined us today, on a visit from his regiment to Thornhill.

April 12th.—Got up at three this morning. Our elephants went off at twelve to a cover in which the villagers assured us a tiger had been seen yesterday, and which had the last night killed and carried away a bullock from their herd. At break of day we entered the jungle, which, to our mortification, we found exceedingly strong. We took the advantage of some open spaces in it, and shot *niel ghy* (wild black cow), two boars, several deer and a great quantity of black partridges.

In trying the last corner on our way back we were suddenly saluted with a tremendous roar and charge of one of the largest royal tigers I ever beheld. So sharp was his attack that we could not without the utmost difficulty keep our elephants steady to sustain his charge and wait his coming sufficiently near for us to fire with good effect. From the desperate manner in which he came on we saw he was not to be trifled with; he came down roaring hideously, lashing with his tail, and looking savage and fierce beyond description.

The sight was truly noble. He commenced his charge at the distance of about two hundred yards from us. Peyron, Martin, Boileau and myself fired at about fifty yards; he reeled very much, and was evidently severely wounded, though not mortally. Unfortunately, the elephant immediately opposite him, as he came down upon our line, was one merely for beating the cover, and was brought out as a spare elephant for that purpose only, consequently there was no gun on it. The tiger closed with this elephant, and dreadfully wounded the two keepers who rode on it, nor could we during the contest get a shot for fear of injuring the people on the elephant. The shock of the tiger was so great that it fairly staggered the elephant, and very nearly brought it to the ground; the latter was sadly wounded by the tiger, and the instant it could extricate itself it ran off with every symptom of being dreadfully scared, and torn almost to pieces about the trunk and face.

Boileau's and Martin's elephants instantly followed at a good round pace. I was the next in the line, on an elephant that was never known to flinch. He came now with redoubled fury on me, but my elephant stood like a rock, expressing his anger only by beating the trunk on the ground. I gave the monster a shot from my rifle at about twenty paces; it entered just above the forehead, and rolled him completely over. He gave such a roar as I never heard, and was striving to recover himself when Peyron and Anderdon both fired.

He then received both the barrels of my two-ounced gun, and we soon despatched him. The runaway elephants, much to the annoyance of their riders, did not stop till they reached the banks of the river, and then it was with difficulty they were prevented from dashing instantly into the stream, so much were they alarmed. Fortunately they met with no groves or wells in their retreat, for when an elephant runs under trees, and into wells (they never alter their course when completely frightened) the consequences are very often fatal.

Our breakfast was prepared for us at a small bungalow built on the banks of the river, to which we returned in great glee, all as happy as princes, excepting only the fugitives, who were not a little hoaxed on the occasion; the fact was that the elephants they rode were not regularly trained for the *howdah*, but were carriage elephants, and not used to shooting or meeting tigers. (N.B.—I had seen the best elephants run on some occasions).

After a hearty breakfast we commenced taking the skin off the "royal game," and from the number of balls we cut out it was evident that very few missed him; he was nearly as large as a heifer, and, consequently, a pretty good mark to us. There is something to a person not in the habit of killing tigers so awful and really tremendous in their charge, the roar, and their actions in attacking, that it is apt to shake the hand a little. I cannot otherwise account for a tiger being ever missed at a near distance. His terrific head we packed in a basket, and sent it, as a trophy and mark of our success, to the gentlemen in cantonments. The day was so exceedingly hot that we resolved to pass the hottest hours in our little bungalow, and to return in the cool of the evening into Bareilly.

We amused ourselves in the afternoon firing ball at a mark, and at five mounted our shooting ponies, and cantered home.

Dressed and dined with Anderdon. Upon the strength of our morning's sport a pretty decent quantum of claret was drunk.

April 13th.—At four this morning Ridge, Guthrie, Peyron, Boileau, Lesley, Blackney and myself met on the edge of a low cover by appointment, the distance not more than five miles from the cantonments. Hogs we found in great abundance, and had most glorious sport. In the course of the morning there were many very severe falls, but fortunately no bones were broken. My grey horse, Major, carried me the two first runs in very high style, and I had the first spear in each boar. They charged most furiously, but with an expert horse, in general, they may be avoided, and you may deliver your spear with little danger. With a hard-mouthed, ungovernable horse, hog hunting is by far the most dangerous sport of any I ever engaged in, and there are few instances of a large boar and a horse coming in contact, without either the former or his rider being much cut, and frequently the horse is killed on the spot.

Our ground today was very dangerous, full of holes and old wells, and many of them quite covered by the grass which grew over them. In those cases it is usual to follow the exact trail of the hog; he is almost invariably well acquainted with the country where you find them. An experienced hunter always sticks as close after them as possible, and by doing so very often saves his bones. Hog hunting, beyond a doubt, requires the most desperate riding of all field sports. The danger of the ground is, in my opinion, much greater and more difficult to avoid than that of the fiercest boar—for, with skill, they are easily struck, but a blind hole, or a well, is the devil. We all knocked up our horses, and returned about eleven to breakfast, with an elephant laden with some of the largest boars I ever saw.

Guthrie ruined an elegant North Country horse this morning, towards the conclusion of the sport, and I considered myself very fortunate to find that neither of my horses appeared at all injured. Peyron, Ridge and myself ordered our servants and clothes to Guthrie's, where we breakfasted on every luxury this part of the country afforded. Guthrie had as good interest as any civilian in the country, and we found him also an excellent good fellow.

April 14th.—The elephants and servants went off this morning before three o'clock. We followed (Peyron, Anderdon and myself), and crossed the Rham Gungah before sunrise. We killed a great deal of game, *viz.*, partridges, hares, two fine deer and a boar, and returned home by ten to breakfast. The weather was so intensely hot that our elephants were completely knocked up for want of water; the servants also were nearly exhausted. We carried with us a supply of cold tea in bottles (the very best of all drink on a hot day in India). A large party dined with us.

April 15th.—Peyron, Middleton and self went this morning at daybreak to shoot on the banks of a small river which runs close to the cantonments. We killed three hares and seventeen brace and a half of quail, and were back to our bungalow and dressed for breakfast by eight o'clock. On my return I was very happy to find a note from my old friend and shipmate Maling, who was passing through with three companies under his command in charge of treasure for our troops at Lucknow. He was immediately invited to pass the day with us, and we talked over ship affairs, and not forgetting our respective friends in old England. Maling is a brother of Lady Mulgrave's, and, like all that family, a very handsome person.

April 16th.—Some accounts of a tiger reaching us yesterday, we despatched our elephants at two this morning, to a jungle about six miles from Bareilly. We followed at four o'clock on our shooting ponies. Our party was Middleton, Peyron, Anderdon, Ridge, Boileau, Guthrie and myself. We tried in vain till nearly ten. Although we could not succeed in finding the tiger, we had otherwise good shooting, and killed on our return (we never shoot at any other game when in pursuit of tigers) many boars, deer, hares and black partridges.

Breakfast was provided for us, and our couches brought down to our villa on the banks of the Rham Gungah River, so that we got under cover the moment we left off shooting. At breakfast we had, as usual, a variety of fish, eggs, cold meat, sweetmeats and jellies of all sorts, and some of the finest bread and butter ever made in India. We afterwards shot with our rifles and ball guns at a mark, and in the cool of the evening mounted our *tatoos* (ponies) and galloped to cantonments. Dressed and dined at Macan's, where we passed a very jovial evening; he gave us some excellent champagne and claret.

April 7th.—At daybreak Peyron, Anderdon and I rode to some dry grass near the cantonments; found our servants, dogs and guns ready. We killed about twenty brace of quail, three brace of hares and six brace of black partridge, and were again at our bungalow at eight o'clock. This was a very pretty morning's sport, and our dogs all behaved admirably. Although we returned so early, the sun was very hot before we got back. I wrote Europe letters today. A large party of us partook of an excellent dinner today at Anderdon's, where the good claret was done special justice to. Walked with Middleton through the different stables of troops before dinner, and the horses appeared very much recovered since our return from the campaign. There is not finer grass in the world for horses than what grows in the vicinity of the cantonments at Bareilly.

April 19th.—Left the bungalow this morning before daybreak, and met Thornhill and Macan at a spot fixed on to course. The greyhounds and servants were ready at the ground. We found hares numerous, and uncommonly strong; they showed us capital sport. Macan's "Norah" and "Gip" ran the two first courses, and killed their hares. The next two courses were remarkably severe between Thornhill's dog "Major" and my "Smoaker"—the first hare went to earth close before them, and the second they killed. The Europe bitch "Trinket" and Macan's "Fly" lost their first hare, and killed the second.

The country over which we coursed this morning was very sound, and afforded excellent riding compared to the ground we in general met with in the country. Thornhill and Guthrie passed the day with us, and in the afternoon we amused ourselves by firing at a target with our rifles and pistols.

All dined with Macan, and met there a very large party; among the ladies was a very nice woman, married to a musty old Major (Mitchell), She was sister to Lady Leigh, and appeared a very gay, charming woman. Her sister, a Miss Vaughan, and another stranger, Miss Ashe, were also of the party. The latter was passing through Bareilly with her father, Colonel Ashe, on their route to join his corps at Amrooah. The ladies did not leave us till nearly eleven, and we drank their health in champagne on their quitting us.

April 20th.—Got up an hour before daylight. Rode the grey horse to Asiff Bhang, found Ridge and Thornhill ready to start. Went to the usual coursing ground, and had excellent sport. Ridge rode the English horse "Pepper Jacket," which went in the true racing style, and mounted, as well as in his stables, showed an uncommon deal of blood. Thornhill kindly offered to give me an opportunity of breeding from him and my Mahratta mare, in consequence of which I despatched a groom this evening to bring her from Shikoabad.

In the evening Anderdon and myself went to shoot otters, which swarmed in the river that ran at the bottom of Thornhill's grounds. We killed several with ball from our rifles, and some good shots were made by both. Anderdon rode my shooting pony, which was one of the best leapers I ever saw. He carried her up to a brook in so careless a style that the mare imagined she was to take a drink, and accordingly put her head quickly down, when the rider, whose thoughts were on the opposite side, went immediately over her ears, and was up to his neck in mud and water; the pony, to my great amusement, stood enjoying her draught, till my friend crept out, and after shaking his ears, remounted.

On our return we found a very snug party assembled for dinner. We dressed in one of the alcoves in the garden; passed a comfortable jolly evening, the claret was circulated very freely, and at twelve Peyron and self got into the buggy and returned to our bungalow in cantonments.

April 21st.—My friend and shipmate, Becher, arrived this morning in cantonments; he was stationed at Bareilly in a civil capacity. I found him the same gentlemanly excellent fellow as ever; passed the greater part of the morning with Becher, the lady (a fine European girl) we did not see; she was too much fatigued by the long march they had made in the morning.

Tiffed with Anderdon, and went in the evening with him to the parade of the 8th, of which corps Anderdon was the staff. Their band was really excellent, owing to the great pains and attention bestowed on them by Anderdon.

The whole party broke up at twelve, after a great deal of singing, and one of the pleasantest evenings I ever passed, all made comfortably happy by a fair quantity of good claret.

April 22nd.—Shot this morning in some barley stubble within a mile of the bungalow. Anderdon to his own share shot eighteen quail without missing a shot. We returned to breakfast with nearly thirty brace, and after one of the prettiest morning's sport I ever saw in my life. The quail fly exactly like a partridge, and indeed are partridge in miniature, in general very fat, and delicious eating. In my opinion the quail shooting is as pretty shooting as any in the world. Breakfasted with Guthrie, who resided in the princely house built by Government, as a residence for the lieutenant-governor of the ceded provinces, the Honourable Mr. Henry Wellesley, brother to the governor-general. Guthrie displayed one of the most elegant sets of china at breakfast that I ever saw, and though not much in the habit of admiring or noticing the ornaments of a table, we were much delighted with these.

We had a large party again at Anderdon's this evening at dinner; the bottle was very freely circulated, and after the party broke up Anderdon and myself on our elephants, and Peyron in his *palanquin*, set off to go to our tents, which we had sent across the Rham Gungah, into the jungle about sixteen miles from Bareilly.

After crossing the river we mounted our horses, and with several torches carried by men on horseback in order to keep off the tigers, we pushed on through some narrow tracks and passes in the jungle, which made it somewhat hazardous, as it is well known that lights and fires are no security against a hungry tiger.

After a rather gloomy ride of nearly four hours we arrived at our tents, and got about two hours' sleep (till day broke).

April 23rd.—Mounted our elephants soon after the dawn of day, and commenced shooting in a strong jungle close to our tents, in which the villagers had reported there were tigers.

We found deer, hogs and partridges in great numbers, but did not fire at them all the earlier part of the morning, for fear our firing should disturb the nobler game, for tigers are sometimes known to slink off when annoyed by noises of any kind.

After trying for nearly three hours in vain, some villagers, who had taken their station on the most lofty branches of the trees, gave the alarm, and we got sight of a tremendous tiger galloping over a clear space to another and a much stronger jungle; we instantly chased him, and every endeavour that could be made was used in hopes of coming sufficiently near to induce him to turn and charge us; in crossing the plain we had a complete race with our elephants, firing all the time at him. Many of the shot from our rifles and heavy guns struck near him, and he positively turned about and looked well inclined to attack us, but on our pressing nearer to him he continued his route, and to our great grief got into a *jow* jungle, which we found higher even than our own heads when in the *howdah*, and so very strong that we could not see our elephant's length in our front.

On entering this jungle the elephants immediately commenced beating their trunks on the ground, and expressing every symptom of rage, which convinced us that the tiger was at hand, and that they winded him; but alas, we were unsuccessful, and after trying till nearly three in the evening in as scorching a sun as ever shone from the heavens we most reluctantly gave him up.

Elephants and the servants mounted with us for the purpose of handing the ammunition as well as the Mahouts (elephant drivers) were so much distressed by the uncommon heat of the sun and wind that some of the men fainted, and we had all enough of it when we reached our tents. Our breakfast was ready for us, and after a sound sleep of a few hours we felt much recovered. Dined in the jungle, and drank "Tiger hunting" in a bumper of claret, nor did we forget our friends in old England, and fox-hunting.

Our party was small (Peyron, Anderdon and myself), but we contrived to pass a very jolly day in the wilds, I fancy it had not often happened three Somersetshire men meeting in so remote a place, and so far removed from their native country, and those they love. We resolved to make another trial for our friend, the terror of the woods, at daylight; but in the evening some villagers came in, and gave us information that he had made off, and was seen to cross the river several miles above us; this caused us to vary our plans of operation, and to determine on returning in the morning to cantonments.

April 25th.—I got on my pony at daylight this morning, and met Thornhill and Ridge with the greyhounds by appointment at the clump of mango trees near the coursing ground. I rode the pony to the spot on which we met, and then mounted a grey horse of Thornhill's, called Kooley Khan.

We soon found a hare, and a strong ditch coming in our way, I rode flying at it, but my steed's heart failed him, and he endeavoured to avoid the leap by trying to turn short on the brink; the spurs were in his sides, and he could not effect his retreat, nor would he make any exertion to cover it, so that we rolled comfortably in together. I soon recovered my footing on the side of the ditch, and with some little trouble we got the horse out without any other inconvenience than the loss of the sport, and a little hoaxing.

After four very capital courses we returned, slept half-an-hour, bathed, and dressed for breakfast. In the course of conversation I found that I perfectly well remembered the mare on which Lord Craven got his death, and which was afterwards my father's, and died, I believe, on Ashill Forest. We played billiards and backgammon all the forenoon.

April 26th.—We shot today a great deal on foot, as the jungle was mostly low, though the risk of meeting with a tiger made it rather an unwise plan, but we had excellent sport, and did not reflect much on the danger. We chose the low cover to give our dogs an opportunity of hunting.

Killed a *florikin*, sixteen brace of black partridge, five brace of hares, and were again at our bungalow before two o'clock. This was as pretty a morning's sport as I ever saw, though somewhat interrupted just before we left off by a savage brute of a bull which had turned out vicious, left the herd to which he belonged, and reigned the dread of the neighbouring villagers in the jungles. The instant he saw us he made towards us, and was actually within twenty paces of us, when Peyron and myself fired, and he instantly dropped. We were not long in despatching him. The first round, either Peyron's ball or my own, entered directly in his forehead, the other shot went through the upper part of his skull.

The instant he fell our servants ran in with their sabres and cut his throat. Anderdon came and *tiffed* with us, and an hour before sun setting we sent our guns, and cantered down to some stubbles, not half a mile from the bungalow. Killed nine brace of quail, and several ducks on a small lake near the quail .ground. Middleton had a very large party today at dinner, and I was introduced by B—— to his fair companion, and a very nice girl she was; exceedingly genteel, and apparently must have had an excellent education.

Of the latter I had some opportunity of judging, as far as my discernment would enable me to decide, by a seat next her at dinner. As an old friend of B——'s, I was very cordially received. Miss W——t was one of the prettiest figures I ever saw, and two finer eyes never illumined a lovely woman's features. Her manners were those of a perfect gentlewoman, and we all agreed that she had advantages which unfortunate girls in her station are not frequently possessed of, and must have been elegantly brought up. She was a perfect mistress of music, and played the most difficult pieces at sight, in a manner really superior.

All those qualifications were not thrown away upon B——, who treated her with the utmost kindness and attention. She was much admired by the men, and that to the annoyance of several of the married families at Bareilly, who affected to decline visiting those that at any time invited her; and the consequence was the almost total break up between the bachelors and married folks, for the former declared that they preferred the manners and society of the young lady to the company of the old ones, and as far as I could judge it would have appeared strange if they had not, for a more stiff set I never fell in with; plain, proud and ignorant,, attempting the airs of gentlewomen, though it was more than probable that previous to their arrival at our markets most of them could not boast a change of dickies twice a month.

April 28th.—Arose this morning an hour before daylight, and rode with Anderdon to shoot at Sirdar Nagur. Peyron was on duty in cantonments, and could not accompany us. We killed three deer, a boar, several brace of partridges and hares, and on account of the heat, which was dreadful, we left off shooting at nine and returned home to breakfast. Peyron gave a great *Connor* (dinner) this evening, and a good deal of claret was drank. We parted as usual in high great good humour at twelve.

April 29th.—Remained at home today and rested our people, shot with our rifles and plain ball guns at a target from the veranda of my room. Dined by ourselves, a very snug party at home this evening, talked as we very often did a great deal of Somersetshire and our absent friends, and I could not help thinking that no men in India could possibly remember their connections at home with more affection than we all did.

April 30th.—Got up at the time this morning that the regiment was sounding to boot and saddle, and rode with Thornhill, who slept at Peyron's, towards Asiff Bhang (his house), and met the greyhounds at the old coursing ground, where they had been ordered: we had some very severe coursing, killed two brace of hares, and I went on with Peyron to breakfast and passed the day with him. We reached the house, and were dressed by eight. Remained all the day with Thornhill, and a little before sunset we got into the curricle and drove into cantonments to dine with Macan, where we all met (our usual party, *viz.*, Thornhill, Seton, Becher, Macan, Middleton, Peyron, Anderdon, Stewart, Doveton and myself). We met either at one house or the other almost every day, and time could not be passed more socially or pleasantly than we spent ours at Bareilly.

CHAPTER 8

Tiger Shooting near Bareilly

Accounts having reached us of some tigers having committed horrid depredations at a village in the jungles about sixteen miles from Bareilly, at daylight this morning our elephants, guns and servants were despatched, and Peyron, Anderdon and myself left Macan's at twelve at night, and about two we crossed the Rham Gungah; a curious circumstance occurred in crossing the river!

One of the party felt quite exhilarated by the wholesome quantity of champagne and claret we had partaken of, and in crossing our boat touched on a sandbank, and it was some minutes before we could get her off! My friend felt quite indignant at being detained, and, mounting his horse in the boat, he clapped spurs to him, and the horse immediately leaped the boat's side, and they plunged together into the river, from which they reached the banks with no other inconvenience than a sound ducking, and that to our great amusement!

We soon after reached our tents, escorted by a strong party of armed villagers with torches, to conduct us in safety through the woods which at many parts were hardly penetrable! We were well assured that the intelligence of tigers being in the neighbourhood was perfectly correct, for about midway between the river's side and our tents we heard them roaring, and howling hideously, and that at no very great distance from us.

Some of the villagers who were conducting us left us, and took to the tops of trees. The men carrying the torches remained with us! We drew our pistols, and at the head of a party of Matchlock men we advanced, and got safe to our tents, which were pitched at the village end. Went immediately to bed, and the villagers remained all night, and promised to take us at daylight in the morning immediately to the spot where the tigers always harboured during the day.

May 1st.—At four this morning we mounted our elephants, and within the distance of half-cannon shot from our tents, the villagers pointed to a brake of briars, in which they assured us there was a tigress and four half-grown cubs! The brake was not three hundred yards round, and we instantly encircled it with our elephants! To penetrate it was impossible, and we commenced shouting and firing into the jungle, but all in vain, no tiger making its appearance! The villagers who for safety had, according to their usual plan, mounted to the tops of the trees near us, persisted in assuring us that the tigers were yet in the jungle, and one of the drivers attached to my elephant dismounted and looked under the cover, which we were unable to do from our elephants. The man instantly remounted, and in a terrible funk declared that he saw one of the young tigers stalking along under the briars.

We commenced again every stratagem we could invent to draw the tigress out to charge us, but she would not come, and I suspected that fear had got hold of the man who dismounted to reconnoitre, and was therefore induced to go down to look myself! I had no sooner reached the ground than I discovered two of the young tigers, and plainly saw the immense feet and paws of the tigress. I instantly ran up the elephant's side by a rope, and communicated this glorious intelligence.

We all loaded a double barrel each with small (buck) shot, and fired in the direction I pointed out. This had the desired effect. The young ones bellowed out a ghastly noise, and the crashing of the jungle soon convinced us what was coming. The tigress, on hearing the cubs roar, instantly sprang forward, bore down everything before her, made a most savage and desperate charge on us. The roar was really like a clap of thunder when she attacked us. Peyron and Anderdon both fired, and wounded her, but she sprang upon the elephant nearest to her, and shockingly wounded three of the people; one of them died almost immediately!

She was fairly fast on the elephant's poll with her teeth sticking in her neck, and the hind claws fast deep in the poor elephant's trunk and face. This was a subject which the best artist would have been puzzled to have done justice to. The tigress was nearly the size of a Bengal bullock, and presented a fair mark to me although closed with the elephant, and I immediately fired my two-ounced double barrel at her; she instantly quitted her hold, dropped from the elephant (which I firmly believe she would have brought to the ground in an instant more), and slunk back, apparently stupefied, into the jungle, all of us saluting her as she returned. She staggered into the briars, evidently mortally wounded.

We now prevailed upon the villagers to come with fire, and soon had the brake in a blaze. The young tigers now came out, and although not half-grown, attacked the elephants with all imaginable fury, and evinced that savage and desperate nature born with them. They afforded us excellent diversion, and we despatched the whole party. The tigress was stone dead in the jungle, and such a monster my eyes never beheld! The poor villagers threw themselves at our feet, calling us the saviours of them and their cattle. We returned with our glorious spoils to our tents, as much gratified with the morning's sport as men ever were.

The inhabitants of the village, men, women and children, came to express their gratitude, and to put up their prayers for us. We had a delicious breakfast on mutton chops, cold fowls, tongue, eggs, and all sorts of good things, and slept till two in the afternoon; walked out upon the banks of the river, and shot two immense alligators. The Rham Gungah swarms with them, and we wounded at least a dozen. In the heat of the day every sand is covered with these monsters; they come up to bask in the sun. At four we mounted our horses and crossed the river about five miles above our tents, at a good ford. Reached cantonments soon after sunset, dressed and dined with Becher, passed a glorious evening, detailing to our friends the sport of the morning, and aiding our repetition with a comfortable quantum of most excellent claret.

May 5th.—Anderdon, Peyron, Middleton and myself went this morning to breakfast with Becher; we found them exceedingly agreeable, and after breakfast the lady played and sung us a great number of songs and fine pieces of music. Hers was a grand piano, braced with brass to preserve it from the scorching winds, and was one of the most elegant instruments I ever beheld, and her superior skill and taste did it real justice.

At noon we commenced shooting with Becher's air gun. Killed a "minor" with a ball from it on the top of the house, and broke several *kedgeree* pots at a great distance. We returned to *tiff* at home with Middleton, and I took with me Becher's double-barrel ball gun, by Nock, to carry with me on our next tiger party, with which, in addition to five double barrels and a rifle, all of my own, I considered myself well equipped in arms. Becher declined accompanying us, on account of the scorching sun and winds which prevail at this season of the year. Our guns, elephants, servants, with a good store of claret, Madiera, fowls, hams, etc., etc., left cantonments today, with orders to remain at the ground we last shot at (in the jungles) till we should come up.

Met Becher, W——t, Colonel Powell, Nuthall, Guthrie, Anderdon, Thornhill, Vernor, Boileau and Montague at dinner this evening at Doveton's, who gave us a sumptuous entertainment. Doveton was Middleton's senior captain in the 3rd, and as friendly a fellow as ever lived. After passing a most sociable pleasant evening, and as the clock struck twelve, Major Middleton, Anderdon, Peyron and self mounted our horses, and rode off for our tents in the jungles, with proper guides, and a good escort of troopers.

About four in the morning we arrived safe at our tents, and went immediately to bed, agreeing to halt tomorrow to take rest, and shoot alligators.

May 6th.—We slept till ten this morning, and after taking a hearty breakfast we left our tents to walk on the banks of the river for an hour with our rifles. The alligators were innumerable, and we made some fine shots, and left several of those monsters dead upon the sands, and wounded many more. If an alligator is not struck either in the head or behind the fore leg where the scale is more tender than at any other part it is a thousand chances to one against its penetrating, or giving a mortal wound. They sleep very sound on the edges of the water, and by making a circuit on the banks you may easily come directly upon them; the banks in general are so steep that there is little fear of their being able to come up the sides to annoy the sportsman.

In the afternoon some villagers came to our tents with news of tigers near a village called Sullamy; we immediately sent on one of our tents, took an early dinner and a bottle of claret each, went to bed, and at two in the morning mounted our horses, and rode on for Sullamy, leaving directions for our equipment to follow immediately. Our breakfast apparatus had been ordered on with the first tent.

May 7th.—Sullamypore. We reached our breakfast tent at daybreak, and got on the elephants instantly on our arrival. The *jemadar* (chief) of the villages had assembled all his people (himself we put on a spare elephant) to attend us, and we set forward, all keen for the expected sport. We agreed to fire at nothing but a tiger, and in consequence the deer and hogs, which we found in greater abundance than I could have believed, all escaped. We beat in vain till nearly twelve o'clock, and although we saw their tracks and dens in the deep part of the cover we could not find.

The jungle was so very extensive that if inclined to avoid us they could easily effect it, and the grass was sufficiently high to conceal them from our sight, unless they came, like the deer and hogs, close under our elephants' trunks. At twelve we left the cover, and I shot a deer (the longest shot I ever made with a ball) on our way to the tents, Middleton and Peyron also killed a boar each in returning.

At breakfast other villagers came in with intelligence of tigers, and we determined to try for them in the morning, but the jungles in this part of the country were so exceedingly strong that it was next to an impossibility to see them. The ground we beat over this morning was a perfect forest, so lofty and thick was the jungle that we could see nothing ten yards in our front, and the elephants with great difficulty moved very slowly through it. Tigers there were beyond a doubt, in great numbers, and we traced them on the sands by the river's side, where their prints were in thousands, and it was evident that at night they frequently crossed the river in quest of prey, and returned to lie in the strong cover. Shot with rifles at a mark after breakfast, and the natives, who many of them had never seen a European before, were much amused at our firing, and showed us every civility, bringing us presents of goats, eggs, milk, etc., etc.

Tiffed at two, and a little before sunset I mounted "Major" and went to try for a hog in a short piece of jungle close to our tents. Many of the villagers, with their chief, accompanied me, and we had scarcely formed our lines and begun to beat when a large herd of hogs got up. I gave chase to the boar, and a noble fellow he was. He soon separated from the others, and took across the country towards a strong jungle. The ground was very bad, and full of holes (which kept the rest of the party at the tents), and my horse was several times on his face with me. I could not choose my ground nor pull up for a moment, but with every prospect of losing him.

We had a most complete race of it for full two miles, when I came near him, and the instant he heard me at his heels, and found that he could not reach the jungle (about one hundred and fifty yards in his front) he turned upon me, and made a most furious charge. I well knew that if I missed my first spear he would be in the high jungle before I could again recover it, and as I was single-handed at him, I could afford to risk nothing. At the distance of about twenty yards, when he was coming down, he increased his speed, and made a most desperate push at me, and was almost close to my boot top before I could give him the spear, and turn off to avoid him. The spear entered just behind the shoulder blade, he staggered a few paces, when the blood poured out of his mouth, and he dropped upon his haunches, and in the act of exertion to tear the spear from him he fell as dead as a stone.

He was an immense boar, and had not mine been a tractable horse with an excellent mouth he would probably have destroyed us both. The horse would assuredly have been upset had he struck us, and as there was not a soul at hand we should both have been at his mercy, and in nature I do not imagine anything can be more desperately furious than a wild boar charging. (I have actually seen a young one, not half grown, come voluntarily down to charge a complete line of elephants!) I was as much gratified with my evening's sport as a man ever was on any occasion, and it proved more than a compensation to me for our disappointment in the morning after tigers.

A camel was sent out to bring in my prize, and they all agreed that it was as noble an animal as was ever seen. Our tents we sent on at sundown to the village of Russanpore, and dined under a mango tree. Drank our bottle of wine, and at ten o'clock mounted our horses to proceed to Russanpore for tomorrow's shooting. We came up with our elephants and baggage upon the banks of the river, where they were detained for boats.

The river here was very deep and wide, but as there was no prospect of the arrival of boats, and as we had news of tigers, we had no inclination to lose our day's sport, and therefore determined to cross. We got on our elephants, with our guns and ammunition, and in the dark they swam the river with us. Our saddles we took with us in the *howdahs*, and each took his horse in tow, and all got safe over, leaving the baggage to cross when the boats should arrive.

Our breakfast tents had gone to the proper passage, and found their way with our beds and breakfast things to Mungarah. Placed our cots in the open air, under some trees, as the night was very close, and slept soundly till nearly five in the morning.

May 8th—Mounted our elephants this morning at half-past five, and commenced shooting at a cover within a mile of Mungarah, in which they assured us they had very lately seen tigers, and several people and many cattle had recently been destroyed by them. We were not long in finding, and after several desperate charges, and nearly twenty shots fired, we dropped an immense tigress. Almost every shot struck her, and she fought with much desperation, bleeding most furiously. At last a ball from Middleton, just as she was in the act of springing on his elephant, gave her a brain blow, and rolled her completely over—several shots from the rest of us, aimed at her heart, despatched her before she could again recover herself.

We loaded the tigress, and were proceeding towards our tent, when one of the elephant drivers discovered in the jungle three tiger cubs, apparently but a few days old, and lying close by them was an immense buck, which appeared to be but just killed. We were back to our tents, had bathed, and dressed for breakfast before eleven o'clock, the morning vilely hot indeed. We had a good *tiffin* on some excellent fish, and at three o'clock again mounted the elephants.

Going out, and not one hundred yards from our tents, which were pitched upon the banks of the river, I being nearest the water, shot an immense alligator; the first shot was through the head with the rifle; he struggled off the sand upon which he lay sleeping, but could not remain under the water, which was quite discoloured with his blood. The second and third shots which I fired from Becher's gun completely finished him, and the villagers, who were always in great numbers attending us, brought him to shore, and one of the baggage elephants with a strong rope dragged it to our tents! He was a tremendous beast, and weighed as much as a couple of good horses.

We proceeded into the jungles, and had excellent deer and hog shooting. My horses were out, and I dismounted from the elephant to ride after a hog, but the cover was so strong that I could not keep sight a moment. This evening I am convinced that besides hogs innumerable, we saw at least a hundred deer, seven of which we killed, and might easily have shot twice that number had we been inclined. The villagers told us that they never recollect to have seen the game disturbed before. They themselves were deterred from pursuing it, on account of the tigers, of which they are never free.

Dressed and dined at seven o'clock, passed a very happy evening, drank to our friends in Old England, and wished only for the society of some of them to complete our happiness. A day never passed that we did not talk of them, and fox hunting was always drank in high glee.

May 9th.—Went from our tents this morning at four o'clock, to a jungle which the villagers recommended as likely for tigers. After beating a considerable time and rousing a great many deer and hogs, our elephants began to roar and to beat their trunks on the ground and spuming in such a manner as left little doubt of tigers being at hand, and the driver of Anderdon's elephant positively affirmed that he saw two large tigers dart past in the jungle. We were exceedingly annoyed at not being able to get a sight at them; the jungle was absolutely higher than our tents, and we could scarcely move in it. In this situation were we surrounded with tigers, and our elephants, by winding them so constantly, became quite furious, and apparently were as eager to get at them as ourselves.

We had not a glimpse of each other for some hours, and kept our direction in the forest entirely by hearing the rustling of our elephants and their roaring, which we could not prevent.

We went directly through the depth of the wood, as there the tigers lay, but did not get a single shot. On passing a low jungle attached to the stronger one we picked up two cubs, and saw the tigress slink in a most unusual cowardly way into the deep cover. I never before either saw or heard of a tigress quitting her young but with their lives. On the contrary, they generally advance the moment you get within their hearing. We saw her and fired at least twenty distant random shots at her, but it only seemed to accelerate her movements.

On our way to the tents we shot a hog and three deer, and arrived to breakfast about twelve, which, after taking a bath and a dry shirty we relished much and stood greatly in need of, as the morning was very hot, and we were a good deal fatigued. Slept till nearly three o'clock. In the evening our people fishing caught a young alligator in their nets, and we spoilt half-a-dozen swords in trying them on the scales of its back, which the best metal and the strongest arm could not cut through.

At four this morning we went off to the jungle in which we yesterday saw the tigress, and took up the cubs. We made our disposition to interrupt as much as possible her retreat to the deep cover. On drawing near the spot we were gratified with a sight of her, not skulking away as yesterday, but the instant she heard us she came on most desperately and evidently determined to rout us, or die herself in the trial. She came down, roaring and lashing her tail in a truly glorious style, apparently frantic with rage. It is impossible to conceive anything more furious than she was, and the sight was really enough to strike terror into the system of any one not confident in his gun and the resolution of his elephant.

On approaching us at the distance of about thirty paces in our front we gave her the contents of four double barrels, loaded with a couple of balls in each barrel. The tigress tumbled completely over, and in a moment recovered her legs again, and closed with the elephant nearest her, which she tore almost to pieces about the face, trunk, and the breasts. She was, however, enfeebled very considerably by the wounds we had given her, which was much in favour of the elephant, and after a most furious fight (which drove us almost mad with the pleasure it afforded us) the elephant shook the monster off, and struck it so violent a blow with the trunk that quite stupefied it for a moment.

The elephant instantly, and in a most sagacious manner, took the advantage of this, and immediately knelt upon the tigress's breast, and endeavoured by all means to crush it to death. It was impossible for us to take a shot, although we were completely round them, so close and entangled were they in each other.

The tigress at length extricated itself, and was advancing to renew the combat when we brought her down, and twenty balls were in or through her before she could get herself again on her legs, and we settled her, after a fight of at least a quarter of an hour from the time we first saw her. The elephant attacked, and its driver (who firmly kept his seat), behaved most gallantly. The man with his sabre (which they always carry on tiger parties) made many good cuts at the tigress, whilst they were engaged. Our elephants were bellowing, and shewed every inclination to join in the combat; they seemed almost as furious as the parties engaged; in short, we were all mad together, and the roaring and shouting might have been heard for many miles in the woods.

Loaded the royal game upon an elephant, and returned by eleven to our tents to breakfast, having first taken a good bathe and dressed. It was quite the thing impossible for a small party to be more happy and comfortable than we were. We had noble sporty and every luxury at command that the country afforded, besides which we were doing no small service to the poor wretches who, with their little property, so constantly fell victims to the merciless monsters we destroyed, and they, poor devils, were most grateful to us in return for the good we did them, calling themselves "our slaves," and bringing us in everything their country produced, which they thought would be acceptable to us.

We slept till four in the evening, and then walked out with our rifles to shoot alligators on the Rham Gungah. Peyron, Anderdon and myself fired at one tremendous brute within twenty yards of us. Each shot went through his head, and he died almost without a struggle. We sent out the elephants to drag him to our tents to shew to Middleton, who was a good deal fatigued with the morning's sport, and did not accompany us.

We dined at seven, and drank "Tiger Hunting," "Fox Hunting," and "Hog Hunting" with each three times three! At ten at night we left Mungarah to proceed on to another village in the jungles, called Nagarah. At this place we considered ourselves to be nearly forty miles from Bareilly, directly in the jungles, and where no European had ever made his appearance, and we all agreed that, give us but the society of the more amiable sex to keep us civilised, and we could be content to pass the days allotted us in India in our present mode of living. We travelled the first seven miles through very strong jungle, on our elephants, when we mounted our ponies and rode about the same distance to Nagarah, at which place we arrived about two in the morning, got our cots upon the plain, posted a sentry over each, and slept very soundly till seven o'clock.

May 12th.—We killed parrots and parakeets with ball, and I shot a *niel ghant* and a king crow from my own rifle. In the evening we shot at a target, long shots with rifles, and at one hundred and one hundred and fifty yards we had some bulls-eyes. We bathed and dressed for dinner at seven, and after enjoying ourselves, drinking to our friends at home, and planning our time when we get there, at ten we left Lowhanpore, Peyron and Anderdon in their *palanquins* (I abhorred a *palanquin*, and mine always went empty) and myself on my pony. About midnight we reached Bareilly.

CHAPTER 9

Social and Sporting Life at Bareilly

May 13th.—Peyron, Anderdon and self went as a compliment due to the commanding officer of the station, Colonel Powell, to breakfast with him this morning, and afterwards to Becher's, where we passed the morning, *tiffed*, and returned to our bungalow about three in the afternoon. Walked, after having dressed, with Middleton through the different stable ranges of his regiment. All the officers were present (at feeding time). Nothing could exceed the style in which this corps was kept, and the horses plainly told by their condition the care taken of them.

May 14th.—Got up this morning at sunrise, and walked my pony quietly down to Asiff Bhang to pass the day with Thornhill. Brown, Ridge, Guthrie, Thornhill, and myself were at billiards and backgammon the whole of the morning, and after *tiffin* we commenced a match of pigeon shooting. Browne and Guthrie shot against Thornhill and self. We brought down seventeen birds out of twenty, and I believe a single bird did not escape without being wounded. We were beaten by one bird only. Middleton, Peyron, Doveton, Anderdon, Stewart and Montague, also Macan, joined us at dinner, and we had really a jolly evening.

May 16th.—At one this morning our tents, servants and elephants were off to the Kiary Lake, and soon after four o'clock Middleton, Peyron, Brown, Bailie and myself crossed the Rham Gungah to shoot. Killed seven brace of hares, nearly twenty brace of black partridge, several deer and hogs, and returned to the lake to breakfast, where Thornhill and Anderdon joined us. Our nets were ordered down, and shortly after making a hearty meal we commenced fishing the lake. The quantity of fish we killed exceeds all belief.

The nets reached completely across the lake, which swarmed with fish, and hundreds of immense ones leapt completely over the nets and made their escape; in order to remedy this we brought from a neighbouring village the *choppers* (covers of thatch, made of grass and bamboo for their huts), and floated them with men on them, armed with large clubs, so that when a fish cleared the nets he fell upon the *choppers*, and was immediately knocked on the head. All the villagers from the neighbouring hamlets came to assist in fishing the lake, and we loaded them all with as much fish as they could carry away with them.

Peyron and myself followed the drawings of the nets in a boat, and many large fish actually leapt into it, and were despatched with a boat hook.

The sun was exceedingly hot this morning, and we all got famously scorched.

It is a fact as cruel and unnatural as it is horrid to relate, that at a village not far from the Kiary Lake the inhabitants conceive themselves to be of a superior race of men to any other, and to prevent their being contaminated by their female children cohabitating with other natives the men actually murder them as soon as they come into the world.

Facts almost as incredible, though not so unnatural, occur daily in India. It would be difficult for a European to believe, without having witnessed such a scene, that beautiful young women will, and in many parts of India almost constantly do, walk deliberately into a fire, and thus put a period to their existence, and sacrifice their lives voluntarily to a barbarous custom of destroying themselves on the death of a husband, who very frequently is a man old enough to be their grandfather, and to get rid of whom one may naturally suppose would as likely prove a source of happiness as to cause any other sensation, married to them, as they generally are, without their own consent, or perhaps without having ever seen them, and after marriage cruelly shut up and deprived of every intercourse except the society of the old savage himself and some female slaves.

We had our *tiffin* at two o'clock, and then commenced shooting with ball at small birds. From my own gun I killed a mango bird, a king crow and a sparrow, with a small green bird very common in India.

We procured some instruments from a village, and, by way of experiment, bored holes in some very large trees on the banks of the lake, and filled them up with gunpowder, to which we set fire with a fuse, and in imitation of mining we blew them to shivers, and made plenty of firewood for our friends of the jungles.

In the evening we mounted our horses, elephants, and some in their *palanquins*, and returned to cantonments, dressed and dined at home, where Middleton had a very large party, and the evening was passed in great jollity and good humour.

May 17th.—It was late before we parted last night, and we did not go out before breakfast. Accompanied Browne to call on Boileau and Martin, after which got into our *palanquins* and went to *tiff* and pass the day at Becher's, where we had music in perfection, and very many of my favourite songs were sung with great taste and very much good humour.

My time now grew short, and I felt uncomfortable at the thought of leaving my Bareilly friends, from whom I had received the kindest and most friendly attention that could be shown to an individual, and which, of course, attached me very much to them all, and I was thoroughly convinced that in no part of the world could hospitality exceed that of India. The society I met here consisted of true gentlemen, and men with whom I should rejoice to spend all that period of time allotted for my absence from my country and friends.

May 18th.—My Mahratta mare came in this morning, and I received Colonel Blair's permission to be absent from my corps till the end of the month. Ordered fresh ramrods for all my guns this morning. At noon we were alarmed with the cry of fire, and with much concern we found that a fire had broken out in the *bazaar* (market) of Middleton's regiment, and our bungalow had a very narrow escape. Many of the huts in the *bazaar* were destroyed, and owing to the dry state in which everything is at this season, when the heat is most intense, the fire raged so furiously that several poor unfortunate children were burnt to death.

May 19th.—Left the lines this morning at four, just as the 3rd were mounting for school exercises; arrived at Asiff Bhang shortly after daybreak. We had a capital run this morning after a fox, with all our terriers packed, and drove him to earth about five miles from Thornhill's house. Returned there at seven to dress and breakfast. My grey mare got a violent fall this morning, and was considerably strained and bruised in consequence. Passed the day at billiards, and as we were all engaged to dine with Becher we left Thornhill's by various modes of conveyance at sunset.

Browne and myself on an elephant, and we went through the town of Bareilly, and from our exalted situation (on our elephant) we had the felicity of beholding many pretty damsels in their compounds who otherwise would not have been visible. We had a very large party at Becher's, and passed the evening very pleasantly indeed. I engaged that the next application I made for leave of absence should be to visit Thornhill, but when that may occur I thought extremely uncertain.

May 20th.— Peyron and myself went off this morning at *reveillé* beating to cross the river

In about three hours we killed thirteen brace of black partridges, three deer and two and a half brace of hares, and, mounting our shooting ponies, we were again in the lines to a late breakfast. We all dined with Macan this evening, and a decent quantity of his champagne disposed of, and most delicious beverage it was.

May 21st.—Peyron, Anderdon and self left the cantonments this morning half an hour before daybreak. The servants and guns went off at one o'clock, and we joined them at a village about three miles from the banks of the Rham Gungah on the opposite side from Bareilly.

We swam the river on our horses, and it was a very unwise, mad scheme, and the consequences to one of the party were near being very unpleasant. Our elephants, servants, guns and dogs we found all ready, and soon after we commenced beating. No less than six *florikin* got up from a small patch of *jow hassie* jungle. They were so very wild that we could not get a shot at them, and flew into an impenetrable jungle on our left. A *florikin* is by far a bird of the highest game and most exquisite flavour of any I ever met with. They are nearly the size of a turkey, but shaped more like a partridge.

A cock *florikin*, on the wing, looks almost milk white, but among fits feathers there are some of the richest colours imaginable. The hen is about the size of a hen turkey, the plumage does not at all resemble the cock, but more the hen pheasant, only darker, and very much richer. It is very difficult to get within shot of a *florikin*, but when you are near them they are very easily shot; indeed, if a sportsman is steady he cannot well miss them.

In trying a grass jungle shortly after we flushed the *florikin*, one of the servants pointed out a tremendous boar rooting very near us. My horses and spears were close to me. Peyron and Anderdon's servants were less cautious, and had left their spears at home. The moment the boar saw our elephants he made off, but at first not in the smallest hurry, and I was soon after him, and after one of the severest chases I ever witnessed, of at least three miles, every inch at speed, I came up with him.

The instant he found me at his heels he turned, and made a most furious charge, and I most unfortunately speared about one inch too high, and it made a horrid wound just behind his shoulders, and passed through. I got out of his way after delivering my spear, without receiving any accident, either myself or my horse. He pursued me a considerable distance, and for want of a spear or other assistance I dared not attempt to dismount, nor could I without some weapon face him.

I drew him off a considerable way, and then made a push back to recover my spear; he took the advantage of this, and got into a jungle close by, in which the cover was as high as my horse's back, and I, of course, lost him. It was one of the stoutest boars I ever ran, and to my great anxiety to kill him single-handed I attribute my missing the first and only spear. He was one of the few hogs I ever brought to the charge that made his escape. If a person is at all collected the spear is generally fatal, unless a horse is untractable, and then the danger exceeds any in sporting.

Major carried me divinely this chase; the holes and broken ground we went over made it a desperate thing, but he rather seemed to fly than gallop at them, and the agility and caution with which the good horse avoided the danger was astonishing. I left everything to him, and kept my eyes on the boar, which I was obliged to do as the grass at many parts was even higher than the hog's back, and his rustling it and waving it was my only guide. Returned and joined the shooting party. We killed seventeen brace of partridges, six brace of hares, five peacocks and a brace of fine deer.

We arrived in cantonments about twelve to breakfast. The weather was very hot, and we got very much scorched. Our faces and hands fresh peeled. We did not quit our bungalow until sunset, and then went to dine with Anderdon. Our party was very large, and we kept it up till about one o'clock.

May 22nd.—Breakfasted and passed the morning at Becher's, where we had a great deal of music and singing. Returned to our bungalow about five in the evening, dressed and went to dine with Seton, where it was past eight o'clock before we sat down. The dinner and wines when it came was really sumptuous, and although Seton himself was no sportsman he very cordially joined us after the ladies had left the room in drinking "Tiger hunting," "Fox hunting," "Hog hunting" and "The Tiger" in champagne. We kept it up to a late hour, and to our shame be it confessed, many of the party saw no more of the ladies this evening; in truth they too much resembled the generality of Indian dames to afford much attraction. The bottle was not unusually preferred, and generally confessed to be the best company.

May 23rd.—At four this morning Peyron, Guthrie, Anderdon and self left the lines to go to the Sirdarnagar Ghaut. Anderdon and Peyron to shoot, Guthrie and I to see what hand we could make at the hogs, though the strong cover left us but little prospect of success. We had one good chase and killed our boar; saw many, but they easily evaded us by getting into the strong jungle. We were fortunate in falling in with no tigers, as they are very often seen, and we had killed them in the jungle we rode through this morning.

Anderdon and Peyron killed eleven brace of partridges, four brace of hares and three deer.

May 24th.—Becher, W———t, Macan and Anderdon came down this morning to pass the day at Asiff Bhang. At sunrise we commenced a match of pigeon shooting at twenty-five and thirty yards. The first match was shot by Macan and Becher against Thornhill and myself. We brought down eighteen birds out of twenty-two, and nearly all the rest were wounded.

For my own part I passed a very melancholy day, and did not at all relish the loss of a society I so much enjoyed, and had such cogent reasons to be happy in. The exceeding kindness with which I had been treated by all at Bareilly merited every return in my power to make. I told them so, and received for answer that the most effectual mode of repaying what I considered an obligation was to return again whenever I should have an opportunity of doing so.

At twelve at night I took my leave, and got with Macan into his buggy, and drove to his bungalow, which was the most immediately in my route to Futty Ghur. My *palanquin* and bearers were all ready at Macan's, and about one I shook hands with him, and sat forward towards Futty Ghur, from whence my friend Wemyss was to lay horses on bearers to convey me the last half way.

CHAPTER 10

Bareilly to Futty Ghur, Mynpoorie, and Shikoabad

I travelled twenty-six miles in my *palanquin* from Bareilly, and at Futty Gunge mounted my pony, which was laid there for me, rode her fifteen miles to a village called Burrah Matahney, at which place I mounted Major, and rode him to Jellalabad, and then I had the pleasure to find Wemyss's *palanquin* and my own tent pitched with breakfast ready for me on the table. A note from Wemyss announced the regular reliefs of bearers to be all in readiness on the road.

After breakfasting very comfortable, and dressing afresh, I took a sleep for a couple of hours, and then got into my *palanquin*, and pushed on towards Futty Ghur. The wind blew after sunrise like flames, and the day was so intensely hot that I had difficulty in proceeding on, notwithstanding the quantity of bearers I had in each set; many of them frequently fainted, and were left at the villages through which we passed. Under every tree I was necessitated to halt to give them a little rest in the shade, and a drink of water, a pretty good quantity of which I drank myself. I was obliged to give the bearers their time; it would have been cruelty to have forced them on, and I gave up all hopes of reaching Futty Ghur in time for dinner.

At every stage I found the bearers in perfect readiness, and about eight I reached the banks of the Ganges; kept along upon the sands, and got to the passage opposite the Futty Ghur magazine, just as the gun fired at nine o'clock. There was not a single boat on my side the river, but by hoisting lights for signals they soon came across, and at ten I once more arrived on the western banks of the Ganges, and soon after at my good friend Wemyss's bungalow, where an excellent dinner was provided for me, and we sat chatting till a very late hour.

May 25th.—Did not leave the bungalow this morning before breakfast. About eleven Wemyss and self went to call on General Ware and others of my Futty Ghur friends. The day was exceedingly hot, and the winds particularly so.

In the evening I met at home a snug party of friends, who Wemyss had asked to dine with him. Among others was Campbell of our corps, a happy fellow, on his way down the country for the purpose of embarking for dear, dear England. I was bent on another kind of expedition, and marching to join my regiment, in the expectation of shortly taking the field with it against the Mahrattas, with which power we were supposed to be on the eve of a war.

About ten we left Wemyss's to go to see a play performed by gentlemen, and arrived just in time for act the second of "She Stoops to Conquer." It seemed to afford the old ladies great amusement, and many of the ladies assembled on this occasion, although from England, I think very probably had never seen a play before. We returned about one to sup at Wemyss's, and it was late before we broke up.

May 28th.—At three this morning Wemyss and myself left Futty Ghur on horseback for Mutdanpore, about twenty-five miles from the cantonment. We expected to have found the tandem at the village of Mahomedabad, half way, but on our arrival there at daybreak we were annoyed to find that the servants had mistaken their orders. Our *palanquins* were there, but the tandem had gone on. To the former we preferred our horses, and rode on to Mutdanpore, where the tent was pitched in an elegant mango grove, near the banks of the Colla Nuddy.

The weather was intensely hot, and the mango birds, crows

and other birds were absolutely gasping on the trees, as if almost expiring with the heat, and which is a very common occurrence in India during the hot season. A little before sunset, although the wind was blowing blazes, we took our guns and walked upon the banks of the river. Saw two hyenas and several wolves, but could not get a good shot at any of them, and they retreated to their earths, which were close at hand, and we had it in contemplation to halt tomorrow, and smoke them out, but as I was under the necessity of being present at muster on the 1st at Shikoabad, we were obliged to give the plan up.

On the river we killed several ducks and teal, and it was dark before we reached our tents. Dinner was ready, and we ordered the table to be removed from the tent into the grove, and dined under the mango trees. Drank each our bottle of claret, and spent the evening very happily together, talking of sporting and our friends in Old England.

May 29th.—Mynpoorie. Wemyss and myself arrived here this morning about seven, came twelve miles on horseback, and the remaining fifteen miles in a tandem. Cunynghame and Mrs. Cunynghame expressed themselves very happy to see us.

We got our breakfast, and immediately went to pay the judge a visit (Mr. Ryley), to whom Wemyss was appointed register. Wemyss went in his own *palanquin*, and I took Mrs. Cunynghame's, it having *khuss purdals*, and in consequence was much cooler than my own. We found Mr. Ryley a pleasant, gentlemanly man. Played a few games of billiards, and returned to *tiff* with the Cunynghames on mutton chops and hock and water. Slept till six, and dressed at the small bungalow, after which I drove Mrs. Cunynghame in the curricle round the estate. At dinner we had Mr. Ryley, Captain White, Browne, and a Mr, Mansell, who was appointed Cunynghame's surgeon.

Cunynghame's gave us, as usual, an elegant dinner, with lots of champagne, hock, claret and Madeira. We went to the drawing room at ten, and Mrs. Cunynghame played and sang us a number of songs, that in *Life*, sent me by Miss Goodford, was most admired, and Mrs. Cunynghame was quite delighted with it. We supped at twelve.

May 30th.—Rode this morning with Wemyss on one of Cunynghame's Arabs; took out the greyhounds, and killed a brace of hares.

On our return we found MacGregor of our corps, who was also on his way to join. We were necessitated to be at Shikoabad by the 1st to muster, and therefore determined to go off together after dinner this evening. We were all engaged to dine at Ryley's.

Drove Mrs. Cunynghame there in the *phæton*, Wemyss and Cunynghame went in a curricle. The judge gave us a sumptuous entertainment, and we passed as pleasant an evening as we could considering we were about to part. Both Cunynghame and Mr. Ryley made me promise to pay them a visit as soon as I could contrive to get leave of absence. At eleven we handed Mrs. Cunynghame to the *palanquin*, and took my leave of the party. MacGregor and myself got on an elephant and went halfway to Shikoabad on it, and there, at the village of Garroul, we found our horses in readiness for us. At daylight we arrived at our bungalows at Shikoabad.

May 31st.—Breakfasted with MacGregor and Weston, after which we put on our swords, and went to visit the colonel. He was very happy to see us, and we passed all the morning with Mrs. Blair.

June 5th.—Received a letter from Wemyss this evening, telling me that Cunynghame intended to make me a present of an iron grey horse, for which he paid eleven hundred *rupees* (£140), out of a string of North Country horses. He is a beautiful horse, and altogether one of the finest figures I ever saw in my life; he had too much spirit for Cunynghame.

June 8th.—Breakfasted with Plumer, and passed the morning at Murray's, where I left a party at two o'clock, playing whist! Went home and slept till five. Purchased a very handsome buggy of Livesey, and this evening I put harness on Major to break him for it. The groom walked him with it for about an hour, and he behaved very well. Dressed and rode to Forrest's, where a large party of us dined, and the evening was passed in great good humour.

CHAPTER 11

Assault and Capture of Buddown (Budaon)

June 10th.—We had a field day this morning, and the battalion paraded at gun fire. Colonel Blair observed that I looked very unwell, and kindly recommended me to fall out, and take a gentle ride, instead of remaining in the ranks. I did not leave my bungalow all this day. Received a letter from Thornhill, Bareilly. At five this evening the following order appeared:—

> A detachment consisting of three companies from the 1st Battalion, 2nd Regiment, to march tonight, with a six-pounder, under the command of Major Hammond.
> The detachment to consist of the 1st Grenadiers, and 2nd and 4th Battalion Companies. Mr. Macaulay, surgeon, to march with the detachment.

In consequence of the resistance I had met with on a former occasion when detached with one company only, and without either a gun or a surgeon to dress my wounded, Colonel Blair had now taken the necessary precautions.

The colonel wrote me a most kindly note, strongly advising me, in my present state, not to think of marching with the detachment. He said it was true that my company of grenadiers were ordered, but added that Sinclair was going with it, and that one officer would be quite sufficient.

I thanked him in the kindest terms I could, but told him that as my company was under orders I should assuredly march with it. (Memo.—Never to remain behind on those occasions.) The major wrote us a circular note, telling us it was his intention to parade and march off when the moon should get up. We met at Mr. Dyer's (our surgeon's) at dinner. He comforted me by telling me that I was in a high fever, and more fit to go to my bed than on a command.

At the rising of the moon at eleven o'clock we paraded, and examined the arms and ammunition of our respective companies.

The adjutant had wisely taken the precaution of sending three bullocks laden with musket balls, ammunition, besides the forty rounds in pouch, so that we were in no fear of falling into the same dilemma which threatened the destruction of my detachment when I was sent to attack the village of Camney.

At midnight we marched off for the fort of Buddown, the place we were going against.

The fever continued severely on me during the night, and I believe that I drank at least a gallon of water. The night was dreadfully hot, and we were obliged to halt at every well we passed to give the men water, many of them fainted during the march.

June 11th.—At daybreak we came in sight of the village of Buddown, and the guides informed us that enemy were in possession of it. Major Hammond halted the detachment about half a mile from the village, and then ordered Sinclair and myself to advance with the grenadiers alone, and commence the attack. The gun and two companies the major kept with him in the rear. We thought this a curious arrangement, and Sinclair could not help expressing his surprise to me that the gun and a second company was not ordered to support us. But no further comments were made, and we advanced, and soon gained possession of the place.

On getting in we ascertained that Rham Bux, who commanded the enemy, and the greater part of his followers, had got into the fort about a mile in our front. We were ordered to rejoin the major with the grenadiers, and advanced immediately towards the fort. The grenadiers and the six-pounder were again ordered to take possession of the *pettah*, about two hundred yards from the gate of the fort. The enemy were strongly posted in it, and a brisk fire immediately commenced.

I was ordered with the leading section of the grenadiers to assist at the drag ropes of the gun, while Sinclair and the remaining three sections of the company continued a very smart fire, and that of grape from the gun was not less effectual. Several of our men were killed and wounded, as we were completely exposed the whole of the time of our advance. I was much hurt at the conduct of one of the artillery men (the man who pointed the piece.) He appeared so exceedingly confused because the shot flew thick about us that I could not prevail upon him to do his duty, and was provoked to strike him a severe blow with the flat of my sword. At this instant a shot killed a *bheesty* at his elbow, and I was necessitated to order another man to his post to point the gun.

We continued pressing down towards the gate of the *pettah*, and suddenly the enemy's fire slackened, and the place was in flames at many different places. We ran up a battery for the gun, and took post at a part where the flames had not communicated. The enemy all ran into the fort. After we had established ourselves in the *pettah*, Major Hammond came down with the 2nd Battalion Company, and relieved us.

We withdrew the grenadiers, and carried our wounded with us to the ground in the rear, and where the 4th Company had piled its arms. A smart fire continued all the morning. I never suffered greater pain in my life than I did this afternoon; the exertion in the early part of the day had increased my headache and fever exceedingly.

At sunset the company in the *Pettah* was relieved by the 4th Company with Livesey and Forrest. We prepared our scaling ladders in the evening, and it was determined to escalade the fort at break of day. About ten at night, however, we heard a smart fire, and on moving down to support the post we perceived that the enemy were evacuating the place, and before we got down our drums were beating the Grenadiers' March on the ramparts, and Livesey and Forrest were in full possession of the fort. After securing the gateways, and leaving a sufficient force to garrison the place till morning we retired to camp, and I got a little rest.

June 12th.—At daylight this morning we discovered about forty of the enemy lying killed and wounded about the glacis of the fort. They fell by our musketry in pushing out to get off. They generally come out with their matches lighted, and thereby discover themselves. At noon we received information that the man who headed the enemy was severely wounded yesterday evening, and that he was then lying at a village at no great distance from us. A company was immediately marched off in pursuit of him. A great quantity of blood was found in the house where he was represented to have been, but they had moved him away.

No plunder was found in Buddown or in the fort of any consequence!

The fever continued to distress me during the day. The party dined with Macaulay, and at eleven at night the General beat, and we commenced our march back from Shikoabad, the weather being so hot as to prevent troops moving during the daytime.

At three in the morning we arrived at the well near the village of Shaik Sarie; here we halted for an hour, gave the men breath and water, of both which they stood in much need; drank some cold tea ourselves, and moved again for Shikoabad. We arrived in cantonments about an hour after sunrise.

CHAPTER 12

In Cantonments at Shikoabad

June 22nd.—At seven this morning Cunynghame and Mrs. Cunynghame, the Honourable Mrs. Carlton, Mr. Paterson of the 29th Dragoons, Richardson of the 14th Regiment, Miss Dunbar (a very fine girl), and Wemyss arrived.

After dressing we all went over to MacGregor's bungalow to breakfast with the ladies. Mrs. Cunynghame introduced us to Mrs. Carlton and Miss Dunbar, and at Shikoabad I think we could now boast three of the finest women in India. They were kind enough to ask me to accompany them, but the surgeon told me that it would be madness to think of stirring at this season, and that a relapse would inevitably be the consequence of my moving in tents.

We were all exceedingly pleased with Mrs. Carlton who, we were told, was not treated in the kindest manner by her husband. She married the Honourable Colonel Carlton; a son of Lord Dorchester; he commanded the 29th Dragoons, and was now with them at Cawnpore. Miss Dunbar was just fresh from the Highlands, and one of the most elegant figures, and finest women I ever saw, except that she spoke broad Scotch. Dined today (a select party) at Colonel Blair's, sat next to my friend Mrs. Cunynghame, and passed one of the most pleasant evenings that I had done since I left England.

July 5th.—Took an early dinner with Colonel Blair, and about six o'clock we left Shikoabad for Mynpoorie. The ladies went in the *phæton*, a *postilion* driving them. At the village of Arroul the roads were so bad that the ladies got out of the *phæton*, and on elephants proceeded to Garroul. At Arroul Wemyss and I took our horses, which had been laid there for us, and Cunynghame, Paterson and Richardson changed their horses; we rode on together to Garroul. We had a beautiful moonlight night, and arrived at our tents at ten o'clock, where dinner and every luxury was prepared for us.

July 6th.—Left Garroul at daybreak this morning. The ladies in the *phæton*, and we all on horseback. The morning was dreadfully hot. We passed Wemyss's bungalow, which was nearly a mile from Cunynghame's, and where he kept his family. We were dying of thirst, and out of sheer vice drank each of us a bottle of beer. This was kept secret, but I never relished a draught so much in my life.

We (bachelors) dressed at Wemyss's house (close to Cunynghame's) after having taken a good bathe, and found breakfast all ready at Cunynghame's. In the forenoon went with Wemyss to Cunynghame's and his own stables, and placed my horses in the coolest stalls. *Tiffed* at two o'clock. Dressed at sunset, but none of the party went out this evening. Dined at eight, and we were splendidly entertained. An elegant dinner with champagne, claret, hock, Madeira in abundance. Went to the drawing room about eleven, and had lots of singing and playing.

July 11th.—Accounts today gave us every reason to suppose that a Mahratta war is inevitable, and very sincere pleasure did it give me, and I am convinced that if an officer would wish to get forward he should pray for opportunities to distinguish himself, and let none escape him that offer. To be first and foremost in danger should be his object; if he falls, he falls gallantly and respected, and it is a thousand to one if he is not rewarded should he succeed in doing his duty, in the style of a soldier.

Peyron wrote me from Bareilly that they expected to take the field shortly, and jokingly told me that Middleton "desired my company at dinner in the Tauge at Agra on the 5th of October next!"

July 15th.—Mrs. Carlton, Wemyss, Paterson and myself left the house at break of day this morning. On our ride we saw a neat fort at a distance, and rode to examine it. It was called Uxowlah, and had formerly been a country residence of the Mynpoorie *rajah's*, at a time when they were greater men and in more power than since they have had the English among them. Near the fort stood the remains of a house and pleasure grounds, which in its prosperity must have been a very delightful retreat.

On our return we had a very heavy fall of rain, and Mrs. Cunynghame, as well as the rest of us, was completely drenched. It had the effect only of making her look more handsome, and if possible better humoured than ever.

Wemyss and I had fixed with the judge to breakfast with him; got into the buggy and found his worship waiting breakfast. Played at billiards till *tiffin*. Joined the ladies as they were sitting down. During *tiffin* about twenty women who were employed at Cunynghame's new house, grinding up paint, came boldly into the dining room, and seized on Richardson, who made a grand fight, to our great amusement, but they overpowered him, and without ceremony carried him off, and shut him up in a room of the new house. This they had been bribed to do by the ladies, who, as well as the rest, were not a little entertained with the gallant captain's defence. Finding force would not prevail with his dingy friends, he offered them money, and fair words to liberate him.

July 17th.—Wemyss and I breakfasted with the judge this morning, and before the table was cleared Cunynghame wrote us a note saying that villagers had just come in with accounts of a tiger about eight miles from Mynpoorie. White called just as this information reached us, and instead of our *palanquins* we got three into his buggy (by way of expedition), and drove home. White, being a great sportsman, agreed to accompany us. Sent off our elephants, guns and ammunition and the Arabs to the jungle. White followed in his *palanquin*, and Wemyss and myself about an hour after in the tandem. On our arrival at the forest we perceived the villagers stationed on the tops of the trees, from which they pointed out the spot of cover into which they assured us they had seen the tiger go.

It was a forest of trees, so thick that an elephant could not without difficulty pass between the timbers, and the drivers assured us that if the tiger should start suddenly upon us, and the elephants run, we should inevitably be dashed to pieces among the trees. All this we were perfectly aware of, but being determined to beat up his quarters, we ordered the drivers to proceed on. The fellows recommended themselves "to God" and began to pray, and we were obliged to have recourse to the butts of our guns before they would enter the forest, reminding them that the danger was greater to us than to them. The cover was exceedingly strong, with a stream of water running through the centre of it, and on the banks of which we relied on finding him, nor were we mistaken.

After proceeding with great difficulty, White on one side of the stream, Wemyss and myself on the other, about two hundred yards into the wood, the man driving my elephant assured me that the tiger was near, and the elephants began to beat their trunks on the ground and to show symptoms of anger. In a few minutes after I perceived his streaked side, through a thick bush of briars, and instantly pointed him out to Wemyss. Never did I behold a more glorious sight. He lay lashing his tail and crouched waiting only for us to near him a little, so that he might make his spring with effect. We were aware of our awkward situation, and the elephants began to back, when Wemyss and I fired together. He gave a most hideous howl, and in endeavouring to make at us staggered back and fell directly into the water, the blood streaming from him as he swam towards White on the opposite side.

We fired three double barrels each at him in the water, but could not prevent his reaching the opposite shore; where he landed and drew himself instantly into the cover, and we as speedily pursued him. About fifty yards down the stream we discovered him lying in the agonies of death, howling in such a manner as to make the forest ring again; he struggled and made every savage exertion to get at us, but was mortally wounded, and could only rise on his forelegs. His tremendous roaring made the elephants appear very uncomfortable, and they showed symptoms of wishing to make off.

We did not wish to despatch the tiger immediately, as the sight of a tiger in such a situation was really a most glorious one. White's elephant backed and squeezed the servant terribly against a tree. The man was placed in a kind of chair fastened to the *howdah* for the purpose of handing the powder and the balls (shooting *howdahs* have all such a contrivance.) The tiger lay under a small tree, the roots of which he tore up, and appeared perfectly frantic with rage and pain. He had killed a man and a bullock a few hours before we arrived, and it was pleasant to see the villagers with their drawn swords around him, but none would venture near him.

After we had enjoyed this sight a full hour, I dismounted and walked up near to him, and with my rifle shot him stone dead. The villagers began to cheer, and made us a thousand *salaams* to our feet for having destroyed a monster which would otherwise most likely have destroyed many of them and remained there the terror of the neighbourhood. We loaded him on a spare elephant and carried him to the village, about a mile from the forest, where our tent was ready pitched and refreshments which had been sent by Cunynghame for us on the table, and after feasting heartily and drinking lots of hock and water, we mounted our Arabs, and arrived in time to dress and joined the party for the dessert and a bottle of champagne.

About nine o'clock the fruits of our labour arrived, and the ladies were the first in the veranda to see it. They thought us amazing clever fellows, and Mrs. Carlton desired his claws might be taken out for her to carry to England. Nothing but the extreme heat of the day prevented them accompanying us and looking on at a distance. It was fortunate, however, that they did not, as they could not possibly have seen anything. We got very gay on this occasion, and it was nearly eleven before Wemyss, White and I left the dining table. We men smoked a little. Sung and played till near one o'clock, when we went to bed as happy as kings.

July 18th.—Employed ourselves this morning in seeing the skin taken from the tiger, and in cutting out our balls. The first round that Wemyss and myself fired at him, our guns were loaded with plugs (double-headed shot), two in each barrel, four double barrels; they were the only shot of that description that were fired at him (being good only at close quarters), and every one of them, eight in number, were cut out of the tiger, and a great number of round shot. He measured eleven feet, and such limbs I never saw to a tiger before. Preserved the teeth and claws and had them cleaned for Mrs. Carlton to take home with her. The ladies were employed this morning in painting, which they did beautifully. In the evening we all went out in the carriages. Dined at eight. This was Mrs. Carlton's last evening, and we were less gay than usual on that account.

July 27th.—The following extract of a letter from Thornhill received this day:—

> Pepper Jacket is related in blood to Boxer, whose grand dam was the great grand dam of Pepper Jacket, which mare was got by Snip, son of Flying Childers; her dam was Parker's Lady Thigh. I think we shall introduce a little good blood into the country.

Pepper Jacket is a Europe horse, just sent out to Thornhill by his father at home.

Received a letter from Mrs. Cunynghame mentioning that Cunynghame expected officers would be appointed to the Mynpoorie Provincials, and desiring to know if Cunynghame should apply for me, and Wemyss wrote by the same conveyance and kindly mentioned:—"As you are not a married man you can have half of my bungalow."

To this I made the same reply as I had done to Thornhill on the same occasion, and although it was never my intention to join one of the Irregular Corps, in times like the present I was exceedingly flattered by the kind attention they had evinced. It would have been excessively comfortable to sit down settled with such friends, enjoying, at no expense, the luxuries of the East, but a soldier should not study comfort, and I should have felt somewhat awkward in the midst of those enjoyments while my corps was gaining fame in the field. To hear my brother officers, some future day perhaps, "fighting their battles o'er again," and telling "how fields were won," would not, to me, have been very pleasant.

July 31st.—Everything of mine in perfect readiness to march at an hour's notice. Recalled my *hackery* and determined to send back my tent and some trunks to Mynpoorie, as there was no talk of troops moving to relieve us.

Packed ten dozen of Madeira and four dozen of port with some beer in grass for the march. Tailors still brushing up the old tent. Livesey and myself having a pipe of Madeira at Futty Ghur, agreed that it would be better for it to remain there, as the risk of losing it would be less than at Shikoabad (close upon the borders of the Mahratta territory).

The people employed making *purdals* for my *palanquin*, which is to be my substitute for a cot, to which it is far preferable, particularly on occasions when in rainy cold weather we may be obliged to remain all night on a plain and exposed to the climate. The day was particularly cool on account of the heavy fall of rain we experienced since yesterday.

I invited all the bachelors to dine with me on the third of August. Packed up my spare saddlery in readiness to send off to Mynpoorie to Wemyss's care, and my guns also (except Baker and my rifle, my constant companions, with my pistols), it being desirable to move as light as possible. By the Calcutta Gazette received today I was happy to see Golding in Orders for a new appointment.

August 1st.—We mustered this morning a quarter of an hour after sunrise, after which I drove to Cumberlege's, and took Mrs. Cumberlege a long drive into the country; the weather very pleasant. Breakfasted at Cumberlege's, and remained nearly all the morning with them, Mrs. Cumberlege employed in copying a curious painting.

Commenced covering the upper fly of my old tent afresh, having otherwise completely set it in order. Vaughan sent a servant of his who understood tent making, to give them instructions. Letters today stated the probability of our not moving out till the rainy season is past; others affirms that the day was fixed (the third) for the troops, with the commander-in-chief, to leave Cawnpore. Despatched my new tent, a box of spare saddlery, three double-barrel guns, and one trunk of clothes to Wemyss at Mynpoorie. Grant and Weston passed the afternoon with me, and at half-past five I marched my grenadiers the butt. Fired six rounds, by sections, and their fire was well directed. In taking a shot at the target with my rifle, I singed the bearskin of my hat.

August 3rd.—Sinclair, Grant, Livesey, Weston, MacGregor, Forbes, Murray, Arden, Harriott, Vaughan and Macaulay dined with me this evening, and we kept it up till an early hour. Sung a great deal, and parted in high good humour. Some of the party who absconded after drinking as long as they thought proper were brought back to the charge, and this ended in one of the hardest going days I ever saw in my life.

August 4th.—We paraded (some of us, others reported sick) at gun fire this morning for exercise. Went through the same manoeuvres and firings as the last day we were out. After exercises I returned home, went to bed, and slept till nearly ten. Bathed and breakfasted at home. Amused ourselves with pipe tailing some *tatoos* (ponies), which annoyed our horses sadly.

All yesterday's dinner party *tiffed* with me today, and after *tiffin* we sent for Weston's antelope and loosed two brace of greyhounds at him; he went off in the most delightful style, and easily bounded out of reach of the best of our dogs. It afforded us very capital sport, and we knocked up our horses as well as our dogs. I was for picquet this evening, and marched them to their post a quarter of an hour before sunset. Drove MacGregor round the course; we passed the gun the moment it fired, and it so terrified the leader that I could not pacify him the whole evening. Dined with Grant this evening, and, as usual, all passed a jolly day.

August 5th.—A melancholy affair is said to have taken place in Candia, on the Malay Coast. Fourteen officers and three hundred men of the 51st Regiment, commanded by a major, are reported to have been put to death by the Candians, and the Malays, who went over to the enemy during the action, are said to have treacherously joined the Candians in this murderous business. The expedition now fitting out below is said to be intended against the Candians.

August 6th.—The battalion at exercise this morning; we went through the most useful and likely manoeuvres to be practised with an army, to get perfect in which, and to make the men steady in their firings, are considerable objects to accomplish. We were dismissed before six. I returned immediately home, slept an hour, bathed and dressed, and breakfasted with Wilson. Called at Grant's on my way home, and stayed an hour with him, firing at a mark with his pistols. Wemyss's *hurkarrah* (running footman) arrived from Mynpoorie with *taut* (canvas) to repair my tent, which Wemyss had kindly procured for me. Wrote to Wemyss and sent a dog of Colonel Blair's to him to procure a breed from a beautiful Europe setter, for which Wemyss paid four hundred *rupees* (equal to £50.)

August 7th.—Letters by this evening's post mention that the troops at Futty Ghur are to march positively on the 17th, or probably sooner. All the heavy guns ordered to be put on transport carriages in readiness to move at the shortest notice, and everything bade fair for a bloody campaign, as the enemy are certainly very numerous, supported by a formidable train of artillery, of which we hope soon to have an opportunity of relieving them.

A report that a picquet of five hundred men of the enemy were seen encamped on brink of the Mahratta country, not seven miles from our cantonments, purposely, it was conjectured, to watch the movements of our corps; it was true that they remained in their own country, but the position they had chosen caused great room for suspicion.

I was on picquet this evening, and thought it advisable to load my sentries in case of any alarm. Returned after dinner to remain all night with my picquet (in cantonments and at out stations this was not generally expected in time of peace).

August 8th.—Joined the battalion with my picquet at gun fire this morning for exercise; performed several manoeuvres, and fired twenty-one rounds of light ammunition. Breakfasted at Colonel Blair's. Harriott returned and passed the morning with me. My company and the 2nd Grenadiers ordered for target practice this afternoon. The rain commenced soon after four, and prevented us going out. It rained till six, and the weather was cool in consequence.

Drove Mrs. Cumberlege twice round the course this evening, and to MacGregor's, where we dined, a large party. Singing after dinner. The ladies left us about eleven, and we set in for a long night. Drank a great deal of claret, and about three in the morning a dance was proposed in honour of the reported campaign. Vaughan and MacGregor at first commenced the music, but we sent for the fifes and drums of the Battalion, and kept it up until the gun fired at day break. Fortunately for us all there was no exercise today.

August 9th.—At dinner today we all met at Weston's, and again drank a great deal of wine. We heard this evening that the commander-in-chief and Cawnpore troops marched on the 7th and 8th. Mrs. Cunynghame wrote me from Mynpoorie that Cunynghame had received instructions to order two bridges to be built across the Esah River, one equal to bear a heavy train, and another for the column to pass over.

The report today was that General Perron (Scindiah's commander-in-chief) has sworn all the chiefs of his army to conquer or die with him. A great number of Sikhs are said to have joined

General Perron, so that we expect some hard work.

Perron making every preparation to oppose us, and to defend himself. All Scindiah's brigades and artillery from the Decan preparing to join him, and as they amount to nearly twenty times our number, both in troops and guns, he is said to be confident of success. His artillery reported to be equal to any in the world, and in that he chiefly depends for our destruction. We flatter ourselves that there will be many broken heads before that is effected. General Lake we heard of today, within thirty miles of us, and we remained in hourly expectation of moving out to join His Excellency.

All anxious for further intelligence, and for the order of march to arrive.

August 15th.—Got up this morning an hour before daybreak, and saw my tent and baggage all laden on the camels and bullocks. At gun fire we paraded, wheeled into line, and then by sections, backward on our left, at six we marched out of cantonments, the drums and fifes playing the Grenadiers' March officers and men in the highest spirits possible. We encamped on a high spot of ground, a short distance to the south-east of Major Hammond's bungalow, and not more than two miles from our cantonment. Harriott had ordered breakfast for the last time to be laid in his bungalow, and after the parade was dismissed and the picquets and guards posted a party of us galloped back to the cantonments and breakfasted.

CHAPTER 13

March to Ali Ghur from Shikoabad

August 16th.—15 Miles. Jussranah. The battalion marched this morning at four. The orders for the picquet on duty to form the rearguard kept me on the ground till late, as it was a long time before everything was clear off. The ammunition bullocks being fresh from so much rest, and many of them quite unaccustomed to carry barrels, gave us much trouble and delayed us considerably, very frequently throwing their loads and running off.

We did not arrive at our ground till nearly four hours after the corps. Colonel Blair sent after me as I passed on with my picquet, and ordered breakfast for me at his tent. The roads today were much better than we expected, considering the immense heavy falls of rain; the roads or rather tracks were literally level, and very little cut, as scarcely any carriages ever pass on them. *Tiffed* with Grant, and at four o'clock Cumberlege, Livesey and myself went out with our guns; killed a great number of peacocks, hares and grey partridges. It was quite dark before we returned. Forbes, Murray and Grant dined with me, and we had a very cheerful evening. Went to bed at ten.

August 17th.—16 Miles. The general beat this morning at three, and we marched off at half an hour after. Found the water high in many places on the line of march, and in crossing a valley in which the water had lodged we were under the necessity of carrying the limber boxes over it on men's heads, and the soldiers were obliged to take off their pouches to secure their ammunition. Most of the officers crossed over standing on the guns and tumbrils. I rode Major, but it was up to the skirts of the saddle. This detained us very considerably, and it was nearly nine before we arrived at our ground.

I breakfasted with Weston, and received a letter from Thornhill, Bareilly, telling me that Mr. Seton offered to apply to the adjutant-general for the adjutancy of the Provincial Corps there, if I would accept it after the campaign; himself giving me, at the same time, an invitation to his house, which he requested I would at all times consider as my own. These attentions proved highly gratifying to me, but under our present circumstances I could not accept their kind offers, being determined to hint at no such thing as long as we had an army in the field.

Tiffed with Forrest, and at three Cumberlege and myself went out shooting. Colonel Blair saw me passing his tent, and gave me a good lecture for exposing myself to the sun. We tried till dark, but found very little game (an unusual occurrence in India). Killed some partridges and two brace of hares. Dined with Sinclair. Dressed after we returned, and was consequently very late at dinner. Passed a jolly evening.

August 18th.—16 Miles. Etah. We marched this morning by the left. The general beat at three, and the assembly at half-past. Owing to having walked a good deal yesterday evening, and blistered my feet, they were so much inflamed that I could neither stand on them or wear my boots.

Colonel Blair's grey charger being much steadier on the line of march than either of my own, he kindly ordered it to be brought up for me, and I actually rode the whole morning with my feet wrapped up in towels, and in the greatest tortures.

The country through which we marched this day was pretty well wooded, and remarkably green. Some of the windings we passed were truly romantic, and it was rendered still more pleasant by the drums and fifes playing marches and country dances as we marched on. This was one of the pleasantest mornings (the weather) I ever recollect to have marched in, and the weather was particularly cool.

About three miles from our ground, near a village we came

to a lake, in the midst of one of the finest brushwood covers imaginable, and the battalion and its guns crossing it was really a most pleasing sight.

August 19th.—A report today that General Perron had threatened an attack on Sarssney (six miles only from his headquarters at Coel), that the corps in garrison there had been kept several nights on the alert, a great proportion of the men were constantly under arms, guns loaded and matches burning. One letter mentioned that the half-cast officers of Scindiah's service had left it in consequence of a proclamation declaring that all people of that description, born of British parentage, who remained in the service of the native powers, with whom war was now declared, would be considered as traitors to their country, and treated accordingly should the fate of war throw them into our hands.

The commander-in-chief and the army expected to join us about the 26th, and we imagined that hostilities would immediately commence. The Mahrattas are said to have collected an immense force on their frontier, and the native powers have joined them with strong bodies of cavalry.

August 22nd.—Breakfasted at my own tent with Forrest, Harriott and Weston. I received a letter from Wemyss, who, I was exceedingly happy to find, was with General Lake, living in his Excellency's family. The commander-in-chief had at home been intimate with Wemyss's brother, General Wemyss, and in consequence showed Wemyss every kindness, and took him from his station at Mynpoorie because he expressed himself desirous (though in the Civil Service) to witness a campaign.

About twelve the quarter-master-general passed through our camp, to mark out ground for the encampment of the army tomorrow, and soon after an order reached us, directing our march at three tomorrow morning. Walked in the evening to the mango grove, where we had sent our horses and dogs to remain during the heat of the day. Swinton of the 12th and Macaulay came into our camp this evening. A large party of us dined with

Livesey, and a harder going day I seldom had experienced.

August 23rd.—The battalion marched this morning at three o'clock, and we came to our ground shortly after daybreak. At six his Excellency the commander-in-chief arrived with H.M. 27th and 29th Dragoons, 76th Foot, 15th Regiment of Native Infantry, four companies of the 4th Regiment and four companies of the 17th Regiment, with the 1st Regiment Native Cavalry.

General St. John also arrived with the commander-in-chief; they all encamped close upon our right, in .a thin brushwood jungle, and on a fine crop of young indigo. Wemyss, who came in with the commander-in-chief, breakfasted with me, as did Livesey, Aubery, Weston, Arden, Murray, Grant and Harriott.

Colonel Blair went after breakfast to pay his respects to his Excellency the commander-in-chief, and returned very much pleased at the manner in which the general spoke of the corps, and told us all that we must avail ourselves of the first opportunity that may offer to convince his Excellency that we were all desirous to prove ourselves deserving of the high estimation in which the commander-in-chief professed to hold us. The colonel was told that he may depend upon us, and that nothing on earth we wished for so much as an opportunity to evince our prowess.

Colonel Blair had formerly distinguished himself on many occasions, and was thought to be also the first drill officer in the service. He was second in command of one of the corps which formed the detachment under General Goddard, famous for having marched through an enemy's country across the Peninsula of India, a most timely reinforcement to Bombay. They captured also the strong forts of Basseen and Amidabad. In the course of the campaign the corps to which Colonel Blair belonged was detached to bring in some provisions and grain from the neighbouring villages, from which it was exacted by force.

The convoy was attacked, and the battalion beset on all sides by innumerable bodies of the enemy's horse. Colonel Blair, perceiving that the commanding officer of the corps was in a very unfit state to command on so serious an occasion, and that the result bid fair to be the complete destruction of them all without hesitation put his commanding officer in arrest, and took the command himself, and accordingly had the credit of saving not only the battalion but the convoy. It was an occurrence almost unprecedented, for a junior officer upon a parade, and in the face of an enemy, to put his senior in arrest.

The commanding officer never afterwards did duty, and was eventually necessitated to quit the service.

Wemyss remained nearly all the day with me, and I was happy when he told me that he had heard the commander-in-chief speak of me in favourable terms. As the general, however, had so many solicitations from Europe to serve officers in the army, and as I had unfortunately no claims of that nature on his Excellency, I did not flatter myself much, being determined at all events to endeavour to deserve well, and take my chance cheerfully with many others, whose expectations were not more flattering than my own.

Wemyss sent for his guns and dogs, and we had a review of them, promising ourselves some sport of that sort occasionally. We mustered between us nine double-barrel guns and perhaps some of the highest bred dogs (terriers and pointers) in India. By all accounts received today the enemy are making the most active preparations, and some large bodies of their horse are said to have advanced towards us from Coel and Ali Ghur. It was conjectured that we should immediately be formed into brigades upon the arrival of the Futty Ghur troops under General Ware, daily expected, and that we shall attack them without delay.

Wemyss left me about eleven, and I remained in my tent the whole morning. *Tiffed* with Livesey; Arden, Aubery, MacGregor, Weston, Harriott, Forrest, Swinton and Grant dined with me today. Passed a very cheerful evening, and broke up about twelve o'clock.

August 24th.—The army marched this morning by the right. Baggage on the right. Our battalion in the rear of the pack. The country through which we marched was very fertile and pleasant, and we arrived at our ground near to Secundra about eleven o'clock. Wemyss, who came on as staff to the commander-in-chief, passed the day with me. General Ware, with the Futty Ghur division of troops expected to join us tomorrow, and we have every reason to imagine that the campaign will commence immediately. The Mahrattas said to be taking the field with all their regular troops and a formidable train of artillery. We dined with Grant this evening, and a great number of songs were sung. We passed a very jolly night, and broke up at an early hour.

August 25th.—Camp at Secundrapore. We marched at daylight this morning, and arrived early at our ground. At seven o'clock General Ware joined us. MacGregor and self went to breakfast with Middleton, and my friends of the 3rd Cavalry (which came in with General Ware, and the Futty Ghur division). Colonel Blair sent for me to his tent, and told me that General Lake had been enquiring of him for me in a very particular manner, and that his Excellency expressed a wish to serve me, and also his intention of giving me an appointment with the army.

This was the most pleasant information I had ever heard respecting India and my prospects in it.

Soon after Wemyss wrote a note and told me that I was appointed quarter-master of a brigade and quarter-master to my regiment in the room of Cumberlege, appointed a major of brigade. Went up to Wemyss in the headquarter line, and met Major Nicholson (A.D.C. to the commander-in-chief and quarter-master-general of the King's Troops.) He congratulated me on my appointment, and told me that the commander-in-chief had often expressed himself pleased at some occurrences which had taken place the former campaign in which it was my good fortune to have been employed. My appointment appeared in Orders this day, and the army was brigaded, and formed as follows:

Cavalry	Infantry
1st Brigade Cavalry.	1st Brigade Infantry.

2nd Brigade Cavalry. 2nd Brigade Infantry.
3rd Brigade Infantry.
4th Brigade Infantry.

General Order of Battle of the British Army at Secundrapore,

August 26th, 1803.
General Lake—Commander-In-Chief.
Infantry Line At Secundrapore.

2nd Brigade: 3rd Brigade:
Brigr. Clarke. Brigr. McDonald.
Bri.-Majr. Anderdon. Bri.-Majr. Christie.
Bri.-Qr.-Masr. Macan. Bri -Qr.-Masr. Wallace.
Staff. Staff!

4th Brigade: 1st Brigade:
Brigr. Powell. Brigr. Monson.
Bri.-Majr. Cumberlege. Bri.-Majr. Ritso.
Bri -Or.-Masr. Pester. Bri.-Qr.-Masr. Gahan
Staff. Staff.

Park of Artillery.
Col. Horsford, Comg.: Majr.-Bri. Butler:
   Qr.-Masr. Browne.

Cavalry Line.
2nd Brigade. 1st Brigade.
Brigr. Macan. Brigr. St. Leger.
Bri.-Majr. Macan. Majr.-Br. Gore.
Staff. Staff.

August 27th.—This morning the army commenced its march, and I, with the quarter-master-general and quarter-master of brigade, went on in front to look out for ground to encamp on, and to mark out the line for my brigade. Arrived and encamped (the army) about ten, a little to the southward of Bechey Ghur, on the Alighur Road. Today we had pretty good information that Perron was at Coel, and that he meant to try his prowess with us, and depended much on his cavalry, which were very numerous, and said to be the finest Irregular Horse that were ever seen in Hindustan.

We heard a distant firing of cannon this forenoon, and were told it was General Perron's Flying Artillery, and that he daily exercised them many hours, and conceived himself perfectly prepared for the arrival of the British Army. We encamped about eighteen or twenty miles from Coel and Ali Ghur today, and some small detached parties of the enemy's Horse were seen by our picquets at a distance, but no shots were exchanged or fired by either party.

Some British officers, late of Scindiah's and Holcar's Service, came into our camp today, and gave us a most formidable account of the power and force of the enemy, and of their being determined to dispute the ground with us inch by inch, and we as eagerly hoped they would not change their plans, but give us an opportunity of closing with them. From the accounts these officers gave of their formidable artillery, and the state of discipline of the troops destined to support it, it is all fair to calculate upon the loss of many officers and men before we gain possession of it, and defeat their troops, which we do not despair of doing whenever an opportunity offers.

The British officers who gave us those particulars of the enemy may be supposed to be well acquainted with the real state of their forces, as they were the very men who had disciplined their troops and artillery, and a few weeks since only were with them, some in command of brigades, others majors, captains and subalterns.

The French officers, of course, remained attached to General Perron, but after the proclamation which had been issued by our Government, it would have been treason in Englishmen to have continued and to have fought against their country. It was certainly a hard case to those people to relinquish a service which not only gave them bread, but many of them were in situations that promised to have gained them in a few years a handsome independency. Wemyss and self rode in the evening round the fort of Bechey Ghur, and we went to the spot on which our batteries were erected when we besieged the place the last year. Wemyss told me in confidence that it was his opinion we should have a bloody campaign, and all those at headquarters as fully expected it.

August 28th.—This morning we marched at daylight, and last evening all the sick of the different brigades were sent into the garrison of Bechey Ghur, in order that the rapid marches which It was expected the army would sometimes have occasion to make may not be impeded. We encamped in a short brushwood cover this morning, and our picquets were strongly posted at a rising ground in front. About eleven o'clock some strong columns of Horse made their appearance, and part of the line was immediately under arms. They approached near the picquets, and by the immense dust that was flying in different directions it appeared as if they were premeditating an attack.

They kept hovering about till about three in the evening, and then drew off towards the fort of Ali Ghur. I went after breakfast this morning to see Wemyss, and we called on Major Nicholson and Major Lake. All in expectation of an action tomorrow morning, as at headquarters they had received intelligence that General Perron, with about twenty thousand troops, was drawn up near Coel for the purpose of giving us battle. As it was expected that the corps would be engaged in the morning, Colonel Blair paid me the compliment to request that I would not go on in front with the quarter-master-general, but remain to assist him when we should get into action, which I did not.

CHAPTER 14

The Storming of Ali Ghur

August 29th.—The army marched this morning at daybreak, in one column, cavalry leading the line. At the distance of about five miles from Coel we heard a salute of twenty-one guns; supposed from the fortress of Ali Ghur, but saw no enemy till we arrived in sight of the place, when we discovered them striking their camp, and forming their troops into immense columns, preserving an extensive line, with a deep morass covering their front.

I was with the advanced guard, and we received orders from General Lake to storm a high village, which was occupied by the enemy, on the skirts of the morass. This we effected, and here we suffered almost the only loss that was sustained during the day. The fire of the enemy's musketry was very hot, till we closed with them. The line coming up, we gained ground to the right in order to outflank the enemy, as well as to march clear of the morass, which covered them.

The 27th and 29th Dragoons led the column of native cavalry, supported by the infantry. The Galloper guns opening was the signal to commence the attack, and the British line advanced in a most steady manner. On our nearer approach they drew off towards the fort, which covered their retreat by continuing a heavy fire on us. The enemy had in the field this morning upwards of twenty thousand men, but they did not choose to risk anything decisive with us. General Perron, the Frenchman who commanded them, we were told by some prisoners, was the first to fly. As we passed over their ground of encampment we saw a great many of the enemy, who fell by the fire of our Flying Artillery; they were so numerous that every shot did execution.

The general did me the honour to send me repeatedly with orders during the affair, as his staff were all employed. I had my grey horse, Collector, shot through the neck in attacking the village with the advanced guard; he bled a good deal, but my other horses were with the line, in the rear, and I could not dismount him for nearly an hour after he was wounded. Soon after two o'clock we commenced pitching our camp within random shot of the fort, covering the town of Coel, into which the commander-in-chief ordered a battalion for its protection. The morning was excessively hot, and the quarter-master-general was near fainting, as we were marking out the line, having exerted himself greatly in the course of the day.

At this moment my groom came up with a fresh horse and some water, which poor Campbell said was the saving of his life. Wemyss passing up the line with his horse much distressed, I mounted him on Major. He was going with orders to the picquets, and did not return till sunset. At five we had the orders out, when the commander-in-chief expressed himself much gratified with the conduct of the troops. It was nearly four p.m. before we broke our fast, and a hotter day in August I never knew. Dined with Forrest this evening.

August 30th.—Frequent firing of cannon this morning, on our advanced picquets; their heavy guns completely reached us, and annoyed us a good deal. Notwithstanding the fire from the garrison, there was a report that a negotiation was on foot, and that Colonel Pedron was inclined to surrender the place. Remained all day in my lines. MacGregor, Weston, Grant, Aubery, Forbes and Livesey dined with me, and we spent a very pleasant, jolly evening.

August 31st.—At daybreak this morning MacGregor, Shairpe of the 12th, and myself made a push, and passed under a smart fire to General Perron's gardens, which were beautifully situated, and in the highest state of preservation. On our return we were again exposed to the fire of the garrison, and several guns were laid for us, and one very heavy shot was near clearing the whole of us, it completely covered us with sand.

Breakfasted with MacGregor; called afterwards on Colonel Blair, from whence I went to headquarters. Wemyss informed me that the garrison had been summoned to surrender, but that it was probable some of us should soon hear more of it. Wemyss mentioned to me "that a Captain Boukett of Perron's Service met the commander-in-chief about an hour before the action of the 29th commenced, just before the armies came in sight of each other. After a short conference, his Excellency requested him to take himself away, and never to return to him with any terms in future—advising him at the same time to be quick, or that he should be with General Perron before him." Signed the quarter-master roll this morning for the first time. Dined with the commander-in-chief.

September 1st.—Left the camp this morning at daybreak, and rode with several other officers to the town of Coel, which we found a large straggling place, similar to all other Indian towns I had ever seen. Buildings mean and irregular. Near the centre of the place stood a Mosque, from the top of which we had a good view of the country, which was in a high state of cultivation. A Frenchman made his escape this morning from the garrison, from whom we learnt that the troops had determined never to quit the place, but with their lives; that they were resolved rather to remain and be buried in its ruins. General Perron said to be collecting the whole of his brigades, and a decisive action in the field soon expected to take place. Called this forenoon on tile officers of our 2nd Battalion and *tiffed* with Walker.

On my way to my tent called on some friends of the 15th, which was stationed near us in the line. My grey horse recovering fast of the wound he received on the 29th August. Rode an Arab of Wemyss this evening. Returned in front of the line, as the troops were beating off.

September 2nd.—Camp before Ali Ghur. A large party of us dined with Cumberlege today. In the night we experienced a severe shock of an earthquake. I jumped out, and laid hold of the pole of my tent, and for a long time could not believe but that I was dreaming, till the noise of the servants and officers in the tents near mine convinced me it was an earthquake. The motion was very like that of a small boat in a moderate sea. It was the severest shock ever remembered by any in camp, and caused a general alarm.

Went with Livesey and Munro, brother to Munro who was killed in a duel with Pattle, this morning through the town of Coel. Breakfasted with Colonel Simpson. A working party and the pioneers employed this morning cutting materials for a battery; a report that the garrison is divided, but that the strongest party are determined to defend the place to the last extremity.

Captain Lucan, late of Scindiah's service, came into camp today from Delhi, the brigades there preparing either to march to the relief of Coel or to oppose us in the field. Those from the Decan Captain Lucan supposed could not be within two hundred miles of the Jumnah. Dined today with Major Hammond; drank more claret than usual all of us. It was reported this evening that the fort would be stormed in the morning.

September 3rd.—Advanced a party this morning into Perron's garden, which they perceived from the fort, and commenced immediately cannonading it. The pioneers employed as yesterday, cutting materials for batteries, which we imagined to be a deception, as it was pretty certain from Wemyss's account that we should attempt the place by a *coup de main*. Saw Shipton at the Park this evening, mounting two twelve-pounders on field carriages, and removing some eighteens from their transports to field carriages. Shipton told me in confidence, enjoining me to secrecy, that we were to assault the place, by the gateways, at daybreak in the morning, and that he was the captain of artillery fixed on for the dangerous service of commanding the guns which were destined to blow the gates open.

Letters this evening mentioned hostilities having commenced

in the Decan, and that General Wellesley had taken the *pettah* of the fort of Ahmidnagur by storm; it was expected that the fall of that place would soon follow. At sunset went to the parade of the 76th to hear their band. St. Aubin showed me a new purchase, a very clever horse, bought of Ridge, and told me that his company (the Light Company of the 76th) would be one of those employed in the assault. We had been long and intimately acquainted, and took a last farewell of each other. I dined at the mess of the 12th Regiment. The orders for the storm were sent to me by Colonel Blair about midnight, and he ordered me to have our regiment under arms at half-past four in the morning on our own parade.

September 4th.—The whole line was under arms at five o'clock; the storming party formed near Perron's gardens, and the covering guns were run down during the night. Those destined to cover the left were three eighteen-pounders; those to the right four six-pounders. Four companies of the 76th, with a proportion of men from the native corps, formed the storming party, and a quarter of an hour before day broke the whole advanced in silence and in a most steady becoming manner. I was ordered by the general to accompany the storming party, and to bring him immediate information if any support should be required. The Honourable Colonel Monson, who headed the stormers, advanced steadily at the head of his column, which was preceded by Shipton and two twelve-pounders, scaling ladders, etc. We were at the entrance of the sortie before they could perceive us from the walls.

Our first salute was from the two half-moon batteries which flanked the gateway, and at the same moment the whole face of the fort was illuminated by the fire of their cannon and musketry. Our covering batteries opened at the same time, and their fire, as we could perceive by the slaughter on the walls, was well directed. In addition to the heavy guns which played upon us In the sortie, the enemy had also heavy mortars loaded with grape and canister shot, and the leading twelve-pounder of ours, was, in the hurry to carry it up to the gate, thrown into a trench which the enemy had made near the entrance of the sortie. This misfortune detained us considerably, and at this time it was that we lost so many of our officers and men.

Never did I witness such a scene before the second gun could be hauled up; the sortie was become a perfect slaughter-house, and it was with the greatest difficulty that we dragged the gun over our killed and wounded. Nothing could exceed the determined gallantry with which our troops struggled under this most destructive fire. The enemy, too, fought desperately, and many of them actually stepped out upon our own ladders which were placed against the wall to meet our men ascending, but British valour prevailed, and although Shipton, who commanded the guns, was wounded, he kept on his legs till two rounds from the leading gun opened the outer gate, when our troops rushed in, and the slaughter among the enemy, in their turn, became very great. My horse was twice wounded this morning, but I, with my usual good fortune, escaped unhurt.

At this time I left the stormers, with the welcome news to the general (whom I found at a village in front of our line) of our troops being in. I told him also that the slaughter had been very great, and that many officers had fallen, also that I had seen Colonel Monson wounded, but whether dangerously or not I could not tell. By this time our troops were in full possession of the place, and I returned with the general down to the fort, and although he was, of course, highly gratified with our success, and spoke in terms of admiration of those employed, I never saw anyone more distressed for a moment when he entered the sortie, and saw officers and men heaped on one another.

My feelings were such as I had seldom experienced when among the dead I recognised poor St. Aubin. I saw him in the heat of the attack, gallantly encouraging his men, within a short distance of the spot on which he fell. St. Aubin was attached to the Light Infantry, and was much beloved. He was shot through the breast, and could have suffered but little. Captain Cameron and Campbell (his nephew) were lying dead close by him, and near them poor Fleming, in the agonies of death. Lieutenants

Browne and Turton were killed close to the gate. Colonel Monson, Lieutenant-Colonel Brown, Captain Bagshaw, Captain Shipton, Lieutenants Ritso, Andre, Sinclair, Fraser, Welner, Berry, and many others wounded.

Many of the enemy were shot in attempting to escape by swimming the ditch after we got in, and I remarked an artilleryman to snap his piece at a man who at the same instant dived to save himself. The soldier coolly waited his coming up, and shot him through the head. As the heat of the business was over, I remonstrated with him on putting them to death at that time, but the man declared that he had lost some of his oldest comrades that morning, and that he wished to be revenged, reminding me also that we had received orders to spare none. A grenadier came up, wounded, to the general at the gate, and "hoped his honour was well," telling him that he belonged to his company in taking of York Town in America. The commander-in-chief desired him to come to headquarters, and that he would see what could be done for him.

Guards were posted over the different magazines, and at each gate, as soon as we had complete possession, and the enemy were all disposed of; scarcely a man of them escaped, for those who swam the ditch were cut up by the troopers on the plain, and all we found in the place were bayoneted. They were told what they might expect if they waited the result of a storm. The storming party were allowed three hours to plunder, and we found several tumbrils of treasure in the garrison.

Monsieur Pedron, the French colonel, had a very narrow escape. One of our Light Infantry men was in pursuit of him, and would in an instant more have come up with and bayoneted him, but Macleod interfered, and, receiving his sword, saved his life by ordering the man to refrain. Colonel Pedron was placed in command of Ali Ghur by General Perron, as a man in whose valour and address he could most rely, and to do him justice he certainly made a very gallant defence, and to our cost.

I returned to camp at one o'clock, when everything was perfectly silent, and breakfasted with Rose of the 14th. Intelligence reached us this day at noon that our cantonments at Shikoabad had been attacked by five thousand of the enemy's Horse, and that after a desperate resistance they were repulsed by Colonel Cunynghame with great slaughter, but we learnt to our sorrow that although the lines were saved, our bungalows (with all we left in them) were burnt to the ground, and the *chounie* of the city also destroyed.

Rode a horse of Rose's this evening; we went down again to the fort, where our pioneers were draining the ditch, and burying the dead. At sunset we returned, and attended the funeral of those gallant and much lamented officers who fell in the morning. The whole of them were carried to the lines of the 76th Regiment, and at six o'clock we moved off in slow time to pay the last tribute, and to perform the usual honours to those brave men who had fallen, serving their country, and this solemn procession was conducted in a manner becoming men who felt for the loss of fellow soldiers.

I felt much distressed for poor St. Aubin, and the circumstance of having at the same hour, the preceding evening, met on the same spot, and conversed with nearly all the party, would have affected any but a very flinty heart indeed. After the usual firings, the funeral party reversed arms, and we marched back to the line of the 76th, and there dispersed.

A large party of us dined this evening with Livesey, and we passed a very gloomy day.

September 5th.—I went this morning and breakfasted at headquarters, and was much gratified at General Lake's taking me aside after breakfast, and, after speaking to me in a manner that could not but afford me the highest gratification, he assured me that he would take the earliest opportunity of giving me a better appointment than that of quarter-master of brigade, and which he had given to me in a most handsome way. Colonel Lake asked me to dine at headquarters this evening. Wemyss and self mounted two Arabs of his, and took a long ride round the picquets. We fell in with the 3rd Regiment of Cavalry, going foraging, and accompanied them. We saw some small parties of the enemy's Horse, which kept far enough out of our reach. Two or three shot from the Gallopers were fired at them. We went purposely to see the country, and to ascertain if it afforded any game. Saw some antelope and a few hares. It was a too well cultivated country for game. The crops very abundant, and the land in a very high state of cultivation.

It was considered Perron's own domain, and given him by the Prince (Scindiah) as his salary and pay, as commander-in-chief of all his forces. The idea of losing his country, and the requisition said to have been made to his prince for the dismissal of all Frenchmen were the supposed reasons for Perron advising Scindiah to go to war with us, and which they no sooner engaged in than the latter seemed to have repented, as well as his employer. Scindiah's Infantry said to be in force near Delhi, and other brigades marching with all expedition from the Decan. We expect an action with them shortly, and .all the officers lately in Scindiah's employ assure us that they depend entirely on the formidable train of artillery to defeat us. They are said to be fine guns, elegantly mounted and well served.

Accounts reached us from Shikoabad today, by which it appeared that on the morning of the 3rd instant, about four o'clock, they were attacked by upwards of five thousand of the enemy's Horse, which, after a most severe conflict that lasted till past two in the afternoon, were completely beaten off, and with great slaughter. Our men were drawn up on our old exercise ground, all ready to receive the enemy. They began the attack in front, and at the same time a considerable body got round to the rear, set fire to the lines, and all our bungalows, which, with the whole of the furniture we left, were completely destroyed.

Poor Mrs. Wilson, who remained only of the ladies, with an idea that there would be no risk at Shikoabad with five companies, was, with all her children, made prisoner, and carried off to the fort of Agra. It did not appear that she had been ill-used, and, fortunately, this party was headed by a Frenchman of the name of Fleury, who treated her very politely, and restored to her as many of her clothes as could be secured; a great part had previously been plundered by their soldiers.

This afternoon Wilson received a letter from Mrs. Wilson dated from the fort of Agra, and as there were several Europeans there (French and Dutch), who treated her and the children with kindness and attention, there was nothing to be apprehended, if her release can be effected before we besiege that place, and which it was fully expected we should do. Colonel Lake, Wemyss and myself went this evening to examine minutely the works of Ali Ghur. It was in the highest condition possible. Ramparts, bastions, parapets and the ditch all in perfect order. The guns and tumbrils (of French model) uncommonly fine. The only entrance was flanked by batteries of heavy cannon and mortars, and from their fire it was that most of our officers and men fell yesterday morning. The camp gun fired before we left the garrison, and dinner was on MacGregor's table before I reached the lines.

We sat talking over the storm till nearly twelve o'clock.

September 6th.—The army halted today. We heard that Scindiah's Infantry and guns were preparing to dispute the passage of the Jumnah with us. They had, of course, secured all the boats, and we heard had raised heavy batteries at the most penetrable places on the banks. The river at this season is nowhere fordable, and it is reasonable to conclude that much blood will be spilt on the banks of the Jumnah before we cross it. Few circumstances, however, come amiss to British soldiers, led on by a gallant general in whom all place the greatest confidence. Wemyss, Peyron and myself rode down the line and to General Perron's gardens this evening.

Dined with the commander-in-chief, who appeared to me more of the finished gentleman the more frequently that I saw him. Some little attentions which they showed me at headquarters were extremely gratifying. A great deal of claret was drunk before we broke up.

September 7th.—Camp at Poomah. The army marched this morning by the right, and the line was counter-marched in consequence. I left the ground at four with the quarter-master-general. The country appeared very little cultivated, and we scarcely saw a tree or a bush during the march. Arrived at the new ground, and marked it out for the line soon after sunrise. The commander-in-chief and his staff passed as I was fixing the camp colours of our brigade. The line was at its ground before seven o'clock. Breakfasted with Colonel Blair, and heard from him that General Perron had actually applied to the commander-in-chief for his protection, and, on condition of obtaining it, it was said that he expressed a desire entirely to quit Scindiah's service and to throw himself on the protection of the British Government. It was added that his Excellency had listened to his proposals.

We heard the particulars of the affair at Shikoabad today, and a very severe business it seems to have been. Colonel Cunynghame, Captain Wimbolt, Captain Lamborne, Lieutenants Heysham and Stoneham were wounded, and a great number of men killed and wounded. Colonel Clarke, with the 2nd Brigade of Infantry, expected to join us tomorrow. Colonel Macan, with one brigade of cavalry, marched last night in pursuit of the troops of the enemy, who, it was reported, were returning with reinforcements of men and guns to make another attack on the handful of men at Shikoabad. In our rear today we had a beautiful and very extensive lake of water, in which the men of the adjacent part of the line bathed, and the elephants delighted themselves by rolling about in it.

September 8th—We marched this morning at half-past three o'clock. Rode on in front as usual with the quarter-master-general; exceedingly admired a chestnut Arab which he rode. Our parties (all the quarter-masters of the line) of a morning were very pleasant, and we escaped the crowd by going off an hour before the line marched, in order to mark out and prepare the ground for them at the new encampment. Soon after sunrise we commenced laying down the camp colours; the direction of the line running across the principal road, the quarter-master-general desired me to throw back our battalions a little, so as to leave it open for the column and guns to pass on. The line came up about eight o'clock, and we conducted the different brigades to their ground. Breakfasted with MacGregor and Weston this morning.

Accounts arrived in camp that on the 5th the Mahrattas returned in force to Shikoabad. Colonel Cunynghame and his small party, consisting only of three hundred men, had retired into a compound, there to defend themselves to the last extremity.

On the arrival of the enemy a summons was sent in, offering them terms, which were, that if the detachment would surrender, it should be allowed to march across the Ganges into the Company's provinces with their gun and all private property. A consultation of the officers was held, and the terms agreed to. The detachment was accordingly marched off agreeable to the above articles, to which was added an engagement not to serve against Scindiah during the present war.

The 2nd Brigade of Infantry, under Colonel Clarke, instead of joining the army, have received orders to march to the neighbourhood of Shekoabad. The 8th Dragoons and a detachment of the 16th Regiment are also reported to be in that quarter. Great hopes are entertained that one of the detachments in quest of Monsieur Fleury may come up with him before he can do much mischief in the Douab or recross the Jumnah. General Perron said to be on his march to our provinces. A strong fort near to our present encampment surrendered to us this evening.

September 9th.—Camp Neem. Marched this morning at three. Right in front, cavalry leading the column. Got to our ground before eight. Encamped the cavalry on the left of the line, in order to bring them near the only water in the vicinity of our camp, a high, small village on our right flank. Two battalions of our brigade keeping in the rear of the Park, did not come up till nearly eleven o'clock. A fine cover in our rear, full of game, but the servants and dogs so completely knocked up by a long and very hot march that we did not go out.

September 10th.—Marched at half-past two this morning. Rode on as usual with Campbell. Encamped the line about two miles on the Delhi side of Secundra. Breakfasted with Rose of the 14th Regiment. Our tents today were pitched in a very high grass jungle, and in swampy grounds. Some of the men employed to carry the camp colours were missing, and we were obliged in consequence to mark out the ground with the sergeant's pikes. The camp colourmen had mistaken the route, and lost themselves in the dark. Dined today with Dyer; at dinner I received a private note from Wemyss telling me that it was the opinion of all at headquarters that we should have an action certainly tomorrow or the next day. Scindiah's troops were said to be at this moment drawn up on the banks of the Jumnah, in order of battle, and ready to engage us. This position said to be a very strong one, supported by a numerous and formidable train of excellent artillery.

We drank an extra bottle of claret upon this intelligence, and without much discussion or reflection on the fate of a battle enjoyed ourselves till near nine o'clock.

Chapter 15

Battle of Delhi (Putper Gunge)

September 11th.—I left the ground soon after two this morning with the quarter-master-general. We were apprehensive of being annoyed by parties of the enemy's Horse, and, therefore, our escort was strengthened by a squadron of dragoons. Soon after daybreak I observed two men quitting the road, and endeavouring to avoid us. I pursued them with a couple of troopers, and soon came up with them. The men appeared a good deal alarmed, and readily confessed they were from the enemy's camp, and were then going in quest of information of our army. They acknowledged their surprise at meeting us, as they had been led to suppose that we were not arrived at Secundra. After a few threats they proceeded to give us intelligence, which rather surprised us, as we did not suppose the enemy had left the banks of the Jumnah. They told us "that Scindiah's army, composed of fourteen thousand men and one hundred pieces of cannon, was at that moment within five miles of us, drawn up in order of battle, waiting our attack."

The quarter-master-general did not credit this account, and it appeared improbable to us that they should quit the banks of the Jumnah. The spies we threatened with immediate death if they gave us information that should not prove correct, but they persisted in their first account. The men were put under a guard, an account of their report was sent back to meet the commander-in-chief and the line, and we proceeded onwards, and at sunrise commenced marking out the ground of encampment unmolested, and without giving credit to one word of information received from the men of the enemy's camp.

After the ground was in readiness and the camp colours of each brigade pitched, we sat quietly down in the shade of some plantain trees, and got a drink of water. At this period we did not know that the enemy's line was within a mile and a half of us, nor had they the smallest idea of our being within fifteen miles of them!

The line came up about nine o'clock; the different corps were dismissed, and the advanced picquets and troops for duty went in front to take their post. The men had begun to undress, and officers' tents were pitching when we heard a straggling fire of musketry in front, and presently a few cannon. Our advanced picquets had hardly reached their destination when we saw them open their guns. A regiment of dragoons were ordered on to reconnoitre; the commander-in-chief went at their head; as they approached the enemy we saw the flashes of more guns, and from that we could plainly make out the direction of the enemy's line, and their position.

The reconnoitring party and our advanced picquets were quickly driven in. The drums on the right of the line now beat to arms, and each brigade took it up in succession. The troops on the right were instantly in motion, and in a few minutes we were all advancing to the attack in excellent order. The rapidity of our advance was so great that our brigade guns and field pieces were obliged to drop in the rear, and we soon found that it was the general's intention to close with the bayonet. The line advanced, silent and determined. Their heavy shot now began to make some havoc among us, and we had yet a full mile to advance under the cannonade of nearly one hundred heavy guns, uncommonly well served, and as their fire seemed every moment to increase, the shot came thicker, and officers and men began to drop fast!

A village on an eminence was immediately in front of our wing, and as we could not pass through it, without throwing the brigade into confusion, Colonel Blair ordered them to wheel back by sections on the right, and moved round its flank in column. The enemy's fire was very destructive on us in clearing this village, and while we were forming again after we had passed it. I was with Colonel Blair at the head of the column receiving some orders from him, when a very heavy shot grazed between us, and most completely buried us in the dust it threw up.

The colonel was nearly dismounted by his horse taking fright. We escaped, but the shot plunged directly into the column, and killed and wounded a great many men in the leading company (the Grenadiers of the 14th Regiment). At this moment another cannon shot grazed my horse, and although it touched him, fortunately but very slightly, he dropped on his haunches, but as it was merely the jar of the shot that shook him, he immediately recovered himself, nor did he appear the least intimidated.

We quickly formed our line after we had passed the village, and closed again with the corps on our right. The cannonade at this time to a calm spectator must have seemed tremendous and awful, and the grape came literally in showers. I had the mortification to see poor Aldin and Harriott of our corps fall, while gallantly leading on their respective companies.

A grape shot passed through the housings of my pistols, and shattered the stock of one of them, and I felt my horse staggering under me; another grape had grazed his side, and lodged under the skin; a third went through him. It entered at his near quarter and passed out at the other. He fell on me, and I was a little bruised. General St. John's orderly dragoon (a man of the 27th) by the general's orders rode to the rear to bring up one of his horses, but I mounted one of Colonel Blair's which was immediately at hand. Our troops advanced most gallantly, without taking their muskets from their shoulders, under this galling fire, and such a rattling of shot as we were now exposed to I never witnessed.

At this moment we were within two hundred and fifty paces of the muzzles of their guns. I was the only mounted officer in front of our brigades. I saw the left a little staggered, and was pushing down in front to encourage them, when General Saint

John from the rear, who did not observe me, gave the word to "Fire," and, most miraculous to say, I escaped unhurt, though I was actually within twelve yards of the front rank men, at full speed, when the whole gave their fire. The volley was instantly followed by a cheer, and the drums, striking up, they rushed on with an ardour nothing could resist, closed with the bayonet, when the enemy fled, and the contest with us on the left was now decided. Our troops, after marching eighteen miles, and being so long in action were, of course, much worn and fatigued, and the enemy had greatly the advantage of us in running.

The peals of musketry on the right convinced us that our troops down the line were also closing with the enemy, and when the smoke cleared up a little, it was a most grateful sight to see the whole of this formidable artillery in our possession, the flying enemy making the best of their way off to the rear. The cavalry now were advanced, and we saw them actively carving in all directions. A proportion of our wing was left in possession of the captured guns on our part of the line, and we advanced to support the cavalry.

We drove them (the enemy) into the Jumnah, and hundreds of them were destroyed in endeavouring to cross it. The Flying Artillery was up, and the river appeared boiling by the fire of grape kept up on those of the enemy who had taken to the river. It was literally, for a time, a stream of blood, and presented such a scene as at another period would freeze a man's very soul. When this was past, we faced about, and returned to the field of battle to collect our wounded men and officers.

The commander-in-chief now came to us, and expressed himself in the most flattering terms on the "steady gallantry" of our wing. The men were all crowding round him, and his Excellency had full employment in returning their salutes. The general had been all day where the battle was hottest, and his heroic example did not pass unnoticed among the soldiers.

Although our artillery had been left in the rear, they had not been idle. The guns were advanced to a rising ground, and as the enemy outflanked us, they were enabled to keep up a spirited fire as we could discern by the noise of the shot which passed our left flank.

It was with infinite satisfaction on the clearing up of the smoke when the firing had ceased, that I observed Sinclair and my grenadiers most actively employed with their bayonets and in securing the guns.

After halting on the field about two hours and collecting our wounded, we moved again towards the Jumnah, in a more northerly direction. It was sunset when we commenced marking out the line of encampment. Our tents and baggage did not come up till nearly nine o'clock. A drink of muddy water given to me by a drummer of the 2nd Battalion, I believe almost saved my life, after the close of the action. We were all dreadfully distressed for something to drink. We had been twelve hours in as scorching a sun as ever shone from the heavens, and nearly eighteen hours marching and in action. Our servants, of course, all remained in the rear, and the first opportunity the troops had of quenching their thirst was in the Jumnah. It was with great grief that I heard from an officer of the cavalry that poor Middleton was among the gallant fellows who had fallen in the battle.

My orderly was shot, and a better soldier there never was killed by my side, and by a cannon shot early in the action, and another, Blair's, fell by a grape as we were advancing from the last village. MacGregor's and Murray's servants were the first up and at ten we drank lots of tea on the plain, while our tents were pitching. Colonel Blair came to me and desired me to march two companies to the General Hospital tents which were to remain as a guard. There the scene was truly shocking.

This was a sight that caused tears to bedew those faces which were not used to turn pale at the approach of death in the most terrific forms. About thirty surgeons were absolutely covered with blood, performing operations on the unfortunate soldiers who had their legs and arms shattered in the action, and death in every shape seemed to preside in this assemblage of human misery. Their exclamations were enough to pierce the hardest heart. Numbers were fainting, and even dying under the operation; others bore the pain with as much fortitude as they had evinced in the early part of the day, gallantly executing that duty in which they had received their wounds. In one corner of the tent stood a pile of legs and arms, from which the boots and clothes of many were not yet stripped off. I delivered over the guard to the head surgeon, and left Lieutenant Jones in the field command of the two companies.

Camp near field of battle, after action. About midnight an order came to my tent from headquarters, addressed to Colonel Blair, directing our wing to halt in the morning to bury the officers who fell in the action.

September 12th.—The right wing of the army marched this morning, and encamped about three miles in front. The report from the opposite side of the Jumnah was that in consequence of yesterday's defeat, the enemy's army had completely dispersed. Their guns, tumbrils, colours and arms having been left on the field of battle, and all now in our possession.

Our wing received orders to march at three this evening, after performing the last honours to as many of the brave fellows who fell yesterday as could be collected. Poor Hill of the 12th, a shipmate of mine, was among the slain, and Preston of the 15th was brought in while the funeral service was reading. Some soldiers brought him, uncovered, and just as he fell; his thigh was shattered by a shot, and having been left in the heat of battle he appeared to have died of loss of blood. We had only time to wrap his body in a boat cloak, and to put him in his grave.

Rose and myself did not wait for the line, but mounted our horses and rode on to the general's camp and prepared the lines for our wing, after which we mounted the horses which our grooms had carried on in the morning with the right wing, and galloped down to the banks of the river to reconnoitre, but with our glasses we could not discover the smallest appearance of an enemy anywhere along the opposite banks.

Returned and took some refreshment with Captain Martin, and conducted the wing, which had by this time come up to the ground. Our grooms each carried a leathern bottle of water strapped over their shoulder, to the sides, and in shifting Rose's pistols one of them by some accident went off, and the ball passed through the bottle, which his groom was carrying; the servant was not hurt.

September 13th.—Camp banks of Jumnah. A general order was issued this morning to collect from the soldiers and camp followers all cattle that had been plundered by them from the enemy after the action of the nth. In the course of an hour our non-commissioned, who were employed to collect those of our corps, cleared from the lines of the 2nd Regiment only one hundred and twenty-three fine gun bullocks; they were sent to the prize agents to be disposed of on account of the army at large.

In the evening, Christie, Wallace, Lyons of the 15th, and myself went to the Park to inspect the captured guns. They were cannon mortars, howitzers and carronades of the finest cast, and most highly finished; in general of a French model. By the most accurate accounts from prisoners taken on the 11th, it appears that the enemy had in the action seventeen complete battalions instead of thirteen as was at first reported to us, each corps with its proportion of guns and mortars, beside their Park.

Opposed to them we had seven battalions only, and, comparatively speaking, no artillery. We had not more than eight guns playing on their line of nearly seventeen thousand men, while they had a hundred pieces of cannon blazing on our handful of troops, not exceeding, cavalry and all, six thousand fighting men. We effected that, in a handsome manner, with the point of the bayonet, which never could have been executed in any other way, when their artillery was so superior. In it it was evident they depended for beating us off, and their surprise must have been great when they found that the awful and destructive fire which they kept up was no check to our advance. They must have seen the havoc their shot made among us, but still they found that those who remained came on with redoubled energy.

Our soldiers saw their officers cheerfully leading them on,

and with the most undaunted gallantry they nobly seconded the example set them. It was imagined that in history there is not a single instance recorded of so formidable a force, aided by even a more formidable train of artillery, being so completely annihilated by a handful of men. Dined with Christie this evening, talked over our exploits on the 11th, and drank a decent lot of claret.

September 14th.—The Third Brigade crossed the Jumnah this morning at daybreak. The enemy in their precipitate retreat, of course, had not time to destroy the platform boats on which they crossed their own troops and artillery, and much time saved was the consequence to us. It proved a most fortunate circumstance to our army, the enemy crossing the Jumnah to engage us.

The river was at no part fordable, nor was it likely to be so for some months to come; they had secured every boat, and how we were to have crossed under the cannonade they could have opposed to us I know not. Boats, or rafts of some description, must have been procured, which would have caused great delay, and given them time to collect the troops said to be advancing from the Decan. The enemy felt so confident of the effect of their artillery that it was said their officers could not restrain them, and that they were resolved to decide the contest on the Dewaub side of the Jumnah. It was an infatuation that terminated most happily to our army.

Received a letter from Thornhill, Bareilly, pressing me to apply for the command of the Bareilly Corps, which I declined, in consequence of my present situation on Actual Service. Went to headquarters to see Colonel Lake and Wemyss; found that they were gone to my tent. Remained in Lake's tent till they returned. Wemyss was a good deal bruised on the nth; his own horse was shot, and the commander-in-chief ordered him to mount one of his, and go with orders to some part of the line during the action; in executing the general's orders, and when pushing the horse through some long grass, he stepped into a hole, and rolled completely over Wemyss, who, though not confined, was black from his shoulder down to his ankle; fortunately the horse was secured, and the orders delivered. Colonel Lake wished me to dine at headquarters, but I had a party at home. Livesey, MacGregor, Weston, Forbes, Grant and Murray dined with me, and we parted about twelve, rather glorious or so.

September 15th.—This morning His Excellency the commander-in-chief, with the 1st Brigade, crossed the Jumnah. At sunrise a Royal Salute was fired from the Park, in honour of the capture of Ahmidnagur.

All the baggage of the 1st Brigade moved from our camp to the banks of the river during the day. Dined with General St. John this evening. We had a very large party, and an elegant dinner and good wine of almost every kind. The subject of the battle was the prevailing one during the evening.

September 16th.—The Park moved out of the line this morning at daybreak, and was at the river's side soon after sunrise; commenced crossing it immediately. We heard today that the commander-in-chief had paid his visit to the Emperor, Shah Allum, who received him most graciously, and bestowed on him every title of honour, with numerous presents, etc. This unfortunate monarch had his eyes put out by Gollaum Cawdor, and had now nothing left him but his titles, and the fort of Delhi to reside in (a miserable instance of fallen Royalty).

He is of the noble House of Timur, and one of the highest born Princes in Asia. A number of his sons, Princes of the Blood, reside also in the fort, the whole objects of charity, and with the King supported by the prevailing powers in that part of Hindustan. He is allowed a party as a guard about his person, and those evinced their fidelity two days before the Battle of Delhi, when Louis Bourguain, the Frenchman who commanded the enemy on the 11th, demanded that the Emperor should be given up to them. His faithful guards, however, shut the gates of the garrison, and declared their determination to perish with their noble and unfortunate master.

Louis opened a battery of six heavy guns against the fort, and which was the firing we heard two days before the battle. This battery we found, complete of itself, but the guns, of course, were taken out, and most probably were among those captured on the 11th and now in our Park. What must have been the feelings of this Royal Family during the action which was to decide their fate, for had the Mahrattas conquered, those unfortunate Princes would, to a man, most probably have fallen victims to their temerity, and for refusing to give up the fort to Scindiah's troops. They witnessed the defeat of the enemy from the walls, and saw us cutting them up on the banks of the river, which runs immediately under the fort of Delhi. The Emperor had sent out instantly to congratulate the commander-in-chief on our victory, and declared that he "anxiously waited to receive the general as his saviour in his arms."

Livesey and myself rode towards the banks of the river this evening, and we brought in with us two wretched sufferers of the enemy, who had laid wounded on the field ever since the 11th. We sent them to our hospital, but they were too far gone to leave any hopes of recovery. We supposed they had been wounded on the 11th, but they were not able to articulate, and could not give any account of themselves. We knew them by their hair, which is never cut like our soldiers. They were a fine soldier-like looking cast of men; their clothes were stripped off them, but the most friendly office of the two was left undone- putting them out of their misery.

Under the heavens there is not a more inhuman, barbarous set of brutes than that blood-thirsty crew who are called camp followers of an Indian Army. They accompany it solely with the intention of plunder, and there have been instances known of wounded officers being put to death by those hell-hounds, with their own swords (no doubt), to prevent the possibility of their discovering who had plundered them. They frequently watch the rearguard of an army passing a village, and then push out from their lurking places, in jungle, or any other secure situation that offers, return to the village, sack it completely, and put every helpless wretch to death who attempts to remonstrate with them. When the army commenced its march, the commander-in-chief most wisely issued an order that all persons detected in plundering should be punished with immediate death. This order was afterwards frequently repeated, and many of the vagabonds in consequence met the fate they so richly merited.

We saw a great many partridges and hares in our ride this evening; the banks of the Jumnah appeared to abound in game, and during the action on the 11th the wild hogs and deer were flying in all directions, scared out of their senses. Dined with Livesey this evening, a small comfortable party.

September 17th.—The whole of the Park crossed today. The artillery officers were ordered to destroy the carriages of the guns captured on the 11th, and to load them in boats in order that they may be sent down the Jumnah to come on to Agra after we shall have laid siege to it. Our brigade directed to stand fast till further orders. Took a long ride in the evening, and carried our spears with us, in hopes of meeting some hogs, but they had taken the alarm and gone off.

Received a letter today from Wemyss from the other side of the river, giving me an account of their encampment, and what was going on at headquarters. I promised in answer to visit him tomorrow, and dispatched his servant at sunset. Dined with Forbes.

September 18th.—Rose and myself crossed the Jumnah this morning at daybreak, and marked out the ground in the line for our brigade. Breakfasted at headquarters, and remained with Lake and Wemyss till near eleven o'clock. Called on Rose at Captain Burrel's of the 15th, and rode to take a look at the famed city of Delhi. Very many of the inhabitants had left it; of the city itself every street almost bore the traces of its former grandeur and magnificence, and presented something unusually superb to arrest the attention. The Jummer Musjeed is the most stately and splendid building I almost ever saw, and a famous place of worship. I cannot conceive a grander sight than was afforded us of the city of Delhi, from its minarets, which are so lofty that you have a perfect view of all the streets, and also of the most luxuriant gardens which are situated in the vicinity of the city.

An order had been issued that no officer should go into the fort without the commander-in-chief's permission or a pass from headquarters, but we had an opportunity of seeing it and all its curiosity without one or the other. In passing the Lahore gate of the garrison we saw the Emperor's Prime Minister returning from a visit to headquarters; he very politely stopped his retinue, and sent to ask if we wished to see the fort, and on our answering in the affirmative, he ordered four of the King's Guards with an officer to escort us through the garrison, and directed that every place should be opened to us in the palace and elsewhere.

The fort of Delhi is very extensive, bounded on the east by the Jumnah, which runs immediately under its walls; on the other faces it is entirely surrounded by the town, not even a ditch between. The walls, built of a red kind of stone, are very lofty but by no means strong. There was a numerous artillery mounted on the works, but much out of condition; the carriages of many of the guns so much decayed that they could not bear firing more than a few rounds.

From the north part of the fort there runs a detached outwork called Selim Ghur, to which the communication from the fort is opened, or cut off by the drawing up or lowering a drawbridge. The sun was exceedingly powerful today, but we were not satisfied till we had gone completely round the works, from which we entered the palace, and every curiosity it contained (except the poor blind monarch himself) was shown us.

The king, unfortunately for us, was asleep. From the palace we went to that part of the garrison allotted to the princes. We saw them, and really they appeared to be in want even of the necessaries of life. They were meanly dressed, and, to our great surprise, began to make known to us all their misfortunes and the hardships they endured in their confinement (not one of them was allowed to go without the limited space pointed out, and guards were placed to see that they did not). They solicited us to make known their grievances to the commander-in-chief, which we lamented it was not in our power to comply with. The princes detained us full an hour, and it was with seeming reluctance that they permitted us to leave them. They paid us numerous compliments on our recent victory, and pointed out to us the bastion from which they beheld the battle, and witnessed the defeat of the enemy. They described their anxiety to have been excessive, and which we could readily credit.

We saw the apartments in which they kept their women, the company of whom would have been quite as agreeable to us as that of the princes. They are said to be many of them exquisitely beautiful, and many of their children who we saw certainly gave us reason to believe that they were so. I never saw finer children in my life. We returned to camp, and called at the lines of the 12th, where Hazard was proposed. We played till sunset, and played deep. We were fortunate, and returned across the Jumnah £150 more worth than in the morning. I had a party to dine with me, and they had very wisely ordered dinner, which was on the table when we got to my tent. We rode furiously from the river to our camp. The 27th and 2nd and 3rd Cavalry crossed over today. Broke up about eleven o'clock.

September 19th.—Camp near Delhi. The whole of the cavalry and their baggage crossed the Jumnah in the course of the day, the 6th Regiment excepted, which corps was detached in pursuit of a body of the enemy's cavalry, heard of last evening, plundering some villages in the vicinity of our camp.

A party of us rode towards the field of battle this evening, the line of retreat was very easily traced by the killed, which remained thickly strewed on the plain, and so offensive that we were obliged to ride in another direction.

September 20th.—At four this morning we struck our camp, and moved immediately down to the banks of the river. At daybreak we commenced embarking the brigade. Our first battalion, and a battalion of the 14th, with the greater proportion of their baggage, were across the river at eleven o'clock. The 2nd Battalion of our regiment ordered to stand fast on the Dewaub side till the hospital and also every kind of baggage had cleared the ford. After breakfast I rode towards the river, and met the corps, to conduct them to their respective lines. We were not much gratified at our new encampment, which stood so immediately upon the banks of the river that every gust of wind smothered us with the sand it brought from the water's edge. Wallace, and a large party of the officers of the 1st Brigade dined today with Christie, who gave us a sumptuous dinner, and some excellent claret. We did justice to both, and congratulated ourselves on being across the Jumnah, without more broken heads.

September 21st.—Rode with Aubery this morning before breakfast through the principal streets of the city. Aubery's groom was thrown from his horse, and while the master was riding on, abusing the servant, his own horse most unfortunately stumbled, and I had the felicity to see them both sprawling on the ground together! Breakfasted with Colonel Blair.

The commander-in-chief went today to pay a second visit to the Emperor; his own staff only attended him, in which Wemyss was included, from whom I had a visit as soon as they returned, and we had from him all the particulars. It was a counterpart of his Excellency's first reception. Arrangements making for our immediate march towards Agra, to besiege that place. A strong garrison consisting of five thousand of Scindiah's best troops, commanded by his most confidential leaders are said to be waiting our attack at Agra.

It was also reported that Scindiah was advancing his troops, with a determination to give us battle, and as we all preferred a field day to a tedious siege, we sincerely hoped he would try his prowess with us again on the plain, as the result of an action may be that they will more probably be induced to surrender the fortress, if they are beat in the field.

September 22nd.—The wounded officers and men, with the General Hospital, moved down to the banks of the river on the Dewaub side this day in readiness to cross before the heat of the morning tomorrow. The 6th Cavalry returned and crossed this forenoon.

Dined with the commander-in-chief this evening. Colonel Lake, Wemyss and myself rode into Delhi before dinner. Drank, all of us, a good deal of wine this evening.

September 23rd.—The sick and wounded crossed the Jumnah this morning before sunrise. Our 2nd Battalion with its baggage followed they had received orders to leave nothing in their rear, and therefore did not arrive at their station in the line till a very late hour. The best accommodations that the city of Delhi afforded were secured, and converted into hospitals for our sick and wounded, and the best situated houses were taken for the wounded officers.

Breakfasted this morning in the cavalry lines with Peyron, returned to the headquarter lines and *tiffed* with Colonel Lake and Wemyss. In the afternoon Wemyss and myself sat down to write Europe letters. I to my father, and Wemyss to his brother, General Wemyss. Rode with Wemyss, Colonel Lake and Duval on the river's side several miles in the evening. Dined at home; Aubery, Forbes, Murray, Shairpe, MacGregor, Weston, Forrest, Swinton of the Pioneers, and Grant of the 15th dined with me. Wemyss never dined out, but always at headquarters; he came, however, to us in the evening, time enough to finish his wine with us, and we passed a very jolly evening, and we were all of us rather high before we broke up.

CHAPTER 16

Siege and Occupation of Agra

September 24th.—Camp near Furreedpore. The army marched this morning, by the left. The cavalry in front, and the Europeans leading the column of infantry. We marched today over as barren and rocky a soil as the imagination can paint, passing through numberless ravines so narrow that the baggage was very tedious in clearing them, and we were in consequence much detained. Several alarms were given during the march that *banditti* were plundering the baggage, and which proved to be the case; these scoundrels rushed from the deepest of the ravines, where they had concealed themselves, upon carts and other baggage that happened to be in the rear, cut up the persons belonging to them, and carried off the contents.

Several parties of infantry were detached in quest of them, and about thirty of the vagabonds were shot. These marauders, with which the banks of the Jumnah swarm, are called *Goojers*, and, not content with plundering, they very frequently (indeed generally) put all to death who are so unfortunate as to fall into their hands.

Grant of ours lost his trunks, containing all his clothes and his wine this morning (no small annoyance to an officer marching in an enemy's country, where neither one nor the other can be procured). We did not arrive at our ground till nearly twelve, and the sun was exceedingly powerful.

September 25th.—Camp near Billumgur. We marched this morning by the left (the General beat at five and the Assembly at six o'clock) in the same order as yesterday.

The soil today very barren, but the country more level than yesterday, as we had drawn off a little from the banks of the Jumnah. The hares and partridges were swarming this morning, and great numbers of the former were knocked on the head by the camp followers. The posts for our camp were cut off today and all our letters lost. About twenty of the *Goojers* were cut up by a *jemadar* party of the 2nd Cavalry, while in the act of plundering some baggage. The quarter-master-general and the rest of us belonging to his party arrived at the ground at eight o'clock, and the lines of the respective brigades were marked out in complete readiness when the commander-in-chief and the army came up,

September 26th.—Camp near Pulwaul. The army marched this morning in the same order as yesterday. The general was beat at four and the assembly at five o'clock.

On our march today we passed through a great deal of jungle, among which grew many caper trees, abundantly laden with very fine fruit. We walked our horses till daybreak, and then galloped briskly on in search of a good spot for the encampment of the army. Saw a good deal of game riding through the cover, and so tame and undisturbed that the black partridge sat and allowed us to pass close without noticing us.

In consequence of some baggage having been so constantly plundered since we crossed the river, an order was issued directing the field officer of the day, commanding the rearguard, not to come into camp till every particle of baggage shall have come up. The guard, therefore, did not arrive in camp till five in the evening. No accounts today of any mischief having been done by the *Goojers*. Several officers lost their tents and camels yesterday. Our brigade today encamped in the midst of jungle, so high that we could scarce see each other's tents. On the right of the line they were more fortunate, and pitched on good ground.

Breakfasted with Colonel Blair, and passed the day with Weston, quietly in my own tent. Issued Regimental Orders for the promotion of some *havildars* and *naiks* in the regiment to fill up the vacancies of those who fell in the battle of the 11th. Wemyss, Gore and myself rode in the evening to hear the band of the 76th Regiment, on its own parade; met Peyron, Doveton, Fitzgerald, Howarth and many others of my friends of the cavalry.

Dined with Grant, and met there a large party of officers of the brigade, mostly of our 2nd Battalion, and we passed a very pleasant evening; talked of our late successes, and promised to do our friends credit whenever they chose to meet us again.

September 27th.—Camp near Mittroul. The army marched this morning at the same hour, and in the same order as yesterday. The cavalry and 76th Regiments countermarched, in order to gain the main road, with their left in front. We went on in front at the usual time, and saw several parties of Hindustani Horse hovering on our flanks. They proved to be the troops of neighbouring *rajahs*, and some approached us, and showed us every possible respect, just as they would have behaved to Scindiah's troops had they been as we were, victorious, such is the policy of native powers, always to join the stronger party, and crush the fallen. The road today on the line of march was very good, and the Park and heavy stores came to the ground at an early hour.

We were much vexed today to hear that several posts, containing Europe letters, stated to have left Cawnpore for the army, had never arrived in camp, and must consequently have been cut off. Mine from my good friends of Yeovil had a narrow escape, and for which I blessed my stars. An overland dispatch also said to have been lost, all since we crossed the Jumnah. The unfortunate *hircarahs* (postmen) some of them came in, horribly mutilated. The right hands and noses of many of them were cut off, and some had been murdered by the cowardly *Goojers*. Met most of the officers of our own corps at Colonel Blair's at dinner.

September 28th.—The army marched this morning by the left, in the same order as yesterday. The general at five and the asembly at six o'clock.

We had a very heavy fall of rain during the night, and it came pouring through our tents on us as we lay in our beds. It actually came down in torrents, and the best tents were not proof against such a deluge. An order had been sent to the Park from headquarters to countermand the beating of the General, but the orderly, in the dark, lost his road, and did not arrive till the drummers had beat off. The commander-in-chief, therefore, determined on marching, as the troops had all turned out and were dressing. At daybreak it seemed to come on with redoubled fury, and we rightly guessed that a great deal of the baggage would be left in the rear, as camels for rainy weather are but indifferent carriage, and from their long legs and immense height very liable to accidents.

We (the quarter-master-general and his party) left the line at daybreak, and galloped on to prepare ground for our encampment. We saw a considerable camp of Native Horse, and on sending some of the quarter-masters of dragoons with a party of our escort to reconnoitre, we found that they were troops belonging to the Rajah of Baraich, and were on an embassy to the general.

We arrived at the village near which it was our intention to have encamped about nine o'clock. The rain fell so thick that we could scarce see each other. Ground did not offer near the village, and we were returning to try for better ground to encamp on.

Peyron and myself at the head of some dragoons were at full speed, retracing the road we had gone, for the purpose of reporting on some ground we had passed. Our heads were literally down on our holsters with the wind and rain beating so furiously that we could not look up, nor without difficulty keep our seats; in this situation we were scampering back when our horses came to a sudden standstill, and when we looked up, to our surprise our horses heads were within a yard of the commander-in-chief and his party, who had left the line and pushed on in hopes of finding his tents up. The general very good humouredly told us we were "formidable fellows," and got out of our way as quick as he could.

We pitched the camp today on high and dry spots of ground, without attending to any other regularity than keeping brigades together. We were driven to this alternative, for the ploughed ground was all a perfect slough, and men and horses were up to the knees on it. The artillery also was kept on the firmest ground, or we must have swamped it.

It was nearly eleven o'clock before the line came to its ground. The principal part of our baggage did not arrive till sunset. Many camels, and a great deal of baggage did not come in the course of the day, part of it remaining in the rear. I did not pitch my tent, but as Livesey's was first up passed the day in his. Dined also with Livesey, as did Murray, whose tent and camels all remained in the rear. I sent an elephant in search of Murray's tent, but the people returned at ten at night without any tidings of it. In spite of our cares and fatigues, however, we passed a very jolly evening. MacGregor, Weston, Forbes and Aubery joined us after dinner, and the bottle was circulated pretty freely.

All accounts seem to agree now in making out the enemy to be advancing towards us with a formidable force and heaps of artillery. We conjectured that anxious as the commander-in-chief is to meet them again, we must halt tomorrow to allow the baggage to come up.

September 29th.—16 Miles. Camp near Hurriel. The army halted today in order to give the baggage in the rear an opportunity to join us. A continuance of rain nearly the whole of the day. The *hackeries*, camels, etc., came straggling in, all the forenoon; the cattle completely fagged, and hardly able to move through the mire with their loads. Part of my tent still remained in the rear, and I was told that one of the camels had met with an accident, by slipping, which detained the tent. Took the advantage of being a quarter-master and sent back one of the Company's elephants to assist.

None but wise officers are quarter-masters in India. A great many camels were disabled yesterday, and can never join us again, in consequence of which many officers' tents were entirely lost, and but for the Honourable Company's elephants mine would inevitably have shared the same fate. It came up about five in the morning, and the elephant returned nearly to the ground we left in the morning before it was recovered.

At sunset the rain somewhat abated, and Livesey, Forbes and myself took a short ride in front of the line. Dined with Livesey and slept in his tent.

September 30th.—15 Miles. Camp at Kossuah. We marched this morning at seven o'clock, the left in front. The weather during the time of march was favourable, and everything moved well on. We had tolerable good ground for our encampment today. After marking out the line, we returned, met our respective brigades, and conducted them to their stations. It was nearly twelve before all our tents were pitched or spread to dry.

Received from the field paymaster this morning the amount of my quarter-master's bill for August (*Rupees* 1,017). The first month in my life that I ever drew more than 250 *Rupees*. A large party of officers dined with me today. The enemy said to be in force near Agra, and we all expected soon to have another field day with them, and nothing was more anxiously wished.

October 1st.—Camp near Chuman. The army marched this morning at five. The country well cultivated, and in far higher condition than any we had passed through since we crossed the Jumnah. Soon after daybreak we passed a curious *puckah* tank, or *bolee*, and near it a remarkable well. It was in length about 100 feet, and 30 broad, with four stories or landing places, railed out in a curious style. We pitched our camp with our right extending near to this place, and just as we had completed marking out the encampment, an antelope three parts grown leapt out of a small patch of cover, and as my groom always carried a spear, I was prepared for him, and after one of the severest chases I ever rode, I speared it.

About nine the army came to its ground. Breakfasted with Colonel Blair, from whom I received a general invitation to dine with him when I was not otherwise engaged. In the evening Colonel Lake, Wemyss, Duval, and myself rode to the parade of the 76th Regiment, to hear its band. Colonel Lake told us that the Chevalier Dudrenec, the Frenchman who commanded two of Scindiah's Brigades, had deserted them, and had surrendered himself to Colonel Vandeleur at Muttrah. The troops, however, had every reliance in their very formidable artillery, and were making every preparation to meet us again in the field.

Thirteen of Scindiah's regular battalions supported by a numerous artillery advancing towards us, supposed with the intention of preventing us laying siege to Agra. (N.B. It will cost them some broken heads to effect that.) By the papers this evening we saw that war was again declared by England against France. It gave us also statements of what had passed between the two nations, and the reasons assigned for the absolute necessity of a war.

Wrote a letter on the service to the adjutant-general, recommending a favourite *havildar* (sergeant) of my grenadiers for promotion. I had often observed this man's gallant and intrepid conduct in the most perilous situations, and he was immediately made a *jemadar* (*lieutenant*).

October 2nd.—The army marched this morning by the left, cavalry leading the column.

As we again approached the banks of the Jumnah, we found the country quite rocky and uncultivated, and the ravines on our line of march were really tremendous, and detained us greatly in getting past our heavy guns. At seven we came in sight of Muttrah, and met Colonel Vandeleur going out to meet the commander-in-chief. Left the town a short distance on our left, and observed Colonel Vandeleur's camp at a distance.

Marked out our line about a mile on Vandeleur's right. We found here H.M. 8th and 29th Dragoons, 4th Regiment of Native Cavalry, one battalion of the 9th, a battalion of the 12th and five companies of the 16th Native Infantry.

Called on Anderdon, Colonel Clarke's major of brigade. I was disappointed to find that Mr. Young was not with his corps; he was left with some dismounted men, for whom horses could not be supplied.

The men of the 8th appeared stout, heavy fellows; too much so, I thought, for Light Dragoons. This place is remarkable for a Hindoo Temple, or place of worship, and many of our rascally servants called (*en passant*) to get rid of their numerous sins, in consequence of which we did not see some of them till night. The tents and breakfast things were all up in good time.

Saw an astonishing number of hares on the line of march this morning, and the ground on which we encamped literally swarmed with them. Two brace were knocked down by the sticks of the camp followers, during the time we were at breakfast, not fifty yards from the tent.

Wilson, a shipmate of mine, and a very fine young man, called and passed the day with me. Colonel Monson, of the 76th Regiment, having recovered of the wounds he received in storming Ali Ghur on the 4th September, came into camp today, and joined his corps, which was encamped on our left.

Wilson and a large party of officers dined with me this evening.

October 3rd.—13 Miles. Camp near Phurrah. We marched this morning by the left. The road today exceedingly uneven, with numerous ravines on our right and left, and but very little cultivation. We were in hourly expectation of falling in with the enemy, who were reported in force between Muttrah and Agra.

Joined Macan during the line of march. We marked out the line of encampment, and the Cavalry came up a considerable time before the infantry, the latter being detained in consequence of the difficulties of dragging the heavy train, and guns attached to the different brigades, through the narrow defiles in the ravines. By ten the line was encamped.

October 4th.—The army marched this morning. We moved off by the left, and the cavalry brought up the rear. This gave us some reason to think that an enemy was in the neighbourhood, and we were in momentary expectation of an action, it having been confidentially reported that they were drawn up in order of battle, near a village which we passed about eight o'clock.

We arrived at Secundra (about five miles from Agra) at nine o'clock. Our party (the quarter-master-general and quarter-master) was ordered not to go in front, but to keep with the advanced guard; all these precautions proved quite unnecessary, as not a sign of an enemy appeared. The commander-in-chief was with us (the advanced guard) all the morning, and we halted near the environs of the city of Agra to wait the coming up of the line.

We were then ordered to proceed, and mark out a position before the fort, commodious for commencing the attack. We encamped on the western face of the place; they began a fierce cannonade on us as soon as we were perceived; fortunately, however, although many heavy shot passed over and near us, their fire had no other effect than shewing us the distance their guns would reach, and thereby enabling us to judge how near we could encamp without being annoyed from the garrison. The ground was not good, on account of the numerous ruins scattered promiscuously about. Advanced our picquets to a garden, three hundred yards in front of the line.

Several parties of the enemy came near us in the course of the day, and guns were fired constantly from the garrison on our advanced post, which Sinclair commanded, and where he had some men killed and wounded, and some very handsome buildings in the garden knocked about his ears. Received a letter this morning from Thornhill. A report that Major Wade has been killed in a duel; a pretty wife of whom he was extremely jealous is said to have been the cause.

Rode a horse of Weston's this morning, Collector being still very far from recovered of his wounds, and Major lame.

In the evening I went in front with Major Lake, Wemyss and Duval to a rising ground from which with our glasses we could distinctly see the men and count the guns on the ramparts and bastions. Scindiah's colours were also plainly visible, flying over the Delhi gate of the Fortress and along the walls. They appeared very superb at the principal flagstaff. It was a red silk ground, with a white snake diagonally.

I dined with the commander-in-chief this evening. The principal engineer and cavalry officers were there, and we had a great deal of conversation regarding the fort and city, and points of attack, etc. Drank a great deal of claret, and passed a very pleasant evening.

October 5th.—Rode down in front this morning at daybreak. The bastions and ramparts appeared crowded with people. Breakfasted with Christie, after which Anderdon and myself mounted our horses, and determined on reconnoitring the fort narrowly, and for which we had nearly paid the forfeit of our lives. About two hundred and fifty yards from the walls of the place, and in a road which ran through the ravines (in which we thought ourselves completely covered from the shot of the garrison, and from the view of the enemy on the ramparts), my groom came up, and told me that he saw several infantry among the broken ground close to us. The man himself immediately turned short and galloped off. We were at this moment entering an arched gateway which extended across the road, but as we had no conception the enemy were so near us we put spurs to our horses and dashed on.

On clearing the arch our surprise was great to find a party drawn up behind it on the road's side. They were actually not fifteen yards from us, when they fired directly in our faces, and most miraculously without effect. It was so sudden that we had barely time to draw our pistols and give our fire. The man nearest us staggered back and fell. We both fired at him; he seemed to be at the head of the party, and was not hardly a sword's length from my stirrup. We pushed on and got clear to camp, completely annoyed at our folly.

The people from the fort had seen us coming, and had evidently sent out this party to cut us off, and a more complete ambush men were never drawn into. This affair was seen from the picquets, and made a great noise in camp. We were very justly blamed for our temerity; had the enemy been but steady, we must both have inevitably fallen, nothing could have saved us. A firing of cannon on our advanced posts all the day, and several shot came into camp. The garrison was summoned by the commander-in-chief, and resolutely returned for answer that "they were soldiers, and would defend the place to the last."

Dressed on a rising ground this evening in the rear of my tent, and dined with Arbuthnot. A heavy shot fell close to the tent during dinner, and a drummer brought it in to us. We had the curiosity to weigh it; it was upwards of sixty pounds. We only requested they would be civil to us during dinner; drank our wine and passed a very pleasant evening. Broke up at eleven o'clock.

October 6th.—A smart firing this morning at our advanced posts, on some snipers of the enemy who came nearly up to the picquets under cover of some broken ground, and the heavy guns continued an almost incessant fire with a view to dislodge our parties in advance. We heard this morning that the line would shift ground tomorrow, and take up a final position for the attack. The enemy very busy mounting fresh guns on the works, and threatening a formidable resistance. We were as zealously employed in preparing for the siege; cutting materials for batteries, etc., etc.

October 7th.—Rode on the flank of the line a short distance. Wemyss, MacGregor and Weston returned with me to breakfast at my tent. A fire of cannon from the fort the whole of the day, and several of our men at the advanced posts were killed and wounded, but no officer suffered that I heard.

At four this morning Colonel Clarke, with the 2nd Brigade, marched and took up a position above the fort, his left extending towards the Jumnah, so as to enable him to cover the boats, which are at Secundra bringing down the guns we had captured in the Battle of Delhi. The carriages of which we had previously destroyed.

Owen, of our corps, with three companies, had charge of the guns down from Delhi, and conducted himself very much to the satisfaction of the commander-in-chief. Colonel Clarke by this position had complete command of the Jumnah above the city, and it was determined at headquarters to dislodge a party of the enemy stationed at the Tauge and the garden, so as to prevent any communication below the fortress. The Pioneers and working parties of infantry employed cutting materials for fascines and gabions.

This afternoon orders appeared for our change of position in the morning; to move from the right. The advanced guard ordered to be reinforced with a battalion and two six-pounders. Some deserters from the enemy came in this evening, and were immediately entertained by us. A severe reprimand appeared in Orders today to some officers who had declined entertaining deserters in consequence of their being under size. Officers commanding corps were directed to send all of that description to headquarters, and not to entirely dismiss them in future. A copy of General Lake's letter to the Governor-General in Council appeared in the *Gazette* today, relating to the glorious affair of the nth at Delhi, and in which we all got lots of praise. *Tiffed* today with MacGregor, after which we took our glasses and went down to the advanced posts to reconnoitre. In front of the picquet nearest the fort there was a mosque, and we contrived, though unwisely, to push on to it. They saw us from the garrison, and the brick and mortar, with some heavy shot, was quickly flying about our ears, and we stayed a few minutes and retreated.

A cannon shot came through the parapet on the top of the post, between MacGregor and myself; it was within three feet of both of us. We now had made what observations we could, walked back to the picquet, mounted our horses, and rode again to the lines. Dined with Livesey this evening. During dinner the fire of musketry was so quick at the advanced post that we thought it was attacked. I mounted Major and galloped down; it proved to be a false alarm occasioned by some gun bullocks, which the enemy had turned out of the garrison to prevent their starving. The night was uncommonly dark, and the sentries in advance had been the cause of the mistake. I reported this to

Colonel Blair.

On my way back I met an *aide-de-camp* of the commander-in-chief's, and told him what had been the cause of the firing. The fort had taken the alarm, and opened some guns on our post, directed by the flashes of the musketry. Several heavy shot passed close to me both going down and on my return, without any other effect than frightening my horse a little.

October 8th.—The infantry marched this morning at six, leaving the cavalry on its ground, except the 8th Dragoons, which came up in the rear of the line. We commenced marking out the ground soon after daybreak, and everything was in readiness when the troops came to their encampment. A very steep, high bank ran directly across our line. I rode at it in order to call some pioneers who were passing at the head of the Park, to cut through it.

The horse made a boggle in attempting to clear it, and I had nearly met with a severe fall; the horse recovered himself in an astonishing manner. Campbell, the quarter-master-general, who was close by me, declared that the circumstance of the horse regaining his balance and coming on his feet to the ground was miraculous. The bank was at least ten feet in height.

When the line came up, MacDonald's brigade, with the advanced picquets and their field pieces, were ordered to move down to the Tauge in which, and in its gardens, it was reported to the commander-in-chief that three battalions of the enemy were posted. The dragoons also moved down to support MacDonald, and in order to cut them up in their retreat to the fort. The Tauge is one of the most beautiful buildings in the world, entirely of marble.

We remained under arms till near nine o'clock, in readiness to support the corps in front should they require a reinforcement. On MacDonald's arrival at the Tauge Garden he found that the enemy were retreating, and the greatest part of them already secure upon the glacis.

A party of five companies and two guns was left to retain the post, which we fortunately got possession of without any loss.

A tremendous blazing of cannon was kept up from the garrison, but the distance was too great for any serious mischief; some straggling shot killed and wounded a few of our men. At ten the whole line of infantry encamped, distant from the walls of Agra about two and a half miles on the south-east face. They threw several shot over our line, but ground did not offer farther in the rear; we were therefore necessitated to take our chance, rightly guessing that as they could not easily see the effect of their shot from the garrison at that distance, the fire would soon discontinue. The whole of the cavalry, except the 8th and the advanced picquets of yesterday, stood fast this morning.

I wrote today to Mr. Young of the 8th Dragoons, and to Thornhill at Bareilly. Wemyss called on me and told me that Guthrie had arrived at Mynpoorie, to take charge of Ryley's appointment, in consequence of his having too speedily left his post at the time of Fleury's visit to Shikoabad, expecting them on to Mynpoorie, and on that account Ryley was superseded.

Wemyss also showed me a letter which he had received from C., who did not appear quite comfortable. They certainly may have remained until accounts of the actual approach of the enemy had reached them, instead of which they made off on hearing of the enemy at Shikoabad, nearly thirty miles distant from them.

A great deal of materials for our batteries was brought in this morning, and all the public cattle and quarter-master's establishments were sent to the Park to assist in making fascines and gabions. It was conjectured that before we could break ground by commencing on our trenches and batteries, seven battalions of the enemy which lay encamped upon the glacis, supported by nearly thirty pieces of artillery and immediately under cover of the guns and musketry of the works, must be dislodged, and from their exceeding favourable situation supported by the garrison, we expected this would cost us some officers and men.

Rode down in front this evening with Major Lake and Wemyss with our glasses to reconnoitre the position of the enemy's battalions on the glacis, and to endeavour to ascertain the best road through the ravines, down to attack them. We carried an escort of dragoons with us from the picquet, and advanced so near that their sentries fired upon us. To our annoyance we found that it would be in vain to carry down guns on the occasion, as they had taken the precaution to cut off the different roads which led to them.

Several deep trenches were cut across the roads, and to carry artillery over them would be attended with much delay. We therefore agreed that the musket and bayonet alone must be had recourse to. We returned to camp at sunset, and they pelted us with cannon as long as their shot would reach us, and we had all of us several very narrow escapes. A thirty-two pounder passed directly through the dragoons, but providentially without killing any of them, or injuring us who were at the head of them. We returned all the way to camp at three-quarter speed.

I was asked to dine at headquarters, but was engaged to my friends of the 3rd Cavalry. Took a fresh horse, and posted off to the cavalry lines. Dined with Peyron, who gave us an elegant dinner and plenty of Kilbey.

Talked a great deal of what we would do if we ever reached Old England again.

We heard a constant firing during the evening, and at times it seemed rather heavy.

The Bhirtpore Rajah, with 1,500 good Horse, joined us this morning. In the evening some parties of the enemy's infantry advanced near enough to fire on our Grand Guard, but some detached parties from our advanced picquets soon drove them in. Accounts today confirmed the report of Colonel Guthrie having taken Teteeah, but the colonel was mortally wounded. They attempted the gate by a *coup de main*, but some unexpected obstacles prevented their carrying the gun up to the gate, and they were repulsed, and obliged to leave their gun in possession of the enemy, who at night fled the place, and our troops took possession.

October 9th.—Went with Shairpe at sunrise this morning to see the Tauge, which appeared, if possible, more magnificent than when I first saw it. We had a post here, and I stayed to breakfast with the officers of the 12th, who were on duty. Our force was five companies and a six-pounder. Shairpe and self returned to camp about ten. A smart fire all the morning from the fort, on our advanced picquets. From one of the minarets of the Tauge we very distinctly saw several battalions of the enemy, with their field pieces, drawn up on the glacis of the fort, and among them many mounted officers. Twenty-five large boats were moored close under the eastern face. Our Pioneers and builders employed as yesterday, cutting materials for batteries. People in the Park making scaling ladders, fascines, gabions, etc.

I received a private note from Colonel Blair, telling me that we were to beat up the enemy's Battalion in the morning, that the attack would commence at daybreak, and requesting that I would be at his tent, mounted, half-an-hour before.

October 10th.—The line was under arms this morning at five o'clock, and a little before daybreak our brigade marched off to attack the enemy. On our arrival at the ravines our battalion was halted, and the 14th advanced and commenced a very vigorous and galling fire of musketry on the enemy. Our battalion advanced in the best order that the nature of the broken ground would admit, to their support. The enemy's battalion on the glacis were completely surprised, and routed with great slaughter. We could plainly perceive by the smoke and peals of musketry on our left that the city was attacked by Clarke's brigade.

The fort was in a perfect blaze of cannon and musketry on every side. We pushed close up to their works, and brought off two guns, having dismounted many others which could not be secured, the enemy's fire was so extremely heavy, and we were quite exposed to every shot from all the works on the southern face. Having completely routed them, we drew off to the ravines, and took post in them, at the distance of about two hundred yards from the south gate of the fort.

The fire from the garrison continued without intermission till nearly ten o'clock, and a small village and mosque close on the left of our post was laid in ruins. The musketry did not cease in the town, and we were for a long time apprehensive that our troops there had not succeeded, and which proved in some measure to be the case.

Brigadier Clarke finding himself hardly pressed, and much galled by the musketry of the enemy from the tops of houses and gateways, actually ordered a retreat, but as his detachment had divided, one part of it, consisting of six companies of the 16th Regiment under Colonel White, fortunately penetrated and established themselves in a good post near the walls of the fort; Colonel Clarke sent orders to Colonel White also to withdraw his men from the town, but to the immortal honour of Colonel White he refused; saying that it would be disgraceful to British troops, and that without the orders of the commander-in-chief he would not retreat as long as an officer or man of his regiment remained.

At the same time he dispatched a letter to headquarters, and the commander-in-chief was so well satisfied and pleased with his gallant conduct that he paid him a handsome compliment in Orders, ordered Brigadier Clarke to return immediately to camp, and left Colonel White with a good reinforcement in command of the town, which in the course of the day he obliged the enemy entirely to abandon, and drove them to a man either to destruction or into their garrison for safety.

Our post was on ground over which we had driven the enemy in the morning, and many of them, as well as some of our own people, were lying killed at it, nor could we remain there, as they continued a heavy fire almost the whole of the day; towards the evening they became very offensive, and in the night insufferably so, and we were obliged at the risk of our lives to draw them off under cover of the night, in doing which we had some men wounded. Rose was brought into our post, badly wounded, and we sent him immediately to camp. About midnight Colonel Blair and I (as his staff) left the post and returned to camp.

October 11th.—Received a note at daybreak this morning from MacGregor, desiring me to order down *doolies* (litters) for our wounded men. When the fort was a little silent I took the opportunity of sending them with some provisions down. Colonel Powell, with a battalion of the 8th Native and the 1st Regiment of Cavalry, crossed the Jumnah and marched into camp this forenoon.

In the attack of yesterday we had seven officers killed and wounded. I went to Rose this morning; found him in tolerable spirits, considering that his wound was a very dangerous one. I passed great part of the morning with him, and it was with difficulty that I got away.

Our battalion was relieved in the trenches this morning by a battalion of the 8th Infantry, and marched into camp at daybreak. We observed a number of the enemy assembled on a large mosque in the town; two howitzers were immediately ordered down to dislodge them. Lieutenant Whitaker of the 9th died today of the wounds he received on the 10th. The death of this officer was particularly lamented, as it was occasioned by his gallant and humane exertions to carry off another wounded officer (Lieutenant Grant, of the same corps).

On hearing that Lieutenant Grant had received a shot and was left behind, he ordered the grenadiers of his own company to follow him; they returned under a heavy fire to the place, but Whitaker was mortally wounded in this generous but fruitless attempt to save his friend, who was cut to pieces by the enemy, and two finer young men the Service could not boast of.

Today I received a letter from Thornhill, Bareilly, and we had a report that two new regiments were to be raised immediately. A talk that the remains of the battalions which we defeated on the 10th were desirous of coming over to us. A very heavy fire of cannon the whole of this day from the fort. A battery of two twelve-pounders, to enfilade some works of the enemy, was opened from the river's side with great effect, and they succeeded in silencing the guns on the nearest bastion of the water face of the fort. Wemyss, MacGregor and myself mounted our horses about five o'clock this evening, and with our glasses went down very near the works, to reconnoitre.

Left our grooms and horses at a small village in the rear, but they perceived our destination, and annoyed us as much as they could by shot from the *fausse braye*. On our return to camp, Wemyss had the most narrow escape of a cannon shot I almost ever saw. It grazed within a foot of him, and passed on between MacGregor and myself. I was on a young horse of Murray's, which actually sunk with fear till the girths nearly touched the ground, at the noise of the shot, which was a very heavy one. Dined with Colonel Blair; we had some officers of the cavalry this evening, whom I had never met before.

October 13th.—The different posts were relieved this morning, and the 8th Infantry came into their lines about seven o'clock. I breakfasted with MacGregor, and afterwards we mounted our ponies, and rode to the lines of the 3rd Cavalry, to see Peyron, who, with Ryder, returned with us to our lines, and we had a jolly party at *tiffin* with Anderdon. About two o'clock we were surprised at the garrison having ceased firing, and in an hour afterwards we heard that the enemy had sent terms of capitulation into camp. Captain Salkield, on our part, was admitted into the garrison, and we supposed everything at the close of the evening to be in fair way, and had hopes of being speedily in possession of the place, without a further effusion of blood.

About nine, however, the fire from the garrison recommenced with redoubled fury, and continued till daybreak on our trenches and working parties at the batteries, killing and wounding a great many of our people.

The terms first proposed by the enemy were to be allowed to march out with their arms and private property, to which General Lake acceded, but they added that no troops should inspect them as they marched out, which was, of course, objected to, as there was reported to be a large sum of money belonging to Scindiah lodged in Agra, of which they would have left but little for us.

The enemy did not wait even till Salkield had quitted their fort, but opened their guns on our works, sending him in a boat down the river to land at our twelve-pounder battery, which circumstances had nearly cost Salkield dear, as in the battery our people hearing a boat pulling towards them, concluded it was the enemy attempting to carry off the treasure under the cover of the night, and were laying a gun loaded with grape for the boat, when Salkield contrived to make himself heard.

A party of *sepoys* were advanced in front of the battery, and the officer was pointing his rifle at Salkield when he made himself known. The boat was not twenty yards from him at the time.

October 14th.—The fire from the fort continued very heavy the whole of this morning, and not the smallest appearance of surrendering; this, however, did not much intercept our working at the batteries, though it cost us some lives. The battering guns were today removed from their transport to field carriages, and as some of our scaling ladders were lost in the attack of the 10th the artillery and engineers were employed in constructing fresh ones. Rode this afternoon to the village in front, where our people were working up fascines and gabions, and paid a visit to Sinclair, who commands the advanced picquets today; his post was in the rear of a mosque between the Tauge and trenches.

This evening seven battalions of the enemy surrendered themselves, with their guns, tumbrils, colours and ammunition to Colonel White, and marched up and encamped on the left of our line, at the distance of about one mile. The terms given them were to employ them in our service with the same pay as they received in Scindiah's, the officers to continue with them, with the rank they formerly held. Colonel White, with five companies of the 16th, took possession of the Jumna Musjeed in which they had been posted, which gave us a communication to the choke of the fort, and annoyed the enemy greatly, as they did not at all relish having us so close to their gate, which, however, from having a drawbridge, was perfectly secure. Many of the enemy who came over this day are very smart fine fellows, and soldier-like looking men.

A heavy fire from the garrison all day, but with less effect than would have been expected, considering the incessant roar of cannon. Our batteries expected soon to be complete. We had a report today that a Frenchman, supposed to have come as a spy, had been apprehended in Calcutta.

In the evening MacGregor and myself rode down in front, and returned through the camp of the battalions who came over yesterday. Many of their officers addressed us in a most respectful way, and told us that some of the men were desirous of returning to their families, and wished to obtain their discharge for that purpose, expressing at the same time the honourable manner with which they had been treated since they had surrendered themselves to us.

October 15th.—At four this morning our regiment marched off the parade to relieve the 15th in the trenches at the left post. We cleared the ravines, and were at the post before the day broke, without the loss of a man, as they could not discover us from the works. They guessed at the time of our relief, and several random shots were fired without effect. The 15th Regiment had marched when day broke, and with it they commenced a heavy fire on us. The post was a very good one, and the men well sheltered, and we lost but few people. We returned their fire from two howitzers and a couple of *cohorns*, and it seemed to have the effect of annoying them greatly.

The enemy continued turning out their cattle for want of forage in the garrison, and several bullocks came into our post this day. We pitched Weston's servants' tent between two deep ravines, and had some victuals dressed in it. The tent was frequently covered with stones thrown up by the shot of the garrison while we were taking a hasty dinner in it, but it was so small that they could not possibly discern it from the walls, and consequently no mischief was done. It was hardly possible to eat anything, the stench was so terrible of the bodies left on the 10th, and the fire continued so heavy from the garrison that it was impossible to remove them far.

Our post was within two hundred and fifty yards of the works, and the cannon shot and musketry went uncommonly sharp over us, and a mosque which stood about the centre of the trench was completely demolished in the course of the day.

It was not possible to continue working at the batteries during the day, as we were so completely within range of grape from the garrison that a man could not show himself without certain destruction.

MacGregor and myself went in front a little before sunset, and took with us about fifty men without their arms, and a covering party, to bring in a gun that lay near our post, left by the enemy on the 10th. We succeeded, and hauled it in under a smart fire; some of our men were killed and wounded, and we had several very narrow escapes. We should have deferred this hazardous undertaking till night, but there was great reason to apprehend that the enemy at dark would attempt to recover it. The gun was an elegant brass nine-pounder field piece.

We saw some other guns with their axles down; they were visible from the garrison, and they had broken them down with their shot to prevent us taking them off. About an hour after sunset the firing of cannon ceased, but the musketry continued all night, accompanied with a shower of grape at intervals on our working parties. They must distinctly have heard us driving the pickets, fixing the fascines, etc. Several parties of Europeans from the different corps were employed in getting up the Grand Battery, and we had hopes that another night would complete them all.

October 16th.—Soon after four we were relieved this morning by the 8th, and marched to our lines by daylight. Went to bed a good deal fatigued, having been nearly all the night on my legs, and slept till eleven.

We all met at twelve at MacGregor's tent to breakfast, went afterwards to see Rose, who was wounded on the 10th, and found him in good spirits; most of the officers wounded on the 10th and during the siege said to be doing well. It was certainly ascertained today that the garrison consisted of five thousand fighting men, and if they stand a storm we may expect some warm work, and there must be a good deal of blood spilt. Our battering guns went down from camp this morning, and it was supposed would open tomorrow; not the smallest probability of the garrison surrendering, on the contrary they had declared their determination to defend the place, or perish in the attempt.

Many of Scindiah's principal leaders and some of his best troops are reported to be in the garrison. Today, thanks from the governor-general and captain-general, the Marquis Wellesley to the commander-in-chief and the officers and men employed with him in the glorious affair of the 11th September at Delhi, arrived in our camp. Honorary colours to be presented to every corps engaged on that day, and the governor-general stated his determination to erect a monument in Fort William to the memory of the officers who fell in that battle and in the assault of Ali Ghur on the 4th. The governor's letter was a very handsome one, and he thanked in cordial terms "The illustrious General and his brave Army."

In the evening Livesey and myself rode down to the Tauge and remained till after sunset, in consequence of which we were near being fired upon by the sentries of the picquet on the right of the line. The day was ushered in by a tremendous fire from our Grand Battery of eight eighteens, four twelves, a mortar battery, and six ten-inch mortars and six howitzers.

October 17th.—The twelve-pounders composed an enfilading battery, erected close upon the brink of the Jumnah; in the rear of it about sixty yards was placed the Grand Mortar Battery, the battering guns on the left of it, and within two hundred and fifty yards from the works. The garrison returned this cannonade by a very spirited fire from every gun they could bring to bear, and the fire from six till nine was truly awful, and as heavy a one from the number of guns as I had ever witnessed.

Before our batteries ceased firing several of the enemy's guns on the face of the fort attacked were dismounted or silenced.

Our fire was uncommonly well directed notwithstanding the number of guns opposed to us and the loss that was sustained in the Grand Battery (where Shairpe and myself had taken post to see the effect of our fire). Nearly all the men stationed at the two left hand guns were twice swept away, and as they were more exposed than the others the enemy's shot every moment came into the embrasures and killed the men. One shot carried away five men, and we were completely covered with the blood and brains of the poor fellows. The officer commanding in the battery then withdrew the men from those guns, and ran them back. When we ceased firing the defences of the Bengal bastion and those of the curtain next it were completely destroyed.

The bombs and shells seemed to be thrown from our mortar batteries with great precision and effect, and we could distinctly hear them burst in the body of the fort. Between ten and eleven the firing ceased, as if by mutual consent, and both parties were glad with a little respite. Shairpe and myself returned through the ravines to the village in front of our line, where we found our horses. Shairpe breakfasted with me, and as it was known that we had been in the battery, a great number of enquiries were made concerning what was going on and who had suffered. Soon after twelve the firing again commenced from our batteries, six guns only from the Grand Battery firing. We continued breaching with little intermission till sunset, and the wall came down in immense flakes. In the evening a summons was again sent into the garrison, to which they replied that they "were soldiers, and should defend the place to the last."

Went to headquarters to take the orders for Cumberlege, who was on duty in the trenches. Called on Wemyss, with whom and MacGregor I went in the evening very near the fort in order to see the effect of our fire from the batteries. We contrived to get in the range of the guns pointed at the batteries on our return, and several shot passed us.

Dined with Murray; at ten at night two *hircarahs* (messengers) were sent in from the garrison, under pretence of treating with us, but it was imagined that their object was to gain time. The firing, however, on both sides ceased, but our people continued to repair the damage done by the enemy's shot at the batteries during the day, and a strong party of Europeans were ordered down to assist in that duty.

October 18th.—Everything perfectly quiet this morning, and we began to think them serious in coming into terms. Two of their principal *sirdars* (commandants) came into camp early to-day, and after some conversation with the commander-in-chief the capitulation was signed by them on behalf of the garrison. Livesey and myself rode down to a hill in front, and knew nothing of the surrender till we saw the garrison marching out. They were allowed to leave the garrison carrying with them their arms and private property. Our regiment was ordered into garrison, and I had the inexpressible satisfaction with my own hands to haul down Scindiah's colours, and plant the British Standard in its stead on the ramparts. We placed proper guards at the different gateways, and admitted none but the prize agents to give them an opportunity to secure all the property on account of the army. Treasure was discovered to the amount of nearly thirty *lacs* of *rupees*.

In the evening MacGregor, Livesey and myself, with Ryder, Anderdon and Peyron, rode round that part of the glacis on which we attacked the enemy's battalions on the 10th.

None of those who fell in that affair had been removed. Hundreds of dogs from the city were preying upon them, and swarms of vultures and eagles were also devouring them. This was a sight too unpleasant for any but perfect savages, and we soon turned from it in disgust. Any person who had witnessed such a scene would know how to estimate the glories of war.

We went on to the breach, and the Bengal bastion was very much cut by our shot, as was the curtain; and the defences were completely destroyed. Another day's battering would have made a practicable breach for us.

Maddoo Ghur, an outwork thrown up for the protection of the bastion which we battered, was completely torn to atoms by the fire principally of the enfilading battery. This evening all the guns and platforms were removed from the batteries, and an order given for them to be immediately destroyed and the trenches levelled.

The garrison consisted of at least five thousand men, and had they waited the result of a storm the loss would in all probability have been great, and many a gallant fellow would have fallen.

It was rumoured in camp that thirteen battalions more of the enemy with one hundred pieces of cannon are not many miles in our front; should this prove true I resolved to use my interest and endeavour to gain the commander-in-chief's permission to accompany the army and not remain here in garrison with the corps. A soldier, in my opinion, should lose no opportunity of seeing service, but show an inclination at all times to be first and foremost when actual service is really expected. It is surely preferable to share the dangers and glory of a battle in hopes of gaining approbation and applause than to walk leisurely round the ramparts of a secure garrison without the prospect of notice or preferment.

We heard from Bundlecund this day that a skirmish had taken place between Colonel Powell's detachment and a body of the enemy; the latter were driven back, but allowed to carry off their gun with them; if Powell had adopted our plan, left the artillery and had recourse to the bayonet (*à la Delhi*), the enemy's guns would most probably have been left behind. Poor Farley Smith, with whom I was in the 18th Regiment, was killed early in the affair by a cannon shot.

October 20th.—Prize rolls ordered to be sent in this morning, and a distribution of prize money to take place immediately.

At four this afternoon Colonel Blair sent for me, and told me that the commander-in-chief had determined to leave our corps in garrison. I made the colonel acquainted with my intention to apply to the general for permission to march on with the army. Colonel Blair at first did not give his consent, but on my pointing out the very material difference it might make to me he approved. Went in the evening to my good friends, Colonel Lake and Wemyss, and the former readily engaged to make my wishes known to the commander-in-chief. During dinner I received a note from Colonel Lake telling me that the general could not consent to my leaving Colonel Blair; at the same time paying me the compliment to say that my services and assistance to Colonel Blair could not be dispensed with, as there were numerous arrangements to make in the garrison, and that as staff to Colonel Blair I must remain in Agra. I began to suspect that Blair had interfered, and contented myself at least with having offered my services.

October 21st.—The treasure found in the garrison was all counted today. It amounted to twenty-four *lacs* and forty-four thousand *rupees*. N.B. I expect six thousand (equal to £800) to be my share. At twelve today three hundred of the Bhirtpore Rajah's Horse made their appearance on the opposite banks of the river, and the boats, such as had not been sunk by our shot during the siege, commenced crossing them. A corps of *Nijeebs* (Irregular Infantry) ordered to be raised in order to protect the town, and that none of our men may be required out of the garrison, but to be confined entirely to the duty of the fortress only. From a bastion on the N.E. face we discovered a fine jungle which looked exceedingly likely for game.

Tomorrow fixed on for me to make the distribution of quarters to officers according to seniority. In the evening I went with Colonel Blair to examine the drawbridge at the Delhi gate; we found it in want of much repair.

October 22nd.—At gunfire this morning I accompanied Colonel Blair round the ramparts to examine the works and to make some fresh arrangements of the artillery. The senior officer of artillery joined us, and gave us his report, by which it appeared that in the garrison and on the different works there were mounted one hundred and sixty-three pieces of cannon of different calibres, with their proportion of ammunition made up.

The commander-in-chief and Colonels Clinton and Nightingale came into the garrison this morning. They joined us on the works, and his Excellency did me the honour to introduce me to them himself.

Then, addressing me in a very good humoured way, he said that he understood I was ready to "cut his throat" for leaving me in the garrison, to which his Excellency added: "You are an old soldier now, and have seen fighting enough, and Colonel Blair will not willingly dispense with your assistance in garrison." Colonel Lake told me that he had tried hard to accomplish my wishes, but that His Excellency did not like to deprive Colonel Blair of any part of his staff, as their services in the garrison were requisite; at the same time he told me that he thought the general wished me to proceed with the army, and that there was yet some chance of it.

In the evening I went down to the great mosque, where all the small arms taken from the enemy were lodged; took the sergeant-major with me to pick out sixty stand of arms, belts and pouches for our recruits. The locks of these pieces were in general very inferior.

October 23rd.—At gunfire this morning I went with Colonel Blair to inspect the carpenters' and smiths' yards, and to examine the arsenals. Found abundance of shot and artillery stores of every kind and description. No garrison could possibly be better founded in every warlike sort of stores. The commander-in-chief and his staff came into garrison this morning. Wemyss remained and breakfasted with me in my new quarters, which I had fixed in Shah Jehan's bastion, so named from being the bastion in which that Emperor was confined for life, shut up from every human being, a faithful daughter excepted, who never left him, but shared with him all his distresses.

Wemyss, Shairpe and myself walked round the ramparts after breakfast. The commander-in-chief's share of the prize money was sent into camp this afternoon. It amounted to forty-four thousand pounds, and the general declared that he had been upwards of forty years a soldier, and never touched prize money till this campaign. Received a letter today from Robert Dawson, dated at Diamond Harbour.

October 24th.—At daylight this morning I accompanied Colonel Blair to inspect the breach, and to give the necessary directions to the workmen who were employed at it. At seven the commander-in-chief came into garrison, and expressed himself highly pleased with the arrangements we had made on the ramparts and the disposition made for the guns, etc.

The general talked of marching tomorrow morning, and asked me if I was yet reconciled to remaining behind. I could not refrain from expressing a desire to proceed on with the army. It was well known that the enemy were not many miles from us, with a force consisting of thirteen battalions and one hundred pieces of cannon, and therefore I knew that my wish to march could not be imputed to any other cause than a desire to let no opportunity escape me of seeing service.

The general repeated that my services in the garrison were so requisite that I could not be spared, adding that he could not but approve of my wish and inclination to proceed on with the army, which he did me the honour to add was very commendable.

Wrote on the service this afternoon to the adjutant-general, forwarding an indent on the camp magazines for musket ball ammunition to complete the men to one hundred rounds in pouch each man. Indented also for muskets, belts and pouches for the use of some fresh recruits. In the evening I went to look out a proper place for the battalion magazine, and ordered the platforms to be laid. Several of my friends in camp, whose rascally servants had deserted them on finding they were about to march into the Mahratta Dominions, sent their *palanquins* and baggage into the garrison to remain with me. O'Donnel's, Shairpe's, Paterson's, Anderdon's, and many others. Colonel Blair desired me to fix on good quarters for myself as near his (in the palace) as possible. This evening we all dined with Sinclair, and passed a very gay evening.

October 25th.—The commander-in-chief came into the garrison this morning, and we pointed out to His Excellency the place fixed on for our hospital. It was the marble hall in which Scindiah held his *durbar* (court), and was exceedingly airy and in every respect commodious and well calculated for the purpose. The surgeons proposed to have it divided, one part for the sick and wounded Europeans and the other side for the natives. The wounded of the battle of Delhi were all in camp except a few of the worse left in Delhi.

The prize money was distributed this morning. Secured all my baggage and that of my friends in Shah Jehan's bastion. Several officers wounded at the battle of Delhi and during the siege of this place came into garrison this evening. A rumour that General Wellesley had given Scindiah a second edition of what he received from our hands at Delhi, but no official despatches from the Decan had reached General Lake.

One of the *havildars* belonging to the breach guard in Maddoo Ghur was badly wounded by an alligator which attacked him. The man had been just relieved, and was sleeping on the glacis when the alligator came from the ditch, and was very near taking the soldier with him into the water. The man's cries alarmed the guard, and the animal made off. It is not unusual among the native powers to stock the ditches of their forts with alligators, in which they only get what prey is thrown in to them, and are consequently dreadfully ravenous and savage, attacking anything and devouring it the instant it is in the water, these modes of defence are among the natives considered very formidable, and men no doubt are often taken down by the voracious devils. The prize agents took a final leave of the garrison this afternoon. We dined with Dyer in the quarters formerly inhabited by Colonel Hessen, a Dutchman, and Governor of the fort of Agra, in which he died shortly before the war broke out. Received a letter from Mrs. C. this evening.

October 26th.—The last night was one of the most boisterous I ever recollect; perpetual thunder accompanied with the most vivid lightning. Ordered the sergeant-major exchange some of the worst of our recruits' arms for the best of those remaining at the Great Mosque (Jumma Musjeed). Visited the works and arsenal with Colonel Blair, and ordered the battalion stores to be removed immediately into the new magazine.

Breakfasted this morning with Livesey in Maddoo Ghur. Livesey had the breach guard. After breakfast Weston, Forbes, Livesey and myself took our rifles and walked on the glacis in hopes of getting a shot at some of the alligators in the ditch, which constantly annoyed the sentries during the night. About eleven o'clock Wemyss came galloping down from the camp, and gave me the most pleasing information I had ever almost heard.

His Excellency the commander-in-chief had sent for Wemyss to his tent, and directed him to go to me in the garrison, to inform me that as I was so very desirous of accompanying him and the army I should immediately address a letter to him (General Lake), and he would see what could be done. I was extremely gratified at this proof of his Excellency's recollection of me, and lost no time in addressing a letter to the commander-in-chief, and Wemyss was the bearer of it to his Excellency.

The general immediately sent for Captain Cumberlege, major of brigade, to his tent, and told him that as I was desirous to accompany the army, he had better return to his appointment of quarter-master to the regiment, as His Excellency wished to give me the Brigade Majorship of the 4th Brigade, to which Captain Cumberlege readily assented. This pleasant information was immediately transmitted to me from Wemyss in camp.

Nothing could have been more flattering to my feelings than this arrangement. When the order arrived in garrison, Colonel Blair presented it to me as my death warrant. The colonel insisted on my remaining to dine in garrison with him, and ordered a sergeant's party to escort me to camp at night.

Dispatched my tent and baggage to camp, as the army was to march in the morning. Colonel Blair was not displeased at my application to march with the army, though he rowed me a little for leaving him. We passed a very jolly evening, and at eleven o'clock I left the garrison with my party. Called at Livesey's post and took my leave of him as I went out of the fort.

My route to camp was through the ravines, and it was rendered very unpleasant by the horrid stench, and by stumbling about in the dark among the bodies which still remained unburied and lying as they did on the day of the storm of the ravines, only in some degree devoured by the dogs and birds of prey. The ravines were swarming with jackals as we passed through them.

Chapter 17

March from Agra to Gwalior

October 27th.—Camp near Kerrouly. This morning I waited on Brigadier Powell at his tent, just in time to get some coffee before we moved off. The general beat at five and the assembly at six o'clock in conformity to yesterday's orders. The country over which we marched this morning was very finely cultivated. The sun was exceedingly hot before we came to our ground, and I was dreadfully annoyed by the headache. Owing to some confusion among the baggage (as is generally the case the first day's march of an army) our tents did not come to the ground till nearly an hour after us.

The troops this morning owing to our having been some considerable time encamped on our last ground, were so completely covered with flies that it was really almost impossible to discern the colour of their regimentals. They almost drove our horses mad by perpetually covering them and stinging them cruelly. We did not come to our ground today till ten o'clock.

On the march we learnt from some *hircarahs* (messengers) from the enemy's camp that they remained in force with thirteen battalions and one hundred pieces of cannon within eighteen miles of us; and we expect a bloody action, perhaps tomorrow or the next day. The enemy's force by the best accounts amounted to at least twelve thousand men, well armed and clothed, and thoroughly disciplined, supported by as fine a train of artillery as was ever carried into the field, and, formidable as they are, we hope soon to see them under British colours.

In going for orders to headquarters this afternoon Colonel Lake called to me as I passed his tent, and showed me the despatches received about an hour before with an account of General Wellesley's action (Assaye). It appeared to have been a very bloody day, and a great number of officers fell. At one period the fate of the day seemed very dubious; the army, greater part of our artillery was in possession of the enemy, but recovered by a timely charge of the cavalry, and the enemy were eventually routed with great slaughter, all their guns, ammunition, tumbrils and colours taken.

The result of this glorious affair, we trust, will prove a prelude to the result of our coming up with the enemy we are now in quest of. Colonel Lake informed me that Scindiah's *sirdars* (commandants) relied on beating us off with their artillery, and there was no doubt of the determination to try the fate of another battle with us. Two days or three days more he supposed would bring us together. Returned and issued the brigade orders in Brigadier Powell's tent. The pleasing news of General Wellesley's action put the brigadier in high spirits.

About five o'clock this evening the most severe hurricane came on I ever witnessed. The greater part of the tents in the line were smooth in five minutes, and nothing could exceed the scene of confusion occasioned by this unexpected salute. The thunder rolled tremendously, and the lightning was most vivid. It was accompanied by a deluge of rain that came down in torrents, and the tents blown down were soon nearly overwhelmed. It ran like a river through those remaining, drenching our beds and every particle of our clothes most completely. I dined with Anderdon, and we were absolutely necessitated to cut a trench round the table in the tent to draw off the water sufficiently to enable us to sit to eat our dinner, of which and a bottle of claret each we made an end about eleven o'clock.

October 28th.—At daylight this morning the country appeared completely inundated, and in consequence of the heavy fall of rain the men (who had been all night exposed to it) appeared miserably uncomfortable in the lines. Their tents were nearly all blown down and swamped. The commander-in-chief passed the rear of our brigade at daylight. We struck all the inner walls of our tents, and put them in the sun to dry. My *classhies* employed in repairing my camel's saddles. Breakfasted with Colonel Powell. At ten a.m. a general order came out for the army to halt today, and I issued a brigade order for all *hackeries* and wheeled carriages of every description to be removed from off the heavy ground into the road in readiness to move off without delay.

October 29th.—The army marched this morning by the left, cavalry in front. It was not without the greatest difficulty that we dragged on the heavy guns this march, the ground over which we moved was a complete slough, and the field pieces even were not easily drawn over it. The elephants this day were of the greatest use in assisting the heavy guns out of the mire. We arrived very late at our ground, and encamped about two miles to the northward of Siekri.

Passed this morning the spot of ground on which Major Collins, Livesey, Marston and myself encamped about sixteen months ago. Breakfasted with my brigadier, and at three went to headquarters for orders. The army to march in the morning. Instead of finding an enemy here, as we were told, ready drawn up to receive us, we received information that they quitted Siekri two days before, and were retreating by rapid marches towards Scindiah's country, and in the direction of Ougene, his capital.

October 30th.—The army marched this morning, the cavalry leading. A report this day that the enemy were two days before on our present ground of encampment. Our brigade was ordered to bring up the Park. The weather cool and pleasant in consequence of the late heavy fall of rain.

November 1st.—Nothing particular occurred since we left the ground at Siekri till this morning. The general and cavalry marched at one o'clock. The 2nd and 3rd Brigade of Infantry with the brigade and battalion field pieces, and our brigade in charge of the Park. About sunrise we heard a most tremendous fire of cannon about six miles in front of the infantry, and rightly concluded it was our cavalry engaged with the enemy. Orders soon came for the line of infantry to advance, and presently several horses came galloping towards our line without their riders. About eight o'clock the cannonade ceased.

The line of infantry still pushing on. At this time accounts met us of the cavalry having made an unsuccessful attack on the enemy's guns; that the cannonade we had heard in front was that of the enemy. The cavalry, we were told, were beaten off, and were then drawn up, out of reach of the enemy's fire, waiting our arrival with the Infantry. We were told the loss of our cavalry had been great in officers and men. About eleven o'clock the attack with the Infantry commenced with great vigour.

Our brigade was drawn up in the rear for the protection of the Park, and when the 1st, 2nd and 3rd Brigades began the attack the enemy's cavalry immediately came round to attack us, but were soon repulsed. The fire was extremely heavy, and particularly from the villages of Lassuary and Malpoorah. In about three hours the whole of the enemy's guns, tumbrils and colours were in our possession, although they cost us dear, as we had thirteen officers killed in the action and about forty wounded; among the former were General Ware, Colonel Vandeleur, poor Campbell, the quarter-master-general, Major Griffith, etc., etc.

November 2nd.—The pioneers and *beldars* employed the whole of this day in burying the dead. The officers who fell, thirteen in number, were buried at sunset this evening with all military honours. All the surgeons of the line ordered to the General Hospital tents to assist in dressing the wounded. All the *doolies* of the army ordered to the head surgeons.

November 6th.—This morning the wounded men and captured guns left us to go immediately to Agra. A party of the 12th Regiment escorted them from our camp under the orders of Captain Wood of that corps. Dined today with Raban of the artillery.

November 7th—This morning we marched, supposed by our direction, in pursuit of Holcar, who was said to be menacing an attack on our conquered country. There was some capital hog hunting this morning on the line of march, and the commander-in-chief did not object to officers quitting the line, a small proportion of each corps, with the permission of commanding officers. Came to our ground about nine o'clock. Dined at headquarters today.

November 14th.—Continued marching in a southerly direction; nothing material occurred, good hog hunting daily, and they were the most delicious eating I ever met with. This was accounted for by there being an immense quantity of sugar cane in the country through which we passed, and on which, to the great discomfiture of the villagers, the hogs fed.

The country was the Bhirtpore Rajah's, who without any hesitation took the head of any of the people who were detected killing the hogs. This day despatched to Colonel Scott at Lucknow an order from the collector on the paymaster-general for *Rs.* 4240, with directions for to have it put in the eight *per cent*, loan; my share of Agra prize money, at least part of it, and the first money I had ever realised.

November 15th.—This morning we marched at the usual hour; the general beat at five and assembly at six o'clock, in the same order as yesterday. Soon after daylight one of the largest boars I ever saw crossed our line. He went directly at the bullocks dragging one of the eighteen-pounders, and put the whole of them to rout, after which, in the most mischievous manner, he cut and attacked several camp followers. The alarm was soon given, and I changed my horse, and mounted on Major. The groom had my spear, as was customary, in his hand, and after him I went.

Ford, Harris and several other officers joined me, and after a chase of nearly two miles, over very bad broken ground, full of wells and every other annoyance that an unsound country could afford, I came near him; he instantly turned and charged me. My spear entered just behind his shoulders, but he did not fall till he had got under my horse, and cut him in a most dreadful manner, and severing every sinew in his off leg behind. My stirrup leather was nearly cut through by his tusk. The moment he had effected this mischief, or rather in the act of doing it, he fell stone dead under the horse.

A servant of Colonel Haldane's gave me some spirits to wash the horse's wounds, which we also sewed up, but found that he was completely ruined. Got him with much difficulty into camp, and gave him to a servant of Wemyss. In this horse I lost one of the best hunters in India, on which I seldom missed a hog. He was uncommonly bold, very active, and had a most excellent mouth. On further examination we found that there was a probability of the horse recovering the wound behind the girths in the flank, but the sinews were so completely torn that the horse must be lame for life. Mr. Burgh, the surgeon of the 14th, who was an excellent horse doctor, as well as a very clever man in other respects, dressed my horse, and gave me dressings for him.

November 16th.—We marched this morning at the usual time. The roads very good, and the country remarkably well cultivated. Got to our ground about eleven o'clock; killed some hogs on the march today. Colonel Powell and self dined with the commander-in-chief; drank much wine.

November 17th.—Camp at Pehaiser. At break of day this morning the army halted. Major Swinton, Campbell, Wemyss and myself left the camp to hog hunt. Wemyss mounted me on Lassuary, the name he gave the horse which he purchased at poor Campbell's (the quarter-master-general's) sale, and the same on which Campbell was killed in the action of the 1st. We remained out nearly all the day, but as we were strangers to the country, and did not know in what direction to go for hogs, we had but little sport.

I never was carried in higher style than on this day, and Wemyss was delighted by the manner in which his new purchase went over the country. Campbell had brought this horse with him from Arabia; he was a real Desert Arab, and for beauty and powers exceeded any horse I had seen in India. Wemyss purchased him for £300, and he was thought a cheap horse. We had seven elephants from headquarters, and a great number of camels out with us to beat the sugar canes, but we fell in with but very few hogs. We returned, and made a late breakfast at Mercer's, agent to the governor-general. Went at the usual hour for orders. Dined today with Macan, and we had a very pleasant day.

November 18th.—Breakfasted this morning at headquarters, stayed till nearly twelve o'clock with Colonel Lake in his tent. He recovered but very slowly of the wound he received on the 1st. It was a grape shot through him just above the knee; great fear is apprehended of his being always lame from the wound, as the tendons were much cut by the shot. Rode with Wemyss in the evening, and dined with General Lake, and, as is always the case at headquarters, drank a great deal of wine.

November 21st.—At four o'clock this morning rode out from the left of the line on an Arab of Wemyss's. We had a large party, and heard of hogs near our camp. Wallace, Ridge, Shairpe, Gilbert, Bolieau, Rainey and Durant joined us, and we found a boar in the first jungle (cover) we entered, which we killed after an excellent chase; he carried my spear, Wallace's and Wemyss's a considerable distance, sticking up straight in his back, before he fell, and made several charges with them in him.

In the same jungle we afterwards found two more boars, which afforded us excellent sport, and both of which we killed. The ground was very bad, and very dangerous riding; there were several severe falls, but no material injury done. On our return to camp we saw a *niel ghy* (blue deer, very fleet, resembling a large deer), and it was a capital opportunity to try the speed and bottom of our Arabs.

Wemyss, Wallace, Shairpe and I had a perfect race for full three miles before we came up with him. The ground was dangerous, and we were literally at speed the whole time, over several wells, and deep, broken ground; this was one of the most desperate things I ever saw attempted, and none but madmen would have tried it.

Wallace had the first spear at him, and missed him. I speared him through the loins, and he staggered a few paces, and fell. Wemyss's spear went to his heart. There was scarcely ever an instance before known of a *neil ghy* being speared. They are full thirteen hands high, and at a small distance look like the large red deer sometimes seen in Devonshire, and which I had seen hunted by Sir Thomas Ackland's hounds, near Dulverton. They are of a light blue colour, with eyes and nostrils resembling those of a high-bred Arab horse. Got to camp in good time to write the general orders of the day, by which it appears that we are to halt here for some days longer.

November 22nd.—Macan and myself left our camp this morning at daybreak with the greyhounds. We had some good sport, but the ground was so excessively hard that the dogs could not bear more than a couple of courses each. Killed two brace of hares; returned and breakfasted with Macan on soused hog's head, which was delicious. The officers of the 8th (Colonel Powell's Corps) dined with us today, and as I was placed at the head of the table I was under the necessity of taking more wine than my usual quantity.

November 23rd.—Left the camp this morning at four o'clock, to hog hunt. Wemyss, Wallace, Ridge, Boileau, Wilson, Bailey, Gilbert, Durant, Shairpe, Rainey and myself. We breakfasted under a tree at a village, and commenced hunting afterwards. In the course of three hours we killed four hogs, and knocked up some of our horses. During the last chase Shairpe's horse fell with him, bruised him much, and the horse got loose in the jungle, nor could we during three hours' searching for him, with all our servants mounted on the led horses, hear or see anything of him.

The commander-in-chief, on hearing that an officer had lost his horse, desired that a party of the irregular troops might be sent in search of it. I dined at headquarters this evening, and the general enquired of Wemyss and myself if there was no danger to be apprehended of our being attacked in our hunting parties by the *banditti* which infested that part of the country, and told us, in future, always to apply to Gerard, the adjutant-general, for a party as an escort when we went on those excursions. We passed a very pleasant day, and the whole party were quite mellow before we separated.

November 25th.—Rode in front an hour before breakfast this morning with Colonel Lake and Wemyss. Colonel Lake on a black Arab called Rockett, Wemyss on Lassuary, and myself on Collector; the former offered me two thousand *rupees* for Collector this morning.

November 26th.—Camp at Helenah. The army marched this morning, agreeable to the orders of yesterday. The roads remarkably firm, and richly cultivated. Marched in a south-westerly direction, and directly in a line for Jeypore. Wemyss, single-handed, killed two large boars on the march today.

November 27th.—Mounted my horse this morning at sunrise, and went with Wemyss and Lumsdaine hog hunting. We were unfortunate, and had but little sport. Returning, we rode at a herd of antelope, but could make no hand of them; they were too fleet even for our Arabs. Breakfasted with Lumsdaine on wild hog, cold, and pork chops; it was the finest meat I ever tasted, and literally as white as snow. Went at three o'clock for orders, and in the evening a large party of us rode to the parade of the 12th to hear their band.

Dined today with Major Witherstone—this officer, though no sportsman, kept half-a-dozen of the most beautiful Europe bred terriers I ever saw; they were all pets, and running about his tent. I had a fancy this evening to walk to my tent, and, owing to the stupidity of my servants, I lost my way, and found myself at last in the cavalry lines, at least two miles from my tent. The fogs and smoke in an Indian camp at this season of the year render it difficult, after the night has set in, to find one's way from one tent to another.

November 29th.—Went with Wemyss to a grass jungle in the vicinity of the camp to shoot peacocks with ball; killed a great many. Macan, Philpot of the 27th Dragoons, and another officer joined us with the greyhounds and pack of terriers. We found hares in great abundance, but the cover much too strong to course. An immense boar got up, but, making immediately to a strong jungle across the sandy bed of a river, he got off before we could get near enough to give him a spear.

December 1st.—Left our camp an hour before daylight this morning, having sent off the servants and breakfast things during the night, and breakfasted at a village about five miles in the rear, after which we tried the sugar canes near the place, and found hogs in plenty. We had a capital day's sport, and killed everything we went after. While we were running a boar a very beautiful Arab of Durant's got from the groom's hand, and, coming loose at speed towards us, fell into a well, and unfortunately broke his back. We shot him on the spot.

December 2nd.—Rode round the picquets with Colonel Lake and Wemyss this morning. Colonel Lake told me that we should change our ground immediately, heard also that accounts of a very favourable nature had been recently received from General Wellesley's Army, in the Decan. The Rajah of Jeypore expected in camp on a visit to the commander-in-chief. Dined with Brigadier Clarke.

December 3rd.—Went before daybreak this morning with a large party to hog hunt. We assembled before daybreak at the headquarter lines, in Wemyss's tent. We had today some of the most severe chases I ever witnessed, and some very serious falls, owing to the badness of the ground, which was full of holes and wells, covered with jungle in such a way that neither man nor horse could see them till the accident had happened.

December 6th.—The army marched this morning by the left. We arrived at our ground about ten o'clock. The country over which we marched this morning afforded but little cultivation, except near the villages. After breakfast I joined Wemyss in the headquarter lines, and we went off towards a range of beautiful hills about two miles in our front. Killed many partridges and two brace of hares. We were shooting in a fine dry grass cover when a herd of hogs got up before the dogs. Our grooms, horses and spears were at our heels; we singled out two very large boars, and separated, Wemyss after his hog and I in pursuit of mine.

The ground was very full of hillocks in the grass, and my horse came down on his face before I had got him into his gallop, but I recovered him, and the boar I was after took the line to our camp. The arms being all piled in front of corps, the hog charged the sentry over a stack of arms belonging to the 9th Regiment, upsetting the whole; he made directly through the centre of the camp, directly towards the Park, and passed headquarter lines, wounding several people desperately as he went on, nor could I, owing to the tent ropes, guns and people get a spear at him till he had got clear to the rear, where I killed him within one hundred yards of the commander-in-chief's tent, after a severe run of at least three miles. Wemyss killed his hog near one of the infantry picquets. Dined with Macan, and passed a very pleasant day; took lots of claret.

December 7th.—The army marched this morning by the right, baggage on the right. The general beat at six and the assembly at seven o'clock. The roads good, and the country well cultivated. Arrived at our ground about ten. Wemyss and myself left the camp immediately after breakfast to shoot; killed a great deal of game, partridge, hares, peacocks, quail and snipe.

December 8th.—Camp at Koorkhah. The army halted today, and after breakfast Wemyss and myself mounted our horses and rode towards some hills on our left flank. We got into a very strong jungle, in which the neighbouring villagers told us there were tigers.

In the midst of the jungle we discovered a fine lake of water, and on its borders we sprung an immense quantity of snipe as we walked our horses along. This was one of the most romantic spots I ever visited, and we resolved, in the event of the army halting a day, to return with our guns in the morning. Breakfast was ready for in my tent, and it was past twelve and very hot before we got to camp. At three I went for orders, and was much annoyed to find our schemes done away for the following morning, the army being ordered to march.

December 9th.—We marched this morning by the left, baggage on the left. A fine range of hills on our right, and the country highly cultivated. The commander-in-chief passed in front of our brigade on the line of march, and sent Wemyss to ask me to dine with him. Arrived at our ground about eleven o'clock, and pitched about three miles from the hills. Breakfasted, and had good shooting till nearly five o'clock. As it was late before I returned to camp, and the orderly hour was passed, Harris very kindly went to take the orders for me. Dined with the commander-in-chief today, a very pleasant and large party; a great deal of singing.

December 10th.—The army halted today. Wemyss and self went out in front to shoot; killed in about three hours four brace of snipe, four and a half brace of quail, three brace of partridge, and after we had given up shooting and had mounted our horses to gallop into camp we discovered a very large boar feeding in some young corn. We had just left the spears with our servants, but we continued to keep sight of him, while my groom rode back for them, and as soon as the spears arrived we made towards him; at first he made a charge at us, without attempting to make off.

I wounded him slightly in the neck, and while we were recovering our spears he made off across the plain, and ran two miles before we could come up with him; on our drawing near him he charged us again in a most desperate manner, and Wemyss, being nearest him, gave him his spear between his shoulders, where it stuck when he attacked me, and I met him and lodged my spear directly in his forehead; he staggered a few paces, and fell quite dead. The spear was full five inches in his skull, and it was with some difficulty that we drew it out.

We hired some villagers to bring him into camp. His size was immense, and from the length of his tusk we imagined him to be of a very ancient family. The country over which we ran this boar was the finest possible, all young corn, less than a foot in height. Sent the commander-in-chief our hog, and dined with Macan.

December 11th.—Camp at Nameedah. Rode out in front this morning with Macan; we had our greyhounds, and found a hare immediately on the skirts of our camp. We had a capital course, but I was very unfortunate in laming Collector. Wemyss sent me Lassuary, one of his Arabs, to ride while my own horse remained lame. The Bhirtpore Rajah, with about three thousand soldiers in attendance, came into camp. The headquarter line was so much crowded by those people that it was with difficulty we got to the office tent for orders. His Excellency returned the *rajah's* visit about five in the evening. An extra dram served out to all the Europeans in camp this afternoon. Anderdon and self went with our pistols this evening to a village in the rear, and amused ourselves with firing at a mark.

December 12th.—13 Miles. The army marched this morning by the left. On the line of march we discerned the famous gateway at Futtypore Seekrie, and about nine o'clock we encamped, having gone through a pass in the hills, which we left about two miles.

December 13th.—Camp at Rhemidah. Wemyss and self had a snug breakfast at my tent this morning, after which we took our guns and rode quietly to a *jow* jungle about three miles to the northward of our encampment. Saw a good deal of game, and many hogs, but the cover was much too strong to ride them, as we could scarcely see each other on horseback.

On the skirts of the jungle we killed five brace of partridge and four and a half brace of hares. Saw Futtypore very plainly. We returned to camp about three o'clock, and I went as usual for my orders. This evening Colonel Lake informed me it was very probable that our Brigade (the 4th) would march shortly to Gwalior. This place is thought to be one of the strongest in the world, and styled the "Gibraltar of India."

December 14th.—This morning at seven o'clock the right wing of the army, commanded by General St. John, paraded for exercise, and our brigade was under arms at the same time for the inspection of General Fraser, who rode down the line and passed in the rear, and expressed his entire approbation of the "veteran-like appearance of the whole"; dismissed the line.

December 15th.—This morning the recruits of the different corps in the line were out at target practice in the rear of the Hindustanee Cavalry, under the range of hills we passed the last day's march. Brigadier Powell requested me to wait on the adjutant-general and mention to him the state of the brigadier's health, which daily grew worse. The commander-in-chief immediately gave him two months' leave, and permission to leave the army whenever he thought proper. I was much concerned at parting with him, as I liked him exceedingly; he was a good soldier, and an excellent man.

December 16th.—At daylight this morning Brigadier Powell left camp, and Colonel White, well known in the army by the appellation of "The God of War," was appointed to succeed him. No officer in the Indian Army is more esteemed as a gallant active officer than Colonel White, and to his meritorious exertions on the night of the 6th of February, when our army stormed Tippoo's lines at Seringapatam, was attributed the saving of Lord Cornwallis, and H.M. 74th Regiment, as stated in the account of Tippoo's War.

After having received my orders at headquarters, I waited on my new brigadier, to whom I was by Anderdon introduced. We found him completely equipped, sworded and sashed, as if he had been prepared for a night's duty in the trenches. He received me with much pomp and politeness, and I issued the brigade orders at his tent, after which Anderdon and self went to the parade of the Dismounted Dragoons. Dined with Shairpe at the mess of the 12th Regiment.

December 18th.—The brigade paraded for exercise this morning at gunfire. We advanced in line, and in open column of companies; changed front by *echelon*; returned by files in quick time, and wheeled into line, when I was desired to order company officers of corps to dismiss their respective parades. Wemyss came to me after the parade was dismissed, and told me that the commander-in-chief was going out to shoot, and that he was desirous I should accompany him.

Breakfasted at headquarters, and, just as we were setting out, despatches arrived, which prevented His Excellency from going out. Colonel Clinton, Wemyss, Rose, Martin and myself went, and we had a famous morning's sport; killed eighteen hares, twelve brace of black partridge, two hogs and several brace of quail. Wemyss and myself dismounted from the elephants and got on our horses when we found the hogs, and killed one each.

Harris took the general orders for me today. Dined with General Lake this evening, and his Excellency greatly lamented that he had not accompanied us. Drank a good deal of wine.

December 21st.—Agreeable to yesterday's general orders, our brigade moved out from the line this morning at sunrise, and encamped near the village of Senedy, about two miles in front of the Army and on the Gwalior road. Marched with the Brigade to its new ground, after which I accompanied the Brigadier back to breakfast at headquarters; when we took our leave of the Commander-in-Chief, and Brigadier White received his instructions. We returned to our camp in the forenoon, and all the officers of the Brigade dined with us, and we passed a very pleasant evening, all in high spirits. Issued orders for the detail of guards, picquets, etc., and to march in the morning at half-past five.

December 22nd.—9 Miles. Camp at Seepow. This morning the general beat at five and the assembly half-an-hour after, when we moved off by the right. We were soon out of sight of the

Grand Army. The country through which we marched today was well cultivated, and the roads were good. We arrived at our ground about nine o'clock; our encampment was on broken ground, with the ruins of an old fort in our rear. A large party of officers of the detachment breakfasted with us this morning, and the brigadier desired that I would live with him at headquarters, and make his tent my home.

December 23rd.—11 Miles. Camp at Futehgung. The brigade marched this morning at six o'clock, and arrived at its ground about ten. The road pretty good, and tolerably level; less cultivation than yesterday. Brigadier White received a note today from Mr. Mercer, who was encamped about six miles in our rear, and very anxious to join us. Mr. Mercer accompanied the brigade as having full powers to treat and make settlements in the conquered provinces, in the capacity of "Governor-General's Agent"; he was Mr. Wellesley's adviser in making the settlements in the country ceded to us by the *Nawab* of Lucknow in 1800, of which Mr. Wellesley was appointed lieutenant-governor.

December 24th.—At ten o'clock we beat the general, and immediately after the assembly, and marched off by the right. About eleven o'clock we entered a pass in a fine range of hills, and soon got clear of it. The country well cultivated, with fine mango groves in abundance After leaving the pass we marched in a south-westerly direction, keeping the hills on our right and the fort of Dholepore about two miles on our left. Dholepore was in possession of the enemy, and we expected they would have tried some heavy guns at our column as we passed, but they did not molest us.

About one we arrived near the banks of the Chumbill, the passes near which are uncommonly strong, and with a few good troops might be defended against almost any force. A small party which we had ordered to cross the river in front of the advanced guard returned and informed us that the pass on the opposite side of the river was occupied by the enemy, and that the ravines were full of men. I offered my services to dislodge them, and the Brigadier desired me to take the command of the advanced guard, and to cross the river, while he halted the column on the Dholepore banks.

I primed and loaded, and at the head of the guard crossed the river; a body of armed men made their appearance the moment we entered the ravines, and a small party of them advanced unarmed, and I soon learnt that they were part of the few men of the enemy who escaped in the action of the 1st November at Lassuary, and came to offer their services to us. I sent an officer to the brigadier to report the circumstance to him, and the column crossed immediately. The brigadier soon dismissed those men, not having any authority from the commander-in-chief to take them into our service.

On the Gwalior side of the Chumbill the ravines exceeded anything I ever saw, and it was with the greatest labour and difficulty that we dragged the guns up some of the precipices with the assistance of the soldiers at the drag ropes. The road was so narrow as barely to admit a gun to pass, and flanked by defiles which made it excessively strong, and, if defended, would be perfectly inaccessible.

The brigadier marched on, and encamped the brigade about three miles from the top of the ravines, and I remained with Lieutenant Morris, an artillery officer, to see all the guns clear of the pass. It was late before we got into camp, and as the guns detained the baggage in the pass our tents did not come up till near sunset. Brigadier White, Mercer, Campbell, Marishall and self took post under a large tree while our tents were pitching. Issued the brigade orders, and dined with Harris of the 14th.

December 25th.—The brigade halted today, and it being Christmas Day, extra *batta* was served out to the Europeans in our camp; here we procured a good supply of flour and grain. The land was poor and thinly cultivated, except on spots near the villages. Received letters today by an express from the Grand Army, from Wemyss and Maling; the former gave me information of the arrival of the *Tigress* and three Company's ships from England, and sent me the heads of intelligence brought out by them. Dined at home today, and the brigadier gave an immense dinner to nearly all the officers off duty in camp. We sat up late, and drank a good deal of claret; a great number of songs were sung, and we parted at a late hour.

December 26th.—13 Miles. Camp at Barokah. The brigade marched this morning by the right, baggage on the right. A finely cultivated country the first part of the morning; the latter part of the morning through deep ravines and broken ground, which, with a small river that we crossed, greatly impeded our progress. Arrived at our ground at eleven o'clock. I rode to a village on our left flank on an alarm being given that the camp followers were plundering it, and with a guard rescued the property of the villagers, and several of the villains were punished in the act of pillaging those helpless people. Many others were brought to a drumhead Court Martial, and punished in a most exemplary manner.

December 27th.—13 Miles. We marched this morning at six o'clock. The roads very level and fine, and the country crossed mostly with grain. About eight we crossed a small river, the banks of which were very steep, and we had much difficulty in dragging up the twelve-pounders. At ten we arrived at Noorabad, a decent town, but thinly inhabited, to the southward of which we encamped, about ten miles from Gwalior. At Noorabad are the ruins of a fine bridge, at this time barely passable for people on foot. The brigade marched over it, but the guns, tumbrils and heavy stores, with the carriages of every description, went a circuitous road to the right, and passed through the water, which was quite shallow at this season.

December 28th.—The brigade marched this morning at seven by the left. The country quite barren, and the soil very dry and sandy. The rains during the wet season seem to have lodged on the greater part of this neighbourhood. At sunrise we saw the fort of Gwalior towering among the clouds, and as we drew nearer it appeared an amazing strong place, very extensive, and the rock perpendicular on all sides as far as the eye could reach.

About nine o'clock we crossed a small river, and encamped. We pitched our camp at about the distance of four miles from the fortress, with the village of Suserara in our rear, and the river on our right flank. The people (inhabitants) from the town of Gwalior sent in a paper entreating that their lives and property might be spared. The brigadier returned them every assurance of his protection as soon as we should gain possession of the city.

Some spies of ours came from the garrison this morning with information that a nephew of Amboojee's (Raganauth Rhow) was in the fort, and that they were mounting fresh guns on the rampart, and making every precaution to defend the place to the last extremity. A strong body of Horse was reported to be encamped under the walls of the town, and within range of shot from the fort.

Received letters from camp stating that the commander-in-chief was moving in the direction of Jeypore; they also stated that a groom of Mr. Higgin's of the European Regiment was murdered near the camp, and the horse taken away. The servant was conducting his master's horse to camp after hog hunting. The brigadier desired me to issue an order requesting commanding officers of corps to caution their men against going without the limits of the camp. A man confined in one of the battalion quarter guards this morning for drawing his sword and threatening to murder a *sepoy* of the 18th.

A paper arrived in camp mentioning that Lord Nelson had captured thirteen sail of French merchantmen, having on board, 200,000 in specie; this intelligence said to have arrived with the *Tigress*. A report that Holcar had put to death every European serving in his army, and which, from his sanguinary disposition, it is feared is too likely to be true. The intentions of that chieftain towards us still unknown. The brigadier sent a summons to the garrison to surrender the place, which they declined in a spirited and soldier-like manner, declaring their determination sooner to be buried in its ruins, and the brigadier assured me seriously that he believed the place would cost us a good deal of blood, and that many officers and men would fall before it would be in our possession. Many of the officers rode a considerable distance in front this evening, which the brigadier desired me to put a stop to in future, by issuing an order to that effect, directing them not to go without the picquets.

Wrote a long letter to the adjutant-general this evening, stating the determination of the garrison to fight, and our preparation to attack them without delay. Went a long way in front with the brigadier this afternoon, and with our glasses we plainly perceived them cutting embrasures and mounting guns innumerable on the western face (the only part accessible on account of the immense height of solid rock which cannot be scaled). The brigadier and myself dined with Stuart this evening.

December 29th.—Ordered a foraging party to accompany the cattle this morning for forage. Two men punished for plundering a village near our camp. Some spies came in this morning with information that the garrison consisted of three thousand fighting men (many more than our detachment altogether). Two guns, not shotted, and pointed at our camp, were fired from the garrison about nine this morning. It was reported to us that about eight hundred of the enemy were posted at the different gateways in the town of Gwalior, at which were mounted some guns.

We determined on attacking the town without delay, and the brigadier desired me to arrange a party for that purpose. I proposed four grenadier and five battalion companies with two six-pounders for the attack, which was approved of, and I issued an order for all officers and *sepoys* to remain in their lines ready to be under arms at the shortest notice.

We had a report that General Lake was moving towards Agra. This evening some circumstances occurred which induced us to defer the attack on the town for a day or two, as the commander-in-chief directed that we should wait the result of another letter from Amboojee, who, like a true Mahratta, was assuring the general of his having given strict orders for the surrender of the fortress, at the very time we were intercepting his letters, directing the garrison to fight to the last, and never surrender it to the English, and promising them further supplies of men and money immediately; this, of course, we lost no time in communicating to headquarters, and forwarded the intercepted letters. Amboojee remained in the fort of Narwar, distance from Gwalior about thirty miles, from whence he kept up a regular communication with that place.

December 30th.—Accounts from Wemyss this morning informed me that the army had been moving in the direction of Jeypore adding also that the commander-in-chief had received letters from Holcar, expressing himself in terms of friendship and peace towards the English, but his sincerity was much doubted. From the garrison we have every reason to expect a formidable resistance. Went after breakfast to reconnoitre the place, but a body of the enemy's Horse menaced our small party, and we did not go beyond a range of gardens, about half cannon shot distance from the fortress. Notwithstanding the solicitations of the town people to give them protection, very few came near us, and the city gates were reported to be guarded and made fast.

This afternoon we had intelligence that Raganauth Rhow was dismantling the town and carrying off some of the light guns on field carriages. We much lamented that the limited time for commencing hostilities not having expired prevented our attacking him. The garrison today sent in a messenger saying that if Amboojee ordered them to surrender they were determined to throw off their allegiance and to defend the fortress. Dined at home today. The brigadier particularly anxious to take the town. Our ally the *ranee* of Gohud with a parcel of ragamuffin troops encamped about two miles from us this evening.

December 31st.—This morning the *ranee* of Gohud paid the brigadier a visit; he came in all the pomp of war, and attended by near one thousand followers, armed. I was desired to attend. After having gone through the usual forms of embracing, etc., etc., and remaining about an hour, His Highness took his leave, and went to his own camp. He appeared about thirty-five years of age, of a sensible countenance, though owing to his mode of life for many years past he was extremely awkward, having lived mostly in the jungles, hunting and shooting, of which he seemed very fond. He was much pleased with our reception of him, and we made him a present of an elephant and a double-poled tent.

CHAPTER 18

Siege of Gwalior

January 1st.—1804. At break of day this morning the brigadier, the quarter-master of brigade (Stewart) and myself left camp determined to reconnoitre the town and fort of Gwalior. We took a strong party with us, and posted them out of reach of shot from the fort to cover us in reconnoitring. They opened their guns upon us the moment we got within range of shot. We pushed on at speed, under a smart cannonade, to a large garden within four hundred yards of the wall; a place well calculated for our purpose. Here we were concealed by the shrubs and trees, though not sheltered from the shot, and they kept up a hot fire of round and grape all the time we were making our observations, and committing to paper some essential observations regarding the entrance of the town, and the road to it.

We had all many narrow escapes whilst performing: this hazardous service, and as on leaving the garden called the Begum's Bhaug (or Queen's Garden) we were again necessarily quite exposed, many shot threw the particles of stone over us, and my horse was wounded above the hock by a grape.

We got safe back to our escort and to camp without any further mischief. I was well assured this morning that the many accounts I had heard of the gallantry of the brigadier, and the numerous instances recorded of his personal courage and zeal did not exceed his merit, and he remained for full half-an-hour exposed to a smart fire of cannon and not at all covered, making his remarks with exceeding coolness and deliberation. Many of the trees were cut to pieces by the shot whilst we were standing under them.

In a letter to the commander-in-chief, which the brigadier, as usual, showed me, he was so good as to mention both Lieutenant Stewart and myself in terms very gratifying to us. The officers in camp having observed a heavy fire from the fortress, many were assembled at headquarters anxiously waiting the result, and we had a very large party at breakfast. The brigadier told me this morning, in confidence, that nothing should prevent his attacking the town either tomorrow or the following morning.

January 2nd.—Changed ground this morning to within two and a half miles of the town, and after having reinforced the Before picquets with a grenadier company, I advanced them to a village on the border of the town. We were cannonaded all the way to the post, and lost some men, but the village afforded good cover for the party when we arrived there, though the fort kept up a heavy but ineffectual fire on the post all day. Having stationed the picquets, and given the senior officer his instructions, I returned to camp, and the brigadier told me that he had resolved on getting possession of the town that night. All the day the fire continued heavy on the picquet, and they threw a few shots into our camp. At sunset I paraded four companies of the 16th Regiment, and with them and two six-pounders reinforced the advanced picquet; composing altogether four companies of grenadiers, five battalion companies and two six-pounders.

At dark we paraded the party, primed and loaded, and with good guides advanced towards the town under cover of the evening. The brigadier himself at the head of the column. We left our horses at the village, with orders to bring them to the town when the firing should cease. On foot I found my scabbard very incommodious, and though with much reluctance, having brought it with me from England and often carried it on the more peaceable parade of Yeovil, I was necessitated to throw it away. At the first and second gates of the town they opposed to us very little resistance; their principal stand was at the last gate (the gate of the choke or entrance up to the fort).

The brigadier gave me orders, on forcing this gate, to follow the enemy, if we found it practicable, into the fort. A very narrow road led up to the last gate, and we were assailed by a heavy fire of musketry; many of our men fell, and there was scarcely a man left at the drag ropes of the six-pounder in front. With great difficulty we succeeded in carrying the gun up to the gate, and nothing could exceed the gallantry of the troops; the lane was so narrow that we could not form to return their fire. The first round from the gun tore the gate very much, and another shot made a way for us.

At this time a shot passed through my boot, and grazed my knee, and I also received a severe blow on the shoulder from either a spent shot or a stone thrown from the top of one of the houses, neither of which I felt much at the moment. We drove those who escaped into the fort, but notwithstanding our rushing on to the fort gate instantly on forcing that of the choke (an outwork from the gate), we found it shut, and in fastening it so very hastily many of their own people had not time to get in, and were bayoneted by us. We immediately formed the leading companies and brought our guns and tumbrils into the choke.

We found ourselves immediately underneath the rock, and soon saw lights moving in every direction on the ramparts, which convinced us of their being in great confusion and at a loss where to direct their fire. After we had been about an hour in this post one of the most grand spectacles I ever witnessed was presented. The rock was several hundred yards in height, and in order to get a sight of us they illuminated the ramparts with blue lights, thrown out and suspended on strong bamboos.

The reflection on the steep and rugged side of the rock had a most magnificent and grand appearance, and we saw them crowding on the walls, but as it was too far for our musketry we did not fire on them. The light was so effectual that on the ground the smallest object was visible, and we were obliged to cover our guns (which with the reflection of the light on the brass would otherwise have been visible to the enemy) with some of the men's clothes. They continued a straggling fire of musketry the whole night, and the moon, rising about midnight, showed us several outworks, and convinced us that the post at daylight would not be tenable for so many men, and it also was commanded completely by one angle of the fort. The tumbrils and ammunition were, therefore, immediately ordered to be lodged in secure places in the town, concealed from the view of the fort. I wrote a letter to Colonel MacCullock, whom we left commanding in camp, directing him to march into the town with the remaining troops and baggage, and to join us. Sent guides to him. Remained all night under arms, expecting a sally from the garrison, and resolved to endeavour to enter with them into the fort if they attempted to attack.

At five in the morning Colonel MacCullock relieved us, and at daylight the fire from the fort increased so much, and we had so many men killed and wounded, that we withdrew such from the choke as could not be well covered, and posted a gun and a strong party at the gateway, with about one hundred men in the choke, disposed in a manner best to screen them from the musketry of the enemy's outworks, The brigadier ordered me to march the troops which had been all night under arms, and engaged, to the best post I could find for them in the town, and I directed them to pile their arms in a dry *nullah*, which led through the centre of the town.

The men who fell during the night and morning were buried the moment the troops had lodged their arms. The *nullah* was not more than musket shot distance from the bottom of the rock, but so deep that they could not discern the troops. I wrote a letter on the Service to Colonel Taylor, commanding the Lahaar division of the Bundlecund Army, directing him to join us with all practicable expedition, without distressing his troops. A very heavy fire of cannon and musketry kept up on us the whole of the day. The brigadier ordered that his tent and men should be pitched in the bed of the *nullah*, and about twelve o'clock we got a little breakfast.

They had discovered the tops of our tents from the ramparts, and soon brought some guns to bear on them. A heavy shot struck immediately between our tents, and a second at the same moment cut the ropes of the brigadier's tent, and we had nearly got it down on our heads; this obliged us to strike the tents, and we finished our breakfast in the sun near the banks.

Issued an order for a return of casualties to be sent immediately to my office. Visited the different posts this afternoon, and made some necessary arrangements with the troops for the mutual support of each other in case of an attempt to dislodge us from the town, of the probability of their accomplishing which we were not at all apprehensive. We dined about nine o'clock under the fly of my tent, and for the first time since we entered the town laid down with our clothes on.

January 4th.—At two o'clock this morning I paraded the 16th Regiment, and marched them to the relief of Colonel MacCullock, which we completely effected before break of day, and thereby saved many lives. MacCullock's Battalion was ordered to take up post in the street leading up to the western gate of the choke, and the brigadier and self, with Stewart, took up our quarters in a Hindoo place of worship, close to the gate of the choke which we stormed.

About eight we visited MacCullock's post, with a small escort to conduct us through the different streets; we were fired on from the enemy's outworks, and two men and my orderly were wounded before we reached the post. Sent off the return of casualties which occurred in our attack of the choke on the night of the 2nd. We lost thirty-one men killed and wounded, but fortunately no officer fell.

I still found it difficult to walk, from the slight wounds I received on my knee, but my services were required, and I was obliged, on horseback, to make the best of it; though the shot but slightly grazed my knee, it swelled considerably and gave me much pain. The brigadier most kindly insisted that I should not use so much exertion for the present. In the evening I visited our different posts on horseback, and as many of the streets were completely exposed, both to the fire of the fort and the different outworks, I was constantly fired upon, but, passing pretty swiftly,

I escaped unhurt. Got some little rest tonight, but, as usual, with our clothes on. A constant fire all night from the garrison.

January 5th.—The different posts stood fast this morning, a hot fire of cannon and musketry on us all the day. Lieutenant Sterling wounded, and a great many men killed and wounded. At noon I mounted the horse I purchased of Weston, and went with orders to the different posts. Dispatched messengers to Colonel Taylor and Major Don, directing them to push on and join us with all practicable expedition without distressing too severely the troops under their command. Many soldiers killed and wounded today by the fire from the garrison, which laid part of the town in ruins, and killed also several of the poor inhabitants. Gave "Goodford" for the parole today, in honour of my friends at Yeovil.

In crossing from one post to another with Stewart this evening we were fired upon by a party of the enemy; who seemed to have been posted there on purpose for us. A ball passed through the skirts of Stewart's coat, and my orderly, who was at my heels, was badly wounded; they were so close to us, and fired such a shower of ball, that it was surprising either of us escaped. Dined at our new quarters, and drank a cheerful glass of the brigadier's claret. A heavy fire all night without any serious loss, except a few men wounded.

Our quarters (the brigadier's, Stewart's and my own) were close under an outwork of the enemy, and we were constantly all night amused with the cracking of their musketry. We were so close that they could not bring guns to bear on us.

January 6th.—With the brigadier I visited our different posts at three this morning, and made some new arrangements in order to give the troops an opportunity to join speedily and assist each other in case of an attack from the garrison.

The fire from the fortress somewhat slackened today, and we lost but few men killed or wounded. Wrote to the adjutant-general. As soon as the evening set in I went with an artillery officer to examine a subterranean passage, said to communicate with Baddle Gur, the principal of the enemy's outworks; we found that it led towards the works, and ordered some miners and pioneers, under an officer, to continue mining on. Ordered a party of the Prince of Gohud's troops to block up a well to the southward of the garrison, from which the enemy was reported to receive considerable supplies of water. A report that two hundred men reinforced the garrison before daybreak this morning and in the night. I posted a strong party of the prince's troops in a position to completely prevent anything of the kind in future; in performing this duty I was discovered from the ramparts, and the garrison, suspecting that we were reconnoitring for the purpose of making an attack, commenced a very heavy fire, and I was under the necessity of drawing off the men under cover, with the loss of some of them, and posted them in the rear of a mosque, which completely commanded the wicket through which it was said the reinforcements entered the garrison.

Wrote to Colonel MacCullock on my return, directing him to join us by the nearest route, in case of any attack on our post during the night, in order to support us. Received a letter by express from Thornhill at Bareilly, and sent a return of killed and wounded to the adjutant-general. Got very little rest this night.

January 7th.—Left our post at six this morning with Brigadier White to reconnoitre the south face of the fort. They opened some guns on us the moment we were discovered, which did not, however, prevent our pushing up to musket shot distance of the rock, which was for the most part perpendicular , and the walls and ramparts all in good repair. Many cannon shot went over us and fell near us on our return, but happily without doing us any injury.

Having in the course of the last night thrown up traverses in the choke, which enables us to pass tolerably secure under cover from the east to the western gate, we withdrew some of the men, a smaller number being capable of defending the post, and the duty on the troops becoming very heavy. The brigadier received a letter today from the adjutant-general, mentioning the commander-in-chief's intention of sending battering guns, also another battalion of *sepoys* and flankers of an European regiment to our aid. Visited the different posts with the Brigadier this evening.

Though within half pistol shot of the enemy's works, we ate our dinner very snugly under cover, without their being able to annoy us notwithstanding their keeping up a perpetual fire of musketry on the spot, and dozens of balls were picked up every morning which had struck in the square of our quarters and flattened against the walls. It was fortunately so near that heavy guns could not be brought to bear on us. Some men killed and wounded today.

January 8th.—Another letter from the adjutant-general this morning stated that four eighteen-pounders, some twelve's, and a battalion with the European flankers under Major McCleod, the whole under the command of Lieutenant-Colonel Ashe, were under marching orders to join us for the reduction of the place.

Stewart and myself left the town at three this morning to reconnoitre the north-west face of the rock, and at the same time to fix on ground for the encampment of the Lahaar Detachment. On our return, as usual, some guns opened upon us, but neither ourselves or a man of our escort was injured by their fire. On reaching the town I received a letter on Service from Colonel Taylor, advising me of his intention of joining us on the 10th. Commenced today cutting materials for the batteries, ordered all the public cattle to be daily employed to assist in bringing them in. Gave orders to the artillery officers to superintend the making of fascines and gabions.

January 9th.—At eleven this morning we were joined by Taylor's Detachment from Lahaar. We encamped them on the north-east face of the fortress, just without reach of cannon shot from the garrison. Ordered Colonel Taylor to march in the morning tomorrow at three o'clock, and to take up a position on the south-west face. All the *beldars* and lascars employed today in making fascines and gabions for our batteries.

At three this afternoon the brigadier, Morris of the artillery, and myself mounted our horses for the purpose of reconnoitring that part of the rock battered in former days by Scindiah (but without effect). At Acbar's Battery (the traces of an entrenchment and battery said to have been erected by Acbar Shah some centuries ago) we dismounted, and were soon discovered, when some heavy cannon were brought to bear upon us, but we made such observations as we thought requisite before we quitted the post.

On our return we mistook our road, and entered a street in the town which ran directly under an outwork of the enemy's; it was too late to retreat; before we could turn our horses they discovered us, and we had nothing for it but to push on, and most wonderful it was that we passed nearly three hundred yards, close under the wall, and quite exposed to the fire of the enemy, without receiving any injury. The brigadier's horse was wounded, and a musket shot passed through the flounce of my holsters, and through the pummel of my saddle without wounding either the horse or myself.

The brigadier expressed his concern for having carried us incautiously into such danger, when it might have been avoided, and declared his astonishment that we all escaped. Lieutenant Morris dined with us at headquarters, and we much enjoyed a bottle of claret. A smart fire all night from the garrison.

January 10th.—This morning at daybreak I left the town with the brigadier, in order to inspect Colonel Taylor's position; found him encamped under a range of hills, on ground that had been pointed out to him by the quarter-master of brigade. Ordered three companies from the 18th Regiment and one from the 11th to parade at five this evening, and at six marched them off towards the south-western point of the rock, to establish a post there.

We arrived undiscovered within three hundred yards of the ramparts, and by deepening some approaches which had formerly been made by Scindiah when he besieged Gwalior we covered in the party by three in the morning, and left the post in command of Major Palmer of the 11th Regiment. The picquets of the 11th and 18th were ordered down to support the four companies under Palmer; dispatched a letter to the adjutant-general.

January 11th.—At daylight this morning a smart fire of musketry opened on Palmer's (the advanced) post, but the distance was rather too great for it to have much effect. Major Palmer wrote to me to request that under cover of the evening some gabions and fascines might be sent down in order to throw up a shoulder to his entrenchment, as the enemy brought a gun which nearly enfiladed him.

This morning, in passing from one post to another, a very favourite orderly sergeant of the brigadier's, who accompanied us, was shot. The brigadier was exceedingly hurt at the loss of this man, as he had distinguished himself on many occasions, and particularly in the Battle of Lassuary, when he carried off the brigadier, who was severely wounded in the action. I met my friend and shipmate, Mr. Ross, this morning; he came with the 18th, of which corps he was the surgeon. Mr. Ross called at my quarters, but I had merely time to shake him by the hand.

A report that a large body of troops are on the point of moving against us from Narwar, for the purpose of raising the siege, but we were under no apprehension of the result, and the Brigadier resolved to march out and give them battle as soon as they may approach, and I was directed to keep the corps as much together as possible, and to have everything in readiness to move out at the shortest notice. Ameer Khan, with 20,000 Horse, said to be marching towards the Bundlecund Detachment.

Dined early this evening, and at seven o'clock Brigadier White, Major Don, Stewart and myself left Taylor's camp, to examine a post for Don's Battalion. We rode close under the rock for a considerable distance, and could distinctly hear them talking on the ramparts, but the night was excessively dark, and the enemy could not perceive us; they heard our horses, and fired some shot at random at us. Our only escort was a *havildar* and twelve from the picquet. Fixed on a spot for Don's Battalion near the north-western point of the rock, in a *nullah* surrounded by gardens, in one of which stood a beautiful temple and a place of worship.

Ours was a very gloomy excursion through the buildings, and we discovered a fine *bolee* (extensive kind of well with flights of steps and lodgements, one storey above another, with elegant apartments). Issued orders for Taylor's camp to be struck at three in the morning; his corps to march to the *Serie* (square) to the east of the *choke*, and Don's to the gardens and *bolee*. An irregular fire of musketry and at times a shot at Palmer's post the greater part of the night. It was two o'clock before we arrived at the choke, where we had ordered our cots.

January 12th.—The enemy, having this morning at daybreak discovered Major Don's post, commenced a heavy fire of cannon on him, and several of his men were killed and wounded. At eight o'clock I visited Don's post; the officers were getting their breakfast on one of the buildings, and as I was delivering the brigadier's orders to Don, who was sitting at breakfast, a twelve- pound shot came through the dome of the building, brought down lots of brick and mortar, broke everything on the table; several officers were slightly struck by the pieces of the wall, and the shot passing through the second wall killed the man standing sentry near the entrance. They were obliged to move out instantly, and in an hour the place was levelled to the ground by shot. It appeared that they suspected the officers had assembled in this place.

On returning, my orderly, a fine young man of the 16th Regiment, was shot at my heels, and in many places I was obliged to pass entirely exposed to the fire of the garrison, and at pistol shot distance from the bottom of the rock. Issued an order that no man should be permitted to pass from one post to another, except the brigadier's and my own orderly with orders. A horse of Don's was killed this morning at his picquets.

Ordered a return of casualties to be sent to my office daily at five o'clock. Letters from the adjutant-general mention that Colonel Ashe's Detachment, with six heavy guns, four twelve-pounders, howitzers and scaling ladders, had left the Grand Army to reinforce us. Another letter mentions Colonel Ashe to have received orders from the commander-in-chief to attack the fort of Dholepore on his march to Gwalior. Dholepore is the place which we passed, on the banks of the Chumbill, and from its appearance we feared Ashe would be some days detained at it. Some men killed and wounded this afternoon. A perpetual fire from the garrison.

January 13th.—At nine this morning the enemy opened five guns on a mosque within musket shot of the fort. We had some intention of removing into it, and of which we imagined the enemy must have had some intimation, as they laid it in ruins during the morning. The brigadier, Stewart and myself, who lived together, shifted our quarters today, for the purpose of having the headquarters in a more central situation. We moved to a large house in the north-east part of the town.

Marched the 16th, and posted them near the *nullah* in which all the baggage was stowed and the cattle kept. Posted Colonel Taylor with the 2nd of the 11th Regiment in the broad street near the southern gate of the choke. From the camp of the Grand Army they write that Holcar's real intentions are supposed not to be most friendly towards us, and a war with him expected. Paraded the relief of the advanced post this evening at six o'clock, to be commanded by Colonel MacCullock. Only one man killed today, and several wounded. Found that our servants had arranged everything as advantageously as possible for us in our new quarters, which were very spacious and handsome, and in which, for the first time, we dined today.

January 14th.—A brisk fire from the fortress this morning, and we were all most anxious to hear of Colonel Ashe's approach with the battering guns. As it was thought necessary to pay the Prince of Gohud a visit, or rather to return his, the brigadier, accompanied by Stewart and myself, Lieutenants Wilson, Durant, Heathcote and Edwards of the brigadier's own corps, left the town and galloped to the prince's camp, distant from the town about four miles.

We were received in all possible state, and with great form and respect. We remained with His Highness about an hour, and on quitting his tent were presented with shawls, muslin and quantities of rich stuffs. On our way into the town we were saluted with several shot from the garrison; they commenced the moment we came within reach, and kept blazing away on us, without effect, till we got under the walls of the town. Several heavy shot whistled over us and some fell close by us.

On our return I changed my horse, and visited the post of the 11th. At sunset a very heavy and sudden fire of cannon and musketry commenced from all quarters of the garrison, which at first gave us reason to suppose that some of our posts were attacked. The incessant roar of the guns for nearly an hour equalled almost anything I had ever heard. When it commenced I was sitting with the brigadier, and, mounting my horse, I immediately rode round the different posts and found the troops all under arms, and all wondering at the cause of this tremendous fire; their guns were all shotted, and the houses in the town began to fly to pieces in high style, but we soon found that their fire was directed against no particular object.

On returning from Taylor's post, against which the fire at first seemed principally kept up, I met the brigadier, and soon after we were informed that all this blazing was in honour of a great day among the Mahrattas; it killed and wounded, however, a great many of our soldiers, and many of the inhabitants fell by it, but not a man of the enemy Had ventured without the works of the fort. By nine everything was perfectly silent except a shot at times from the garrison and a straggling fire of musketry.

January 15th.—We were much annoyed this morning to find that Colonel Ashe's Detachment was likely to be detained many days at Dholepore. Aghe himself wrote to me, and truly lamented the delay which presented itself.

The people on being summoned returned for answer that they were determined to defend the place to the last extremity, adding that "when the English had taken Gwalior they would surrender Dholepore!"

The brigadier received a letter this forenoon from Jougy Rham, commandant of Gwalior, in which he stated that he had been placed in command of the fort by Cundajee (Amboojee's brother) under the most solemn injunctions never to give it up without the orders of Cundajee; that besides the Mahrattas in the garrison he had brought with him from Minior five hundred men, of proved courage, chosen for the purpose of defending the place; he assured the brigadier at the same time that the garrison was provided with ammunition, provisions and stores for a two years siege.

To all this no answer was returned nor any notice taken. I forwarded his letter in the evening to the commander-in-chief. A brisk fire all day from the garrison, and many men fell in the town. Received a letter from MacGregor, and replied to it in haste.

This evening a few officers dined at headquarters, a circumstance which had seldom occurred during the siege; at meals we were very irregular, and often went without our dinner when duty interfered.

January 16th.—The brigadier having some reason to suspect the fidelity of Chumper Rhaum, the person who conducted us to the different gates of the town on the evening of the 2nd, requested me to order him in from Mercer's camp, but nothing appearing sufficiently clear against him to induce the brigadier to confine him, he was liberated. Chumper Rhaum was suspected of holding a communication with the garrison, but in my opinion, very unjustly suspected, as in many instances he had so strongly proved himself a friend to the English, that his conduct could not be mistaken.

At two this afternoon I received a letter from Colonel Ashe, stating that that instant he had received orders from the commander-in-chief to raise the siege of Dholepore, and to proceed with his detachment to reinforce us at Gwalior, with all possible expedition. We much lamented that Colonel Ashe had ever been detained at that place, as the circumstance of having left

Dholepore, a fort of considerable strength compared to Gwalior, was likely to be attended with serious consequences, as giving the enemy confidence and spirit to hold out to the last, and we fully expected a deal of bloodshed.

Colonel Ashe expected to join us on the 19th or, at farthest, the 20th inst. Wood and Fordyce of the engineers, with three companies of pioneers, were to leave Dholepore the evening on which Colonel Ashe's letter was dispatched, to join us by forced marches, in order to fix on a post for our batteries, and to hasten the preparations for the siege. This evening we erected a battery for one six-pounder at the advanced post, and strengthened the entrenchment considerably, having from some observations reason to conjecture that the enemy was meditating an attack on the post.

Ordered a detachment of *beldars* to throw up some traverses at Colonel Taylor's post for the better protection of men passing from one street to another in relieving sentries and on other duty.

January 17th.—Soon after daylight this morning a smart cannonade opened from the fort, but without destroying many men, as by throwing up traverses and cutting entrenchments we had secured the different posts tolerably well against cannon shot, and particularly the openings that were before much exposed. Received a letter today from my friend Maling, who was staff to Colonel Ashe, mentioning their having crossed the Chumbill River and encamped on the ground we were on, the 23rd of December. They expected to halt a day to get up the baggage, the heavy guns having detained it in the pass the day they crossed, and scarcely anything but the stores and officers' tents cleared the ravines the first day.

This forenoon a brother of the famous Cheit Sing, who committed the horrid massacre of Banass, when the officers and three complete companies of *sepoys* were butchered, visited us; this surprised us a good deal; he appeared one of the best bred native gentlemen I ever saw. He had been concealed in the town from the time we took it, but had never confidence before to make his appearance.

January 18th.—The six-pounder at the advanced post opened with good effect this morning, and the enemy were soon driven from the *oruvy*, an outwork in front, with the grape; the fire was returned from all the guns from the garrison that they could bring to bear on the post, but with very little effect. About twelve o'clock today Captain Wood and Ensign Jones of the engineers arrived in Macan's camp, with two companies of pioneers. At two the officers waited on the brigadier at our quarters in the town.

At three we mounted our horses, and with the engineer officers went to reconnoitre the south-west face of the rock, which, in spite of a smart cannonade at us, we completely effected, and remained out till quite dark. There was a smart fire on the town during our absence, and four men were killed at Captain Vanrenon's post.

The engineer officers dined with us, and we were much of one opinion respecting the point of attack, indeed there appeared one place only in the rock that was accessible, exclusive of the ramparts; the solid rock in other places was so steep that no ladders could be made sufficiently long to scale it, and the engineers declared that except the point alluded to (in a re-entering angle) they thought the place completely impregnable.

Captain Wood had been at Seringapatam, Chittle Droog, Nundy Droog, Bangalore, and at all the chief fortresses in India, and he declared Before to us that he never saw any place to be compared to Gwalior, nor did he hesitate to express his doubts if our artillery was sufficient to breach the place, but this last opinion we were determined to pay very little attention to. Several cannon shot passed near our quarters during dinner time.

January 19th.—Received a letter this morning from Wemyss, telling me that an overland dispatch had arrived in Calcutta, of so late a date as September, extracts of which had been sent to Colonel Lake. They stated that a serious disturbance had taken place in Ireland; that Lord Hawarden and his nephew, with two dragoon officers, had been wounded on their way to Dublin. This morning about ten Colonel Ashe's Detachment encamped at four miles to the north-east of Gwalior. Some of the officers off duty came into the town. This evening I despatched an order to Colonel Ashe directing him to march at three in the morning, and take up his station in the line, which had been previously marked out on the south-western face of the fort, just without range of cannon shot.

January 20th.—This morning at three o'clock the 2nd Battalion 11th Regiment and 1st Battalion 14th and a detachment of the 16th marched out of the town to the new encampment, leaving Major Don, with the battalion of the 18th and the Rohillah Infantry, which arrived with Colonel Ashe, to occupy the town. The brigadier and myself left the town about five, and at daybreak met, by appointment, the engineer and artillery officers, at a garden to the northward of the fort, in order finally to determine on the place to be breached.

An angle called Ginguapore, and the point first intended, was resolved on to be the place. Ordered our tents from the town to be pitched in camp, to which about nine we returned to breakfast. Issued long morning orders respecting the tours of duty for the detachment, which now composed nearly half the army in the field, and as I had every arrangement to make, and the tours of duty for every officer and soldier in camp to attend to, I soon found that I had enough myself to employ every moment of my time.

January 21st.—This morning it was finally determined to erect three batteries, *viz.*: one for four eighteen-pounders, two for two twelve-pounders each, with the ten-inch mortars. The cattle of the detachment employed as yesterday, and the people at work in the Park completed a great number of fascines and gabions. Owing to the great distance we were obliged to send for our materials, the cattle could not make more than two trips a day. No grain sticks (which were what we generally used) could be found within twelve or thirteen miles of our camp.

A villager came to me today with information of Raganauth Rhow being at a place called Subbul Ghur, about fifteen miles from us, with a large body of Horse. Ordered a stronger party to accompany the working parties, and fifty Europeans to parade at the Park. The enemy this morning opened some fresh guns from the south-western face of the fort, and continued a very heavy fire during the early part of the morning.

Received a letter from MacGregor, mentioning that five Companies of the old Veteran 2nd were under orders to march with Hammond, to join the Grand Army. Vaughan, with four companies of the 21st, had been ordered into garrison at Agra to supply their place. Today we received intelligence that a peace was concluded with the Rajah of Berar, in consequence of which a Royal Salute and three volleys had been fired in camp, but as we had a full employment for our artillery in a duty of a different nature, we declined the honour till a more suitable period. The materials in a great state of forwardness for our batteries, and every officer in the detachment seemed emulated in a desire to forward the service with aiding it by sending their private cattle to assist in bringing materials, etc.

Collector was taken dangerously ill this day, and my duty, which was now become rather arduous, would not admit of my paying attention to him Wilson and Durant, two officers of the 16th, with whom the horse was a great favourite, by great attention, were the means of saving his life. Purchased Weston's bay pony, as I found three horses hardly equal to my work now.

The enemy during the whole of the day were by every means endeavouring to annoy our camp and picquets, and some shot fell among us, though with little execution, their guns being so much elevated that their shot never rose, but fell dead on reaching the ground.

January 22nd.—My horse, apparently well this morning, and I refused for him 1,200 *rupees*, which Harris of the 14th offered me. Gave my poor grey, wounded as he was, to Wemyss's *moonshey*. This forenoon I strengthened the picquets, and issued

Brigadier White's order for all reports from them to be made to me, and for officers commanding to wait on me for their instructions when going on duty.

Ordered an officer and twenty men from the European flankers to parade with the men employed in the Park. The gabions nearly all completed. Issued orders for the recruits of the detachment, together with one hundred and fifty *sepoys*, to parade at five in the van of the Park as a working party.

At sunset sent down a great number of fascines and gabions to a *paun* garden in the rear of a village, near the spot intended for our Grand Battery. A tremendous fire all day, and the garrison evinced the most determined resistance, and nothing could exceed the vigorous measures adopted in our camp to bring the siege to a speedy termination. Before break of day this morning we discovered in the rock a passage sufficiently wide to admit of a single man, by stooping considerably, to ascend to a considerable height on the rock—by this means we were informed a communication with Holkar, with Amboojee, Cundaji, and the garrison had been kept up. Posted a party, under cover, for the purpose of intercepting their correspondence. Captain MacLeod of the 11th having quite recovered his wounds, joined his corps this morning.

January 23rd.—A constant and extreme heavy cannonade on our advanced post kept up this morning. I was ordered down, under a very hot fire, to give orders to the commanding officer, as the fort seemed to threaten an attack on the post. Brigadier White complimented me for carrying his orders on so important an event as that which menaced the post. The pioneers employed as yesterday, and we had hopes of opening our guns on the 28th. All the recruits and a proportion of old soldiers employed this evening in shifting the fascines and gabions to the garden in front of Acbar's redoubt.

January 24th.—Brigadier White and myself visited the different posts and works this morning about two, and returned to camp at sunrise. Several guns were laid for us on our return, but without effect. During breakfast a sudden and very heavy cannonade commenced, followed by a brisk fire of musketry, which in a moment convinced us that our advanced post was attacked. The drums beat to arms, and the brigadier and myself were instantly on our horses. I proposed that he should order on two battalions to the support of the post, and I immediately rode directly down to be a better judge of the nature of the attack.

This post was within musket shot of the fort, and the cannonade on it as I galloped down surpassed everything that I had witnessed. Until I rode into the battery I had no shelter, and there, being on horseback, I was exposed to the musketry from the walls. Upwards of thirty pieces of cannon were blazing on the post, and my horse was stupefied nearly by the noise of shot. I had soon the pleasure to observe that our grape and musketry had capital effect from the battery trenches, and in a short time the party which made the sally were retreating precipitately towards the garrison, many of them dropping from our fire.

Their defeat seemed only to increase the fire from the garrison, and Major Palmer, who commanded the post, pressed me to dismount, and not to quit it till the fire should slacken, but I was anxious to make the brigadier acquainted with what had been done, and put spurs to my horse to return. The shot fell uncommonly thick, and several were very near knocking us both over; and when I had nearly got without range of the guns in the rear of Acbar's battery I perceived the brigadier, very anxiously beckoning to me to increase my speed and to get out of the range of the shot.

After hearing my report he shook me very heartily by the hand, and in front of the line paid me many compliments, and thanked me very cordially for what he termed this essential piece of service. Two companies from each battalion were left to support the post, in case of another attack, and I had settled with Palmer and fixed a place where troops should be lodged to support him if they tried his post again. The companies were left under cover of a hill near Acbar's redoubt, and two six-pounders with them, under command of an officer of the 9th Regiment.

Everything soon became perfectly silent in the garrison, and all firing ceased before we got back to camp. A *dawke* came into camp this morning, and I received a letter from Dawson, of the *City of London*, which I had barely time to reply to. About seven this evening Colonel Shepherd came into camp from Bundlecund; he had formerly been in Amboojee's service, and affected a great knowledge of the fortress of Gwalior, in which he completely failed.

January 25th.—On a very near reconnoitre this morning the engineer and artillery officers reported to Brigadier White their apprehensions that our artillery was not equal to breaching the place, which they declared all "in the field" was not more than sufficient to effect, and this greatly disconcerted the brigadier, as by a fresh arrangement of the artillery department he must inevitably have been superseded by Colonel Horseford, who was in command of the remaining artillery with the army, and who was to have accompanied it if we found our force inadequate.

On my return about nine o'clock from visiting the different posts, the brigadier came to my tent with this unwelcome intelligence, showing me at the same time a letter which he had written to headquarters, stating the report of the engineer and artillery officers, and proposing to the commander-in-chief that, sooner than the service should be delayed, as it appeared that difficulties presented themselves as insurmountable and more than our artillery was equal to, he would, however, reluctantly wish the remaining part of the Park to be sent, although the consequence would be immediate supercession to him, still that he conceived it to be his duty to represent the state of affairs as they really appeared.

This letter the brigadier showed to me (as he did all his public ones), and asked my opinion. I felt much mortified, and did not hesitate a moment to declare that nothing in life should prevent me (were I in his situation) from proving whether or not our force was insufficient, before any representation was made to headquarters, or any difficulties stated to the commander-in-chief; and that I thought he ought to attempt to breach the place and risk everything in preference to the alternative.

This struck him very forcibly, and he instantly tore the letter into a thousand pieces, sent immediately for the commanding officers of the different departments, and very deliberately told them his full determination never to apply for a reinforcement till he had tried to the last extremity what his present force could effect, but the artillery and engineer officers did not cheerfully accede to his resolve.

I was surprised when the business was first made known by the brigadier to me, to find how their persuasions had operated on him, who in a thousand instances had proved himself a most gallant and zealous officer. It could only be accounted for by the responsibility of the situation and command which he held. I told him that I was convinced that our gallant commander-in-chief would assuredly approve of our giving it a trial, the result be what it may. Brigadier White now, if possible, redoubled his efforts, and everything was carried on with the utmost vigour.

He did not fail now and then to remind the artillery and engineer officers that they must do their duty, nor did I fail to make them my enemies by the part which I took in this decision, and which I had no wish to prevent their being made acquainted with.

Resolved immediately to breach Baddle Ghur, ordered two twelve-pounders down for that purpose to the *Choke*.

January 26th.—A letter received this morning from Colonel Powell, requesting a reinforcement, which Colonel White did not hesitate to refuse. This evening at seven o'clock we commenced our batteries and entrenchments, and about nine a heavy but ill-directed fire was opened on our working parties. By daylight, 600 *sepoys* were completely covered in, on the flanks of the battery.

January 28th.—This morning at break of day, our batteries opened. From the four eighteen-pounders they immediately commenced breaching the rampart, whilst the twelve-pounders were dismounting the guns which bore on the battery, and

Lieutenant Hay with great precision commenced his fire from the mortar battery, and his shells seemed much to disconcert the enemy. A heavy fire was returned from the fortress, but those of the enemy's guns which were nearly in front of our batteries were soon silenced by our twelve-pounders.

I was with the brigadier in Acbar's redoubt, some distance in the rear of the eighteen-pounder battery, from whence we could see the effect of every shot, as well of the enemy as of our own. Our fire continued without intermission from daylight till near eleven o'clock, when the men in the batteries left off in order to gain a little rest, and get some refreshment. Considering the short space of time our guns had opened, we thought the effect had been great on the ramparts, which were considerably torn. From the garrison they continued an almost incessant fire on the batteries, and we perceived them erecting a battery in the descent of the hill, which could be brought to bear on us, and from the low situation of our batteries we could not in return point a gun at them.

About twelve o'clock our fire recommenced, and the wall coming down in immense flakes, discovered to us a flight of stairs which led up the side of the rock, very narrow, but such as we expected would afford us a footing in the assault, and assist us considerably in ascending the breach. We were also by this circumstance convinced that the wall we had battered was merely a shell to screen the stairs, and strengthen the works, behind which we plainly saw the real rampart, and commenced instantly on it.

The firing continued with very little intermission on either side till sunset. A straggling fire of cannon, at times, on our batteries during the night, which was returned with some shells from the ten-inch mortars, howitzers and *cohorns*, with a round of grape at different periods from the eighteens, to keep the breach open and to prevent stockading it.

January 29th.—Our batteries opened a tremendous fire at daylight this morning, which was as furiously returned from the garrison. I remained in the batteries till they ceased firing at eleven o'clock, and mounted my horse at the *paun* gardens, galloped into camp. Many heavy guns were fired at me as I returned, with no other effect than the shot alarming my horse a little.

The brigadier was much pleased at the account I was enabled to give him of the effect of our shot on the rampart of the place. Sergeant Parsons and some men were killed this morning. Our fire continued heavy all day, and the enemy brought three guns into the battery we saw them preparing yesterday. They were, however, soon silenced, and the men driven from it by the shells of our mortar battery. The masonry of the wall appeared inferior to what we were led to expect.

January 3rd.—We heard this morning from Amboojee's camp, near Narwar, that he was absolutely preparing to march, and as our force was much divided, having the town, the trenches and the camp to protect, we resolved if possible to take up a stronger position, and about ten o'clock the brigadier, Stewart, Rose and myself got on our horses, and marked out a fresh position for our camp. We threw back the left of the line, and by that means pointed outwards from the range of hills, keeping the high and commanding village of Julean on our left flank, to the top of which we could without difficulty carry cannon if we found it expedient.

The fire from our batteries this day had a fine effect, and the breach was considerably widened. A hot fire also from the garrison, and some casualties occurred in the trenches. Lieutenant Richards, artillery, badly wounded today.

Received the artillery officer's report of eighteen- pound shot expended this day, which amounted to nearly six hundred.

January 31st.—Some letters this morning from camp mention the peace as having been certainly concluded with Scindiah, but the intentions of Holcar still remain a mystery. With the Grand Army they were in daily expectations of moving towards him as soon as Gwalior falls. A private letter this morning from headquarters to the brigadier mentions that the report circulated by Amboojee of Gwalior being given up in the treaty to Scindiah is false, and urging us to use every vigorous measure for its reduction.

Wrote on the service to Major Don, directing him to proceed early in the morning to camp with his battalion, and there to take up his station in the line. At six this evening ordered two of the Prince of Gohud's Battalions to march into the town to supply the place of Don's Corps; the whole to be under the command of Captain Vanrenan with the Aligoles, and one hundred regular troops, with two six-pounders.

Went to the batteries this afternoon, after having issued the detachment orders. The breach was much cut by this day's firing, and we anxiously hoped that two days' more battering would render it perfectly practicable. Captain Greene reported to me five hundred and sixty eighteen-pound shot expended this day; they ceased firing at dark, and I met the relief going down as I was returning to camp.

February 1st.—The Prince of Gohud paid us a visit this morning, to our great annoyance, as the attention and parade with which we were ordered by the commander-in-chief to receive him interfered with our duty, and took up a portion of time that might have been employed to a better purpose; the prince expressed a wish to see the effect of our fire on the ramparts, but to get rid of him I told him that to approach the batteries would be attended with great risk of his life, upon which he quietly took his leave.

About five this evening two men were announced to me as I was writing some orders in my tent, and I was not a little pleased to find that they came from the garrison. I conducted them to the brigadier, and they informed us that Jougghie Khan, the commandant of the fortress, wished to consult Amboojee at Narwar regarding the surrender of the place, and camp before they requested permission to wait on Amboojee to that Gwalior. effect; this was absolutely refused them, and we ordered them to tell the commandant that if he persisted in the defence of the place, the whole of his garrison would be put to death; not a man should escape the bayonet.

The men declined returning this evening, and I gave them over to the *havildar* of my guard, ordering that they should be allowed to proceed at daybreak to the fort. As we had some reason to imagine that the men coming was a fraud, merely to gain time, we resolved to push the siege with the utmost vigour, and it was reported to the messengers from the place, that the breach would be immediately practicable, and that no lives would be spared.

February 2nd.—The men returned into the fortress early this morning. The artillery and engineer officers reported to me in writing their opinion that the breach would at least require another day's firing to make it practicable. The brigadier came to my tent early this morning, and desired me to arrange the troops for the storm, requesting me to employ such a proportion, and of such corps, as I thought proper, which I considered a very high compliment.

He informed me of his determination to head the storming party himself, adding, "We will never return, if we do not succeed in carrying the place." The brigadier wished to give his friend Colonel Ashe an opportunity to distinguish himself, and therefore desired me to put him in orders to command the column destined for the attack. I witnessed the brigadier's will this morning. A *vakeel* arrived in camp this day from Ameer Khan, who was still reported to be advancing towards Bundlecund. A heavy fire all the forenoon from our batteries, and from the enemy in the garrison, and during the early part of the day we heard nothing more of terms, or saw anything that did not tend to a most obstinate resistance.

At four o'clock this evening a despatch arrived from Amboojee at Narwar with a copy of the articles of the peace concluded between General Wellesley, Scindiah, and the Rajah of Berar. Two messengers came in from the garrison, and were told that the place would be stormed immediately. On the part of the garrison they at length demanded a cessation of arms till the morning, with which the brigadier complied, telling them that by ten o'clock he should expect a final and decisive answer. I wrote immediately to the officers commanding in the batteries, to forbid firing either of shot or shell till the time specified should expire.

Received a letter from Captain Vanrenan, commanding in the town, stating that three hundred men from Baddle Ghur, the enemy's principal outwork, had expressed a wish to be allowed to evacuate it, to which they received for answer that they would be permitted to march out with their arms and private property. In case of stratagem on the part of the garrison, I proposed to the Brigadier to march myself to the town with five companies to support Captain Vanrenan in case he should be attacked, and at one in the morning I left the camp to reinforce him. Lieutenant Meredith (brother of Sir George Meredith) was the senior officer on duty with these five companies; he delayed in coming to the parade, and I marched off without him. We arrived in the town about three o'clock, but for reasons unknown to us the enemy had changed their plans, and declined marching out.

February 3rd.—No reports from the town, nor intelligence from the garrison; everything remained perfectly silent agreeable to the terms agreed on. Received letters from headquarters, from Wemyss, and answered them, and told him that "if ever he heard again from me, it was my intention that it should be from the top of the Rock."

Letters from the commander-in-chief directed the brigadier "after the fall of Gwalior" to proceed immediately to invest Gohud and Dholepore, for which purpose the battalions of the 9th and 14th Regiments were to remain with our division of the army, instead of joining at Headquarters.

At three o'clock hostilities commenced afresh, and a very heavy fire opened from the guns and mortar batteries, and also from the garrison, and we concluded that the treaty was merely a subterfuge to gain time. The brigadier resolved on storming the place the following morning, and I drew out the annexed orders, of which he approved:

The storming party to be composed of corps as follows: Parole, Death; Countersign, Glory."

European Flankers.

The 2nd Battalion 9th Regiment.

The 2nd Battalion 11th Regiment.

The 2nd Battalion 16th Regiment.

The 2nd Battalion 18th Regiment.

The European Flankers to lead the column, supported by the Grenadier Companies of the Detachment, completed by one hundred men H Company, followed by corps according to seniority.

The stormers to parade at two o'clock tomorrow morning, the Grenadiers on the right of the 2nd Battalion 9th Regiment, and the European Flankers on the right of the whole. On the arrival of the troops, composing the storming party, at the batteries, the officers on duty at the advanced post and in the trenches will fall in and proceed with their respective corps.

Lieutenant-Colonel MacCullock, with the battalion companies of the 1st Battalion 14th Regiment (with the exception of such men of that corps as may be on duty) and the picquets on duty, to remain under arms for the protection of the camp during the assault.

The officers and men on duty in the trenches, and at the advanced post, belonging to the 1st Battalion 14th Regiment to remain as a Battery Guard during the attack. The ammunition to be completed to one hundred rounds in pouch, and two spare flints each. Officers in command of corps will be held responsible for the arms of their respective corps being in the highest order, and their bayonets well sharpened. The brigadier has the fullest reliance in the troops, having recourse to the latter on gaining the enemy's works; the effect of which is well known to British soldiers.

The strictest silence to be observed as the troops approach the breach, and officers in command of corps and divisions are enjoined to give the most positive injunctions to their men not to fire without orders.

John Pester,
Major of Brigade.

Camp before Gwalior.
February 4th, 1804.

The brigadier told me that he would in person head the storming party, and that I should accompany him at the head of the column, and we determined never to return if we did not succeed in carrying the place. Drew out a hasty soldier's will, and two officers signed it. Went down with my glass to the Battery, to look at the breach, which was as practicable as shot would make it, and the defences on each flank of it appeared totally destroyed.

It was the opinion of the engineer and artillery officers that, from the natural situation of the rock, and the immense height we should have to ascend, that the troops must inevitably be a considerable time in gaining the ramparts, and that our loss would undoubtedly be very severe, and those were occurrences to which we had made up our minds.

Joined the brigadier as I returned from the battery; he was reconnoitring the breach from the *paun* gardens, and was well pleased with its appearance. A most tremendous fire continued the whole of this afternoon from our batteries; that from the garrison was less spirited than usual.

At eight o'clock we were surprised at receiving a letter from the commandant, proposing to meet the brigadier the next morning, to treat with him for the surrender of the place. It appeared from the tenor of his letter that he junked a little, and we were inclined to suppose him serious, and the brigadier was desirous, if possible, of sparing the effusion of blood which would inevitably be the result of a storm. I therefore circulated an order, countermanding the parade of the storming party in the morning, and the relief of picquets, guards, etc., as usual.

This morning at daybreak the brigadier went by appointment to meet the commandant, and the former received him very politely, and with that respect which was due to a man who had really made a gallant defence. The brigadier assured him of his anxiety to save the lives of men, and of his willingness to give the garrison permission to march out with their private property, their arms, and all the honours of war, but that if he persisted in defending the breach he could not answer for the slaughter that would probably ensue.

The treaty was carried on till five in the afternoon, when it was agreed that we should immediately take possession of six of the gateways, and the garrison surrendered on being allowed to march out with the usual honours, and with their private property. They were to evacuate the fortress at daybreak next morning. I rode to camp in the evening, and, meeting the relief for the trenches going down, ordered them to change their route and proceed immediately to the town in readiness to take possession in the morning, or to support our parties at the different gates, should that service be requisite. I went on to camp, gave some necessary orders, and carried a guard of Europeans, with a Union Flag, back to the town. Major Palmer (and a few men) was admitted into the upper gate of the garrison during the night. We all anxiously awaited the appearance of daybreak and our men at the different gateways were all night under arms.

Chapter 19

In Garrison, Fortress of Gwalior

February 5th.—At dawn of day we drew up our troops, and shortly after the gates were thrown open, and with my own hands I had the pleasure to plant the British Colours on the ramparts of the renowned and hitherto almost impregnable fortress of Gwalior. The garrison marched out in a most orderly manner with their matches alight and carrying their arms. They amounted to nearly four thousand fighting men, and I conducted them all clear of the town and dismissed them.

Posted the necessary guards in the fortress, and went to look at the breach, which we found extremely steep and very difficult of access; rendered still more formidable by immense pieces of timber cut into junks of about three feet long each; these were lodged on the edge of the breach, could with ease have been rolled over, and from the great height which they would have come hurling down on us they would most certainly have proved very destructive.

A Scotch officer (Lieutenant Oliphant), looking down the breach, very feelingly exclaimed, "That place would have been the grave of many a brave fellow had it been defended."

The breach was flanked with cannon, and mined, and a dreadful slaughter would assuredly have been the result of a storm. I was many minutes ascending it, without any opposition, and troops, under such a fire as they would have opposed to us, would have found it a very formidable breach. Lieutenant Morris, of the artillery, in ascending with me, fell, and was so much bruised as to be unable to quit his couch for many days without exceeding inconvenience and pain.

By ten o'clock a man of the garrison (the enemy's) was not remaining in the place. Jougghie Khan, the commandant, marched out at the head of his troops, accompanied by his nephew and other principal *sirdars* (commanders). He was a small man, stooped a good deal, but with every appearance of a veteran; he seemed to possess great influence over everyone about him, and his countenance expressed much sagacity and energy. He took his leave of us in great form.

By twelve o'clock the 2nd Battalion 16th and 2nd Battalion 18th Regiments, with their guns and tumbrils, were in garrison.

The brigadier ordered my baggage to be carried with his into the palace, which we fixed on for the headquarters and for our own residence.

The European flankers, 2nd Battalion, 9th and 2nd Battalion, 11th Regiments, changed their ground, struck their camp, and pitched it near the bottom of the rock. All officers off duty in the different corps came in to see the place which had afforded them so much entertainment, and before which most of them had several narrow escapes of their lives.

Issued orders this afternoon for Lieutenant-Colonel Ashe, with the 2nd Battalion 9th, 2nd Battalion 11th and the European Flank Companies, with the heavy guns under Captain Greene, to march tomorrow morning towards Gohud.

Ordered also Lieutenant-Colonel MacCullock to march in the direction of Dholepore. A large party of the officers belonging to the corps in garrison dined at the palace with us today, and we had a very jolly evening; to me interrupted a little at times by letters on the service from the corps under marching orders. It was a late hour, and a decent quantity of the brigadier's claret was disposed of before we parted.

February 6th.—This morning Lieutenant-Colonel Ashe's detachment marched towards Gohud. We saw them at nine o'clock from the high bastion on the north face of the fortress, many miles distant, and moving direct by north. Rode round the fort this morning with the brigadier, and examined the breach very minutely, and it was the opinion of the brigadier that owing the very bad footing which the large loose stones afforded we should have found it a tedious duty in ascending, and that much blood in consequence must have been spilt, and many a gallant soldier would have fallen.

We should without doubt have carried our point, but if they had defended the breach it must have been at the expense of much blood. We found the interior of the fortress of extent sufficient to contain an army, and in this particular Gwalior differs much from Bangalore, Chittle, Droog, Ramah Droog, and other famous hill forts, which are shaped like a sugar loaf, and consequently easy of access and capable on the summit of containing but a small garrison.

Gwalior is perpendicular on all its faces, and nearly as extensive within the ramparts as at the bottom of the rock. The ramparts we found in excellent repair, and on them was mounted during the siege about two hundred pieces of cannon of different calibres, all of which had been playing on our handful of men more than a month. Towards the south angle of the fortress there is a bend in the rock in which are several fine wells, which furnish the garrison with excellent water when all the wells on the top are quite dry; this recess is called by the natives the *Orwy*, and is secured to the garrison by a wall of about thirty feet thick of the finest masonry in the world, and well guarded with cannon above.

The *Orwy* is completely cut off from the fort by blocking up a wicket, the only communication with it, so that, if an enemy could possibly succeed in breaking the *Orwy* wall it would be impossible to maintain it as a post, every inch of it being completely exposed to the fire of the garrison. The wells are remarkable for having fine flights of steps leading from the top to the bottom of it, and the *Orwy* is altogether one of the most romantic places possible to conceive. The height of the solid rock round it has a most terrific appearance, with as much grandeur and sublimity as the imagination can form.

February 7th.—Received a letter from Wemyss congratulating me on the fall of Gwalior, and expressing the concern he was in at a report which prevails in camp that Gwalior had been taken by assault, that many officers had fallen, and among them the brigadier and myself; the first intelligence they had to the contrary was my official letter to the Adjutant-General. Wemyss in the kindest manner expressed his anxiety till the official account was received. From the army they wrote that they expected to march immediately towards Indore.

Made the necessary arrangements respecting the military stores in garrison. Two drummers of the 14th Regiment lost their lives this morning. They were blown to atoms on the ramparts by an explosion of gunpowder that had been left scattered about by the enemy. Mounted one of our twelve-pounders on the bastion north of the *Orwy.* Ordered that the gates of the garrison should always be shut at sunset, and the wickets at nine o'clock, to continue fast till gunfire in the morning. Fired the garrison gun for the first time this evening. A large party partook of the brigadier's good fare this evening, and we sat late, talking of the siege over a cheerful glass of claret. Took a regular night patrol on the works.

February 8th.—The rock on which this celebrated fortress stands runs from north to south-east. Length within the ramparts about two miles. The height at the north point we conjectured to be about four hundred feet. At this end is the palace, in which Brigadier White and myself took up our quarters. Some of the rooms appeared to have been altered after the European mode, supposed at the time Popham was in the garrison.

About the centre of the fort stand two remarkable pyramidal buildings of red stone. They are in the most ancient style of the Hindu architecture, and we were informed were built for the residence of some of the *rajah's* family, who reigned in a very remote period, when this fortress was the capital of an extensive empire. A rampart and parapet runs all round upon the brow of the rock, which is so steep that it had been always judged perfectly secure from assault, till Popham took it by escalade on the 3rd of August, 1780, and by cutting away the rock he rendered that particular part quite as inaccessible as the strongest part. The parapet, too, at that point was considerably heightened, no doubt, by Popham, as it was evidently the masonry of Europeans.

The only outer gate is towards the northern extremity of the rock, from which by several flights of steps, and passing seven intervening gateways in thorough repair and well defended, you ascend to the top of the rock. Within the ramparts are several natural cavities in the rock, which contain a perpetual supply of excellent water. On the outside about half-way up are many cells, which contain the figures of gods, men and animals, carved in the same manner as those excavations themselves out of the solid rock. Along the eastern face and near the summit runs a line of blue enamel, looking as brilliant as the day on which it was placed there; a strong proof that this manufacture attained considerable perfection in Hindustan at an early period. It had a very handsome effect as you ascended the staircase, and formed a sort of border to the rock and ramparts.

The town runs along the east and north-east face of the fortress; it is large, and contained many good houses, but these we found quite deserted, as all the most respectable of the inhabitants quitted their hitherto peaceful dwellings on the approach of our division. The town is entirely built of stone; the

Fortress of ceilings were composed of slabs, or rather flakes, of stones, about four or five inches thick, and thirty long, resting on beams of stone in the place of wood. I do not recollect to have seen a particle of wood used in any part of the buildings, either in the garrison or the town, the doors only excepted. The stone they procured in great abundance from the neighbouring hills, which form a kind of amphitheatre, surrounding the fort and town for nearly four miles. These hills are of a reddish hue, and are said to contain iron. Their surface is uncommonly rugged and quite barren, not affording a single atom of vegetation.

To the eastward of the town runs the river of Soonrica, which at this season is quite dry, and it was on the bed of a branch of this river, which runs through part of the town, that we took post on gaining possession of the town on the morning of the 3rd of the last month.

At about one thousand yards distance from the northern extremity of the fortress is a conical hill, on the top of which there is a curious stone building. It consists of two lofty pillars arched together, and is apparently of very ancient workmanship. We had a picquet here for many days after we took the town, as one of the principal entrances runs close to it, and the building from its commanding situation afforded an excellent post, and one that a few good troops would easily defend.

Across the river Soonrica is a handsome building of stone, and a cupola on it covered with blue enamel, of a similar workmanship and pattern to that on the eastern face of the garrison; this is the tomb of Mahomed Ghous, a man celebrated for learning in the time of the Emperor Acbar. Within the enclosure which surrounds this stately monument is a smaller tomb to the memory of Tansien, a musician of great skill, who resided at the court of the same monarch.

His tomb is overshadowed by a tree, concerning which the natives have a superstitious notion that the chewing of the leaves gives an extraordinary melody to the voice.

The district depending on Gwalior, which includes also the country of Goad, yielded to Amboojee twenty-five *lacs* of *rupees*, fifteen of which went into the treasury for Scindiah, and the remainder to Amboojee for the expenses of the collections. In the absence of Amboojee, Cundaji, his brother, was usually employed to make the collections, and to this brother that scoundrel Amboojee laid all the blame of breaking the treaty, in which he had agreed to give up the fortress to us without resistance, although we constantly intercepted his letters to the garrison, holding out a promise of money, men and lands, as an inducement to them to defend it, assuring them at the same time that it was not in our power (the English) ever to breach the place; such is the treacherous, rascally conduct constantly practised by the native chieftains.

Cundaji also frequently held the temporary command of the fortress in his brother's absence, but they both of them took great care to be out of the way during the siege.

A considerable trade was formerly carried on at Gwalior of cloth from Chanderi, and indigo, and we learnt that about fourteen miles distance on the Narwar road at a village called Beerie is a mine of iron.

The garrison itself, from its great security, was made use of by the Prince Scindiah as the place of confinement for his state prisoners, and it was also the grand repository of his artillery, ammunition and military stores; the quantity of each of which we found in the place was almost incredible, and it will prove a tedious employment to ascertain the quantity of powder, shot, shells, etc., lodged here.

From Gwalior the straight road to Scindiah's capital, Ougene, runs close to Narwar and Seronge, and the *rajahs* in the districts through which this road lies constantly employ a troop of *banditti* to plunder the helpless traveller.

A *sepoy* on guard on the south ramparts declared to me this evening that he saw a tiger on the side of the rock at noon day when he was standing sentry. Several immense wolves were constantly seen prowling at dusk among the chasms of the rock, and I concluded the soldier must have mistaken one of them for a tiger, as from the nature of the place it was impossible the latter could lay there, as the rock did not afford a bush even to shelter him, and I never heard of a tiger earthing.

Many of the natives assured me very confidently that in former days the neighbouring hills abounded with small black lions, and an old mason employed in repairing the ramparts pointed out a spot on which he positively declared he had been at the death of many of them. This account amused us greatly, and we had almost prevailed upon the old bricklayer to acknowledge that elephants also had been inhabitants of the hills of Gwalior in former days. I had a good night's rest tonight, the first, I with truth may affirm, for more than five weeks, during which time I never slept but with my clothes on.

Forwarded a general return this morning of killed and wounded officers and men during the siege.

Ordered all the pioneers under Lieutenant Swinton and Ensign Jones of the engineers to be employed in erecting a temporary wall on the top of the breach, to secure it against any sudden attack, and whilst the breach was clearing away and repairing. The rubbish near the summit was first ordered to be removed, to render it as steep and difficult of access as possible.

Received a letter on the service from Colonel Ashe, announcing the surrender of Gohud to the troops under his command last evening. Terms:

"The grain and stores shall be sold to pay the arrears to the garrison, who shall be allowed to march out with their arms and private property. The officer commanding the British troops to allow a native officer and thirty *sepoys* to proceed as an escort fifty miles with the garrison."

This being complied with, our troops took immediate possession of the town and fort of Gohud.

The brigadier wrote a letter this morning to his Excellency the commander-in-chief, the contents of which were a source of much gratification to me. Sent off a confidential man of rank in the service of the Prince of Gohud with powers to receive over charge of the garrison from the officer left by Colonel Ashe in command. Gohud was the prince's capital, from which by unfair means he had been driven by Scindiah and his allies.

February 10th.—A large packet of general orders reached us this morning, and it appeared that my friend Harriott, who, poor fellow, unfortunately lost his leg in the Battle of Delhi, whilst advancing with our battalion to attack their batteries, was appointed Persian interpreter to Courts Martial at Dinapore.

Private letters from Wemyss mention the order of march of the army. Received in a return of ammunition in the fort. The powder amounted to three thousand barrels, equal to one hundred and twenty thousand pounds weight. Letters mention the capture of Gwalial Ghur, taken by storm by our troops in the

Carnatic—the garrison all put to the sword—the loss on our part but trifling compared with that of the enemy, and the nature of the attack.

Went down from the rock this evening with the brigadier, and rode through the town, and to our old quarters, where we had remained during the siege. We were surprised to find the streets so rapidly filled with people; they came flocking in from all parts of the country, and put themselves under our protection. The sun set as we were mounting the rock, and the gates were kept open for us.

February 11th.—This morning Lieutenant-Colonel Ashe marched in, and encamped on the ground he had been on previous to his marching to Gohud. Ordered Captain Greene to send two twelve-pounders with their apparatus and fifty gun lascars into the garrison. Issued the orders of march for the 2nd Battalion 9th and 1st Battalion 14th Regiments, with the eighteen-pounder, and flank companies of the European Regiment, under Colonel MacCullock towards Dholepore.

Went down to Baddle Ghur in the evening to see if the twelve-pounders had arrived; found them safely lodged in the works, but a complement of twenty-eight instead of fifty gun lascars with them. Wrote immediately to the artillery officer to know why he had not obeyed his orders, when the remaining men were sent in with a paltry excuse for an officer to make. Dined out today (the first time for a long while) with Major Don, and we passed a very jovial evening.

February 12th.—Got up this morning at four o'clock, and sent immediately for the key sergeant, when the brigadier and self descended the rock. We were without the seven gates when the day broke, but descending the staircase on horseback before daylight made it very unpleasant, and we were a long time going down.

Went with Browne this evening round the ramparts of the fortress, and to the *Orwy*, which, as he had not seen it before, struck him with astonishment. The immense figures cut in the solid rock were great curiosities; some of them were sixty feet in height and large in proportion. Posted two twelve-pounders to flank the breach.

Saw the baggage of MacCullock's detachment a great distance off, marching in a north-west direction, and on the same road we followed on our route hither. The brigadier sent off an express to the commandant of Dholepore, telling him the consequence of any resistance on his part, and recommending him to deliver the garrison over immediately on the arrival of the troops. Rode round the garrison this evening, making some arrangements with the engineer and artillery officers; advanced the former one thousand *rupees* towards repairing the breach. Dined with the brigadier.

February 13th.—Walked round the different ramparts on the town side of the garrison this morning, and it was a matter of astonishment to us how we held the town, exposed as we were for so many weeks to the fire of great guns and musketry in almost every street, all of which were raked by guns in one situation or another. Received letters from headquarters of a very pleasant nature respecting our proceeding before this place. An extract of one of them was as follows:

"Both Lake and Clinton told me in how very handsome a manner you have been mentioned by Brigadier White in his despatches to his Excellency the commander-in- chief."

Posted a six-pounder at the main guard, so as to command the upper gateway, and ordered that a round of grape should be always kept in the muzzle, and a slow match burning. Ordered one hundred rounds of ammunition to be lodged with every gun on the ramparts, ready at a moment's notice. Talked with the brigadier on the necessity of training some of the *sepoys* to the gun exercise, as our proportion of artillery was by no means equal to manning all the guns. Rode in the evening round the south ramparts, observed the sentries to be too thinly posted, and ordered additional parties from the 2nd Battalion 18th Regiment. Did not return till very late to the palace. Dined by ourselves.

February 14th.—Nothing material occurred during this day, and brigadier to detain Colonel Taylor's Battalion and a the evening's *dawke* brought a letter authorizing the guns in garrison. Brigadier White also showed me a proportion of Golundauz to assist in working the private letter from the commander-in-chief, an extract of which was:

> I am very happy to find by your letter of the 7th inst. that you approve so much of Lieutenant Pester. I have a very high opinion of him, and mean him extremely well.

February 15th.—I received a letter today announcing the surrender of Dholepore to Colonel MacCullock's detachment the latter had left a garrison and was pushing on to join the commander-in-chief with the corps he commanded.

February 16th.—At gunfire this morning I accompanied the brigadier out of the garrison, and we rode entirely round the rock. The engineer and an artillery officer were of the party. We discovered many impressions of shot on different parts of the rock, and an attempt seemed to have been formerly made to batter a high bastion at the southern point, but with little effect, and had they succeeded in breaching it the solid rock on which the bastion stood was so extremely high, and quite perpendicular, that no troops could have scaled it. There appeared no trace of trenches nearer than one thousand yards of the foot of the rock. The sun was scorching hot before we got into garrison, and I suffered dreadfully with the headache.

February 17th.—Rode in the evening and particularly examined the works of the citadel; found it well constructed, and the masonry excellent. The citadel was commenced by Old Scindiah, and had it been completed would have been one of the finest works in the world. It had regular redoubts, and was reckoned by the engineers a pattern of fortifications of the kind.

Returned, dressed, and left the rock to dine with Mercer, the governor-general's agent, previous to his leaving us to join the commander-in-chief. Passed a very jolly evening, and returned into the garrison at twelve o'clock on horses of Mercer's.

The brigadier had ordered the key sergeant to be Gwalior. in waiting to admit us. We reached the top of the rock soon after one in the morning.

February 18th.—This morning Mercer, with his escort, consisting of a company of the 14th and some Irregular Horse, marched for the Grand Army, and soon after the Prince of Gohud struck his camp and proceeded towards his capital, with a vast concourse of followers, the veriest of wretches, of which his army was composed, and their deeds did not excel their appearance, few of them deserved the name of soldiers—miserably armed, and worse mounted than accoutred.

February 19th.—An express reached us this morning from the governor-general in Council, enclosing a copy of the Treaty of Peace between the Honourable Company, its allies, and Doulat Riah Scindiah. A Royal Salute and three volleys of musketry at the stations of all the land forces serving in India.

February 20th.—This morning I issued the following garrison orders:

> In conformity to the general orders received yesterday, a Royal Salute and three volleys of musketry to be fired this evening by the troops of the garrison, for which purpose the battalions will parade at four o'clock, and fire three rounds alternately.
> The 2nd Battalion 11th Regiment to commence, on the cessation of the cannon from the North Square, and each corps to beat a point of war after every discharge.

At four the troops paraded, the 2nd Battalion of the nth on its own ground, and the 16th and 18th in the North Square. On turning sharp at speed round the flank of the 16th Regiment to give some orders during the firing, my horse lost his footing on the rock, and came down, and bruised me a good deal. I was going to give directions to the centre gun to continue firing, and not to wait for the right gun, which was rendered useless in consequence of some mistake in making up the cartridges. Opened one of our own twelves to finish the salute.

February 23rd.—The artillery all employed this morning exercising the guns. The weather tolerably cool, and no appearance or symptoms of hot winds. Ordered a flagstaff to be erected, and timber to be cut out for platforms, which were much wanted at some of the heavy guns. Employed a number of masons in repairing the battlements in the North Square, some of which had been much shaken during the siege by the constant fire of the heavy guns in that square; they were all two and thirty and sixty pounders, and had been principally employed in firing at our camp and batteries.

Went as usual this evening to my stables, and ordered all the stalls to be immediately planked, and racks and mangers made up. The horses began to recover the hard work they had during the siege; one of them was always at my tent or quarters saddled, and as our posts lay so wide I was frequently on horseback all day, and sometimes nearly all the night long. It was full five miles from the camp to the town and trenches, and I had some- times four or five times a day occasion to visit each post. Ordered the grooms to purchase cloth and make them up new sets of body clothes. We had a small party at headquarters at dinner this evening.

February 24th.—A letter from Wemyss this morning mentioned Colonel MacCullock's arrival in camp with his detachment. Rode out this forenoon for an hour with the greyhounds, and tried the country to the west of the fortress, but found no game. This being the time of the famous Hindu festival (the Hooley) the soldiers of that caste were permitted to be absent from parades for two days. The shouting and noise of the Hindoos on this occasion never fails to annoy all within hearing of them, and their ceremonies are dreadfully unpleasant and troublesome to all but themselves.

They more resemble madmen (beating their breast, tearing their hair and using all manner of frantic gestures) than people in their senses. They stain and paint themselves in a frightful and disgusting manner, and their behaviour is at times, as well as their conversation, very indecent. Dined at home with the brigadier; as our quarters were immediately projecting over the town, the noise during the night prevented our getting much sleep. On this occasion they blew the conch (shell) and beat immense drums, etc., to the discomfiture of all near them. The town was lit up, and from the rock had a pretty appearance.

February 26th.—Left the garrison this morning at gunfire, and rode to the gardens of a native gentleman, on the Gohud road, about one mile from the town. Returned into garrison to breakfast, found Collector lame, and soon discovered that it proceeded from a thrush in one of the fore-feet. Sent the bay horse to a stable at the entrance of the staircase, there to remain, as moving them up and down the flight of stairs was attended with great inconvenience and risk of laming them.

Wrote to Captain Stevenson, infantry prize agent, to request that whatever prize money of mine may remain in his hands may be put into the eight *per cent.* loan. Hannay of the 17th Regiment (brother of Sir William Hannay) came to my quarters this morning, and we practised some pieces of music, and continued playing nearly all the day.

February 28th.—This morning the brigadier received a very timely supply of claret and port wine, of which we began to run short. Rode Collector before breakfast, to see the artillery exercise the guns on the ramparts. Received abstracts this day from Mr. Crawford, surgeon, to enable him to draw for the wounded men of the 4th Brigade at the time Colonel Powell commanded it.

Received a note from Brown, in Taylor's camp, requesting me to go with some of the officers on a hunting party, but my duty in the garrison would not admit of my joining them just then.

The brigadier this morning received a letter from Rajah Amboojee complimenting him on this successful result of the siege of Gwalior. Brigadier White was a great deal surprised at this man's conduct in addressing him, after the duplicity he had evinced during the siege, when by his intercepted letters it appeared he was holding out every inducement to the garrison to defend the place, and assuring them that we could "never take Gwalior." The brigadier declined entering into a correspondence with him, and forwarded his letter to the commander-in-chief, asking his Excellency's instructions.

February 29th.—Rode round the garrison this morning before breakfast. Went with the brigadier to see the *sepoys* exercising the six-pounders in the redoubt nearest the citadel. Brigadier White expressed himself much pleased at the progress they had made, and the men at the Spunge Staff were really as expert after seven, days' practice as many who had been all their lives in the corps of artillery.

March 1st.—Mounted our horses this morning at gunfire. After mustering the troops rode through the garrison with the brigadier; dismounted at the *Orwy* wicket, and walked through the works. Below we found it cool and pleasant, but on reaching the top of the rock again we felt the sun quite scorching, and the weather much changed within these few days. We all dreaded the approaching hot season on the rock of Gwalior, which is said to be very unhealthy, during the hot months particularly.

The brigadier was authorised to order a Union Flag and flagstaff to be up for the garrison of Gwalior.

March 2nd.—Left my quarters this morning with the brigadier at daybreak to examine some spacious buildings near the main guard, and determined to remove the detachments of the 16th and 17th Regiments into them, as the men daily fell sick in great numbers, as the sun became dreadfully hot for them in their tents. Removed the tumbrils from the artillery parade, and fixed on it for the parade of the 16th and 17th Regiments.

Ordered also the European sentry over the Park to be discontinued during the heat of the day, as many men had severely felt the effects of the sun on that duty, and in garrison it could be dispensed with. Went with the Brigadier to examine the ordnance and stores in the arsenal; found many of the dismounted guns quite unserviceable. Walked in the evening alone round the north ramparts, and returned soon after sunset to my quarters, but found it excessively hot after dinner, and removed into the balcony to drink our wine. The balcony projects in an extraordinary manner from the rock, over the town, and from it we were much entertained with illuminations and a procession of a marriage in the town.

The fireworks and music had a very good effect from the rock. Broke up at eleven o'clock.

March 3rd.—Captain MacLeod of the 11th and Lieutenant William, garrison officer of the day, breakfasted at headquarters this morning. Hannay came after breakfast, and we played over a great deal of the music which my European friends had sent me, and which was uncommonly pretty. Despatched by this day's *dawke* one thousand five hundred and thirty *rupees* to Cunynghame, the collector, for the eight *per cent*, loan, being the amount of my Delhi prize money.

News reached us this day of the unfortunate result of an action between some Irregular troops of ours, commanded by a Major Brownrigg, late of Scindiah's service, and a body of Sikhs, near Delhi. Major Brownrigg and a Captain Swinton, with nearly three hundred men, fell in this contest, and three pieces of cannon were left in the enemy's possession. Brownrigg's detachment marched from Agra, at the same time we left it with the Grand Army. It was principally composed of men formerly belonging to Scindiah, and many of them were men who surrendered to us at Agra on conditions of being entertained in our service.

Their arms to my knowledge were infamous, as I went to the place of arms in Agra, and chose the best of them for the recruits of the 2nd Regiment, and reported to Colonel Blair that none of them were serviceable; these were the same those unfortunate men had to use, and to which the failure of the attack was attributed. The action was fought near Hansy, above Delhi.

March 8th.—Went with the brigadier to see the people employed in levelling the ground for a grand parade. We remained out till the sun became extremely hot, and breakfasted later than usual. Was taken dangerously ill this day, and unable to dine out or leave my couch all day.

April 28th.—In continuance from the 8th of March, having been prevented writing by a dangerous illness, during which my life was for many days quite despaired of. Continued exceedingly weak and unable to sit up more than a quarter of an hour at a time.

April 29th.—Rode the bay horse (the first time of my leaving my quarters since the 28th March); went first to my stables, and found things in tolerable order considering the long time of my absence. Sold the bay horse, Capsicum, this morning to the brigadier, and purchased a very handsome, well-bred Dukan mare off Friele of the 11th.

Declined by letter this day the appointment of adjutant to the Bareilly Corps, not thinking it proper to join any corps not on actual service in such times as these, and while the army continued in the field. Wemyss, who knew my determination respecting the adjutancy, wrote me that the commander-in-chief highly approved of my conduct, and informed me that Colonel Lake had very kindly interfered for me, and mentioned my objections to the general.

April 30th.—Rode for the air this morning a short distance in my *palanquin*. The wind during the day very hot and uncomfortable, and the only water we could get to water our *kuss* was what had been so long lying in the ponds on the top of the rock that the stench from it was hardly bearable. My friend, Mrs. Cunynghame, who had heard of my illness, wrote to me and kindly entreated me to change the air of Gwalior and to go immediately to them, offering to send tents, elephants and a carriage to meet me at any place I should appoint, but with my kind acknowledgments I declined it till the end of the campaign, and then promised to join them with all expedition.

May 1st.—The wind blew excessively hot all this day, and the thermometer was up to one hundred and fifteen at noon. The fever continued hanging on me, and I did not in the least gain strength.

May 4th.—As I recovered so slowly the surgeons again urged me to quit Gwalior for change of air, and they seriously assured me that it would not at all surprise them to find me some morning a corpse on my bed. I resolved (perhaps unwisely) to abide by the consequences, and not to quit the fortress as long as there appeared a shadow of a chance of our being attacked. Nothing could possibly exceed the kind treatment I experienced from the brigadier, who generally passed the greater part of the day in my quarters, and sat many hours on my bedside every day. Every comfort that our situation afforded was obtained for me, and I was nursed with every care that my unpleasant situation required. The wind continued blowing flames, and the officers declared they had never felt heat equal to what we experienced in Gwalior.

May 5th.—The cannon of the garrison was exercised this morning at daybreak, and the officer reported that the *sepoys* in training at the guns made astonishing progress. I rode a very steady horse of Wilson's a short distance this morning, and went to the Fakeer's Temple in front of our quarters. A *rajah* from the town visited us this morning, and the Brigadier received him in my apartments. The usual ceremony of throwing *otta* and rose-water was attended to, and I was happy when this chief took his leave.

A dreadful accident happened this morning. Seven men at work in the arsenal on gun carriages were unfortunately blown up by the bursting of a shell which had remained charged, and to which some sparks of fire, it was imagined, had communicated. These unfortunate men all lost their lives.

This evening we had a sudden alteration in the weather, and at sunset a violent *tofaun* (hurricane) commenced. Even on the rock it was rendered almost dark by the immense clouds of dust, and it continued nearly an hour blowing most tremendously, and at dark it rained extremely hard for a short time, which cooled and refreshed us much.

As the surgeons recommended me to take as much exercise as I could bear, without too much fatigue, rode this morning on Fidgett (my new mare) to the breach, to observe the alterations and the progress made in repairing it since my illness. Returned early exceedingly tired.

Received this morning a letter from Thornhill, detailing his severe loss in the Euphrates of four chest of claret and one of hock. At sunset Friele, Wilson, Stewart, Nesbit and myself left the garrison and proceeded to the rose garden, where I had ordered dinner. I found the change rather reviving, and my spirits were better than they had lately been. At ten o'clock it came on to blow a hurricane, but the wind soon subsided, and a gentle shower of rain afforded us great relief, and I was enabled to sleep tolerably well, to which I had long been unaccustomed.

May 8th.—Rode Fidget this morning on the eastern face of the fortress, and returned by the way of the breach, and on the new-made road near the *Orwy*. Breakfasted with Friele, from whom, during my illness, I experienced the most kind attention; he passed the greatest part of his time at my quarters, and his pleasant, gentlemanly manners, and the solicitude he always expressed on my account, attached me exceedingly to him. We made a plan today to go together to Bareilly after the return of the army, and when everything should be finally settled in the field. Friele had a sister (Mrs. Welland, wife of Mr. Welland, Second Judge of the Court of Appeal) living at Bareilly, and as my most intimate friends resided there, we "built our castles" accordingly.

May 12th.—We had the honour of a lady's company (Mrs. Griffin, wife of Lieutenant Griffin of the 11th Regiment) at dinner today, the first European female most probably that ever dined on the rock of Gwalior.

May 14th.—No *dawke* from the army this morning. Pitched

the fly of the brigadier's breakfast tent on the top of the palace, in hopes of getting more air there than in the gardens below. The weather dreadfully hot and oppressive, and the thermometer upwards of one hundred and twenty, after the sun had set! It was hardly to be borne by men in health, and I suffered more than can be expressed. To gain strength in such a climate perfectly out of the question. At ten at night I got into my *palanquin*, and accompanied the brigadier round the ramparts, it being the only time possible to leave one's quarters, and even at that hour we felt all the horrors of the hot wind.

The sentries we found very alert, and observed that the rounds went most punctually, as well as the patrols in the intermediate time. We knew the enemy were in the neighbourhood, and that we could not guard too much against a surprise, which was all we had to apprehend. It was nearly three o'clock before we got back to our quarters.

May 15th.—Breakfasted with Friele this morning, and found myself somewhat better than I had been for many weeks. The brigadier received accounts that Raganauth Rhow remained encamped at Subbul Ghur with nine thousand horse, and that he intended to take up a post so as to intercept the supplies to this place. At noon I sent off my servants to prepare dinner for a small party in the rose garden, and at six o'clock Friele, Wilson and myself left the garrison, the two former on horseback and I in my *palanquin*.

We ordered all our dogs down (about thirty), and let them loose in the garden. Found our dinner ready, and passed as pleasant an evening as the weather would allow.

The day was dreadfully hot. For the first time since my illness I left my quarters this evening to dine with Browne, and the evening was so hot that the wax candles on the table at dinner actually melted, and sunk down on the cloth. This had never been witnessed before by any officer at table (there were more than a dozen present), and we had the curiosity to send for a thermometer from the next room, and it absolutely stood at upwards of one hundred and twenty-five!

May 17th.—In the evening we received a public letter from the adjutant-general, stating that Don had taken Rampoorah by assault, and it appeared that the *sepoys* behaved with their usual gallantry. Our loss reported to be but trifling, considering the nature of the attack. It was a second Ali Ghur business, only that *sepoys* alone composed the storming party. Three gates were blown open under a heavy fire, and nearly all the troops composing the garrison were put to death.

May 18th.—Received a letter from headquarters this morning from my friend Wemyss, telling me that the army would immediately commence its march towards cantonments, some of the troops to canton at Muttrah and Agra (on the banks of the Jumnah), others to proceed on to Cawnpore and Futty Ghur. Colonel Monson to advance towards Boondah, with a strong detachment, to a *ghaut* of that name, and his position is intended to prevent any of Holcar's predatory horse returning immediately to the Jeypore country. As I did not recover my strength at all, and the surgeons' constant persuasions were to change the air, I resolved, in case of the return of the army, to proceed to Mynpoorie and pass a month with my good friends the Cunynghames.

May 19th.—Vilely hot, and all declared they never before experienced anything equal to the sun and wind at Gwalior. Men daily dropping off.

May 21st.—Accounts from the army this morning related to nothing more than we were before acquainted with. They continued marching. The Europeans were very sickly, and many died from the effects of the climate, which is always particularly destructive to troops marching at this season. Some villages were plundered, and many of the inhabitants murdered within three miles of the garrison this morning. This dreadfully annoyed the brigadier, and we much lamented that our authority did not extend beyond the garrison and the limits of the town, past which we could not act without express orders from headquarters. The plunderers were reported to be nearly four thousand strong, and our friend Raganauth Rhow supposed to be at their head.

May 24th.—This morning the Bundlecund post brought me letters from home. The happiness they afforded me was much damped by accounts in the same post of the unfortunate fate of a part of the Bundlecund army, which had been cut off and destroyed by Ameer Khan. My most intimate friend, poor Morris of the artillery, whose gallantry and good conduct I had often witnessed during the siege of this place, was among the officers who fell.

Captain Teade, Lieutenants Hooper and Gellispie were also killed, with upwards of fifty European artillerymen and three hundred *sepoys*.

Colonel Taylor died suddenly in the garrison this evening, much lamented by us all. He was a zealous officer.

May 25th.—At five this morning they buried poor Taylor under the flagstaff, with all military honours. A confused account of the melancholy fate of the officers and men in Bundlecund reached us this day. It appeared Ameer Khan was still hanging upon their rear, but nothing had occurred since the 2nd.

May 26th.—As far as we could judge the heads of the detachment in Bundlecund appeared highly culpable, and their conduct was most extraordinary in not having advanced to endeavour to recover their guns. The affair took place six miles only from Koock (at a mud fort, and where Colonel Fawcett, who unfortunately commanded in Colonel Powell's absence) was encamped. Letters from the commander-in-chief's camp inform us of their being in full march towards Agra.

Received a letter from Wemyss, requiring a promise from me to quit Gwalior immediately, and to meet him at Mynpoorie. Remained all day in quarters.

May 27th.—No accounts this morning from the Bundlecund army. In the evening we received accounts that the enemy had destroyed the country around them, and it appeared that they were in a very precarious situation. The brigadier expressed his apprehension of being ordered away himself to take the command from Colonel Fawcett, not doubting but that as soon as the accounts should reach headquarters some officer would be sent to supersede him.

The brigadier asked me if, in my present weakly state, I would accompany him, to which I most readily assented, though the medical men comforted me by telling me that to attempt to take the field in my reduced state, and in such a season, would inevitably prove fatal. I resolved, however, to go, and lamented only the dread of not being able to do my duty as I would wish. Another express from Fawcett received this evening stated that the enemy hourly threatened an attack on their line. This was a burning day.

May 31st.—Prepaid people this morning to go off towards Gohud with my baggage. This forenoon I had the satisfaction to receive letters from England. Those letters came by Welstead, and had been lying for many weeks in a village near the fortress, and were stopped by a party of the enemy, and afterwards politely sent on. They were unopened and unhurt. Wemyss wrote to me from the army; they were at Indown, a place at which we lay many days encamped after the battle of Lassuary, on the 1st of November.

This evening at sunset (it being so hot during the day that the camels even could not travel without being injured much), I sent off my tent and baggage to Beharderpore, half way to Gohud, determined to follow the next day.

June 1st.—The brigadier, on my account, ordered an early dinner. He passed the whole of the day with me in my quarters, and made me promise to join him again as soon as the fever had quite left me, and the weather became more temperate. At eight I took my leave of the brigadier, and most of the officers (my intimate friends whom the brigadier had asked on the occasion of my leaving the garrison), and got into my *palanquin*. By gunfire (nine o'clock) I had reached the foot of the staircase.

Chapter 20

From Gwalior to Bareilly

June 2nd.—Camp at Gohud. I had with me a guard of fifty men and twenty horsemen, and considering the very unsettled state of the country and that the enemy were daily committing depredations in the neighbourhood, I considered myself fortunate in reaching Gohud in safety. Passed Baharderpore about one in the morning, and arrived at Gohud about six, where I found my tent ready pitched in a fine mango grove, and breakfast on the table. I found great relief from the burning rock of Gwalior, to a fine, fertile country, and the trees completely shading my tent made it tolerably cool compared to what I had been lately accustomed to. Most of the respectable inhabitants of Gohud paid me a visit, and sent me presents of various kinds.

June 3rd.—15 Miles. Camp at Mahamooah. Arrived here this morning before break of day. My tent pitched, and breakfast comfortably laid in readiness. Felt very weak, but revived by the change of air. Lost during my march last night a very beautiful terrier, and a great pet; she was always miserable when out of my sight, and I was obliged to carry her with me in my *palanquin*, from which, by some accident, I imagine, she fell in the night, and lost us. I never saw her again.

This place afforded but very little shelter for my tent, and it was a vile hot day. I, notwithstanding, evidently daily gained a little strength. The villagers brought me kids, milk, fowls and everything that I and my servants stood in need of. At four I dined, drank my pint of claret, and sent on my tent and baggage.

The country near this place very much burnt up, and the land seemed poor, and little cultivated. The heat was so great that it was impossible to march while the sun was up.

June 4th.—15 Miles. Arrived at Bhinde this morning at sunrise, after experiencing one of the most dreary nights I ever marched in. Sent on an express to my friend Major Palmer, commanding at Etyah. The weather after breakfast was cool and pleasant, and I felt quite gay and in good spirits. The people from the town brought me everything I had occasion for, and behaved with the greatest attention. My horses here got some fine hay (the first time since we left Gwalior). Stopped the post and opened it. No letters for me. Dined at three; drank my pint of claret; forwarded my tent and baggage at sunset, and got into my *palanquin* about ten at night.

June 5th.—30 Miles. Left Bhinde last evening at ten o'clock. After going about two miles lighted my mussalls. Arrived at the banks of the Chumbill about midnight, and found great difficulty in discovering the ford. The ravines on the banks of this river are really tremendous, and a small force might always defend the different passes. At daylight reached, and once again crossed, the Jumnah. Found my friend Major Palmer with his elephant ready to receive me; got to his bungalow about eight, and made a very hearty breakfast. Slept nearly the whole of the day, and dined with Mr. Macvitie.

June 6th.—Received certain accounts this morning that the general, with the cavalry, was advancing towards this quarter; found the people here under some apprehensions of the approach of an enemy, and letters from my Gwalior friends express their anxiety for my safety. Visited the different fords with Major Palmer (commanding the station), and resolved on erecting a one-gun battery at each ford. Kept the troops under arms during the nights. Ate some fine grapes this morning, the first of the season.

June 7th.—This morning's *dawke* brought us information that the general had crossed at Agra. Received a letter from Thornhill, most kindly offering me his advice to go to Europe on account of my health, and, at the same time, requesting me to accept the loan of one thousand pounds to make myself comfortable during my stay in England; declined so doing with every suitable acknowledgment to him for such kind and friendly conduct; such friends are rarely met with.

June 13th.—Dined with Captain Drummond, and at nine o'clock left Etawah for Mynpoorie. About twelve was awakened by the *palanquin* stopping, and hearing at the same time a noise, on looking out perceived several men with drawn swords round the *palanquin*; got hold of my pistols, but found no occasion to use them, as the people proved to be a party of Frith's Irregular Horse on their way to join him; proceeded on, and at daylight met Cunynghame's chariot (which he had kindly sent out to bring me in); about seven met Wemyss and Campbell; the former came on with me in the chariot to Wemyss's little bungalow, where we all dressed, and breakfasted in Cunynghame's new house.

July 11th.—Passed my time very pleasantly at Mynpoorie, and this morning at six o'clock went in the buggy to Bugong, and in my *palanquin* from thence to the Colla Nuddy; found Wemyss there, who had arrived an hour before me.

July 12th.—Left the Colla Nuddy this morning at daybreak, and arrived at Futty Ghur to breakfast, which, with a very hearty reception, I got at my friend Christie's. Sent immediately for some cloth and purchased a sufficiency to make a dozen suits. Employed all the tailors that could be found. The weather very cool, and the old Ganges (on the banks of which stood Christie's house) afforded a very gratifying sight.

July 14th.—Remained the whole of the morning at home, and at half-past four in the afternoon got into my *palanquin* in the most rainy, disagreeable weather I had almost ever witnessed in the country. Got across the Ganges a little before sunset, and found the country nearly inundated. The bearers going constantly knee-high in the water.

Soon after dark I was under the necessity of quitting the *palanquin* in order to proceed, and was carried a considerable way on the men's shoulders, the *palanquin* on their heads in order to keep dry the bedding. The rain continued with unabating violence till daylight. Crossed the Rham Gungah at six o'clock, and arrived at Burrah Matahney at nine, where I found my friend Thornhill had sent a tent, a very comfortable breakfast, and a couple of bottles of claret, should I have been disposed to spend the day there. Halted here about an hour, and again set forward towards Bareilly.

This afternoon proved singularly fortunate to me. About four o'clock, and within five miles of Bareilly, I discovered at a small distance three elephants and a couple of gentlemen. On our approach I was happy to find them Peyron and Anderdon going in pursuit of a tiger; got out of my *palanquin* and on the spare elephant with a double barrel of Peyron's; we had not proceeded a mile when we discovered him stalking majestically across the plain. We instantly pushed for him, and he no sooner discovered us than he turned about and came on like a gallant fellow to charge us. Peyron's elephant fled. When he arrived at about forty yards in front of our elephants, Anderdon and myself fired, and with effect. It, however, only served to bring him on with increased fierceness, roaring at the same time tremendously.

At about fifteen yards from my elephant's trunk I fired again, and my shot entered exactly above the eye, and he fell stone dead. He had, a few hours before, destroyed two poor unfortunate villagers, and being on the roadside (within one hundred yards of the spot over which I had passed in my *palanquin*) he would inevitably have done much more mischief. The villagers were soon in crowds about us, returning us thanks, and one old man remarked that whether tigers or goats it was the same thing to the *sahib logue* (gentlemen). After talking over our game for half-an-hour, I got into my *palanquin*, and went on to Asiff Bhang, where I arrived, exceedingly fatigued, about eight o'clock, having been twenty-six hours on the road. Thornhill, not expecting me today, had gone into cantonments, but his servants soon got me a comfortable dinner, after which and a bottle of claret I got my *hookah*, had a famous smoke, and went to bed.

July 16th.—This morning soon after daybreak Thornhill and Ridge arrived in a tandem. We all three got into it, .and went round to see the colts, and Pepper Jacket, the English horse. Returned to breakfast, and, shutting out the hot winds, passed a pleasant day in my old quarters, where I was received with all possible kindness, and a most hearty welcome. I received a letter today with the very welcome news of my friend, Captain (now Major) Sinclair having, in a most gallant manner, carried the fort of Hinlass Ghur by assault, at twelve o'clock at noon. Sinclair was my Captain of Grenadiers for a long time, and we had witnessed some hard knocks together. I truly rejoiced at his success, knowing him to be as brave an officer as ever drew a sword.

July 20th.—This morning the natives had a report that Colonel Monson, commanding the detachment in the Jeypore country, had met with a check, and was under the necessity of falling back, but this we did not credit. Took my usual ride round the racecourse this morning. Passed the day quietly at home, and drove the tandem in the evening for about an hour. Found my time so much taken up with sporting, visiting, etc., that I could not journalize so regularly as usual, or as I could wish. We all felt much concern for the fate of Monson's detachment, as the unfavourable reports from that quarter seemed to gain ground, and some letters of a very unpleasant nature were received this evening.

July 25th.—I received letters this morning, stating that on the 7th Monson was attacked by thirty thousand of Holcar's horse, which he succeeded in beating off, with great slaughter. Poor Lloyd of the 12th (a particular friend of mine) was shot through the heart in the action.

July 26th.—I received a letter from Macan this evening, informing me that Colonel Martindale, commanding a detachment in Bundlecund, had been repulsed in storming a fort. It was found impracticable to carry a gun up to the gate; the sortie would not admit of it, and their scaling ladders, as is too frequently the case, were not long enough to scale the walls. In this unfortunate affair my old corps, the 18th, was employed, and Vanrenon, Fagan, Colier and Baynes, belonging to it, were wounded. Captain Robinson of the artillery was also wounded.

The troops appear to have behaved very gallantly, but under the disadvantages in which they commenced the attack, it was next to an impossibility that they should succeed. A report that the army will take the field again immediately. The surgeons seriously advised me not to think of marching in my present weak state of health, but I resolved, the consequence be what it may, to leave Bareilly the moment General Lake marches from Cawnpore, and the troops begin to assemble.

July 27th.—Called this morning on Mrs. Elliott and Mrs. Welland, the latter my friend Friele's sister, and a pleasant woman, good looking, but a bad squat figure. Mrs. Elliott a very genteel woman, and exceedingly pleasant. At Welland's we played billiards, and the lady sang and played us several favourite songs.

July 28th.—Got up this morning at gunfire. Thornhill's Capsicum Colt was ready for me at the door, and we rode away to commence marking out a new racecourse, the square of which we finished this morning. We had a match of pigeon shooting this morning. Major Doveton, Ryder and myself shot against Thornhill, Anderdon and Peyron. Ryder shot very ill, and we were beat. A large party dined at Asiff Bhang with us this evening, and a great deal of claret was drunk. I took, as usual, a very moderate share. Many of the party had taken too much of the goodly stuff to go further, and almost every couch in the house was occupied for the night.

July 29th.—Ridge left us this day, a report having prevailed that his corps is under marching orders, in consequence of unpleasant news from Monson's detachment. I mounted the Capsicum Colt at daybreak this morning, and added a circle to the racecourse, which, when finished, will be one of the prettiest courses I ever saw. Drove Thornhill in the *curricle* to Peyron's in the evening, where we dined and slept. A good deal of hard going again today, and the party did not break up till every man had taken his two bottles at least.

July 30th.—Coursed this morning, but a smart gallop after the first hare we found gave me so severe a headache that I was obliged to leave the party and to return home. This morning intelligence of a most unfavourable nature reached us from Monson's detachment. It related to the action of the 10th in which poor Lloyd fell. The enemy were driven back with considerable loss, notwithstanding which it appears that the detachment was falling back for want of provisions, and Colonel Murray from Bombay, with whom they expected to have formed a junction, had not advanced.

The enemy took every advantage of their situation, and increased their difficulties by setting fire to all the villages in their route, and thereby preventing them from obtaining supplies from them. They continued daily to harass their line during the march, but why Colonel Monson, instead of retreating before the enemy, had not marched to give him battle, was more than we could account for. On the 15th Holcar, with his whole force, encamped within two miles of our troops, and his flag was plainly discovered, flying in the evening, and all the officers felt assured that an attack would be made on him in the course of the night, which the most experienced in camp had recommended to the brigadier.

At twelve that night an order was issued to strike tents, and parade immediately, but instead of advancing to attack the enemy, who had so much annoyed them and taken a considerable portion of their baggage from them, what must have been the feelings of our brave officers and troops, when, instead of moving towards the enemy at a time when everything promised them success, they received the word, "Right shoulders forward," and commenced their retreat (or rather continued it)?

This was a movement most truly disgraceful to the officer who conducted it, as the consequences plainly evinced. The enemy became more spirited as the fire of our brigadier became damped, and they continued the pursuit, with redoubled ardour. Nothing could exceed the disgust of our officers on this occasion, and even the soldiers in the ranks asked "why they were retreating before an enemy they were conscious they could defeat?"

It could only be accounted for by the panic which had so unfortunately seized on the commanding officer, and it will be ever a cause to be lamented that he had not been put in arrest, and a man with better nerves taken charge of the detachment. They continued flying in a most unhappy manner, and on the fourth day of their retreat the brigadier ordered all his cannon to be spiked and abandoned to the enemy, and such was their distressed situation when the last despatches left them, the enemy hourly harassing their line. We were all much distressed at this information, and felt much for the fate of our friends. Sinclair and our 2nd Battalion were with Monson's detachment. Dined at home this evening, some officers of the 3rd dined with us.

I rode the English horse Pepper Jacket this morning, and Thornhill and myself finished the racecourse, and it was a very complete one; as level as possible, and the finest turf I almost ever saw in India. I expected to join immediately, and therefore did not promise myself much sport on the course I had taken some pains to complete.

August 7th.—A fever prevented me journalizing since the end of the month, the effects of which I still seriously felt. This morning we received information that Monson had recrossed the Chumbill, on his way back to Rampoorah. He took the precaution to destroy the boats, and thereby delayed the crossing of the enemy, who continued to hang on his rear and to distress him exceedingly.

Letters from Rampoorah mentioned that the artillerymen belonging to the guns which had so disgracefully been disposed of had arrived there in a most distressed condition; half-starved, and scarcely any kind of covering on them. It appeared that this unfortunate detachment had lost the whole of their baggage, cattle, camp equipage, etc., not a shirt even left them, and were in a most miserable situation. They were obliged in the most severe rains ever known, and with scarcely any provision except what they gathered from the fields on their route, to continue making the most long and fatiguing marches.

This was the most unpleasant affair that had ever happened since the recollection of the oldest officer I had met with, and it seems to have been all occasioned by that ill-judged measure of sending a man perfectly unqualified for such a command on a service of so serious a nature.

Had he but attacked the enemy as soon as an opportunity offered, instead of avoiding him and commencing a shameful retreat, the villagers of the country through which he passed would have brought more than a necessary supply constantly to his camp, as they had done before, but when they observed him flying, as they always do, they joined that which they considered the strongest party, and became the avowed enemies of our detachment, plundering them, and cutting up their straggling camp followers whenever an opportunity offered. Thornhill and self passed the day at Elliott's and Welland's. Feeling much as every man must have done for the fate of my numerous friends of Monson's detachment, I was very anxious to hear further from them, as it appeared that the worst may be apprehended. We remained in cantonments and slept at Peyron's.

August 13th.—I returned alone in the *curricle* this morning to Asiff Bhang, after breakfasting with Becher, and passing a couple of hours with him and the ladies, who sang and played a good deal, and better private performers on . the piano than W——I had seldom heard. Went, on my arrival at Asiff Bhang, to see my camels in the mango grove near the house, where sheds had been erected to shelter them from the rains, which to camels are very destructive. We daily, almost, experienced showers of rain, more or less heavy. Shot two jungle dogs this morning. Thornhill did not come from court till *tiffing* time. As judge and magistrate and collector he had a great deal on his hands.

In the evening we drove the tandem round the course, and had a quiet comfortable dinner and a bottle of claret by ourselves. The evening we passed in talking of England, dear England, and of our friends there.

August 14th.—At daybreak this morning I mounted Horatio, and we took the greyhounds to the coursing ground, and had five of the best runs I ever saw in any part of the world. We killed a leash of hares, a fourth went to earth close to the dogs, and the last hare, after as severe a run as I ever witnessed before, Norah and Major got into some high grass, and we lost her. I rode Horatio the two first courses. The Capsicum Colt the two second, and Thornhill's famous grey pony (Khondrum Khan) the last course, and returned as much fatigued as I ever had been by the longest marches I had made in India, and in the hottest days.

August 16th.—We all went this morning to the Kiary Lake to fish. The tents had been ordered down, and pitched on the banks of the lake in a mango grove, last evening. We had a large party of gentlemen at breakfast. Miss W—— and Mrs. S—— also joined our party. Thornhill had provided a splendid breakfast for us, with every luxury the season afforded.

About nine the nets were run across the lake, and we began to draw them. It was a very fine sight, the immense fish, some plunging in the nets, others completely sprung over, and the natives with floating choppers (grass woven on bamboo) by following the nets received a great number of the fish on them which otherwise would have escaped. Two small boats also belonging to the lake, Peyron and myself in one, and Thornhill and Doveton in the other, followed the nets, and some immense fish leaped into the boats. The lake seemed almost swarming with them. This diversion lasted till twelve o'clock, when we took some refreshment, and commenced firing ball from our rifles at marks on the lake. Some of the finest shots were made that I ever saw.

Peyron and I and the others went to lounge, took our guns,

and, near mounting the elephants, went to the banks of the Rham Gungah, about three miles from the lake, and had a famous evening's shooting. Killed several deer, some hogs and seven brace of partridge. At sunset, some on horseback, some on elephants, others in carriages, left the lake to return into cantonments, about four miles, to dine with Major Doveton, who had provided a dinner to correspond with our morning's entertainment, and at one in the morning we parted after passing as pleasant a day as I remember in India.

August 17th.—Rode Horatio this morning; cantered gently round the new course, and home by the banks of the river, on a pleasant road which had been cut by Mr. Wellesley when he lived in (now) Thornhill's house, Asiff Bhang. Received letters stating that Monson's detachment had arrived at Rampoorah in a most deplorable condition, with the entire loss of the guns, camp equipage, and without provisions or any clothes but those on their backs. Their legs so swollen with extreme fatigue, and not having for so many days taken their boots off, that they were under the necessity of cutting them from their legs.

Every article except what they carried about their persons had been left behind, and with them, it may be truly added, went the honour and credit of the person who conducted this ill-fated detachment. Holcar had found means to cross the Chumbill, and was advancing rapidly in their rear, directly In the route they had taken. We much feared that Monson would be unable to remain long at Rampoorah, as they cannot have supplies there for his detachment to subsist many days on. Great apprehensions, therefore, are still to be entertained for their safety, for without grain they cannot long remain at Rampoorah, and no supplies can be procured nearer than Agra.

August 22nd.—Took my gun this morning down to the river, where I had seen several otters, and had some capital ball shooting at them. Killed several. Peyron, Doveton and Nuthall passed the day with us, and in the evening we went to bathe in the river, and dressed on the banks. Returned on elephants to dinner. A small snug party, and we talked over the feats of the last campaign.

August 23rd.—Coursed this morning, and had capital sport. Knocked up all the dogs, as usual, and killed everything we ran. The neighbourhood of Bareilly I thought the finest I had ever seen for coursing, and the hares ran far stronger than those of any part of India I had coursed in. At sunset we went in the curricle to dine with Becher, and W——t seriously told me it was her intention to return immediately to Europe, as she found her health daily declining. We had a very gay party at dinner, and the evening was passed in great good humour.

August 25th.—This day's post brought the long-expected letter from Wemyss, to prepare immediately to take the field, and by the same conveyance came an order for the 1st, 2nd, 3rd, 4th and 6th Regiments of Native Cavalry, together with the 8th, 27th and 29th Dragoons, to prepare to march. Also the 1st Battalion 2nd Regiment, 15th Regiment and 1st Battalion 21st Regiment to hold themselves in readiness to march at the shortest notice. The 3rd (at Bareilly) ordered to proceed immediately by the nearest route to Muttrah. I resolved on joining the army, and not to go back to a sickly garrison, as Gwalior was well known to be, many fatal proofs of which I had witnessed.

It was my plan to march with the 3rd Cavalry, which corps was ordered to join the headquarters of the army at either Agra or Muttrah. The general orders left it optional to me, as absent by leave on a sick certificate, either to remain at Bareilly, return to my brigade majorship at Gwalior, or join.

I determined, of course, on the latter, though very much against the advice of the medical men, who declared and offered to testify it to Government, that I was not in a fit state of health to join in the fatiguing hardships of a campaign, and further they assured me seriously that by marching at this season I evidently endangered my life. But I had not been accustomed to remain behind on such occasions, and therefore told them my resolve to risk everything, and to join the army. We all dined this evening with Gillman, and Thornhill and self slept at Peyron's bungalow.

August 30th.—Breakfasted and passed the day at Welland's. Mrs. Welland and Mrs. Elliott sang and played a good deal, and we had some matches of billiards. I found that the march of the 3rd would be more tedious than I at first expected, and determined, therefore, to go express to Futty Ghur, and thence, by the same mode of conveyance, to Agra, where the army is to assemble. Wemyss wrote me that General Lake could not arrive at the place of rendezvous sooner than the early part of October. I resolved, however, to go with all expedition, and wrote this evening to Christie, at Futty Ghur, to lay bearers on the road for me.

We dined this evening with Seton, and during dinner the post came in, and Gillman received a letter from Monro, stating Monson to have left Rampoorah, where he could not longer remain for want of provisions; he, therefore, recommenced his retreat, and on the 24th instant Holcar came up with his detachment on the banks of the Banass river, and a very bloody business ensued.

Among other gallant fellows, my worthy and ever-to-be-lamented friend, Major Sinclair, unfortunately fell, a more cool and gallant soldier than whom the Service cannot boast. Many a time had I been an eyewitness of his heroism and undaunted courage, in the most severe and trying occasions. In the storm of Sarssney, Ali Ghur, at Agra, and the Battle of Delhi and Lassuary, we belonged to the same grenadier company (*viz.*, Right Grenadiers, 1st Battalion, 2nd Regiment.) He was promoted to a major, and commanded the 2nd Battalion of our regiment, which unfortunate corps formed, with the picquets, the rear guard, on the day which Monson crossed the Banass, and as all the other corps of the detachment had succeeded in crossing the river, when Holcar and his guns came up, they bore the brunt of the attack.

Sinclair was drawn up on the banks of this river when the enemy opened a most destructive cannonade on him, and at the same moment pressed down on him in heavy columns. He, in this situation, had no alternative. The river had risen so high that he could not cross, and rather than surrender himself and his officers and men into the hands of so sanguinary a butcher as Holcar, he took the colours of his corps in his own hands, and most gallantly stormed the enemy's guns, the greater part of which he had actually gained possession of when an unhappy grape shot killed him on the spot.

Most of his officers had also fallen, and this disaster in front of his men threw them into some confusion, and the enemy, who were before panic-struck at what they saw, took the advantage of this disorder in their line, and poured in upon them in numbers which nothing could withstand, and of this handful of heroes, eight hundred strong, when they went into action, with nine officers to lead them on, one wounded officer and about seventy men only escaped. Becher, W———t, and Nuthall dined at Asiff Bhang with us this evening. I drove W———t in the *curricle* into the country this afternoon. This melancholy news damped the spirits of us all, and it was the only gloomy day I had ever passed at Bareilly.

September 3rd.—The post brought us accounts that Monson's shattered detachment (the sad remains of it) had positively arrived at Agra, and also that three new regiments would immediately appear in orders. I received a short letter this morning from Jones of our 2nd Battalion, the only surviving officer of the corps present at the bloody and unequal contest at the Banass. Jones, knowing my regard for Sinclair, and the friendship which existed between us, told me how gallantly he fell, carrying the colours up to the muzzles of the enemy's guns, and describing as well as he could in his wounded state the nature of the action.

September 4th.—Rode the Capsicum Colt this morning with W———t, who rode Horatio, and a finer lady's horse I never saw mounted. We went quietly, about six miles, and returned soon after sunrise. The party who came down yesterday passed the day with us, and at five in the evening, rather gloomy at the thoughts of leaving my friends, I got into my *palanquin* after taking a farewell of W———t, Thornhill, Becher and Nuthall, and set forward, post, to join the army at the place of rendezvous, near Agra. The surgeons insisted on the impropriety of my journey, and I certainly was in a very bad state of health, but determined at all events to take the field. I crossed the Bareilly River at sunset.

CHAPTER 21

From Bareilly to Agra

September 5th.—After travelling all night, I arrived this morning at daybreak on the banks, and crossed the Rham Gungah River. I found at Jellalabad the bearers just laid, and had I started an hour sooner, I must have waited for them. I immediately pushed on, giving the bearers money to be as expeditious as possible, and at twelve I once more crossed the Ganges, and arrived at my friend Christie's bungalow at Futty Ghur at one o'clock.

September 6th.—At twelve o'clock we saw my horses and camels crossing the Ganges, about a mile above Christie's house. Procured from the Europe shops a few necessary articles, and received from Mrs. Christie two dozen suits of clothes of every description, which she had kindly made up for me at Futty Ghur. Christie dined early, on my account, and my friend Colonel Ralph, from whom I had experienced great kindness during the short time I belonged to the 18th, met us at dinner, looking exceedingly ill, but with his usual flow of spirits. About nine o'clock I got into my *palanquin*, and slept the greater part of the road to the Collah Nuddy (Black River).

September 7th.—Crossed the Collah Nuddy about three this morning, and arrived at Bewar at daybreak, at which place I found Cunynghame's *curricle* and the crossed mares in waiting for me, and I arrived at Mynpoorie in time to dress for breakfast, and from my friends, Cunynghame and Mrs. Cunynghame, I met with a most unreserved welcome. Russel (Cunynghame's collector) and my friend Macan were also here, the latter on his way to join at the rendezvous of the army.

We passed a very pleasant day, and I was less annoyed by the headache than I had for many days been. Mrs. Cunynghame most kindly played over the greater part of my old favourite pieces and songs, and the harmony of her piano was a very different kind of music from that which we shortly expected to be amused with in the field. After dinner Mrs. Cunynghame left Mynpoorie to go by *dawke* to Futty Ghur, on her way to Calcutta, where she expected to meet her relations, Sir John and Lady Doyley and two Miss Doyleys. I very faithfully promised to correspond regularly with her, and to give her an account of the movements of the army. Ryley and a Captain Hearsay, late of Scindiah's service, dined with us today.

September 8th.—We dined at seven o'clock, and at ten, having taken a decent quantity of champagne and claret, we took leave of Cunynghame, and Macan and myself, well armed (and with about thirty of Cunynghame's troopers as an escort) got into our *palanquins* and were soon upon the Agra road.

September 9th.—60 Miles. After travelling all night, unmolested, we reached Shikoabad at daybreak; we passed over the ground on which Cunynghame's detachment fought in September, and I visited the poor remains of my bungalow, except the walls of which nothing remained, and those of the other officers shared the same fate. The lines, also, had been most completely destroyed. We pursued our journey, and about eleven arrived at Ferozeabad, where we found Colonel Macan and the 4th Cavalry encamped.

The last stage was uncommonly hot, and we relished our breakfast (which we got immediately on our arrival at the colonel's tent) exceedingly. We were alarmed a little at a report which had reached Colonel Macan, intimating that one of the regiments of cavalry in front had actually refused to cross the

Jumnah, and remained encamped on this side, near Agra. This account made Colonel Macan very anxious to arrive with the 4th Regiment, and he declared his determination to put to death every man who hesitated. In the night accounts reached us that the regiment had crossed, and were marching quietly to their destination.

We dined this evening at the mess of the 4th Regiment, at which I met the Ridges and many of my old friends, who had called on us in the morning. The weather was exceedingly hot, and I slept in my *palanquin* on the plain.

September 10th.—This morning I alone proceeded on by post. I left the encampment of the 4th whilst they were striking their tents. About ten I arrived at the Raje Ghaut (King's Ferry), and once again crossed the Jumnah. I dropped down to the fort, and landed at the water gate of the Maddoo Ghur outwork (which we breached in October when we took the place). I met with a most kind reception from my friend Colonel Blair (who commanded the garrison) and Mrs. Blair; the latter immediately ordered a famous breakfast for me. All my baggage, except some clothes with two servants, was in the rear. I made Forrest's my headquarters.

The battalion was encamped at Secundra, four miles from Agra only, at the place appointed for the army to assemble. I heard this morning the particulars of Browne's retreat (or rather of his running away) from Muttrah. Monson's appeared but little more inglorious. Most of the officers lost their baggage and all the stock they had laid in for a campaign. Colonel Browne was encamped at Muttrah (about thirty miles from Agra), with five battalions of infantry and a corps of cavalry, with a body of Irregular Horse in our pay (troops enough to have marched through Hindustan).

Holcar was encamped near him at Muttrah, where Browne received orders to return to Agra, which order he interpreted into one to run away, and instantly struck his camp, took to his heels, leaving all his baggage to be plundered by the villagers, nor did he call a halt till his arrival at Agra (thirty long miles).

My friend Colonel Ball, who commanded one of the corps under Browne, took the liberty of telling him that his mode of retreat was disgraceful to the British arms; but the colonel was in such a junk that the more he was entreated not to abandon his baggage the faster he went, taking care always to keep at the head of his column, that being the post most distant from the enemy.

Holcar, who had received immediate information that Browne was striking his camp in a violent hurry, concluded it could be for no other purpose than to attack him, and without more to do commenced his flight in a contrary direction, but as soon as he learnt the true state of affairs, returned and took possession of Muttrah without opposition, and in consequence of this ill-judged retreat, the inhabitants of the country conceived that we had the worst of it, and instantly, to a man, became our enemies, plundered the baggage, and cut up every unfortunate fellow who had not strength or was unable to keep pace with Browne, and very many suffered.

A large party of us dined today with my old friend and shipmate Maling, and we had a very jolly evening. Slept at Forrest's, where Smith of the engineers was also staying. Smith was employed in completing our route the last campaign, having surveyed the country for that purpose.

September 12th.—This morning at break of day Smith and myself rode to the camp near Secundra. The 1st Battalion 2nd Regiment, 2nd Battalion 4th, 1st Battalion 4th and 2nd Battalion of the 15th remained encamped on the ground we took up on our arrival before the place, to besiege it. The 1st Regiment of Cavalry was also encamped near the flank of the infantry line. We passed down the front, and galloped back into garrison to breakfast, to avoid the heat of the sun.

Duncan and Gordon *tiffed* with us today. In the evening my baggage, horses and half a pipe of Madeira all arrived safe from Futty Ghur. Wrote to Mrs. C—— and to Thornhill. The 4th Cavalry crossed the Jumnah today, and the army assembled quickly. We dined with Colonel Blair, and sat playing cards with the ladies till a late hour. The night was particularly cool and pleasant, arid a party of us took a long walk on the ramparts, and it was nearly two o'clock before we reached our quarters.

September 13th.—Breakfasted with Cumberlege this morning. Macan by appointment met me there. I rode a horse of Cumberlege's on trial this forenoon, but did not like him. Called after breakfast on Colonel Blair, who informed me that he had received accounts that Holcar had been employed collecting boats at Muttrah, with an intention to cross a force over the Jumnah into the Dewaub.

Wemyss wrote me from a village near Mynpoorie, and by his accounts we expected the arrival of the commander-in-chief about the 20th. Murray and Forbes called on me today. This evening we had a report that Holcar was bringing on all his infantry and guns, at which we all rejoiced, not doubting the event of an action with him, and we only hoped that chief would not alter his plans.

September 14th.—Rode Mrs. Blair's horse to the Tauge Gardens this morning with Forrest, and the sun was exceedingly hot before we returned. Went to the sale of the late Colonel Sutherland's baggage, of Scindiah's service.

Forrest had a large party of ladies at dinner today, and it was very late before we broke up.

September 15th.—We dined with Cumberlege this evening, and I sat near Miss Browne, who I found had sailed with Welstead in the *Tellicherry*; she was a buxom lass, but in point of figure and carriage a much less pleasing girl than her sister, Mrs. Casement, who was just married to an officer of the 4th Infantry. We had a very gay evening, a great deal of card playing, and a great deal of cheating. It was nearly one before we broke up.

September 16th.—By accounts this morning from Muttrah, we ascertained that Holcar's cannon had come up, and that, with nearly one hundred guns, and all his Infantry, he remained encamped in a strong position. In consequence of this information, I got on Mrs. Blair's horse and rode out to camp, in case a forced march should be made to attack him. But on my arrival Colonel Macan assured me that he had received positive orders to attempt nothing until the arrival of the commander-in-chief and the Cawnpore troops.

As I was daily annoyed with pains of my side and head, and every symptom of the liver complaint, I was advised to return again into garrison, as it was much cooler in a house than a tent, and not to expose myself till it was indispensably necessary.

September 17th.—Wrote to Mrs. Cunynghame this morning, and received a letter from her, dated Futty Ghur. Her *pinnace* was daily expected to arrive from Bareilly. Cunynghame had purchased Major Milhill's for her,, at the price of four thousand *rupees*.

September 18th.—Received a letter from Wemyss, who informed me that he had spoken to Colonel Lake, and told him of my wish to march with the army, instead of returning to the garrison of Gwalior. Colonel Lake mentioned my wishes to the commander-in-chief, and he most readily complied, and promised me a brigade-majorship in one of the brigades of the army, and assured me also that my appointment as major of brigade to the Station of Gwalior should not be done away; that after the campaign (God willing) I may return to it, and this, of all things, was what I would have wished.

A letter from Colonel White this evening greatly damped my spirits—it brought the melancholy account of my friend poor Friele's death. I sincerely lamented his untimely fate. During my sickness at Gwalior he paid me the kindest attention, and it was my firm belief that owing to his care I was principally indebted for my recovery.

September 19th.—Reached camp near Secundra just as dinner was going on the table, and dined with Arbuthnot. The line had changed its position of encampment since I was in camp a few days ago. We were now about half a mile to the north-east of Acbar's Tomb, our right within musket shot of the wall, and running nearly parallel with the Tomb.

September 20th.—This morning a body of the enemy made their appearance at the picquets. They came down in great numbers, and seemed to threaten an attack. Macan (Colonel Macan's brother and *aide-de-camp*) came to my tent and requested me to accompany him in a reconnoitring party in front. We galloped off to the cavalry picquets, and with a squadron of the 1st Regiment, and a galloper, we advanced within musket shot of a body of the enemy, who were concealed in some high corn; they opened a galling fire of musketry on us, nor would the nature of the ground admit of our effecting a charge, but we soon cleared the corn of them by a few rounds of grape from the gun.

The infantry picquets were in motion to support us had it been necessary, which, the enemy observing, drew off towards Gow Ghaut, where we heard they were encamped in force. We withdrew our advanced party, reposted the picquets, and returned to Colonel Macan's tent to breakfast.

Two twelve-pounders, in consequence of our report, were ordered out to a deserted village in front of the line. We had a straggling fire of musketry, and a shot at times from the cavalry gallopers at the picquets, constantly during the day.

September 21st.—This morning at daybreak I relieved Western at the right picquet, and on posting my sentries I found that Anderdon commanded the picquet on my left. Nothing occurred during the day, and not a man of the enemy could we see.

At sunset some of our spies came to my picquet, and assured me that seven thousand of the enemy were encamped within five miles of us, and that they intended to attack our picquets in the course of the night. Paraded my grenadiers and examined their arms, flints, pouches, etc., and ordered them to fill their muskets on a rising spot close to the picquet, and to lie by them during the night. Communicated the information to the commanding officer, and to all the picquets down the line, in order to be prepared for their reception.

Fixed with Anderdon to join our picquets instantly, in case

of an attack, and to take post on the flanks of a large reservoir which stood between us, and there to defend ourselves. A twelve- pounder was also sent to my post, and we were all night under arms, every moment expecting an attack. A proportion of the troops in the lines were also on the parade, ready to support us, but we were disappointed; not a man made his appearance.

September 22nd.—At daylight this morning I marched my company into the lines. Breakfasted with Weston and MacGregor. Purchased a nice snug compact horse this morning of Captain Skinner, price five hundred *rupees*. He was exactly the size and colour and much resembled the little dun mare of my father's, and I only hoped would turn out so well. General Lake arrived on the opposite banks of the Jumnah this day, and the 8th Dragoons crossed over. Accounts from the enemy's camp state that he remains in full force, drawn up at a lake about three miles on our side of Muttrah, where it is said he means to wait our attack. The encampment of the enemy's horse still remained about five miles from us, at Gow Ghaut.

September 23rd—The European troops continued crossing the Jumnah all this forenoon. Received certain information this forenoon that my new tent (which I had supposed was plundered between Futty Ghur and Agra) had safely arrived in the garrison, but as it was expected that we should make rapid marches, in order to come up with the enemy, I determined to leave the new tent, and march with the old one, as being much lighter, and better calculated for a Mahratta campaign.

The commander-in-chief came over the Jumnah this morning, and pitched his tents between the river and our encampment. All accounts agreed respecting the enemy and his supposed intentions to await our arrival, and we anxiously hoped he would do so.

September 24th.—Went to the parade this morning, and rode afterwards with Forbes on the flank of the line, and pointed out to him the spot where, two years since, I was encamped with Collins, Livesey and Marsden, all of whom were now dead; we were then on a party of pleasure, and it was one of the most pleasant trips I had ever made.

We were returning to our tents to breakfast, when we saw General Lake and his staff coming round the flank. Banner rolls had been stationed, and the salute commenced as soon as he entered in front of the line. Rode up and made my bow to the commander-in-chief, and went down the line with Colonel Lake and Wemyss. Breakfasted at headquarters, and his Excellency asked me a great many questions about Gwalior, and paid us some compliments.

As many of my friends had been persuading me to come forward as a candidate for the prize agency, and as it would be a most gratifying circumstance to me to be chosen for that honourable station by the officers of the army, I determined to try it, and as it had been hinted to me that I ought not to accept a brigade-majorship till this point was settled, as many would be of opinion that one officer could not attend to both duties, I stated all this to my good friend Colonel Lake, who thought I would be quite right in declining the brigade-majorship just then, and assured me that, after the prize agency business was settled, I should positively have the first that was vacant, and in the meantime draw my allowances at Gwalior, which was my station.

The Europeans and artillery continued crossing the Jumnah all this day. A report that the enemy had quitted his position near Muttrah, and was marching towards Delhi. In consequence of Wemyss's gallant and active services with us, the last campaign, General Lake got him appointed Collector of Agra, with a salary of three thousand *rupees* a month. Received a note from Young of the 8th Dragoons. Dined at headquarters this evening, and we had a great deal of hard drinking, and it was a late hour before we broke up.

September 26th.—Breakfasted this morning with Wemyss, who made me a present of a beautiful chestnut Arab, for which he paid £300 at poor Campbell's sale. Campbell was riding him in the Battle of Lassuary, and was on his back when a cannon shot cut him asunder. We named the horse Lassuary, and after breakfast Wemyss sent him to my tent, with all his clothes, nets, combs, brushes and three sets of shoes made by a farrier of the dragoons. Gave Wemyss the dun horse which I purchased of Captain Skinner, and which promised to turn out a very clever hack.

Cunynghame came into camp today, to pay a visit to the commander-in-chief before we march off. Cunynghame offered his Arab for sale for *Rs.* 3,000, and had not I met with a friend in Wemyss I should certainly have purchased him.

This evening we stopped some people at the picquets, who gave us information that the enemy had certainly decamped from Muttrah, and had declared his intention of attacking Delhi, in which we had but a small force. The whole of the corps came into their respective stations in the line today, and I received a note from headquarters to know if I was still resolved on coming forward for the prize agency; or if I wished now to be appointed major of brigade, and which, with suitable thanks, I declined, though I almost despaired of success, as several officers of rank and long standing in the army were candidates, and it was reasonable to apprehend they might have more friends than myself.

Macan sent a roll round to be signed by different corps giving their vote for prize agents, and I was told that the number was far in my favour.

I never experienced an anxiety equal to what I felt on this occasion, for I considered that to be chosen by a majority of the officers of the army was an honour that any man might be proud of, and would be a most convincing proof that one's conduct had gained their notice and approbation. I had the satisfaction of seeing many an officer's name down for me, to whom I had considered I was a perfect stranger. I found that both the commander-in-chief and Colonels Lake and Clinton had been using all their influence for me, and every officer of the general's staff and in the headquarters line had given me their names.

A little before sunset Wemyss and myself mounted our new

horses, he on the dun I had sent him and I on my Arab. We rode to Acbar's Tomb, and cantered gently from thence to the right flank of the line and down the front. MacGregor, Weston, Wemyss, Forbes, Murray, Grant and Arbuthnot, with two officers of the reserve, dined with me this evening, and it was past one in the morning before we broke up.

CHAPTER 22

With the Grand Army from Agra to Muttrah and Delhi

September 27th.—This morning the army was brigaded as follows:

1st Brigade Cavalry.
To command Lieutenant-Colonel Vandeleur.
Corps H.M. 8th Light Dragoons.
Corps: 2nd Regiment Native Cavalry.
3rd Regiment Native Cavalry.
6th Regiment Native Cavalry.

2nd Brigade Cavalry.
To command Lieutenant-Colonel Browne.
H.M. 27th Light Dragoons.
Corps: 29th Light Dragoons.
1st Regiment Native Cavalry.
4th Regiment Native Cavalry.

1st Brigade Infantry.
To command The Honourable Lieut.-Col. Monson.
H.M. 76th Regiment Foot.
Corps: 1st Battalion 2nd Regiment (ours).
1st Battalion 4th Regiment.

2nd Brigade Infantry.
To command Lieutenant-Colonel S. Browne.
Corps: 1st Battalion 15th Regiment.

2nd Battalion 15th Regiment.
1st Battalion 21st Regiment.

3rd Brigade Infantry.
To command Lieutenant-Colonel Ball.
Corps: 1st Battalion 8th Regiment.
2nd Battalion 22nd Regiment.

Reserve
To command Lieutenant-Colonel Don.
Corps: Flankers H.M. 22nd Regiment Foot.
1st Battalion 12th Regiment.
2nd Battalion 12th Regiment,
2nd Battalion 21st Regiment.

Prize agents for the Grand Army under the personal command of his Excellency General Lake, commander-in-chief for the campaign of 1804-5.

Prize Agent for Headquarters, Captain Covill, 27th Dragoons.

Prize Agent for King's Infantry, Captain Boyce, 76th Regiment.

Prize Agent King's Cavalry, Captain Smoke, 27th Dragoons.

Prize Agent Native Cavalry, Captain Houston, 6th Regiment.

Prize Agent Native Infantry, Lieutenant Pester, 2nd Regiment.

Prize Agent for the Artillery, Captain Hay, Artillery.

October 1st.—9 Miles. Camp near Gow Pass. This morning at five the army commenced its march, agreeable to the general orders of yesterday, and in the order there directed. The country today was finely cultivated, and the morning dreadfully hot. We arrived at our ground about ten. I suffered extremely by the headache. Encamped in our station in the line (on the right flank), with the 76th Regiment on our left. A small village extended along our front. A great deal of corn around the line in every direction, and much was unavoidably destroyed by the troops and baggage. The officers of our battalion dined with me today. The evening was very close, and all complained much of the heat.

October 2nd.—The army marched this morning by the right. The line in some confusion at marching off, and our battalion, which should have led, was headed by the 2nd Battalion of the 8th. We did not recover our station till broad daylight. I had the command of the flankers this morning. At seven o'clock we heard a firing of musketry in front, and soon afterwards the Horse Artillery and cavalry gallopers opened. Large bodies of the enemy's cavalry were discovered hovering round our line.

About two miles from our new ground the cavalry line formed among some high corn fields, and it had a very grand effect. We formed our line also, and moved on to support the cavalry. The enemy showed a front, and appeared as if they intended to make a stand. On our coming up to the cavalry they wheeled by troops to the right, and both columns advanced parallel to each other, and heads of columns dressing to each other. The enemy drew off as we approached them, and all we could effect was to send the shot from the flying artillery and some shells among them. They were very numerous, and every discharge had apparently good effect.

Encamped about twelve o'clock on a spot of ground, surrounded by the finest crops of grain I ever beheld. Some parties of the enemy's horse continued all day to annoy our picquets, and the guns at them were frequently firing, to prevent their coming too near.

October 3rd.—This morning we marched at half-past five. I lost one of my camels in the night, which occasioned great inconvenience, not having cattle sufficient left to move without difficulty. At daylight we perceived the enemy round us in every direction, and they greatly harassed the flankers during the march, and killed many of our men numbers of them were also shot. A smart cannonade was at times kept up by the rearguard, and a considerable body of the enemy made a dash at our baggage, and were driven back with slaughter.

About eleven o'clock I was ordered with my grenadier and the 1st Battalion Company to take post in some ravines; a squadron of cavalry and galloper were also detached under my command and I used every endeavour to outflank a body of the enemy which threatened our baggage, and to bring them to action, but they cautiously avoided me, never coming within musket shot or allowing us to get nearer to them. I remained at this post till all the baggage had passed, and marched into camp with the rear guard.

Saw the faces of the enemy's lines and encampments in several places during the march today, and at one of them we were told that Holcar in person, with twenty thousand Horse, was yesterday encamped; he moved off on hearing of our approach. We passed a lake this morning which afforded a very strong position to an army, and on that spot Holcar had once drawn up his troops with a determination to fight us, but changed his mind and moved off with all his artillery (nearly one hundred guns) and infantry.

We encamped today about eleven, two miles from the city of Muttrah, into which Colonel Don and the Reserve immediately marched without opposition. Lost my horse tent on the march this morning, and pitched the upper fly of my own for them. The picquets were not much annoyed this afternoon. By the different accounts it appeared that we had upwards of one hundred camels taken off by the enemy's horse during the march this morning, and with them went many of the officers' tents and a great deal of baggage. A great number of their horsemen were shot In the act of plundering the baggage, and many lives lost of both parties.

October 4th.—The army halted today. A report that the enemy in full force were encamped eight miles distant from us with upwards of one hundred pieces of cannon. Our battalion on picquet this morning. I found myself extremely feverish and hardly able to sit on my horse. I relieved the right picquet with my grenadiers and a six-pounder. Soon after daybreak a great deal of skirmishing took place at the picquets, and in front of my post I observed the enemy drawing down as if to make an attempt on a party going with bullocks laden with ammunition and provisions for the troops in the town, with Colonel Don.

I instantly mounted the troop of cavalry stationed under my command at the picquet. The enemy, as I expected, dashed down on the convoy, but the cavalry came up in time to rescue it. A large party of the enemy, observing this at a distance, were coming briskly down to reinforce the others who were skirmishing with my troop of cavalry and as if determined to carry off the convoy.

I instantly ordered the six- pounder to be wheeled round, and opened on them.. They had no idea of our having a gun at the picquet,. and the whole of them immediately took to their heels,, and we pelted them with round shot as long as they continued in the range. The commander-in-chief was all the time on horseback on the brow of a hilt very near my post, and saw all that passed; he came afterwards to the picquet and paid us a compliment for our "vigilance" and "timely support of the convoy," which was all saved, and brought by the troop of cavalry into my post, there to wait a stronger escort. There was no officer at the picquet (European) but myself. Colonel Vandeleur rode into the post while we were blazing away from the field piece, and much admired the effect of the shot and the skill with which the sergeant who belonged to the gun pointed it.

Posted some small parties concealed in the high corn in front of my post, and as they were all choice shots from the company, they succeeded in dropping some of the most daring of the enemy who came near the post, and thereby kept the others at a more respectable distance. I took up my quarters in a *pagoda* near the picquet, and did not pitch my tent today. When everything was perfectly quiet, and 1804. the enemy had retired, the grenadiers piled their arms camp, under the *pagoda*, and I got my breakfast.

At five in the evening they came down again, and continued to exchange shot and to annoy the sentries. During the night we had a good deal of firing, and I was not a minute off my legs. About one in the morning I doubled the sentries, and was soon after reinforced from camp with an officer and one hundred and fifty men of the 4th Regiment. We were under arms all night, every instant expecting an attack, but they contented themselves with annoying us at a distance. The musket shot flew thick about the post, and I lost several men. By way of securing the Arab (Lassuary), I ordered him into the *pagoda*.

October 5th.—I was relieved this morning at break of day by a grenadier company and a gun from the 15th Regiment, under the command of Lieutenant Hartley. The orders for the army to march this morning were army, countermanded. The enemy appeared in strong columns on the right and left of the line soon after sunrise. They did not approach very near to our line, and a couple of shot only from the left picquet were fired at them from one of the gallopers. Some recovered men of the different corps having been very injudiciously sent from Agra to join their respective corps in camp were attacked, overpowered by immense numbers of the enemy's Horse, and nearly all cut to pieces.

Twelve *sepoys* only of the party escaped, and those dreadfully wounded. A great number of camels also sent with them were captured by the enemy. Immediately on this unpleasant intelligence reaching camp a detachment was ordered to march under the command of Colonel Dubois to save if possible some of the unfortunate fellows, but they succeeded in bringing in only the twelve wounded men. Upwards of one hundred bearers sent from Bareilly by Seton to carry the sick and wounded of the army were also cut up. Holcar's guns and Infantry said to have marched towards Delhi, and some apprehensions were entertained for the safety of that city, as the garrison was but weak in regular troops, and the inhabitants, most of them reported to be disaffected.

October 6th.—The morning was as usual dreadfully hot, and I was very unwell; did not quit my tent all day. Purchased a camel this morning for one hundred and ten *rupees*. A rumour this evening through the camp that our brigade would march in the course of the night to attack an encampment of the enemy. Much firing all day at the picquets, and several men killed and wounded. In order to distinguish the Irregular Horse in our pay from those of the enemy the commander-in-chief ordered that the flags of the former should be a dark blue ground with a white St. George's Cross, and officers were directed to pay particular attention to the distinguishing colours.

In the evening General Fraser issued a line order for the whole to be under arms at a quarter before four o'clock tomorrow morning. This evening I put the sergeant-major of our corps in arrest for insolent, unsoldierlike conduct. Two men of my company when I paraded them to examine their arms and ammunition had not their complement of the latter, nor could they account for the deficiency; this, in the face of an enemy, I considered to be of the greatest consequence, and immediately reported it to the adjutant and to the commanding officer; to the shame of the latter, be it said, he merely reproved the men, and without ordering them any punishment.

I was determined that no soldier in my company, and immediately under my command, who could not account for the expenditure of his ammunition, or who paraded without his proper complement, should go unpunished, and therefore ordered my *subadar* (black captain) to parade the company at sunset, and in front of the rest *rattan* the two men in question.

The *subadar* was obeying my orders, when the sergeant-major ordered him in an insolent manner to refrain, while he went to inform the commanding officer; this the *subadar* instantly reported to me; and I ordered him to inflict the punishment, which was accordingly done. I then put the sergeant-major in arrest. This man had often behaved in a like insolent manner to other officers, and I determined on bringing him to a sense of his duty to his superiors. He was a smart officer, and on that account was upheld in his impudence by the commanding officer, who, in fact, was incapable of ordering the detail of duty of the battalion, without the sergeant-major's assistance.

A request was made to me by the commanding officer to excuse the sergeant-major; in answer I told him that on a former occasion (at Sarssney) he had behaved to me with great insolence, but that at the desire of Colonel Blair, then in command, I excused him, but as he had again behaved in a similar manner, I could not put up with it, and therefore was sorry that I could not comply. The commanding officer expressed himself offended at this, but it had no weight with me, as I well knew that without subordination there could be no discipline, and without discipline the most spirited troops cannot be depended on.

October 7th.—We paraded at three o'clock this morning, and about an hour before daybreak we advanced in three columns to attack an encampment of the enemy about five miles in our front.

The cavalry formed the right column, the reserve the centre, and our brigade the left column. We primed and loaded before we marched off. About two miles in front we drove in a strong picquet of the enemy, and an irregular fire of musketry immediately commenced with our flankers and their advanced sentries. This firing gave the alarm to their camp, and we found the whole of them, amounting at least to twenty thousand men, all under arms, and drawn up in order of battle. They were strongly posted, with a lake along their front, and the high village of Arlem on the right flank. They got into motion as we were gaining ground to our right, to clear the lake, and we soon found that they were making off.

As there was no likelihood of our closing with them, or of our getting any nearer to them, the Horse Artillery and cavalry gallopers were advanced, and opened a smart cannonade on them as they retreated. The cavalry at the same time endeavoured to charge, but could effect nothing. The enemy after they had moved off their line still retained possession of the village of Arlem, and our battalion was ordered to break the line, and storm the village. We immediately advanced under a smart fire of musketry, which brought down some of our men, and gained possession of the post.

The line still pressing on, and continuing a distant cannonade on the enemy, I was left with five companies and a field piece to keep possession of the village, and the remaining five companies of the battalion pushed on in pursuit of the enemy, and again took their station in the line. As soon as the army had passed on about a mile, a large body of the enemy's cavalry made a movement round the rear, and advanced boldly, as if to retake the village in which I was posted. I had posted the five companies in a manner I thought most favourable for their reception, and waited their approach. General Fraser, who had observed the enemy getting round the rear, sent an officer to know if I could maintain the post without a reinforcement.

I assured Menzies that as long as our ammunition lasted I was convinced I could keep my ground, with which answer he returned by a circuitous route to General Fraser. The enemy advanced, preserving a front which to troops less acquainted with them than we were would have had a formidable appearance. I allowed them to approach till their musket shot reached the village, and then opened a smart fire of grape on them; they still advanced very boldly until I ordered my men to commence file firing, which was continued very briskly till the enemy became staggered, and began to fly.

Every discharge from the field piece brought down great numbers of the enemy, and many fell by our musketry. The gun continued firing on them as long as our round shot would reach them, and they made off with great precipitation. Finding, with the line, that they had no chance of coming up with the flying enemy, who were also completely dispersed, the general faced about, and passed close to my post, when I received an order to join the rear guard, and with it to march into camp.

We got to our lines about eleven. The sun was exceedingly hot, and we all lost the skin from our faces this morning. On our return we passed a great number of men and some fine horses which had been killed by the Flying Artillery in the early part of the day.

October 8th.—As usual the line paraded this morning an hour before daybreak, and remained until arms till six o'clock. I marched off the battalion guards as officer of the day, and rode with Young round the *videttes*. A report from a prisoner that Holcar in person commanded the troops we saw yesterday, and that he had a very narrow escape of a cannon shot, when our Flying Artillery first opened. Breakfasted this morning with Colonel Macan.

October 10th.—Late last night an order came out directing the troops of the line to be under arms at four o'clock, and this morning we paraded accordingly. The commander-in-chief with the cavalry and some corps of the infantry not employed on the 7th marched to make another attempt on the enemy's camp.

I was posted on the right of the camp with three companies of infantry, three twelve-pounders, and two sixes, to protect that flank in case the enemy should make a dash with their cavalry.

At six o'clock we heard our guns open, and rightly concluded that the enemy had again declined making any serious stand. Some bodies of the enemy's Horse wheeled round towards the flank of our line, but kept at a very respectable distance. Our matches were alight, guns primed, and all in perfect readiness for them, but as they did not approach I threw no shot away at them.

The commander-in-chief returned into camp about ten, and I withdrew my party, and ordered the artillery officer with his guns to rejoin the Park. Some of the enemy fell again this morning by the shot of the Horse Artillery and Cavalry Gallopers, and some prisoners wounded and taken assured us that Holcar himself headed them in the morning. Grain from Agra crossing the river this day, and a report in the afternoon that we were to change ground immediately.

We dined with Colonel Macan this evening, and, it being the anniversary of taking the town and of storming the ravines at Agra, the bottle circulated freely. Accounts of our posts being cut off and the postmen murdered between our camp and Agra.

The letters carried into the enemy's camp.

October 11th.—This morning our battalion being for picquet I marched off to the right of the line at gunfire and took post with my grenadiers and a six-pounder in the *pagoda*, relieving a Grenadier Company of the 8th commanded by Lieutenant Kerr. The brigadier of the day visited my post soon after I got to it, and General Fraser remained with me nearly an hour, observing the movements of some columns of the enemy. We had a good deal of skirmishing during the day, but with little effect, as the enemy declined coming very near the *pagoda*.

We marched this morning (the army) at half-past five o'clock. At five I joined the field officer of the day at the centre picquet, and our battalion with our field pieces and a regiment of cavalry with its gallopers formed the rear guard. We were exceedingly harassed during the march, and our guns were open nearly the whole way. We were obliged to unlimber every ten minutes. They made several desperate pushes at the baggage and cattle, but were as frequently driven back with loss. I found myself exceedingly ill today, and the fever attacked me most severely immediately on our arrival at the new ground.

October 25th.—A raging fever (in consequence of which my life was for many days despaired of) prevented me journalizing since the 12th. This morning I found that the fever abated, and I had no doubt but a short time with care would recover me. I was so much reduced and cut up that my friends scarcely knew me. We arrived here (Delhi) on the 17th. Colonel Lake rode up to my *palanquin* as we were marching into the encampment, and most kindly insisted on my going instantly into the city, as I should find a house much cooler than a tent, and in I was carried accordingly, with the fever raging upon me, and in almost a state of delirium.

My friend Rose, who was stationed at Delhi, and who had behaved most gallantly during the siege, as I had often witnessed his doing on former occasions, particularly in the Battle of Delhi and at the siege of Gwalior, heard of my illness, and sent an orderly to my tent to conduct me to his quarters in the city, in which I was as comfortably lodged as the unpleasant state in which I was would admit.

We found that the enemy had gone off towards Lassuary, leaving four complete breaches in the town wall, which, however, they had not the spirit to assault. They moved off on hearing of our leaving Muttrah, and being in motion towards Delhi. It was the intention of the commander-in-chief to have halted here one day only, and to have pushed on with a view of coming up with Holcar's guns and brigades, but this plan was frustrated owing to a scarcity of grain in our camp and the uncertainty of getting supplies in the country we should have to march through.

The army encamped about a mile from the city, on the banks of the Jumnah, the cavalry line facing the river. Rose took his leave of me this morning, and crossed the river with his corps (2nd Battalion 14th) on the route to Seharanpore. An Irregular Battalion and a body of Hindustani Horse marched with the 14th under the command of Colonel Burne. The day after our arrival at this place Colonel Dubois's Battalion was detached across the river for grain.

October 26th.—About ten this morning the whole of the cavalry moved out, in consequence of some large bodies of the enemy's Horse having made their appearance on the left flank of the line. Our brigade also got under arms, but the enemy fled as we advanced. Ordered the groom to walk out the Arabs daily in front of my quarters. Continued swallowing bark in great quantities, and still to remain exceedingly weak. Accounts received that the cantonment and town of Khauss Gunge is destroyed by the enemy. This appears to have been done by the disaffected inhabitants in that quarter for the sake of plunder as well as to invite the enemy.

October 28th.—A report today of the death of poor Ford of the 12th, and of Aldin of our regiment in consequence of the wounds he received in the Battle of Delhi, at which time I left him for dead in the field, so dreadfully was he wounded. A camel laden with letters which had been detained at Agra in consequence of all communication being cut off in our rear came into camp today, having passed up the opposite side of the river with grain, under an escort commanded by Captain Munro of one of the new corps. Gave the Arab Lassuary *nitre* this morning in consequence of some blotches in his skin, occasioned by his high living and want of work.

I had him daily exercised in front of my quarters by his groom during my sickness. No accounts from the enemy's camp had reached us for many days. This morning we heard a distant cannonade, but from what quarter we could not exactly ascertain. Several officers visited me today, and some remained with me till evening.

October 29th.—It was currently reported this forenoon that the Bhirtpore Rajah had actually taken the field against us; if this proves correct he will have acted a most diabolical part, as our Government had showed him the most pointed favour, and from our own conquest we added very considerably to his estate, and on every occasion he had been dealt by with the greatest lenity and attention to all his requests.

It was also said that the *Begum* (Queen) Somereau had also marched troops to his aid, and had declared her determination to join him in opposition to us. By a long letter from my good friend Brigadier White, commanding at Gwalior, it appears that things wear a very unpleasing aspect in that quarter; he represented the inhabitants to be in a state little short of rebellion.

A party which the brigadier had detached to meet and escort treasure from Agra to pay his troops had been attacked by very superior numbers and forced to retreat for shelter into an adjacent small fort, there to remain till a second party was sent to their relief.

The brigadier mentioned also that the most horrid murders and depredations were almost daily committed in the vicinity of his garrison, beyond the walls of which, and those of the town, he had no authority to interfere, nor indeed would the numbers of his troops admit of his doing it, even if he had been authorized, as he had barely men sufficient to man his works and to furnish the necessary number of night guards and sentries. A report that Colonel Burne's Battalion, which crossed the Jumnah from this place a few days since, was entirely surrounded by large bodies of the enemy's cavalry, which had crossed purposely after him some miles above the city of Delhi.

Our foraging parties for the last two days experienced no kind of annoyance, and it was evident that the enemy had withdrawn his cavalry to act in force against some particular object, and we thought Burne's Battalion very likely to be his point of attraction. The commander-in-chief and staff passed my quarters this evening on their way to visit the Emperor. The general was escorted by a squadron of dragoons, and returned to camp soon after sunset.

October 30th.—This morning at daybreak the reserve of the army, under Lieutenant-Colonel Don, crossed the river into the Dewaub; supposed in consequence of a confirmation of the report of Burne being surrounded. Ridge, whom we left sick at Agra, arrived in camp this morning, and came to me at my quarters in the city.

The air was somewhat fresh and cool, and it was more like a morning of the cold season than any we had yet experienced; towards noon, as usual, the sun became very powerful.

Today I received a letter on the service from the field paymaster, and two from my agents, with Company's paper to the amount of one thousand two hundred *rupees*. A Calcutta post came into camp this day, and some despatches were also said to have been received at headquarters from the Decan, stating the capture of Indore, Holcar's capital, by the forces under Colonel Murray. It was also reported that Murray had received General Lake's orders to march in a direction to form a junction with our army.

Colonel Murray's detachment is very strong, particularly in European troops. In our camp it was the general opinion that things were never known to wear a more unfavourable aspect than at the present period. In our own provinces the different *rajahs* and every petty *zemindar* having at command a small force showed every disposition to be hostile and rebellious, and in many parts of the Dewaub (to the northward of the Jumnah) have already evinced the most disaffected conduct; and if the enemy should have crossed to them in any force, the worst may be apprehended, and at all events it will be the thing impossible for us to advance at any great distance to the southward, and to quit the borders of our own provinces.

In the evening I received some notes from my friends of the cavalry, telling me that they were to cross the Jumnah tomorrow at daybreak, all except two regiments; the infantry to stand fast.

October 31st.—This morning the commander-in-chief, with His Majesty's 8th, 27th and 29th Light Dragoons, 1st, 4th and 6th Native Cavalry and Flying Artillery (Horse), crossed the Jumnah after Holcar, who had actually surrounded Burne's Battalion, and commenced burning and laying waste our country. The whole of the infantry, except the reserve, which had crossed the river with Don, remained on their old ground of encampment, under the command of Major-General Fraser.

The 2nd and 3rd Native Cavalry also remained attached to General Fraser's Division of the army. This forenoon I felt somewhat recruited, and the fever less violent than it had for many days been. Wrote to Colonel Ashe at Agra, to send me by the first escort some dozens of Madeira from a pipe which he had kindly taken charge of for me. Several Europe letters and extracts from English papers were this evening received in camp; some of so late a date as May.

November 1st.—We heard no tidings of the commander-in-chief since his departure yesterday. Grain was crossing the river the whole of this day, brought by a detachment from Agra. A report that we (the infantry) should march as soon as the whole of it was over.

Forage for two days ordered to be brought into camp. Lieutenant Plunkett of the 4th died this evening, and was buried in the city.

CHAPTER 23

Siege and Capture of Dieg Fort

November 12th.—We marched from Delhi on the 5th. Our original route on leaving Delhi was back to Muttrah, but on the 9th accounts reached our camp that Holcar's Brigades and guns had left Gassouly, and were on their route to Dieg. General Fraser determined in consequence of this information to strike off on the 10th (next day) and to proceed towards them. He accordingly sent orders for the European Regiment at Muttrah to join us at Goberdown, at which place we arrived on the 10th, after a march of twenty-three miles, and found that the Europeans had arrived.

After so long a march it was thought necessary to halt on the 11th, and on the 12th we marched to within a short distance of Dieg. This day our cavalry had a skirmish with a body of the enemy's Horse. After encamping, and the dust clearing away, we plainly saw a very large camp, extending with their left close on the fort of Dieg, to a large high village on the right, an immense lake all along their front, and another covering their rear altogether as strong a position as could be conceived.

Finding them thus advantageously posted, and not having any satisfactory information, the general did not think it advisable to attack them this day, but having reconnoitred from a high village in front of our line, and ascertained the road down to the enemy's right, it was determined to fight them next morning. About four in the afternoon the enemy brought out four heavy guns to their front, and cannonaded our camp across the lake, without, however, doing much execution.

November 13th.—At three this morning we were all under arms, and moved down to the attack in three columns, infantry on the right, guns in the centre, and cavalry on the left. We had to make a circuit of nearly three miles, to get round the lake which covered their left. On our way we fell in with several bodies of the enemy's Horse, and soon drove them in. They gave the alarm to their camp by communicating the approach of our line. We drew up in two lines before daylight, with our right on a mosque, and, as the day was breaking, faced to the left, gained ground, so as to attack them immediately in front.

The two regiments of cavalry (2nd and 3rd Native Corps) were ordered to keep their cavalry in check during the attack, and to prevent them cutting in upon our rear. The baggage had all been packed, and left on the ground of encampment, with the 3rd Brigade (Ball's) for its protection. The corps destined for the attack were H.M. 76th Regiment, 1st European Regiment, 1st Battalion of the 2nd Regiment (ours), the 1st Battalion, 4th Regiment, the 15th Regiment, amounting in the whole to about three thousand men.

The leading line of infantry supported by the second commenced the attack on the high village of Aow. At sunrise their cannonade began, and awful and destructive it certainly was. The high village lay immediately in the route of our corps, and we charged, and were soon clear of it; here poor Forbes fell by a cannon shot. He was riding my little mare. MacGregor's horse was shot at the same moment, and he rode her during the remainder of the action. Shot, stones and brick were flying at a tremendous rate, and many men of our regiment were killed and wounded by the two latter, as well as by shot. The cannonade of the enemy seemed every instant to increase till we reached the muzzles of the first batteries.

In descending from the village General Fraser was wounded, and lost his leg by a shot. Many a gallant fellow fell also at this period. Their guns were judiciously posted in tiers, and after pushing on from the first line of guns to the second we observed those who had escaped the bayonet getting round our rear, and again opening them on us. They were soon retaken, and spiked with our bayonets.

We now began to close with them in earnest, and the slaughter among them, in their turn, became great, and at length they fled with precipitation. We pressed on them close down to the glacis of Dieg, and the carnage among the enemy was such as on cool reflection would make the hardest heart relent. At this instant we were checked by a heavy fire of round and grape from the walls of the fort and tower, and we drew off with the captured guns, and took post at some salt pits, from which we completely commanded the field of battle, and at dusk we dragged off the captured guns, amounting to eighty-seven fine pieces of ordnance, in the highest possible condition, and elegant guns.

The enemy were most completely defeated, and had not the fort fired on us, every man of them almost must have been put to death. Murray of our battalion was wounded near the salt pits by a grape shot, but we hoped not dangerously. Poor Forbes, who fell in the village, we all lamented most sincerely; he was leading on his company in a most gallant style, when a cannon shot struck him to pieces. After General Fraser was wounded the command fell on Colonel Monson. We pitched our camp after the battle in front of the village of Aow. This glorious affair was attended with great loss on our part, and several gallant officers fell.

Officers Killed.

Captain Norford, 76th Regiment.
Lieutenant Forbes, 1st Battalion 2nd Regiment.
,, Burgess, 4th Regiment.
,, Faithfull, 4th Regiment.
,, Hales, 15th Regiment.
,, Boyd, 15th Regiment.
,, Lyons, 15th Regiment.

Wounded.

General Fraser (died of his wounds).

Captain Chisolm.
Captain Boyce.
Lieutenant Mansell.
,, Murray.
,, Maxton.
,, Wood.
,, Hunter.
,, Garner.
,, Scuell.
,, Perry.
,, Nicholl.
,, Bampton.
,, Glubb.
,, Smith.
,, Chatfield.
,, Morris.
,, Bryant.
,, Merriman.

Total:—Seven officers killed, and nineteen wounded; of the latter, several died of their wounds.

General Fraser's leg taken off, and he doing as well as could be expected, and no danger apprehended.

Colonel Ball, with the brigade which had been left in charge of the baggage, advanced to the salt pits, and relieved the troops stationed there, and which had been all the morning in action.

At dusk the whole of the enemy's guns were dragged off the field of battle, and safely lodged in our Park. The pioneers employed all night in burying the dead and clearing the field of the wounded, as our camp was pitched on the very spot where the battle had been hottest. Our surgeons most humanely amputated on a great number of the wounded of the enemy, and dressed the wounds of as many as they could attend to. Poor Maxton of the European Regiment received a grape shot, which literally went through his head; he continued alive, but little hopes were entertained of his recovery.

Among the guns taken from the enemy this day were those lost by Monson in his inglorious retreat; they were perfectly complete in everything, and the ammunition which the colonel reported he had destroyed was all found in high preservation in the tumbrils, excepting only what the enemy had expended in the action. We also took six elegant eighteen-pounders, which had formerly been given to the Peishwah by Lord Cornwallis, and taken from him by Holcar. Before the fort of Dieg opened its fire on us we did not know the *rajah* had determined to act against us; he never declared himself till our troops were upon the glacis, bayoneting the enemy.

The evening before the action General Fraser wrote him a letter, desiring to know whether we were to consider him our friend or our foe, to which no kind of answer was returned. It was now concluded that we should immediately invest Dieg and Bhirtpore, and as both places are said to be very rich, we flattered ourselves with the hopes of benefiting considerably by prize money, and as prize agent my prospects were good.

November 14th.—Upon a return of casualties being made out, we found to our sorrow that our battalion had again suffered considerably. Four hundred and thirty men only marched out to the attack, of which number ninety-three were killed and wounded, and two officers, a great proportion for so weak a battalion. This action, considering the uncommon strength of the enemy's position and the numerous and powerful train of artillery opposed to comparatively speaking a handful of men, may be reckoned among the most brilliant victories that were ever obtained.

Nothing could exceed the silence and promptitude with which our troops advanced, and everything seemed equally determined on the part of the enemy. They did not open a gun till they heard our bugle sound the signal to advance, and at the same moment the dawn of day presented our line moving on to the attack, from which period, till we reached them with our bayonets, their cannonade was extremely heavy, and our men fell very thick. General Fraser was heading us, and descending from the village of Aow, when he fell, wounded, and nothing could exceed the conspicuous gallantry and heroism he evinced in leading the line into action. We were in action nearly six hours, and a hotter day Britons had seldom experienced in any quarter of the globe.

November 21st.—About nine o'clock this evening accounts reached us that the commander-in-chief, with the cavalry, had come up with Holcar on the 17th instant, under the walls of Futty Ghur. He attacked and routed him, taking all his camp equipage, cattle, etc.; about five thousand of the enemy are said to have been put to death. The rest fled towards Mynpoorie.

November 22nd.—This morning we fired a Royal Salute and three volleys of musketry in honour of the commander-in-chief's victory at Futty Ghur. The Bhirtpore Rajah said to have offered a *crore* of *rupees* as an atonement for his rascally conduct in firing on our troops in the Battle of Dieg, and thereby declaring himself our enemy. This, we hoped, would not be attended to, and we looked forward with pleasure to the time of the arrival of the commander-in-chief in our camp, when we expect to proceed, and take our revenge by battering his fort about his ears, for his conduct on the 13th.

Letters received this day from the adjutant-general give the particulars of the defeat of the enemy. It appears that the commander-in-chief, with the cavalry alone (having left the reserve in the rear), came up with Holcar on the 17th, after a march of seventy-two miles. A tumbril belonging to the Flying Artillery most unfortunately blew up a few miles before they arrived in the enemy's camp, which alarmed them a little, and was the cause of the surprise not being so complete as it otherwise would have been.

They, however, had not an idea that our troops were within fifty miles of them, and many of them had not got on their legs when the general attacked them at daybreak; they were soon routed, and dispersed in all directions. Holcar himself, and two thousand scattered Horse made off early in the morning, in the direction of Mynpoorie.

Upwards of two thousand of the enemy were said to have been killed and wounded, without the loss of a single man of ours. They thought not of making any resistance, but fled on the first alarm. It appeared that our troops at Futty Ghur, consisting only of a few raw recruits, had remained under arms two nights previous to the arrival of the enemy. On the evening of the 16th they discovered them advancing in great numbers, and encamped near the cavalry lines, which they immediately set fire to, and completely destroyed. The few officers at Futty Ghur with the recruits had taken post on the infantry parade, with ravines in their front, and there waited the attack of the enemy, which they were in instant expectation would take place.

Two heavy guns were carried down to a bridge at the entrance into the infantry lines, and the enemy were cannonaded from them, while they were destroying the cavalry cantonment on the afternoon of the 16th. Our troops were all night under arms, drawn up on the infantry parade, and from the immense numbers of the enemy they had much to apprehend, and Holcar sent to them in the evening and threatened to take their lives at daylight, but our gallant commander-in-chief told them another story.

At break of day on the morning of the 17th our troops were all under arms, momentarily expecting an attack; their surprise was great at hearing a very sudden and smart cannonade open very near them, and their joy was, of course, great when day, breaking, discovered our dragoons charging the enemy in every direction, who were flying in all quarters. The cannonade from the Flying Artillery and Gallopers, it appeared, was very heavy for a short space of time, until they were completely dispersed. They fled without making any kind of stand.

Holcar himself did not halt till he reached "poor Mynpoorie," where he destroyed the lines of White's Provincial Corps, and Cunynghame's elegant house, coach houses, stables and all its buildings shared the same fate. White took post in his own house, round which he had thrown up a strong ditch, and raised some small bastions which flanked it. His men were posted on the top of the house, and behind a parapet within the ditch. The enemy made a faint attack, but were driven back by the musketry.

Cunynghame's house, which cost him full half a *lac* of *rupees*, was nearly ruined; all the windows and doors destroyed; the beams set fire to, and they had used every means to fire the house, but could not effect it.

Ryley's bungalow shared the same fate, and all the furniture it contained was destroyed. Accounts came into camp today of Colonel Wallace having taken a strong fort in the Decan.

November 25th.—Major-General Fraser having unfortunately died of the wounds he received on the 13th, whilst leading us on to victory, was buried this evening with all the honours of war, near the town of Muttrah. All officers off duty attended, and deep affliction for the loss of so gallant an officer was visible in the countenance of every individual who attended on this melancholy occasion.

For many days after he received the unfortunate wound, no apprehensions were entertained of his danger; the shot struck him about the ankle, the leg was taken off just above the wound, and he appeared doing well till a day or two previous to his death.

December 5th.—The commander-in-chief having joined us, we proceeded to commence the siege of Dieg, and this morning we encamped within sight of the fortress. The enemy's Horse continued to hang on our flanks and rear, and some men were daily killed, of ours as well as of the enemy.

The Bhirtpore Rajah sent *vakeels* into camp this morning, but they were received in a manner the conduct of their *rajah* had merited.

December 6th.—We moved ground this morning, and encamped between Goverden and the field on which the battle of the 13th was fought. Several hogs were seen this morning during the march, but the enemy were so thickly hovering round our line that it was impossible to pursue them. The whole of the troops that escaped on the 17th near Futty Ghur, and all the Bhirtpore Rajah's own cavalry, were constantly harassing our picquets and the baggage during the march.

A strong party approached our picquet on the right of the line, and a smart cannonade from the two six-pounders commenced on them (at the picquets). Rode a long way down in front this evening, and saw the enemy plainly on the works of the town, and an immense encampment close under the walls. Dined with MacGregor this evening.

December 7th.—The army marched at daybreak this morning in two lines, the cavalry and two battalions forming one, and the remaining corps of infantry the second line.. The baggage moved between the two columns, and was perfectly secured by the rearguard in the rear. The enemy endeavoured to annoy us by throwing rockets, but a few rounds from the guns with the advanced guard kept them at a respectable distance. We did not make a march of more than four miles this day; we passed over the skirts of the field of battle, and saw the skeletons of many poor fellows who fell with us on the 13th. Encamped about four miles from the fort of Dieg, with the high village which we stormed on the 13th on our right flank.

Went round the picquets in the evening; the officer commanding that on the left of the line was amusing himself firing at a small party of the enemy crossing on his flank, but it was a waste of ammunition, not a shot taking effect. Dined at Arbuthnot's, and about nine o'clock orders came in for our Battalion to be under arms at ten, as we supposed, to beat up an encampment of the enemy, but soon after ten we marched off to a lake of water about one mile and a half in our front, with three companies of pioneers, to cut through an embankment with a view to overflow that face of the fort.

We soon reached our destination, and remained all night under arms, whilst the pioneers were working. It was strange that the enemy did not discover us, as we could plainly hear them shouting in their camp, across the lake, and see their lights going the rounds on the ramparts of the town. We completely finished the work, and returned to camp before sunrise.

Having been all last night under arms, we took the advantage of the halt today, and brought up our arrears of sleep. Rode down in front this afternoon, and saw a great deal of the ground on the east face of the fort under water, and the enemy endeavouring in vain to stop it. It appeared to rush out most furiously, and we did not doubt but that they would have infinite labour to check its progress. Dined with the commander-in-chief today, and gave him the particulars of our last night's employment. As usual at headquarters, we all drank a good deal of wine.

December 9th.—We halted this day, and the *hircarahs* were employed in gaining information respecting the strength of the place, and ascertaining the most vulnerable part of the town. Firing at the picquets all day, at some advanced parties of the enemy.

December 10th.—This morning we marched at daybreak, in the same order as on the 7th; in getting round a large piece of water, of some miles extent, we were obliged to pass through a thick jungle, in which the enemy was concealed, and several of our men were shot by them, without discovering the enemy or even the quarter from whence they fired, so thick was the wood. Our flankers were soon out, and a brisk fire commenced in all directions. I was employed in this duty, in command of the flankers of our own battalion; some of them were shot, and I had many narrow escapes myself.

We killed a great many of the enemy, and at length succeeded in beating them quite off, and the line passed unmolested through the latter part of the wood. We encamped about nine, not more than four miles distant from our last ground. Here we supposed we should remain, as in a position proper to commence our approaches against the town and fort of Dieg, which was about two and a half miles in our front. I found myself much annoyed by a violent headache, in consequence of having exerted myself a little with the flankers in the morning. Did not quit my tent the whole of this day.

December 11th.—We moved about one mile this morning, in order to take up a final position for the siege. Soon after we left our ground a considerable body of the enemy were seen collecting under a hill about a quarter of a mile from our line. Colonel Monson, who commanded our brigade, desired me to endeavour to surprise them with three companies and a six-pounder. The army passed on, but the rear guard was at hand to support me if I should have been hardly pressed by superior numbers. By a circuitous route I gained the top of the hill undiscovered, while the gun moved round one point of it, to open on them as they made off. Nothing could exceed the surprise of the enemy when I gave them my fire from the hill; they were immediately under me, and so close that almost every shot had effect, and numbers of them fell, whilst others made off under a smart fire of grape from my gun, which mowed them down in dozens.

On hearing my fire the line was halted, and they all witnessed the surprise and the slaughter which took place among the enemy, who had never dreamt that it was possible for troops to ascend the hill on the part next our line of march. I rode Lassuary this morning, and was not off his back the whole of the time; he carried me up the precipices on the side of the hill in a most astonishing manner, and where very few other horses could have gone. By the time I joined the line the rear guard was come up, and the army was nearly encamped. MacGregor kept breakfast ready for me in his tent. Some guns opened from the town on our picquets, and their Horse annoyed our *videttes* and advanced sentries. Dined with Colonel Macan.

December 12th.—Our corps on picquet this morning. Colonel Ball was the brigadier of the day. I was posted at the centre picquet, and several heavy shot passing over my tent I quickly sent all my horses to the lines, out of the reach of shot. Graham and a party of the 3rd Cavalry was posted at my picquet, and some men of his were injudiciously placed in front of my sentries, and having pistols only they were no match for the enemy, who came deliberately down, took a cool shot with their matchlocks (with which most of them kill certain at eighty and a hundred yards) and galloped before off without danger from the troopers with pistols.

One man was shot in this manner close to the picquet, and another came in at speed, with his horse wounded, and which dropped dead as soon as he reached his picquet. I represented this to Brigadier Ball, and was ordered to withdraw the *videttes* during the day. Some of the most daring of the enemy then came down, and exchanged some shot with my sentries, who, with their muskets, were a much better match for them.

With my rifle I went out in front, and one of their horsemen galloped down, presented his piece, and fired at me. The shot passed very close to my face, and as he was going off I fired, and evidently wounded him. He continued, however, to sit his horse till he nearly reached the party to which he belonged, when we saw him fall and his horse run off. I never saw a horseman of the enemy within musket shot distance of the picquet afterwards. All the cattle and people employed bringing materials and making fascines and gabions. Graham dined at my tent.

December 13th.—A battalion of the 8th relieved us this morning. Every preparation making in camp for the commencement of the siege, and on reconnoitring it was found that our batteries could be formed at a convenient breaching distance, by cutting through a mound of earth in front of a village near the fort, and this evening a battalion of the 12th Regiment and some Companies of Europeans advanced to break ground. The rattling of the gun carriages and tumbrils alarmed the enemy, who had some parties advanced in front, and who gave their fire, and ran under the walls of the garrison. The party ordered for this duty was commanded by my Gwalior friend Colonel Don, who, after dislodging the enemy, took post in the village, and commenced his entrenchments. No firing during the night.

December 14th.—The enemy having discovered Colonel Don's party at daybreak this morning, commenced a heavy fire of cannon from the town and from as many of the fort guns as they could bring to bear on the grove and village. Some twelve-pounders were run down to a well in front of the picquet this morning, and we observed the enemy bringing out guns in all directions from the town, and erecting batteries. On the right of the village from which we commenced our approaches was a great deal of broken ground, and a small redoubt occupied by the enemy; from the former they kept up a constant fire of musketry on our troops, trenching, and many of our men were killed.

At sunset this evening the relief of the trenches took place; the troops paraded in front of the 76th Regiment. Rode to the picquets, and remained till dark; saw the enemy with our glasses, erecting batteries in all quarters, under the wall of the town. The general officer of the day was ordered to mount in the evening, and to command in the trenches, the field officer of the day to have charge of the picquets. Dined with Weston this evening.

December 15th.—By this day's orders the brigadiers of cavalry were directed to take the duties of the day, as formerly, and the brigadiers of infantry the duty of the trenches. A Royal Salute was fired this day in honour of the capture of Gaulney by the detachment under the command of Colonel Wallace. The 1st Battalion 4th and 1st Battalion 15th Regiments, with two hundred men of the 76th Regiment, were in the trenches today. A smart fire on the working parties all the forenoon, and when the salute opened in camp the enemy, as if enraged at our rejoicing, redoubled their fire, and continued firing platoons of cannon for nearly half-an-hour on our trenches.

The commander-in-chief came in front of our parade to ascertain the occasion of so heavy a fire. The relief of the trenches took place at the usual hour. Dined with the commander-in-chief this evening. The general was in high spirits, and expressed his hope soon to have an opportunity of punishing the *rajah* for his infidelity and treacherous conduct.

December 16th.—A foraging party ordered to parade tomorrow morning, and three days' forage to be brought into camp.

The relief of the trenches to be on the parade of the 76th, at six o'clock, and to move off immediately after. The general officer in the trenches was directed to send a non-commissioned officer from each party posted in the trenches to the parade of the 76th at sunset.

The different parties for each post to be told off before they move down, and the non-commissioned officer to conduct each relieving party to its destined post, as soon as they get near the centre of the grove. I was in the trenches this day, and commanded a detached party, posted on the right of the village, for the purpose of keeping the enemy in the broken ground on the right of our batteries in check and to prevent their coming sufficiently near to fire with effect on our men in the trenches.

On this post the enemy kept up a constant heavy fire, and I lost a great many of my men, and had myself many narrow escapes. Lieutenant Dickson of the 4th, with three companies of that corps, relieved me. I cautioned him on the necessity of keeping his men as much under cover as possible, as there was literally an uninterrupted and perpetual shower of ball on the post, and the enemy were so spread in the broken ground that we could not give our fire with the effect that was wished.

I took my leave of Dickson, and returned to the trenches, which I had scarcely reached when an orderly came running to inform me that poor Dickson was shot through the head. He was giving his orders to his men to fire on some of the enemy, who were drawing near his post, when a man from an embankment on the flank of his parapet shot him dead; he was a very worthy young man, and a gallant officer. His body was immediately sent to camp, and the following general after order appeared:

> A funeral party of one company from the 1st Battalion 4th Regiment to parade immediately in front of that corps to attend the remains of the late Lieutenant Dickson to the grave. All officers off duty are requested to attend.

The enemy kept a very heavy fire of cannon from near thirty heavy guns on us in the trenches, and the men employed in erecting the batteries were necessitated to leave off their work till the cover of the night enabled them to continue it. Many poor fellows fell this day, and one of our twelve-pounders which we had in a redoubt to strengthen the trenches was dismounted, the axle being struck in shivers by a shot. The engineer and artillery officers declared they had never witnessed such a fire at a battery, every shot either struck the batteries, or the top of the trench, and many came through the loose earth, and killed our men. The European Regiment and 2nd Battalion relieved us this evening, and we reached camp about eight o'clock, and all dined with me.

December 17th.—A working party of forty dragoons was ordered to accompany the relief this day to the trenches. After before breakfast I went with Macan to the advanced picquet, and we had the satisfaction to observe that the shot from two of our twelve-pounders in advance seemed greatly to annoy some parties of the enemy posted near the glacis. Ridge commanded the centre picquet, and we *tiffed* with him.

Two heavy shot passed over the tent and killed one of the gun bullocks. An artillery officer told us that they expected the batteries would be finished in the course of the night. An order appeared this afternoon directing that whenever working parties of Europeans were sent to the trenches liquor equal to afford two drams to each man is to be sent and served to them during the time they are working.

The person in charge of the liquor is to carry a note to the commanding officer, and to be instructed to serve the liquor at such time as he shall direct. Two hundred of the 76th Regiment and a battalion of the 15th, and one of the 12th, for the trenches.

December 18th.—This morning our batteries opened on the Shah Burge, or King's bastion, and continued a heavy fire the greater part of the forenoon. The mortar battery, which was sunk in the rear of the village, commenced its fire at the same time. This was returned by a very spirited fire from as many guns as the enemy could bring to bear on our batteries and trenches. An incessant roar of cannon continued with but little intermission the whole of the day, and our shot made a considerable impression on the bastion and a gateway close on its left, which seemed to have been blocked up.

A foraging party ordered to parade in front of the centre of the cavalry at eight o'clock tomorrow morning; forage for three days to be brought in. All spare musket balls ordered to be sent to the Park. The general officer when relieved from the trenches is to send a return of casualties which may occur in the corps under his command to the adjutant-general, and all occurrences of an unusual nature in the trenches to be reported immediately to headquarters.

December 19th.—Mounted Lassuary at daybreak this morning, and rode round the picquets, and down to the guns in advance. Shairpe was with me, and we rode very close to a post of the enemy, and were saluted with two shot which passed very close to us. The firing from our batteries continued very heavy, and with considerable effect. Last night new trenches were commenced on, about a quarter of a mile on the left of the Grand Battery, there to raise a two-gun battery to knock down the defences of a couple of bastions from which the enemy could otherwise keep up a flanking fire on the storming party, and in all probability terribly annoy us. I went down to the trenches this evening.

We marched off at the usual hour; some confusion occurred during the relief, owing to the enemy keeping up a smart cannonade on us, which in the dark caused some hurry and irregularity, and which officers in such situations always find a difficulty in putting a stop to. Our battalion was posted in the trenches on the left of the Grand Battery, in which several men had been killed during the day, owing to the enemy having brought some guns round so as to completely enfilade the trench. The corps we relieved gave us this information, and in consequence of which we immediately commenced throwing up traverses, to prevent their cannon shot ranging down the trench. This employed us the greater part of the night, officers and men in parties continuing it all night.

December 20th.—At daylight a smart fire opened from our batteries, which was as briskly returned by the fort, town and batteries of the enemy on the glacis. The enemy threw several shells with great precision at our trenches in the forenoon. Lieutenant Groves of the artillery was killed in the mortar battery this day. He was a brave officer, and much lamented by all who knew him.

About three in the afternoon the enemy opened a fire which enfiladed our trench. The fire appeared to be from two guns, and but for the traverses we threw up in the night the post would not have been tenable. I had as narrow an escape this afternoon as I ever had in my life. A shot carried off a soldier's arm who was sitting in the bottom of the trench. I was using my endeavour to keep them as much as possible under cover, when a cannon shot grazed on the top of the trench, took the bearskin of my hat, tore it to pieces, and lodged in the parapet, burying itself nearly two feet in the side of the trench.

It was within half a foot of carrying away both Durant's legs; he was standing on the parapet, looking over at the enemy on the works of the town. It was a twelve-pound shot. This escape was a very providential one to us both, and a hearty shake of the hand with mutual congratulations followed. Had the enemy continued this enfilading fire we must have suffered exceedingly, as their shot completely raked the trench, and went through the traverses often. Fortunately they fired a few rounds and discontinued it, not knowing, as we concluded, the effect of their fire.

Brigadier MacRie commanded in the trenches this day, and at sunset Durant and myself, as the two senior officers in the Corps, went to him, and offered our services, with our Battalion, to storm some batteries of the enemy's, which lay to the left of the trenches, and to spike their guns if we found it impossible to drag them off, and which it appeared to us could be effected. Brigadier MacRie very handsomely thanked us, and told us that he should report our offers of service to the commander-in-chief, but it appeared to him to be a service that would be attended with severe loss, as their guns were all drawn up under the cover of fire from the ramparts, and therefore he thought that he could not with propriety allow us to make the attempt without the commander-in-chief's order.

About half-past seven the relief of the trenches arrived, and we moved out from the different angles and assembled by appointment in the rear of the grove near the village, and out of the usual range of the enemy's shot. Our battalion arrived in camp before nine, and we all dined with MacGregor, and passed a very jovial evening.

December 21st.—Breakfasted at headquarters this morning; met Fraser near the picquets, and returned with him to the general's tents. The commander-in-chief was pleased to express his approbation of Durant's and my own proposal to Brigadier MacRie last evening in the trenches, and which the brigadier had reported to his Excellency.

Passed an hour after breakfast in Colonel Lake's tent, with the Colonel, Menzies and Fraser. Went afterwards to the advanced picquets with Macan and Peyron to see the effect of our batteries this morning on the works; their fire was very effectual, and particularly that of the new battery directed principally against some defences which flanked our intended route to the breach.

This new battery was completed the last night, and consisted of three eighteen-pounders, of which my friend and brother prize agent, Hay, had the command; Hay kept up an almost incessant fire nearly all the day, and the cross fire of his right-hand gun, which alone bore immediately upon the breach, had great effect in breaching; his other two guns were entirely directed against some defences on the works. Several of the enemy's troopers came very near our picquet, and a horse was killed by a shot fired from one of the field pieces, which kept them at a more respectable distance; the trooper escaped.

A little before sun setting Shairpe and myself mounted our Arabs, and rode out in front of the line of picquets, and round the right flank of our encampment. An advanced sentry from one of the enemy's picquets was patrolling within half cannon shot distance of the flank, and we walked our horses quietly towards him; which the fellow observing, and seeing that we were unattended with any escort, came boldly towards us; he was elegantly mounted, his piece was slung over his shoulder, and he had a spear in his hand.

On approaching sufficiently near to speak he commenced his abuse, and, at the same time, prepared his piece; we determined to take a shot at him, and both drew our pistols, walking still towards him without noticing his salutation till we got pretty close, when we put spurs to our horses and pushed directly at him; he fired his piece, and the shot passed close to us; at the same moment, turning his horse, he made off towards the party to which he belonged.

I was alongside of him in a very short time, and at a distance not exceeding five yards fired directly in his face, but owing to the rate at which we were going (at speed) I missed him! Shairpe then went within a sword's length of him, and gave his fire, also without effect—by this time the picquet to which the soldier belonged became alarmed, and we saw a strong party of them mounted and galloping towards us, and we now thought it high time to move off. The man had depended on the speed of his horse, which was a beautiful animal, and none but an Arab could have gone near him.

The prospect of securing his horse it was, added to his uncommon insolence, which induced us to risk a shot with him, and though it ended without accident to us, we both agreed after it was over that it was a very unwise scheme of ours. About fifty of the enemy followed us down within range of shot of our picquets, but by keeping our horses in a smart canter we kept easily out of their way. The reliefs of the trenches were marching off as we reached the parade. I dined at the mess of the 12th with Shairpe this evening.

December 22nd.—Our corps was on picquet this morning, and after posting our advanced sentries and distributing the companies along the front for the protection of the lines, we got our breakfast about eleven o'clock. About twelve the commander-in-chief came to the centre picquet (where I was posted) to observe the effect of our fire on the breach. The enemy's fire of musketry at this time from the broken ground to the right of our trenches was exceedingly heavy, which his Excellency remarked, and asked if there was no mode of silencing them. I took this opportunity to before describe the nature of the ground in which the enemy were posted, and told the general that it was impossible our cannon shot could have the smallest effect, as the ravines where they were were so steep that the shot passed over them.

I then took the liberty of mentioning to his Excellency that from the village, a couple of howitzers, or *cohorns*, it appeared to me, when I was down at the post, could be used with great effect, as the shells would annoy them certainly, although they were quite secure from shot. An *aide-de-camp* was immediately despatched to the commandant of artillery, with orders to him to send down either a couple of howitzers or *cohorns*, which could be best spared, to the village in the rear of our trenches. A very heavy fire continued the whole of this day upon the breach and defences of the town, and we suspected that the storm would take place in the course of the day or night tomorrow.

My friend and ship-mate Captain Robinson of the engineers, who had been down reconnoitring in front, came into my tent on his way back to the lines, and in confidence assured me that the breach would be reported practicable with another day's firing from our batteries. Robinson remained and *tiffed* with me.

Many of the cavalry officers (who had very little else to do) came daily to lounge at the picquets, and to enquire "when the breach would be practicable," expressing their surprise at the "deal of battering it required"; few of these knowing gentry had ever been in a breach, at least not till it had been rendered easy of ascent by many hundreds going before them, and then when they could with ease and safety take their time for it, without an enemy to oppose them, or the risk of getting a broken head.

Several of the enemy approached our picquets at sun setting, and we mounted a squadron and detached them with a galloper upon the flank, to keep them at a more respectable distance; seven or eight shot were fired at them.

An incessant fire the whole of this day from both our breaching batteries. That of the three-gun battery in front of the centre picquet seemed to have very fine effect, and the defences came down in great style.

We were fully prepared in our arrangements for the storm, expecting it to take place in the course of the evening or night. No regular relief at the trenches took place this afternoon, and at sundown orders arrived for us to be under arms at night at ten o'clock without our battalion guns.

Soon after ten we began to assemble, and at eleven marched down to the attack; we formed (under cover of the night) in three columns, upon the left flank of the Grand Battery. Brigadier MacRie commanded the whole of the storming party, Captain Kelly the right column, and Major Ratcliffe the left, all under the directions of MacRie, who himself led the centre column to the breach.

The rising of the moon was the appointed signal for us to advance, and the cavalry in camp were to mount at the same time, for the protection of our lines. Captain Kelly was ordered to storm the enemy's batteries on the left of the breach with our right column, and Ratcliffe the guns on the right of the breach with the column he commanded, and an artillery officer prepared with a party carrying hammers and spikes accompanied each of the flanking columns to spike their guns if they could not possibly be brought off.

Between our batteries and the breach the ground was very much broken, and in the dark it was utterly impossible to preserve such distance and order as could have been wished; the troops were as silent as death on our approach, but we were no sooner discovered from the works than the whole face was completely illuminated by the enemy's cannon and musketry. The shot flew like hail, and many a gallant fellow dropped; it was, however, no check to us, and instead of returning a single shot we rushed on, with the bayonet, and gained the summit of the breach, in spite of the formidable resistance opposed to us and the obstinacy with which they disputed every inch of ground.

We immediately scoured the works of the Shah Burge, and were shortly in possession of the whole; about twenty minutes as sharp righting as was perhaps ever witnessed put us also in possession of all their batteries under the walls on the flanks of the breach. I was well aware that the tremendous fire they had kept up on us must have caused us great loss; for a very considerable time we were literally exposed to a shower of shot, and the blaze of cannon and musketry from the works was so very brilliant that we could plainly see the flanking columns closing with the enemy, although at a considerable distance from us. By twelve the enemy had all retired (those who escaped) into the fort and to those parts of the town under its fire, and almost all firing ceased.

On enquiring after the officers of my own corps, I was distressed to find that the 2nd had again suffered considerably; poor Bowyer was killed, and Forrest lost an arm and was otherwise dreadfully wounded; he appeared quite senseless and in a dying state. I found him lying at the foot of the breach, and Bowyer was shot a few paces only distant from it. In the breach I heard Anderdon's voice (my Bareilly friend). He had received a dreadful wound in his shoulder, and was almost fainting with loss of blood, and begging for assistance to be carried to camp, which we instantly procured him.

Near Anderdon lay Captain Young of the same corps (8th Infantry), a very intimate friend of mine; he had received a grape through his breast and was dying in horrid agonies, entreating those about him in a most distressing and earnest way to put him out of his misery. We sent him off in a litter, but he expired before he reached camp.

About twenty officers were killed and wounded in this assault. I, thank Providence, escaped with no further injury than some severe blows from splinters and stones thrown up by the cannon shot.

The only officers now left of our battalion out of eighteen were Hammond, MacGregor, Weston, Grant, Arbuthnot and myself; a more cruel slaughter in one battalion during three campaigns had perhaps seldom been known. We were all this night under arms, and the fort kept up a random fire upon us with very little effect except that of destroying the houses of the town. The shot from a seventy-pounder mounted on a high cavalier came frequently among us, and killed most of our men during the night. Not a moment's rest this night.

December 24th.—At daybreak this morning we discovered heaps the enemy lying killed and wounded in all directions around and among us. The proportion of wounded was very trifling to the amount of their killed.

We had no leisure for removing the dead, but the wounded were treated with much humanity by our surgeons. About six we advanced to endeavour to find a way from the Shah Burge (of which we were in complete possession, and our guards all regularly posted) and the town. Colonel Ball (my Lassuary friend) offered his services to reconnoitre in hopes of discovering the communication, and the colonel paid me the compliment to ask me to accompany him. We advanced with one hundred and sixty men, and the enemy from the town commenced a very galling fire upon us. We continued skirmishing with them, and they fell back to a gateway in their rear, which we plainly saw was the communication we were looking for.

We were planning the best mode to force it, when Colonel Ball, with whom I was then conversing, received a musket shot through his right breast; the shot after having gone through his breast entered the fleshy part of the right arm and passed out near the elbow. The party of the enemy from whose fire he fell were within thirty yards of us behind a parapet which covered them completely, but we quickly dislodged them.

The manner in which Colonel Ball fell and the blood streaming from his breast made me very apprehensive that he was mortally wounded. I ordered two grenadiers of the 8th to remain with him, and we rushed on and gained possession of the gateway. Brigadier MacRie was made acquainted with what we had done, and immediately on learning that Colonel Ball was severely wounded and that we had taken post at the gate which led into the heart of the town he advanced and joined us with a battalion of the 8th and one of the 15th Regiment, headed by two hundred men of the 76th and European Regiments and eighty men of the 22nd Flankers.

The enemy had suffered so much in the assault last night that they showed no very strong inclination to oppose any formidable resistance to us this morning; to do them justice, they undoubtedly fought very gallantly, and made a desperate resistance to our cost as well as their own.

We met with no serious resistance till we reached the Palace Gardens, which are within half-musket shot distance of the fort from the walls of which opened a smart and galling fire of grape and musketry. I was with Brigadier MacRie and Colonel Haldane at the head of the column; several men were shot around us, but we all escaped. I advanced with MacRie, for as prize agent I considered it a point of duty to be foremost in order to secure any property that may fall into our hands and prevent the soldiers plundering it.

This check near the Palace Gardens induced us to halt, and we withdrew the troops out of sight and posted them in the palace, and some were drawn up under the walls of the garden, which sheltered them from the musketry of the garrison and also prevented their being seen.

The enemy lost no time in bringing some guns to point in the direction of the palace, but the walls of the fort were so lofty, and we were so close under them, that they found it no easy matter to bring their artillery to bear on us, and almost every shot whistled over our heads, and made great havoc among the houses of the town.

There were many rooms in the palace nearly full of rose water; the soldiers, some of them, got hold of it, and came out highly perfumed, having thrown it at and over each other. We posted guards in all the different avenues leading to the palace and gardens to prevent a surprise; this was one of the sweetest spots I ever beheld. The palace itself was built of fine stone, very lofty and elegant, and had a most stylish appearance; it was supported within at many places with marble pillars of an immense size, and beautifully inlaid with cornelian, agate and various other kinds of valuable stones. The rooms were forty and fifty feet in height, and eighty feet long or upwards.

On the top of the palace was a reservoir of water, which supplied the fountains immediately in front of the building; any of which could instantly be set playing by drawing certain plugs. There were numerous fountains in every part of the gardens, which were very extensive and elegantly laid out. It contained ranges of myrtle and orange trees of the finest kind I ever saw; the oranges were hardly ripe, but the men helped themselves plentifully. The walks were all paved with the same kind of stone as the palace was built of. They were about thirty feet wide, all regularly laid out and kept in the highest possible condition.

The *rajah* was particularly fond of seeing and feeding fish in the ponds of his garden, and on going from one guard to another I met a soldier of the 22nd Foot with a very fine fish in his hand, just fresh from the water, and on enquiring where he had procured it and how, the answer was "With a sharp-pointed bayonet, sir; that's how I catch my fish," and then pointed out to me a pond about thirty feet square only in which were nearly as many soldiers sticking fish with their bayonets. They had, of course, been preserved, and were as thick in this place of confinement as they could possibly swim. We were told the *rajah* himself always fed them daily.

As soon as we had stationed the necessary guards in the vicinity of our post we began considering the best mode of gaining possession of the fort, which we had reason to believe could not long hold out, as the houses of the town enabled us to approach so near that we could easily beat them from the works with our musketry, and a few hours' bombardment, we concluded, would make the garrison too warm for them. A flag of truce was despatched to them from the Palace Gardens, but, unfortunately, just as the native officer who carried it approached sufficiently near to be heard from the works and a soldier of the enemy was preparing to communicate with him, a sergeant of the 76th Regiment from behind a building fired at the man on the ramparts, and they, of course, instantly returned it on the flag. The sergeant was not to blame; he knew nothing of what was going on, and had been sent down under cover of some ruins with a party to snipe at the enemy on the works.

This put an end to all prospect of treating, and the garrison continued a smart firing all the afternoon. We proposed to send to camp for a couple of twelve-pounders, and to attack the gates as soon as the dusk of the evening set in; the guns were accordingly sent for and arrangements made for the assault, but the former did not arrive till the relief came; it was then too late to effect it, and the commander-in-chief sent Menzies and Fraser down to us to give us notice that he had received information which gave him reason to think that there was a probability of the enemy evacuating the fort in the course of the night.

At eight this evening our battalion and one of the 4th were pushed on to the Palace Gardens, and Brigadier MacRie was relieved by Brigadier Sackville Brown. My old servant managed to find me out with a bottle of claret some cold meat, upon which Kerr, Lumsdaine and myself made a good meal on the ground, and felt much refreshed by it. We had been all the night and all day without a morsel to eat.

About ten at night Brigadier Brown assembled the commanding officers and staff of corps on duty, and made them acquainted with his intention to attack the fort by the gateway at daylight in the morning. A proportion of us laid down on the stones, and got a little sleep. I posted a sentry of my own company close to me, to give me immediate notice of the smallest alarm, and ordered that he should be relieved hourly.

December 25th.—About an hour before daybreak this morning we all paraded for the purpose of storming the gates of the fort.

A party was advanced to reconnoitre, but just as storming

we were prepared to move off an artilleryman came running to inform us that the place was evacuated. We went instantly down with two companies (the grenadiers of our regiment the senior corps) and about one hundred men of the 76th Foot.

The gates we found jarring open, and the garrison completely empty of troops.

I posted my grenadiers on the ramparts and with my own hands planted our battalion colours on the works at the principal flagstaff on which we found the *rajah's* standard still flying. At daybreak they were pleasantly surprised in camp by seeing our colours flying in the garrison. As soon as we had taken full possession I commenced and secured all the property in the place by posting guards at every store-house, magazine, etc. Some very fine horses were left by the enemy; we found them all standing at their picquets; a great deal of cattle belonging to their guns were also left, and was secured, and sent with the horses to camp, to be disposed of for the benefit of the army.

Captain Boyce of the 76th Foot, Captain Hay of the artillery, and myself, as prize agents, as soon as everything was secured without, commenced searching the most probable places for treasure, nor were we unsuccessful. In one of the buildings near the *rajah's* quarters we found three *lacs* of *rupees*. It was concealed in a vault, the communication to which was down a very dark, long, winding staircase, covered on the top with a flat board, so contrived that perhaps none but soldiers in pursuit of plunder would have discovered it. We instantly secured the treasure, and sent it with a guard to camp to be lodged in the Park for the present with the artillery, till we should be at leisure to divide it.

We found also large quantities of cotton, ghee and other valuable stores and pits containing, by the invoices buried on the top of them, nearly one hundred thousand *maunds* of wheat and other grain. (A *maund* is 80lbs.) Many granaries were also discovered in the town, and guards planted over them. There was also a great variety of linens, chintzes and valuable cloth; these were sent up to the lines to be immediately disposed of.

The different gates leading into the town were all guarded to prevent camp followers from getting in to plunder; hundreds of these scoundrels were disappointed of their aim by this mode of keeping them out. I was extremely anxious to see my wounded friends, Anderdon and Forrest, in the lines, and, mounting Lassuary, I galloped up to camp. Anderdon had received a dreadful sabre cut down his shoulder, and lay in a very precarious state, much weakened by loss of blood. Poor Forrest's left arm was taken off near his shoulder, and he had some very severe wounds in his head. He knew me, but was unable to speak. It was fortunate that so soon after the accident we were enabled to find him, though we had no hopes of his life.

At six this evening I mounted my horse and rode over the ground on which we charged the enemy on the 23rd. The slaughter among them was horrid, and they actually laid in heaps in their trenches and batteries. Nearly all their artillerymen were bayoneted at their guns, and they fought like brave fellows. The ground was become extremely offensive, and a general order was issued for the pioneers to be employed in burying the enemy's dead. They were covered up in their own trenches. Our loss on the 23 rd was very severe, but did not exceed what might have been expected from the nature of the attack, and under a very destructive fire from the ramparts of the town. At sunset I went to camp, and found that my servants had gone to the fort in search of me. Slept in my boat cloak, in MacGregor's tent.

December 26th.—Destroyed all our batteries today, took up all the platforms, and carried all the battering guns to camp, lodging those taken from the enemy on the 23rd safe in the garrison. We had altogether discovered in a store-room and in the fort three *lacs* of *rupees* and as many *maunds* of grain. The captured property was disposed of in camp this morning for the benefit of the army. The commander-in-chief came into the garrison this morning, and, calling me to him, desired me as prize agent to give orders that no grain should be carried out of garrison, and added that "we were near losing Ali Ghur owing to their having emptied all the granaries."

December 27th.—The commander-in-chief came into garrison this morning, and desired me to point out to him the arsenal and principal store-rooms in the garrison, all of which I had searched in quest of prize property, and knew their contents. The general left the garrison about twelve o'clock. Colonel Lake requested that I would come to camp in the evening, and dine at headquarters.

We were employed the greater part of this day in placing guards over the captured property, and in preventing the camp followers from making away with any part of it. Guards were placed at the different gates in order to prevent any being carried out, but we discovered them throwing it out at many places over the ramparts, and then saw them swim the ditch with it. Of a few we made severe examples, in order to deter the rest, but some of them lost their lives before it could be put a stop to. We delivered over the treasure found in the fort this day to the deputy field paymaster, and received his acknowledgments on behalf of the Army.

All loose property found in the town was sold in camp this afternoon, also a great deal of the cattle taken from the enemy. Colonel Browne received orders to commence immediately the repair of the breach and to cut away some gardens in the neighbourhood, which might afford shelter to an enemy, and of which we had availed ourselves during the siege. They were beautiful gardens, but we had destroyed them in a great measure by cutting the trees down to make picquets and for other uses in the batteries. Orange trees, mango trees and myrtles all went to wreck, and the enemy themselves destroyed several beautiful buildings in firing on us. Such is the unfortunate situation to which a country, the seat of war, is liable, and of which we had very many times been a witness.

At sunset I galloped to camp, dressed in the headquarter lines, and dined with the commander-in-chief. We passed a very pleasant evening, talking over the siege, and in pushing the bottle pretty rapidly, as was generally done at headquarters. All were in high spirits, and looked forward with pleasure to the approaching time for the attack of Bhirtpore, against which we were now marching.

CHAPTER 25

The Siege of Bhirtpore

December 28th.—The army marched this morning from Dieg, and encamped near the field of battle on the 13th of the last month. In the evening a party of us rode to the ground on which those gallant officers who fell in that action were buried, and near to which we ordered a tomb to be erected to their memory. Nothing could exceed our disgust and anger, on going to the spot, at finding that the graves of those unfortunate fellows had been opened, and their corpses lay strewn on the plain.

The infernal inhabitants, knowing that officers were buried on that spot, had, on our marching towards Muttrah, taken up the bodies and stripped them of the covering used on those occasions, and left them to be devoured by birds and jackals. We reported this to the officer left in command at Dieg, and entreated him to use his endeavours by offering a handsome reward to get hold of the merciless wretches who had thus disturbed the remains of our brave and lamented friends.

January 2nd.—1805. This morning the army arrived at Bhirtpore without anything materially occurring on the march from Dieg. All the cattle and public establishments employed in collecting materials to make fascines and gabions. The enemy appeared to be making every preparation to defend the place. The *rajah* sent *vakeels* (ambassadors) into camp, and it was reported that he offered a *crore* of *rupees* if the British troops would leave him unmolested.

The engineer and artillery officers employed reconnoitring the place, and a talk of breaking ground immediately. A report that Ameer Khan with a numerous body of Horse and some infantry and guns is marching towards Bhirtpore. His intentions he had carefully avoided making known. Holcar continued in great force near us, but would never risk anything decisive, even with our cavalry. The batteries were expected to be in readiness to open at furthest on the 4th.

January 4th.—Everything in readiness, and the guns being conveyed down to the batteries; they opened a tremendous fire this morning, and the fort commenced playing on our trenches and posts in advance. The wall was considerably shattered, and the shot seemed to have very good effect.

January 9th.—An almost incessant fire from our batteries from the 4th until this afternoon brought down the wall and defences, and the breach was apparently practicable; accordingly, about eight o'clock the storming party paraded for the assault, led by Colonel Maitland of the 75th Regiment. On the arrival of the party at the breach the ditch in front was found to contain a great depth of water; many of our gallant fellows, however, crossed, and every effort was made by both officers and men to mount the breach, but it was so excessively steep that it was not in the power of men to ascend it.

Under those unexpected and insurmountable obstacles, we were obliged to retreat, with the loss of many a gallant officer and soldier. Brigadier Maitland, who led the assault, and poor Wallace, his brigade-major, both fell. Lieutenants Glubb and Waterhouse were also killed, and Lieutenant Percival was killed during the assault, by a cannon shot, in the Grand Battery.

Killed.

Brigadier Maitland.
Captain Wallace, Major of Brigade.
Lieutenant Glubb.
Lieutenant Waterhouse.
Lieutenant Percival.

Wounded

Major Campbell.
Captain Cresswell.
Captain Hessman.
Captain Brutton.
Captain Welner.
Major Gregory.
Captain O'Donnell.
Captain Fletcher.
Lieutenant Crossgrove.
Lieutenant Byne.
Lieutenant Tully.
Lieutenant MacLaukland.
Lieutenant Mathewson.
Lieutenant Wood.
Lieutenant Hamilton.
Lieutenant Browne.
Lieutenant Latter.
Lieutenant Kerr.
Lieutenant Turnbull.
Lieutenant Shairpe.
Lieutenant Barker.
Lieutenant Tetcher.
Ensign Hatfield.

Many of the above wounded officers were struck by grape or cannon shot, and consequently several of them died of their wounds.

Our battalion (1st of the 2nd Regiment) was destined to scour the flank of the breach, and to storm the enemy's batteries; which was completely effected. We gained possession of their works and spiked or brought off all their guns, bayoneting and putting to death all who opposed us.

In the assault we lost, besides officers, upwards of two hundred Europeans killed and wounded, and nearly three hundred native soldiers.

January 13th.—Major-General Smith, with the 2nd Battalion of our regiment, 1st Battalion of the 9th Regiment, and 1st Battalion 14th, with about one hundred recovered Europeans, arrived today in camp, having performed a march of fifty miles in twenty-four hours.

January 16th.—This morning our new batteries opened. They consisted of two twenty-four-pounders, ten eighteens, six twelve and eight mortars, and continued an incessant fire.

January 21st.—A large and seemingly practicable breach was made. The enemy had found that they could not silence our fire from their guns and ramparts, and that by exposing them they risked having them dismounted, they used the precaution of drawing them behind the parapet, reserving them to fire on our storming party, and this precaution cost us dear. From the unfortunate affair of the 9th, the commander-in-chief was aware of the consequence of advancing a second time without ascertaining the breadth and depth of the ditch. Three broad ladders covered with hides had been prepared for pontoons, and the following gallant and dangerous stratagem was practised at noon this day by a *havildar* and three troopers of poor Middleton's Regiment (the 3rd Native Cavalry).

About three o'clock these brave fellows sallied out, disguised in the common dress of the country, from the neighbourhood of our trenches. As they went off a party of *sepoys* stationed for the purpose commenced a brisk fire of blank cartridges on these supposed deserters, in order to deceive the enemy, who were looking on from the walls. On reaching the brink of the ditch one of the troopers, as if by accident, fell from his horse, and whilst the others were employed in extricating him, the *havildar* (native sergeant) addressed the enemy on the works, begging to be shown the way into the place before they were shot by the English.

The enemy, falling completely into the snare, pointed out one of the town gates to him, and the moment the *havildar* saw the trooper mounted they put spurs to their horses, and galloped along the brink of the ditch, looked at the breach very minutely, and then, turning their horses upon the glacis, they returned at speed to our trenches. The enemy, finding out the stratagem, positively howled with rage, and commenced a fire of musketry from the works, but this gallant party came off unhurt, and received the promised reward of five hundred *rupees* each, and were promoted.

By their report there appeared no doubt but that the breach could be easily ascended. The depth of water in it, of course, they could know nothing about, but the breadth appeared to them not very considerable, and it was in consequence resolved to carry the whole of the troops intended for the storm into the trenches during the ensuing night, which was accordingly done.

At noon this day our troops advanced from the trenches. The parties employed were one hundred and fifty chosen men of the 76th Regiment, one hundred and twenty men of the 75th Regiment, one hundred of the Company's European Regiment, with the fifty remaining men of the 22nd Flankers; the latter, with Captain Lindsay and Lieutenant Manserg of that corps, were to lead the advance. The pontoons were carried by picked men of the different corps, and part of the 75th and 76th received their orders to continue a brisk fire, to drive the enemy from the parapet, whilst the pontoons were throwing over.

On the arrival of the party at the breach it was found, however, that the pontoons would not reach across by nearly twenty feet. The water during the night had been dammed up below the breach, and a very tall grenadier, jumping into it, showed it to be upwards of twelve feet deep. Notwithstanding these unlooked-for obstacles, several swam across the ditch, and some ascended the breach, but their ammunition was perfectly destroyed by the water, and most of these gallant fellows were shot.

Brigadier MacRie, who commanded, seeing the impossibility of taking any number over, so as to be able to act with effect, recalled the foremost, and retired to the trenches in good order, considering the destructive fire to which the party was exposed. The whole of the advance, delay at the breach, and retreat, was performed under a most galling fire of grape, canister and musketry, and many a gallant fellow was laid low. Of the 22nd Flankers only ten men escaped unhurt. The 75th Foot had one hundred and forty killed and wounded; the 76th about sixty, and the Company's European Regiment nearly eighty. Thirty officers were killed and wounded in this assault.

We were again compelled to leave many of our wounded behind, to be mutilated and murdered by the merciless and cruel swords of the enemy. During these transactions at the breach the whole of our cavalry attacked the confederates, who were encamped on the south side of the city, but could not bring them to anything decisive.

The flower of the European infantry of our army and the native troops engaged suffered severely on this day, and the unfortunate cause of the failure made it the more to be lamented. Sacrificing officers and men, who are at all times ready to lay their lives down for the service of their country, without even the possibility of success, is a most deplorable circumstance, and one not to be sufficiently regretted; every generous and feeling mind must think so.

Ameer Khan joined the enemy on the 15th. Six *lacs* of *rupees* sent to him in Bundlecund brought him from that province, but he carefully avoided and abstained from any depredations on his march from Gwalior to this place, and expected to gain terms for himself, in case Bhirtpore should have fallen, and at the same time he demanded twenty-eight *lacs* of the *rajah* before he would join, and in the skirmish with the cavalry on the 21st he kept aloof, but our failure caused him to close a bargain, and all his infantry and cavalry joined the *rajah* and Holcar on the 22nd. This added to their force at least eight thousand men, besides thirty-two pieces of ordnance.

The *rajah* took immediate advantage of Ameer Khan's joining him to attack one of our detachments from Agra, with grain, shot and various stores. This detachment consisted of a battalion of our *sepoys* and a regiment of cavalry, commanded by Welsh; it escorted a convey of twelve thousand bullocks, laden, and on approaching camp on the morning of the 23rd they were attacked by Ameer Khan, who, to show the prowess of his troops, by a *coup d'éclat*, marched his whole force against Welsh's party, which, consisting altogether of only fourteen hundred men, could not possibly cover so many bullocks and wagons when attacked by upwards of ten thousand of the enemy.

They, therefore, immediately took post in a village, covering part of their convoy; in this situation they were assailed on all sides, but the musketry and six-pounders attached to the two corps did such execution that the enemy were, notwithstanding their very great superiority of numbers, repeatedly repulsed. At length two of our guns were disabled, when the enemy's Horse and Foot made a charge, and possessed themselves of one part of the village. Such was the state of things at eight in the morning, and the enemy were waiting a reinforcement of artillery which Ameer Khan in person was bringing up.

Our men's ammunition and that of the gallopers and field pieces was nearly all expended when the 27th Dragoons and 1st Cavalry, which had been hurried out of camp, directed by the loud peals of cannon, appeared. The *sepoys* hailed the cloud of dust approaching on the plain by cheerful shouts, and exulting, as they thought, at the arrival of General Lake, sallied forth upon the enemy's guns without waiting the coming up of the reinforcement, and carried them all with the bayonet, whilst the Cavalry dashed at the cowardly fugitives and cut them up almost to a man. Ameer Khan's nephew, who commanded, threw off his armour, and, mixing with the crowd on foot, was ignominiously slain.

The plain was shortly covered with their killed and wounded; at least one thousand were left by them on the field, and those who remained completely dispersed.

The cavalry joined the *sepoys* near the village which had been the scene of action, showing the enemy's guns, the trophies of their valour, and fifty stands of colours were taken by them and the cavalry.

Part of the grain was recovered, but the enemy's Horse had so dipped their spears in the unoffending blood of the Binjarah bullocks that many of them were lost. It was, of course, a matter of pressing necessity to send another detachment to Agra, where a large supply of grain and stores was waiting for a convoy. At Agra also there were eighteen thousand rounds of eighteen-pound shot and five *lacs* of *rupees*.

January 24th.—This morning the 29th Light Dragoons, two corps of native cavalry and three battalions of *sepoys*, under Colonel Don, marched for Agra, and arrived in safety on the 26th, where they found fifty thousand bullocks and eight hundred wagons with shot, grain and military stores, all in readiness to start.

January 29th.—This morning Colonel Don's detachment, returning from Agra, fell in with the enemy about fifteen miles from our camp, but General Lake, who had intimation of their motions, advanced to Don's support with the remaining cavalry and two corps of infantry. The enemy's cavalry were very numerous, with seven battalions also of Ameer Khan's infantry; the latter, however, immediately returned to Bhirtpore on hearing of General Lake's approach.

Their Horse faintly attempted to assault the convoy, but with very little effect; and the commander-in-chief's party from camp joined them without either having sustained any loss. The detachment encamped at Orma, about half-way between Dieg and Bhirtpore, in the form of a square, and the enemy, who were extremely numerous, pitched all round them, as if ready to swallow them up in the morning.

January 30th.—This morning the detachment joined us in camp, without the loss of a man; the enemy endeavoured during the morning's march to harass them, by throwing rockets, etc., etc., but, finding all their attempts vain, retired to Bhirtpore, after suffering considerably by our grape from some guns which had been concealed in different spots in a wood, and by the swords and carbines of some dragoons of the flankers of regiments.

February 20th.—The siege had been carried on with its usual forms, etc., and nothing very material happened since the beginning of this month until this morning, when the enemy made a desperate attack on our trenches. They sallied out, sword in hand, and came on so rapidly that the foremost of them were in the works before our men were well on their legs. Our troops at first fell back from the part of the trenches immediately assaulted by the enemy, but owing to the gallant exertions of my friend Lumsdaine, who put himself at the head of the Europeans and *sepoys*, they instantly repossessed themselves of the works our troops had quitted, bayoneting every man of the enemy, whose temerity had carried them so forward on the occasion.

Lumsdaine followed the fugitives up to their very gates, and few of the enemy who formed the party for the sortie ever reached the garrison again. The party of Europeans with Lumsdaine belonged to the 76th Regiment, and the officer of that corps immediately attached to them did not show any inclination to lead on his men to retake the trench after our troops had been driven out; on the contrary, he kept aloof, and behaved in a very unbecoming manner, for which he was immediately obliged to quit the regiment.

At half-past three this afternoon we made a general attack on the town and batteries of the enemy. Colonel Don commanded the whole, and at the appointed hour ordered the men in the trenches, who were intended to assault the breach, to move out to the storm.

The Europeans (part of His Majesty's 75th and 76th Regiments) refused positively to quit the trenches. Don harangued them to no purpose, asking them if they wished to bring an everlasting stain upon their country and themselves, and telling them that such conduct was unprecedented and such as British soldiers were supposed incapable of; but all to no purpose, and they persisted in their own declaration that "they would not go to be slaughtered."

Colonel Don then addressed the two *sepoy* battalions on the left of the Europeans, and ordered them to follow him. They left the trenches in the best order, and were presently at the breach, where they struggled like gallant fellows to surmount difficulties which were perfectly impracticable; the ditch was like a sea, and so deep that the instant a soldier jumped in he went completely down, yet, notwithstanding, the colours of the 12th Regiment of Native Infantry, to the immortal honour of that corps, were planted on the top of the breach, but, owing to the tremendous ditch, the party with them could not be supported, and were in consequence almost to a man cut to pieces, or shot in the breach; every attempt was fruitless, and we were necessitated again to retire to the trenches with dreadful slaughter.

Poor Lumsdaine, who behaved so meritoriously in the morning, was killed by a cannon shot. Kerr of the 8th Native Infantry, and Lieutenant Stewart also fell, with a great many others. Twenty-three officers were killed and wounded; of the latter, many mortally.

On seeing the *sepoys* move out to the assault many of the veterans of the King's Infantry also accompanied their officers. Another officer of the 76th Foot was obliged to resign the service in consequence of his conduct this afternoon. At the same time that Colonel Don stormed the breach another attack commenced on one of the gateways, by a division of the Bombay Army, commanded by Colonel Taylor; they could not carry their guns up to the gate, as the sortie was completely cut off.

They then attempted to escalade the walls, but failed, and were beaten off with great loss. A third attack was also made on a village, possessed by the enemy, close under the walls of the town. This post was soon carried, the enemy were completely routed, and thirteen pieces of cannon brought off to our camp. Our loss of men, as well as officers, was exceedingly severe; this evening it was, however, rumoured that another assault would be made in the course of the day tomorrow.

February 21st.—As many of the officers as could be collected from the slaughter of yesterday were buried with military honours this morning, and their remains were attended by several whose fate it was to survive them but a very few hours, and whom, although then in perfect health, were laid low and carried themselves to their graves before the same hour of the following morning; but such is the chance of war and the soldier's fate and glory.

As soon as we had paid the last honours to our gallant countrymen, the line of European infantry was turned out, and the commander-in-chief most strongly expressed his disapprobation and disgust at their conduct yesterday, in refusing to move out to the attack; he told them they had lost all the fame which they had acquired on former occasions; the result of this address was that, to a man, they volunteered for another storm, and accordingly paraded at three o'clock, supported by our battalion (the 1st of the Old 2nd).

The whole moved off in the best possible spirits, and everything seemed to ensure us success; the point of attack was to be the bastion on the flank of the breach; we were fully prepared for a very bloody business, and the moment we arrived within reach of cannon shot they opened a very heavy cannonade, which was followed by showers of grape and musketry from the ramparts, which were lined by the enemy. Officers and men began to drop in great numbers.

On the arrival of the head of the column at the breach it was again unhappily checked by the very same obstacles which prevented our getting in before. In this situation, exposed to a tremendous fire, did we remain a full hour, struggling to get in, but all in vain. The slaughter during this period was dreadful, and our own battalion again had its share of it; we (the second line) lost upwards of one hundred and eighty men, and poor Colonel Hammond and Major Hawkes (of ours) were mortally wounded, and Arbuthnot shot through the back.

Grant, Weston and myself were now all that remained. Several officers and a great many men of the King's two regiments and the European regiments of the Company's were also killed and wounded. Poor Menzies, the commander-in-chief's *aide-de-camp*, Captain Corfield, 76th, Lieutenant Gowing of the artillery, Lieutenant Templeton of the 76th, and Hartley of the 15th were among the gallant fellows who fell, and we had about forty other officers killed and wounded in this attack. The Honourable Colonel Monson led the assault, which was our fourth storm of Bhirtpore! Our fatal loss amounted in the different attacks to at least one hundred officers and three thousand men killed and wounded.

We retired to our trenches, leaving too many of our wounded to be butchered by the enemy, who were thirsting after European blood, and not a soldier or officer of ours who fell into their hands escaped their merciless swords.

This morning we withdrew our guns from the different batteries, and the troops on duty in the trenches returned to the lines. All our eighteen-pound shot expended, and the guns with so much perpetual firing were, many of them, rendered perfectly useless; their vents were quite blown, and we found that it would be absolutely necessary to drill them afresh to make them at all serviceable. The British arms in this part of the world had never before experienced such a check and a loss so severe, and without carrying our point. We were summoned again this evening to attend the remains of more of our friends to their graves; some of the poor fellows were yesterday performing the same office to those who had fallen the day before, although they did not themselves live to see the setting of that sun.

Hammond of our battalion and Major Ratcliffe of the 12th died this evening of their wounds, as did also Captain Moreton of the Bombay Division, and several other officers, and we apprehended that Hawkes could not long survive. The ball went in at his right shoulder, passed through his body and out at the left shoulder.

February 23rd.—This evening we buried poor Hammond. The other officers who died yesterday were also interred with military honours. General Lake and all his staff attended Hammond's funeral; the other officers were buried in front of the lines of their respective corps. Captain Moreton's case was a very melancholy one; he lost his leg, and was also shot by a grape through the body; the anguish of his wounds were so cruel that he prevailed on a servant to carry him his pistols, with one of which he shot himself, but not effectually, and in this horrid state, poor fellow, he lived nearly one whole day and then expired, in agonies too shocking to be described. Moreton was a gallant, fine young man, and had been distinguished for his manly, intrepid conduct on many occasions.

March 3rd.—We remained since the 23rd of last month waiting the arrival of shot and stores. The time was principally employed in collecting fresh materials for new batteries, and in reconnoitring the place, for the purpose of fixing on a spot for another attack. The 2nd Battalion of the 8th Native Infantry and the Bombay Grenadiers' Battalion marched this morning to Dieg, for some supplies which they had prepared there. Two more officers died today of their wounds.

March 5th.—Our battalion, with one of the Bombay Regiments of Infantry and the 4th and 6th Regiments of Native Cavalry, marched this morning from camp, in order to reinforce the detachment sent to Dieg, and which it was supposed would be attacked on its route back. This party arrived at Dieg about ten p.m., and encamped near the fort, on the ground upon which we fought the battle of the 13th. Holcar's and Ameer Khan's cavalry constantly hovered round the detachment during its march, and many men and horses of both parties were shot in skirmishing. Our gallopers in the rear were open the greater part of the morning, and by their fire the enemy were kept at a pretty good distance.

March 6th.—This morning at five the convoy marched from Dieg, escorted by four corps of infantry and two regiments of cavalry. It consisted of seven thousand bullocks, laden, and about as many hundred wagons, containing eighteen and twenty-four pound shot, grain and stores of various kinds. Arrived at its ground about eleven o'clock, and encamped about half-way between Dieg and Bhirtpore, at no great distance from the town of Wier, where the *rajah* had a strong party.

March 7th.—The enemy's cavalry continued to harass the picquets all the night, but were cautious of risking anything serious.

The Dieg detachment with its convoy all reached before camp in safety this morning, and with the loss only of a very few men. We had a report that Ameer Khan, who left this quarter soon after our last failure and crossed into the Dewaub, had again retraced his steps across the Ganges, with General Smith and the cavalry at his heels. Ameer Khan was said to be marching towards Seerdhanah, the capital of the Begum (Queen) Samereau, very probably in expectation of her joining him against us; and her late conduct gave us some cause to be apprehensive that he would not be disappointed; it had always appeared suspicious, and her battalions of infantry and guns would prove a very valuable reinforcement to the rebels in Rohilcund, to which quarter it was imagined Ameer Khan would direct his course. Thornhill wrote me today from Bareilly that the rebels had drawn off from that quarter.

March 9th.—An overland despatch brought us the very pleasant information of General Lake being made a peer, no news later than September. It was said at headquarters that, in consequence of the severe loss sustained by our regiment (the 2nd) in officers and men that it would be ordered down the country immediately after the campaign.

March 12th.—Intelligence reached our camp today of General Smith having come up with Ameer Khan near a place called Affzul Ghur that an indecisive action took place; all the enemy's cavalry escaped very leisurely, and about two hundred only of their infantry were cut up.

In camp we had everything in a state of great forwardness for another attack. Six eighteen-pounders arrived this morning from Muttrah; gabions, fascines, etc., daily making for our new batteries.

March 13th.—Today we received accounts that Ameer Khan had destroyed the cantonments of Chandowsy, and the town was ransomed at half a *lac* of *rupees*; this happened on the 6th. General Smith was encamped on the 5th at Marahabad; had he advanced immediately the town and cantonments would have been saved, or the enemy been forced to another action.

March 15th.—This morning our battalion, with one of the 15th Regiment, a Bombay corps and the cavalry, marched with all the captured guns, sick and wounded officers and men for Agra.

Ameer Khan, by the last account of him, had altered his route, and instead of the Ganges he was reported to be moving again towards Rampoor, in Rohilcund.

A salute was fired this morning in camp, in honour of General Lake, now Lord Lake, Baron Delhi and Lassuary.

The *rajah*, who had heard the salute and found out the occasion, sent in his congratulations to the general. The commander-in-chief returned a polite reply, and told him (the *rajah*) that he had made a gallant defence, but that "his fort must be taken."

March 20th.—This day we received accounts that the enemy had recrossed the Jumnah, from Rohilcund; that part of his force was marching in the direction of Dieg. One account stated that some columns of his Horse had gone down the banks of the Jumnah, for the purpose of plundering the country there.

Received a letter today from Young, whose corps formed part of General Smith's Detachment. They were encamped at Ali Ghur on the 9th.

March 21st.—This day the detachment, with guns, stores and grain, marched from Agra. It was rumoured in camp today that the *Nawab* of Lucknow had taken the field, with a strong force and ninety piece of cannon, with which he remains encamped a few miles from Lucknow. I received a letter from Thornhill telling me that in consequence of Ameer Khan having quitted Rohilcund, they had all left the gaol (their post in times of danger) and taken again to their houses. They had been shut up in this garrison for nearly a month. Intelligence reached us today of the arrival of a fleet from England at Madras, they sailed in

September.

Ameer Khan's whole force again in this neighbourhood, and General Smith with the cavalry daily expected to join us again, after his wondrous feats in Rohilcund.

March 22nd.—This morning the detachment arrived from Agra, with one eighteen-pounder and about fifteen thousand rounds of 18 lb. shot. Fascines and gabions making, and it was expected that the siege would recommence immediately; and another point of attack fixed on. Wrote a private letter to Colonel Lake this morning regarding prize affairs. Received letters from Thornhill and Wemyss. General Smith and the cavalry came into camp today, not, we imagined, very proud of his services, or remarkably well received on that account.

March 30th.—Nothing material occurred since the 22nd till this day. The picquets received orders to admit the *rajah's vakeel* (messenger), and he was accordingly received in camp this morning; he remained some hours at headquarters, but the intention of his visit, or the result of his conference with the commander-in-chief, was kept perfectly secret.

The engineer officers still employed making fascines and gabions, and every warlike preparation for another attack going on.

March 31st.—The *vakeel* was again at our camp early this morning, and from terms which he proposed it was generally conjectured that a peace would be concluded with him. After so much bloodshed, and the loss of so many gallant officers and men, it was expected that nothing short of giving up possession of the place would be attended to. But, situated as we were, all our battering guns rendered useless nearly, by continual and almost incessant firing, our heavy shot completely expended, nearly one-third of our officers and men killed and wounded (the infantry, for the cavalry were never within range of the shot), and those who remained, worn out almost by constant severe duty; under all these calamities, a peace, an honourable one, was to us an object desirable to be obtained.

Our troops had now, for five complete months, been exposed continually to all the hardships and fatigues attending sieges in this fatal climate; constantly distressed by the scorching beams of a vertical sun in the trenches by day, and watching with that vigilance necessary to be observed before an enemy by night. None murmured, and I do believe no soldiers under the heavens could have gone through five months of perilous and arduous service with more cheerfulness and alacrity than did the Indian Army on this occasion, and General Lake very often did them the honour to tell them so.

April 5th.—This morning Colonel Don and the reserve marched out of camp to the southward, imagined towards Rampoorah, to bring up a part of the Bombay Division, left with treasure. The *vakeel* still passing to and from our camp; the result still very dubious. The points in dispute said to be fifty *lacs* of *rupees* demanded by Lord Lake on the part of Government (not on that of the army, I am sorry to say!) and which the *rajah* vows his inability to pay.

The carriages in the Park ordered to be loaded, and a talk of changing ground to take up a fresh position for another attack! We received intelligence that Royall had come up with Hernaut Sing, a rebel, near Dholepore, whom he completely defeated, took all his guns, ammunition, colours and baggage, and bayoneted all who fell into his hands.

April 7th.—The army shifted ground this morning, and took up a fresh position, and another attack seemed certain. The treaty, however, still on foot. The weather daily growing hotter, and the sun more and more destructive, so that we may calculate upon the certain loss of many of us from its effects, exposed to it as we are in the trenches, as well as by the enemy's shot. Guns and ammunition expected immediately from Allahabad. All above that station we had expended; the magazines at Cawnpore, Futty Ghur, and Agra entirely emptied of battering guns and heavy shot.

Scindiah, having heard of our failures at Bhirtpore, and of

the shattered state of our Army, thought it a very favourable opportunity to break his treaty, and join the confederacy against us. We were surprised to hear of him advancing towards us with an immense army, and one hundred and eighty pieces of heavy artillery!

He was drawing towards the country of our staunch but weak ally, the Ranah of Gohud, who without our assistance, can never oppose Scindiah in the field. Scindiah had not declared war against us, but the moment he infringes on the Ranah's territory it will, of course, be considered an open declaration, and we must expect a further effusion of blood before we quit the field; even after the fall of this place, before which so many gallant fellows have fallen, but such is the sad concomitant of war, and the soldier's fate and glory.

The accounts of Scindiah's movements will of course be an additional inducement to General Lord Lake to endeavour to come to an honourable reconciliation with. the *rajah* here.

April 10th.—This day it was much believed in our camp that a peace would immediately be concluded with the *rajah*. The report was that terms had actually been agreed on, and the *rajah's* son was hourly expected in camp, to remain as a hostage till they shall be fulfilled. Several thousand cattle left our camp this evening for supplies from Dieg, and we expect to march instantly in pursuit of that artful scoundrel Scindiah, who had now entered the Ranah's country, and was in the neighbourhood of Narwar, or Gwalior.

Received a letter from Thornhill, telling me of his having marched with Colonel Hawkins in quest of some rebel chiefs in Rohilcund (his district). The collector, it appears, also accompanies him. The country in that quarter still in a very unsettled, turbulent state, the Rohillas continuing very refractory.

April 14th.—Our picquets were now reduced, and the outposts all withdrawn. I was brigade major of the day, with Brigadier Need, who left me to post the picquets, and returned to the lines.

At sunset I waited on the brigadier, and received his instructions to carry out an inline picquet from any corps I thought proper, and post it midway between a high village in front and the left picquet of the reserve. Galloped down to the lines of our corps (the 2nd) and took out a company with me! posted them, and gave the officer in command his orders. The detachment which marched on the 11th to Agra daily expected again to join us, and we positively march immediately to give Scindiah battle.

All our heavy guns and stores sent into Agra, in order that our movement towards Scindiah may not be retarded.

The weather getting dreadfully hot, and many officers left the army on sick certificates. I was told by the surgeons that no one's health was more likely to suffer, or their lives be more endangered by the approaching hot season than my own, and they offered to furnish me with certificates, and recommended me to go into cantonments; but I made known my determination to them to take my chance, and not to quit the army on any earthly consideration.

Dined at headquarters this evening, and a battle with Scindiah was all the rage.

Lord Lake introduced me himself to General Smith, and General Doudeswell, and to General Jones, of the Bombay Division (commanding). His Excellency lamented that my prospects in the way of prize money were altered so much for the worse, and told me that I must content myself with the honour that had been done me by the army at large in appointing me their prize agent.

April 18th.—This morning Mercer, Wood and Metcalfe passed our tents on their way into the town to pay the *rajah* a visit. It was a deep scheme sending Wood with the party, as, being an engineer officer, he would have a fine opportunity of observing on the gates, ditch, etc., and we were told that the howdah on which Wood rode unfortunately got loose at the gate, and the party was detained at if a considerable time, whilst the servants were setting the *howdah* to rights!

April 19th.—Mercer and his party were received in great state by the *rajah* yesterday. Tents were pitched, and great preparations made for their reception. The *rajah* made a present of a fine elephant to Mercer, and some horses to Wood and Metcalfe.

The *rajah's* son continued as a hostage in our camp, and is to accompany us if the engagements are not fulfilled before we march. Our detention here supposed to be occasioned on account of the *rajah* not paying us the stipulated sum, in doing which he seems very backward, and constantly making various excuses of inability, etc. Young dined at Anderdon's tent with me this evening.

April 20th.—This morning was excessively hot, and a quarter-master of dragoons dropped dead from the effects of the sun. Everything settled with the *rajah*.

Dined at headquarters this evening. We had a very large party there, and all in full expectation of soon having a brush with Scindiah.

CHAPTER 25

In Pursuit of Scindiah

April 21st.—Camp near Cazzoovy. The army marched this morning, agreeable to yesterday's orders. Owing to the space left for corps composing the Agra detachment, we had a very considerable break in the line in the left wing of the army at marching off; it was, however, soon remedied after the corps in the rear got in motion. Precautions had not been taken to close the line to the marching flank.

The country over which we marched this morning was completely destitute of every kind of forage; it had been completely destroyed during the long siege (nearly four months since we arrived before Bhirtpore). The numerous bodies of the enemy's horse had devoured almost every blade of grass; hardly a vestige of any kind of forage remained! The trees and bushes had been destroyed to furnish materials for carrying on the siege, and the boughs had all been lopped off for the elephants and camels of either army. Not a more melancholy sight than the country for many miles around Bhirtpore afforded, cannot well be conceived. We arrived at our ground about ten. An order was issued requesting commanding officers of wings to give particular injunctions to the different brigades to have the tents struck in time, loaded, and ready to move off at assembly beating.

The 2nd Battalion 15th (of our brigade) to relieve the weekly guards and orderlies tomorrow.

April 22nd.—We marched this morning precisely in the same order as yesterday, and came to our ground about nine o'clock.

As brigade major of the day I accompanied the general officer round the camp, and assisted in posting the different picquets and guards in front for its protection. It was a ride of nearly six miles round the encampment, at the different picquets, and we tried our Arabs handsomely in visiting the posts. The orderly dragoons which accompanied us could not come near us.

Brigadier Brown was the general officer today, and he was mounted on an elegant good leaped Arab, and, as he himself told me afterwards, he saw that I was well mounted, and was therefore desirous to see what I could do with him. I rode Lassuary, and some banks which we had occasion to cross in going our round proved not too high for us, though they at length caused the Brigadier to pull up. Brown was a cavalry officer, and had been reckoned a crack rider, but he had never rode a fox chase in a deep, strong country, at least so I suspected. It was twelve o'clock when we went to headquarters to report the picquets posted. The commander-in-chief was standing at his sleeping tent door, and expressed himself in high terms on the appearance of my horse, which had long been in his family; first the property of Campbell, the quarter-master-general, who was killed on his back by a cannon shot at the Battle of Lassuary, and latterly Wemyss.

Lord Lake said that he thought him one of the highest bred Arabs he had ever seen. In our gallop this morning my sword flew out of its scabbard, but an orderly in the rear by accident saw it, and brought it to me. We encamped today with the village of Kenwa on our right: this place we destroyed the last campaign, in consequence of some of our soldiers discovering many bodies of Europeans who had been recently murdered by the villagers, and on that occasion many of them fell victims to the rage of the soldiers, and it appears to have been but little frequented since.

April 23rd.—Camp at Rubass (Rupbas). The army marched this morning by the right; and the Bombay column by the left.

I came up with the brigadier of the day (Brown) in command of the rearguard; the roads today were excessively sandy, and the baggage in consequence moved very slowly indeed. We were frequently obliged to call parties of the men to assist the wheeled carriages in the deepest sand. The wind today literally blew flames. In passing back to give some orders in the rear, 1 observed in the long grass a cart laden with hampers of wine and other necessaries, belonging to an officer. The cart had stuck in the sand, and the servants, to save the bullocks, had taken them off, and left the rest at the mercy of plunderers.

I had a party of a dozen troopers with me, one of whom I dispatched in search of one of the company's empty grain carts, and with the assistance of some villagers the things were soon shifted, and I sent them under charge of a trooper to be delivered to the officer who owned them, and from whom I received every polite acknowledgment, as the trooper had told him the manner in which we fell in with his good things. We were out with the rearguard nearly the whole of this day, and had, every soul of us, the skin completely peeled from our faces.

Went with the brigadier to report to the commander-in-chief. We observed some villages blazing as we passed on with the rearguard, and the following reprimand appeared in general orders this evening:

> The Right Honourable the commander-in-chief has beheld with equal mortification and displeasure the outrages committed today by some of the troops and followers of the army. His Lordship, in order to prevent a recurrence of behaviour so disgraceful to the army, and so pernicious in its effects, has directed the safeguards in the different villages instantly to put to death any person, whether European or native, who shall be caught plundering or offering any violence to the persons or property of the inhabitants, and should any person be seized, and upon enquiry shall be found guilty of setting fire to houses, and plundering, he shall be immediately hanged.
>
> Commanding officers of wings and divisions were directed to order the troops under their respective commands to be pa-

raded at sunset, and to have the above orders explained to them in the fullest manner,, and at the same time to enforce strict obedience.

The general officer of the day ordered always to give particular injunctions to the picquets not to allow any European soldier to pass without a written pass from the commanding officer of his corps.

The whole line was under arms this evening a quarter before sunset, and the General Orders were fully explained to the men.

April 24th.—We marched this morning, the Bengal column by the right, and the Bombay column by the left. Passed over the ground today on which we frequently hog hunted and shot, the last campaign, on our march towards Holcar after the Battle of Lassuary.

Several hogs and deer were killed this morning on the line of march. About nine we cleared the pass of Rhemidah, and encamped with the hills in our rear. The Bombay line faced inwards to the hills, whilst the front was preserved by the Bengal Army. The sun and wind excessively hot today before we arrived at our ground, and I began to feel the return of the pain of my side. Inglis gave me medicine, and blamed me much for having marched with the army from Bhirtpore. We heard today that Scindiah, with his troops and guns, is waiting our arrival on the banks of the Chumbill, towards which we are moving with as much expedition as the season will admit.

We hope to have one glorious day with him ere many pass over our heads; most sincerely did I pray for health to keep the field and to do my duty.

April 25th.—Camp at Rattary. We had some confusion in marching off this morning. The corps to the right of the European regiment countermarched in order to gain the road. This brought the column of cavalry, which was moving parallel to us, close upon our reverse flank, and into the thickest of our baggage. The cavalry, being near us, I rode to the 8th Dragoons and had a *Coze* with Young for a mile on the march. The season of the year obliged us to make short marches, to save the European soldiers, who began, notwithstanding, to drop off. We came to our ground today soon after nine, the weather was parching hot.

A fine friendly tree in front of our brigade afforded shelter to a great number of officers, who flocked to it till their tents were pitched, but there was no shelter against the hot blasts of wind, which were dreadfully severe today. A private of the 75th shot himself just before the corps left its ground this morning. Did not quit my tent this day.

April 26th.—Camp near Parbati. We marched this morning in the order directed yesterday, with the baggage between the columns. This morning we came upon the road we took in our route from the Grand Army to besiege Gwalior, the last campaign, and soon after daybreak crossed the sandy bed of a river which I perfectly recollect passing on that occasion. It was generally said today that Scindiah was encamped in what he considers an impregnable position on the banks of the Chumbill, but of that he may be a better judge by waiting our arrival. We shall instantly attack him, no doubt, and though some must fall, still the result no one doubts.

The burning sands over which we marched this morning seemed greatly to distress the European soldiers, and I remarked an increased number of elephants laden with them. We arrived at our ground about nine o'clock. In consequence of Brigadier Ashe being appointed to command our brigade, his tents were pitched with us today.

April 27th.—The army marched this morning at the same hour as yesterday.

Brigadier Ashe was one of my Gwalior friends, and a great favourite of Brigadier White's; he dined last evening at headquarters, and His Lordship requested that the brigadier would desire me to accompany him in all his visits to Headquarters without a further invitation. About seven this morning we came in sight of some mountains on the banks of the Chumbill, which we remarked on our route to Gwalior. At nine we encamped about three miles from the fort of Dholepore.

The weather was excessively hot indeed, and it was with great difficulty that we got the men to pass the numerous wells on the march containing stagnant water, which would have proved the death of many had they been suffered to drink. We encamped with some fine mango groves on our right flank, into which the European corps were sent by way of shelter from the extreme heat of the sun. We marched over a great deal of ploughed land to get from the road to our lines, and the soldiers, as well as the cattle, of every description were dreadfully fatigued. Brigadier Ashe's tent, going on elephants, was generally one of the first up in the lines, and we always got from the sun and had our breakfast among the first, after which we usually took a bathe and went to rest.

Brigadier Ashe and a large party dined with me this evening, and it was very late before we broke up.

April 29th.—The cavalry and reserve marched at four, towards the river Chumbill, and our wing (the left) got orders to hold itself in readiness to march at a moment's notice. I was brigade major of the day, and at sunrise Brigadier Simpson and myself mounted, and proceeded to post the picquets. Four pairs of boots came safe to me this morning, which set me completely up again; they were from Calcutta, and uncommonly fine.

April 30th.—This morning at five o'clock our wing (the left of the army) marched by the right.

Owing to the stillness of the morning we were completely buried in the dust occasioned by the movement of the line. Soon after daybreak we passed the mountains leading down to the Chumbill, and at eight o'clock entered the ravines precisely at the same place we did on our march to Gwalior. Before ten we encamped on a part of the bed of the Chumbill River, and close upon the water's edge. The commander-in-chief, with the cavalry and reserve, left the ground we encamped on, and crossed the river this morning; a great deal of their baggage was not yet off the ground.

The sands were so deep that the cattle could not, without extreme labour, drag the carriages through it, and which prevented the party in advance from crossing yesterday. Nearly the whole of the men of our wing off duty were stripped and bathing in the Chumbill within a few minutes after our arrival. The elephants, camels, and the poor cattle of every description seemed truly to enjoy the luxury of the water.

Brigadier Ashe and myself dined with General Doudeswell, and I think the evening was as oppressive and dreadfully hot as anything I had ever experienced. Not one of us ate a mouthful of dinner, but the general's claret had better custom. During dinner a letter came in from Lord Lake to General Doudeswell, mentioning that Holcar's principal *sirdar* and chief advisor, Bawany Sunker, might probably arrive in our camp tonight or join us in the morning, and it was requested that every politeness may be shewn him. His Lordship in his note also mentioned to General Doudeswell that he had receive positive information that Scindiah had commenced his retreat, and with Ameer Khan was rapidly retiring towards Ougene.

This may make a serious difference in our future movements, and we began to talk again of returning to cantonments if Scindiah continues his retreat and declines fighting us. The determined manner in which we were advancing seems to have been too much for Scindiah's nerves.

May 1st.—Camp at Jettore. This morning at five we marched by the left, the 76th leading the column. We were across the river by six o'clock, and the wing proceeded through the ravines with very little delay, leaving a battalion to come up in the rear of the Park and baggage. The steep part of the ravines, where poor Morris of the artillery and myself laboured so hard to get up our brigade guns on our march to Gwalior, was now rendered quite easy of ascent by the pioneers, who had been some days employed levelling it. The battalion guns of the wing kept their ground exceedingly well, and cleared the ravines in their stations without causing the least detention to the line.

About eight we met some officers of the Bundlecund detachment, which had received orders to join us on the banks of the Chumbill. Colonel Martindale, an excellent officer, was in command of the detachment. Before nine o'clock we saw the encampment of the cavalry and reserve, with His Lordship, and soon after we encamped about a mile from them, with a high village in the centre of the wing.

Owing to the misconduct of the brigade quarter-master, our lines were not marked out when we arrived, and great confusion ensued. The encampment among broken ground and ravines, but no better offered so near the banks of the Chumbill. Brigadier Ashe's ground, and my own (for our tents) was amidst a grove of thistles, and General Doudeswell, close in our rear, was in the same predicament.

May 3rd.—I was most agreeably surprised at sunset this evening by a visit from my friend and shipmate, Ramus, who came from Martindale's camp to see me. We had not met since our first separation at Dinapore in 1801. I had a great regard for Ramus, as well on his account as on that of his amiable relations, and was much concerned to find how considerably he had involved himself. I was assured that seven thousand pounds would not pay his debts; and this he told me himself lamenting at the same time, with the tear in his eye, that chance should have separated us.

Ramus lived with me entirely the first year nearly of our arrival in India; he was then quite a lad, and I managed all his matters for him, and no doubt could have prevented his present unfortunate situation had we remained together. This money, it appeared, had been all spent in Arab horses and claret! Feeling as a brother for Ramus, I was exceedingly distressed at his embarrassment, from which it appears he never can clear himself. This is one of the many instances of the ill consequences of sending lads too young to India without an advisor.

May 4th.—Walked my Arab quietly this morning to Martindale's camp, and saw his line under arms. The corps, compared to ours, appeared uncommonly strong; they had seen no service, and one battalion, in point of strength, nearly equalled two of ours. The dress of the men also set them off much; their clothes had been worn only on parade duties, whilst our men's regimentals had been soiled with gunpowder and dirt in the trenches, to which they had been accustomed without intermission for the last five months. Nor were they a little proud of their rags and tatters, and assured their smarter friends that they wore their fighting coats.

May 6th.—This morning Brigadier Ashe and myself breakfasted with Lord Lake, and we were asked why we did not come more frequently; the severity of the weather was thought a very sufficient excuse. We sat till nearly ten o'clock. Called on my way home on Young, whose lines were near headquarters.

The sun and wind was scorching today and the road from our camp to Lord Lake's led up the bed of a dry river, on the sands of which the sunbeams were so powerful and the glare so bad that it nearly took one's sight away for the time. Engaged to dine at headquarters tomorrow. Received a letter from Colonel Lake soon after I got home offering me an appointment on MacGregor's promotion.

Accounts reached us today of poor Christie's death, on the banks of the Jumnah, where he was employed with his corps. I had experienced much kindness from Christie, and had a sincere regard for him. As soon as accounts of his death reached me I went to Butler's tent in the Park, and proposed to him immediately to set a subscription on foot for Mrs. Christie. Butler was also a particular friend of Christie's, and we drew out a paper and immediately sent it in circulation.

The number of sick in our brigade daily increasing, nearly fifty were returned to me unfit for duty, in addition to the number of the last week.

May 7th.—Ramus and Grant passed the day with me at my tent. The weather dreadfully hot, and I was on my couch the greater part of the morning.

In the evening Brigadier Ashe and myself went to dine at headquarters. We met in the audience tent our old friend the Prince of Gohud, who had just arrived to pay Lord Lake a visit. His Highness remained till dinner was announced, and then retired to his own camp. During the dinner I unavoidably drank too many glasses of claret, and a certain great personage remarked to me across the table that it was "hard going." As usual at headquarters, we passed a very jolly evening, and a great deal of wine was drank.

I returned with Dickens (General Doudeswell's major of brigade, a very fine young man, Captain in the 34th Foot) on his little elephant. We rode on a pad, and in going up and down the steep ravines in the road to our camp we found we had too much wine to sit steady, but managed to hold each other on, and to get home without falling.

May 8th.—This morning my friend, Brigadier White, arrived from Gwalior, on a visit to the commander-in-chief, and I was truly rejoiced to meet him. His four horses were picketed at my tent, and he passed the morning with me, and returned in the evening to dine with Lord Lake. At noon today we had a complete hurricane, and a slight shower of rain which accompanied it afforded us a momentary relief by somewhat cooling the atmosphere.

Many officers' and privates' tents were scattered upon the plain by the violence of the wind. Anderdon came in this morning in charge of some cadets from the camp at Dholepore; many of them appeared fine lads, and may truly be said to have all their troubles before them.

May 11th.—Visited several of my friends of the 18th, my old corps, some of whom I had not met for many years. The day was intensely hot, and I was by no means well. In the dusk of the evening I mounted, with my groom and a servant, all armed, to return to camp. We had to pass through many very deep ravines, and several murders had been committed in the neighbourhood of the camp, which rendered our ride not the most agreeable, as we were liable to be surprised and struck from our horses, owing to the deep narrow tracks we had to pass.

I borrowed Ramus's pistols, and we rode with one cocked in each of our hands; besides the risk of meeting with *banditti*, the ravines on each side of the paths at many places were so steep that it was by no means pleasant travelling in the dark, and I was very well pleased to find myself snug in our camp about nine o'clock. We missed our road, and returned by a very circuitous route.

May 12th.—The weather intensely hot in our camp, and the officers who came to my tent to receive their orders in the heat of the day were frequently almost exhausted on their arrival, so distressingly hot was the wind and sun.

The thermometer considerably above one hundred and ten. Officers and men daily falling sick in great numbers; it was not without the greatest care and hardly ever quitting my tent unless on duty, that I continued to get on without being laid up.

May 15th.—Wemyss galloped over from Bowey's detachment at Dholepore, took a hasty breakfast with me, and went immediately to headquarters; left his Arab at my tent, and rode to the headquarter lines on my pony. Wemyss was on his collections, and Bowey's detachment was aiding him; without a military force to assist, the collectors in this part of the country would make a sorry hand of it, as no man would pay his quota but at the point of the bayonet!

A captain of the 76th and two lieutenants of the 15th Regiment (of our brigade) reported sick to me this morning, and the number of men daily increasing. The weather so intensely hot as to make severe impressions on the constitutions even of the strongest natives, and to that of Europeans it was considered exceedingly destructive.

May 16th.—Forrest, of our battalion, who lost an arm in storming Dieg, appointed fort adjutant and barrack master at Agra. No fresh accounts from Scindiah's camp, and all talk of the return of the army to cantonments at an end, though not the less likely to happen on that account.

May 17th.—Did not move out this morning. The sun, half an hour after it had risen, was so hot that it was scarcely to be borne, and none left their tents but on indispensible duty.

May 23rd.—Rode through the ravines upon the left of our lines, f the and away about five miles in front, with Colonel Lake. The morning was particularly cloudy and cool com- pared to any we had lately experienced. Breakfasted at Lord Lake's; sent for my clothes and dressed in Colonel Lake's tent. Remained at headquarters till nearly twelve. *Tiffed* with M., where there was a gambling party, and some very high play. Ridge, Peyron and a large party of cavalry officers dined with me this evening. The brigadier was also of the party.

May 24th.—This morning I took my usual ride to inspect the picquets and guards of the brigade, and proposed to the brigadier to reduce them by day, on account of the number falling sick. Brigadier Ashe desired me to make any alteration I may think requisite, and we withdrew most of the subaltern (European) officers, and reduced their guard to a *subadar's*.

After breakfast I wrote to the Honourable Mr. Addington, but owing to the uncertainty of the posts did not despatch my letter. Remained all day in my tent. The weather was dreadfully hot, and the sun shone through our tents as hot as fire, and they had been perfect ovens ever since our march from Bhirtpore. It became a common practice with us to remove the bedding from our couches, and to spread it on the carpet of our tents, as it was generally somewhat cooler on the ground than above it.

May 26th.—This morning Lord Lake, with the cavalry and reserve, marched to recross the Chumbill, and our wing ordered to be held in readiness to follow.

The wind continued all this night to blow exceedingly hot, and it was impossible to rest, which distressed us all very much. The soldiers as well as the officers appeared in general very much worn and enfeebled by the heat.

May 27th.—We marched this morning by the right, the 76th leading the column.

The wind, long before the sun rose, became very hot, burying us in a cloud of dust; we had a burning march of about eight miles, the soldiers constantly dropping from fatigue and overcome by the extreme heat, some of them never to rise again. We crossed the Chumbill about eight, and it was with difficulty that we got the men through the water, so dreadful was their thirst that they seemed determined never to be satisfied. About nine we encamped on the eastern banks, upon the spot Lord Lake had quitted in the morning.

The rearguard of our wing came up before eleven o'clock. It blew a hurricane all day, and it literally was a hurricane of flames. We had great difficulty in pitching our tents. Employed our camels today to bring water for our *Kuss*.

May 28th.—This morning we marched by the left. We cleared the deep ravines with little delay, as every precaution had been taken to prevent any wheeled carriages entering in our front. We heard this morning that fifty bullocks, laden with flour, and some camels which went wide of the line, were carried off by *banditti* during the march yesterday. The Patan Horse made an ineffectual attempt to recover the property, but everything was carried clear off. It was said that they actually came up with the marauders, but retreated on their drawing up and showing them a front; and this had been the conduct of our gallant allies on almost every occasion when their services were needed.

Received letters on the march from Inglis and Ramus. We got sight of the encampment at Dholepore about ten, and soon after took up our station in the line.

The weather was intensely hot today, and officers and men appeared completely worn out. I was so distressed with the heat that it was not without difficulty that I kept my horse.

May 29th.—Dined at headquarters, and as usual the evening was very gay. We broke up about eleven. Lord Lake made no secret of his intentions to march in two days for Agra and Muttrah, and repeated his hope of getting the troops under cover before the commencement of the rainy season.

May 30th.—Orders for march in the morning were issued today, and officers as well as men were in general much rejoiced at the prospect of passing a couple of quiet months in a cantonment, and to relax awhile from the arduous duty to which they had been so long continually exposed, and which had visibly made a very serious impression on the constitutions of nine out of ten; and unfortunately for me, on few more than my own.

June 1st.—Camp at Mineah. The road today was good, but the country, great part of it, very rough and uncultivated. About two miles before we arrived at our ground, the Agra troops, under General Doudeswell, stretched away to the right. Our brigade continued its route with Lord Lake and the Muttrah Division, and we encamped about eight o'clock.

From our encampment we could easily see that of the troops destined to Agra, which was a fortunate circumstance for many of the officers, as their baggage being with the head of the line, continued on with it, their servants nor ourselves being aware that the army would divide during the march. My tent fortunately kept on the flank of the brigade, and was up almost the first in the line.

An officer of the 15th and a female friend of his (a European) were sitting on the ground, both exposed to the inclemency of the wind and sun, their tent having gone to the Agra camp. A servant of mine mentioned it, and I went to them to request they would come to my tent and breakfast with us, to which Captain A. and the poor girl readily assented, and if I ever felt for a countrywoman I did sincerely for her on this occasion; she was a remarkably well-behaved woman, and could boast a finer person and had more genteel manners than the greater part of her fair friends in this quarter, who were more fortunate in their circumstances, though perhaps not much more deserving. It may be supposed that we were not wanting in showing her attention, and she was very profuse in her acknowledgments on leaving us.

I was not off my couch the whole of this afternoon, and by the positive orders of the surgeons I agreed, if the army should break up, to obtain leave, and, instead of proceeding to cantonments, to try the change of air in Rohilcund, and go to Bareilly to pass a month with my worthy friend Thornhill, from whom I had received numerous pressing invitations.

June 2nd.—Both divisions of the army halted today, all in anxious expectation of learning their certain destination. Brigadier Ashe and myself breakfasted with Lord Lake this morning. His Lordship remarked to me that the severity of the season had made an impression on me, and Colonel Lake, next to whom I sat at breakfast, advised me by all means to quit the camp as soon as possible, and to get into a bungalow, as every prospect of service was at an end; he most kindly offered to procure me leave immediately, and as the army was now broke up, and there could be no possible objection, I got my leave for two months on a sick certificate.

Lord Lake, as usual, enquired very particularly after "the chestnut" (Lassuary), and mentioned to Colonel Malcolm, who knew the horse, and was with Campbell when he brought him from Arabia, that he was mine; Malcolm assured me that he was a "high bred, real desert horse," and of the first cast in Arabia.

June 3rd.—Camp at Soomnah. This morning the Muttrah and Agra divisions took their respective routes. The day was cursedly hot, and many European soldiers dropped dead on the line of march. It was a melancholy procession, and really the British soldiers appeared more as if they were marching a funeral party than anything else. Men who left the ground apparently in tolerable health were frequently buried at the next, and it is not possible to convey an idea of the sufferings of European troops marching at this destructive period; they were occurrences seldom known in India till our late and present campaigns.

At sunset I went to headquarters and took my leave of Colonel Lake, to whom for his marked attention and kindness, I shall ever consider myself extremely indebted, and not less so to His Lordship, for the many instances he has evinced of his notice of me. Brigadier Ashe and myself struck our tents and had them ready packed to move off at midnight toward Agra.

The brigadier slept on the plain, with a small awning over his couch, and I moved mine, with Lassuary, into his tent. At twelve at night we left the camp, with a strong escort which Lord Lake had granted us, composed of a formidable party of Patan Horse. We were unacquainted with the road, and marched slowly on till daybreak, taking villagers from the places we passed through to conduct us from one village to another, towards Agra.

Chapter 26

On Sick Leave

June 4th.—At sunrise we heard them firing a salute at Agra, in honour of the king's birthday, and soon after saw the fort, into which Brigadier Ashe marched, and I arrived at Secundra (about three miles from Agra) at Wemyss's, about eight o'clock, and from him experienced the most kind and friendly reception. Wemyss being appointed collector of the Agra district, in consequence of his gallant conduct during the last campaign, when he acted in a military capacity in Lord Lake's family, had the range of the whole country to fix his residence.

I found him in a beautiful garden, upon the brink of the Jumnah, living in a tomb, (Etamaut Dowlah's) which he had elegantly fitted up, and in which he allotted me most comfortable apartments. Major Morrison, A.D.C. to Lord Lake, arrived at Wemyss's soon after me, having also come in sick from camp. Morrison pitched his tent in the garden, close to the tomb, to sleep in. Colonel Black and Colonel Wood also breakfasted at Wemyss's this morning, and passed on to the city of Agra the former, and the latter to his camp at Secundra, not more than two miles from Wemyss's garden.

We all felt relief and the very great difference between a tent and good quarters. Received a note in the evening from Brigadier Ashe, who met his daughter in Agra, the first time since the death of her husband, poor Lumsdaine, who was killed by a cannon shot in the trenches before Bhirtpore. She is said to be a very fine young woman, and they had been married but a few months. Lumsdaine was a gallant officer, and has distinguished himself on many occasions, and particularly in retaking our trenches the morning on which he fell.

We had a large party of officers from the Secundra camp to dine at Wemyss's this evening. I did not get off my couch all the day, not even to go to the stables to see the Arabs. Wemyss assured me he should hardly have known me, so much had the dreadful hot weather of the last month altered me, and I was quite as weak and enfeebled as I appeared to be.

June 10th.—Remained quiet in Wemyss's paradise ever since the 4th, till this morning, never quitting the gardens except to take a short ride after sunset on the elephant for fresh air. At daybreak I left Wemyss's quarters to cross the Jumnah, and pass the day with my friend Cunynghame, who was appointed Judge of Coel, and had taken up his residence on the Dewaub side of the Jumnah, during the hot weather, in a tomb and garden very similar to Wemyss's on the opposite bank.

Cunynghame, as usual, gave us a sumptuous breakfast and dinner.

June 11th.—At daybreak this morning, Cunynghame went off "post haste to Cawnpore to meet Mrs. Cunynghame on her way up from the Lower Provinces. I got across the Jumnah before sunrise, and found an elephant of Wemyss's waiting for me, on which I mounted, and got to the tomb to breakfast. Galloway, of the 14th, being on his march to Futty Ghur, I sent off my horses, camels, etc., with him, and determined, in order to be exposed as little as possible to the violence of the weather, to proceed *dawke* (post) myself to Futty Ghur, and from there to Bareilly by the same mode of conveyance. Sent a guard expressly to protect my horses and camels from thieves during the night time.

Colonel Black passed the day with us, and Bailey and the Ridges, of the 4th, dined with us. A serious accident had nearly happened in the evening. As Ridge, in passing under a gateway which led into the garden, on an elephant, was nearly crushed severely, as one part of the arch of the gate was not sufficiently high to admit him through, and he was squeezed between the iron in front of the *howdah* and the upper part of the *howdah*. The elephant felt it, and with the sagacity peculiar to themselves, instantly stopped, and Ridge came off a good deal bruised for his temerity in attempting to enter the garden on his elephant.

We had letters from headquarters this evening announcing the appointment of Lord Cornwallis to the Government of this country, and mentioning that His Lordship was positively to embark for India in April. This arrangement, we expected, would cause a wonderful change in the politics of this country, and peace, instead of war, be the order of the day.

We were much surprised that the Marquis Cornwallis, at his advanced period of a life already entirely devoted to the service of his country, should have been prevailed upon to quit his native country, almost with a certainty of never returning to it: we thought, acting nobly, and perfectly according with every other action of his honourable career.

June 12th.—At daybreak this morning I mounted Lassuary, and walked him into the garrison to pay my friends a visit before I proceeded to Rohilcund. Breakfasted with Colonel Blair and passed the morning there and at Cumberlege's. It was very hot, and I made excuses to several of the officers, whom otherwise I intended to have called on. *Tiffed* with Mrs. Blair, and immediately afterwards got into my *palanquin* to return to Wemyss's. Grant was on duty at the main guard and posted at the Delhi gate.

I got from my *palanquin* and sat an hour with him and Murray. Before sun setting I reached Wemyss's, very much tired, and with a severe headache, occasioned by this little exertion. Wemyss and I dined alone this evening, and talked over past events, some of which had afforded us great pleasure.

The nights were so vilely hot that to sleep indoors was impossible, and we always moved our couches under a fine mango tree in the garden. Jones, of the engineers, a first cousin of the Honourable Mrs. Carlton, leaving Agra also on account of his health, fixed to join me tomorrow.

June 13th.—At sunrise this morning I took my leave of my friend Wemyss, and found breakfast ready for me at Cunynghame's, but the worthy host and his amiable partner were wanting to make the day a pleasant one. Dined early, took a bathe afterwards, and in our shirts and muslin trousers, Jones and myself left the tomb at four o'clock. The wind and sun both dreadfully hot indeed. Several of our bearers dropped under the *palanquins*, and we were able to go but little faster than a foot pace.

About twelve at night we arrived at Colonel Frith's, at Ferozeabad, near my old station, Shikoabad. Colonel Vandeleur and some officers who had crossed from Muttrah had gone on with the bearers, and we were consequently detained. Set down our *palanquins* upon the plain under a tree, and slept till the morning.

June 15th.—Colonel Blair had given me a letter of introduction to Colonel Frith, which secured both Jones and myself a hearty welcome, and everything the house afforded. We did not quit the bungalow all this day, which, in spite of Colonel Frith's attention to us, and desire to keep us cool, was one of the hottest ever known. The colonel asked some officers from the garrison to meet us at dinner, and at nine o'clock Jones and myself got again into our *palanquins* and set forward towards Futty Ghur. About midnight we passed poor Shikoabad, and the remains of our bungalows, now in ruins. We bribed the bearers to push on with us, and at seven we arrived at my friend White's at Mynpoorie.

June 16th.—Passed close to Cunynghame's house, in which I had spent the most pleasant days (though too few) I ever passed in India. The collector who succeeded Cunynghame had now taken up his residence in it. White entertained us with every luxury Mynpoorie afforded, and we remained with him during the heat of the day, when it was impossible to travel.

At five in the evening, after an early dinner, and just as we were getting into our *palanquins*, a letter arrived from the judge, requiring of us to give up the bearers, as a friend of his (Colonel

Vandeleur) was proceeding on, and wanted them. I made immediate enquiries of the bearers, if they had received any previous order to attend at the judge's, and they assured me they had not.

I therefore in reply to the judge's note, told His Worship that, as the bearers in question were laid on the road by government for the benefit of the service at large, and not on account of individuals, and that as they assured me they had received no previous engagement, I could not think of giving them up to anyone, but should carry them Futty Ghur. on for my own convenience. There was something rather peremptory in the worthy magistrate's demand of the bearers, which induced me to hint to him the impropriety of presuming to stop officers, and I recommended him to be cautious how he acted in future and not to interfere where he had not the smallest right so to do. To this I received no reply, and at sunset we took our leave of White and proceeded onwards.

About twelve at night we crossed the Black River, upon the banks of which there was a party of dragoon officers encamped for the night, and on their way sick from the army. At six in the morning we once more got sight of the Ganges, and arrived at Futty Ghur at sunrise. Dressed and breakfasted with Abernethy of the 27th, and made his my headquarters for the short time I may remain here. Macan came to me at Abernethy's and asked us to dine with the colonel, his brother, commanding the station, but I was too much fatigued to have any inclination to leave the bungalow. A party of officers belonging to the 27th dined with us at home.

June 17th.—Breakfasted and dined today at Paton's; met there an old acquaintance of mine, Mrs. B., a nice little widow with a *lac* of *rupees*. All my friends declared that the climate had changed me so materially while campaigning that they scarcely recognised me.

June 18th.—Called on Mrs. Christie this morning, who I had not seen since the death of my poor friend Christie; my having been in continual habits of friendship with Christie, recalled past events to her remembrance, and she appeared much distressed at first. Dined with Colonel Macan this evening; drank more wine than usual, but retired early, leaving a very large party, who seemed all disposed to do justice to the colonel's excellent claret.

Macan and I fixed this evening to leave Futty Ghur for Bareilly, in Rohilcund on the night of the 20th.

June 21st.—At sunrise this morning our horses crossed the river, and the grooms were directed to proceed half-way to Burrah Matahney, and there halt the night. Abernethy went with me this evening to dine with Colonel Macan. We had a small party, and at ten o'clock Macan (the colonel's brother and A.D.C.) and myself got into our *palanquin*s, and commenced our run for Bareilly.

We arrived on the banks of the Ganges about half-past ten, got our *palanquin*s and servants into the boats, and were across the river soon after eleven o'clock. We found our guard drawn up on the sands, waiting for us, and immediately pushed on. It was a dreadful hot, sultry night, and the bearers were not able to go faster than three miles an hour with us, and at that rate many of them dropped under our *palanquin*s. This part of the country is much infested by thieves and murderers; we were well armed ourselves, and we had besides with us a strong guard from Futty Ghur.

We passed on unmolested, drinking immense quantities of water, for the heat almost parched us, and prevented me closing my eyes all night. The *palanquin* bearers and servants were also drinking at every one of the numerous wells on the road's side. Their stopping so often made our progress very slow indeed. This was as uncomfortable a night as I ever passed. My fellow traveller, in good health, made a far better thing of it, and I believe did not once awaken during the whole night.

We crossed the Rham Gungah river about two this morning, at Jellalabad, where boats were all ready for us. Soon after sunrise we arrived at our tents at Burrah Matahney, and found breakfast all laid in readiness for us. I slept till nearly nine, when we bathed, dressed, and got our breakfast. Our tents were well sheltered from the sun by a noble *tamorin* tree, and a fine *puckah* well afforded our servants and horses plenty of excellent water. The horses came up about eight o'clock. Here we passed the day, as travelling during the heat of the day was impossible without destruction to our servants. Our *Kuss* was famously watered today, and the tent was as cool as we could possibly make it.

We had our dinner at four, and drank each our bottle of claret. At sunset our people were all ready, and we started for Bareilly. It blew exceedingly strong soon after we left Burrah Matahney, and very hot. Our *palanquins* went very slow indeed, and the violence of the wind continually extinguished the flambeaux, and we were detained much on that account. To travel without a light in this part of India is very dangerous indeed, owing to the numberless wells, which are frequently in the middle of the road, and during the march of an army by night, when lights are not, of course, allowed, men, and often horses and elephants, are destroyed by falling into them, very many melancholy instances of which I had often witnessed.

June 22nd.—We arrived at a village ten miles from Bareilly soon after daylight, where we found Thornhill's tandem ready for us, into which we got and drove to a small village half-way (five miles) to Bareilly, through a very heavy sand, and although the carriage was a very light one, both horses had enough of it before we reached this second village; here we found the curricle and greys, which I had driven many a time, and knew well their excellent qualities; they were both Arabs, and Thornhill prized them exceedingly.

They took us with great ease to the hall in half an hour, where we were welcomed with apparent heartfelt pleasure by our worthy host, and were truly congratulated on our return from the campaign with our heads upon our shoulders, and without the loss of legs or arms. Thornhill had prepared a sumptuous breakfast for us, of which I could scarcely eat a morsel. I was very unwell. After breakfast I went in the *tonjon* to the stables to see the stud.

June 23rd.—After breakfast this morning Macan and myself got into our *palanquins* and went to pass the day at C.'s. We found a very large party there, and among others my friends Elliott and Mrs. Elliott, Becher and several others. We had music and billiards all the morning; with the former I was delighted, but neither my strength nor my inclination permitted of my playing at billiards. I sent for my clothes and dressed at C.'s, where we all dined, and the evening was a very cheerful one to those who were able to enjoy it. As an invalid, I was allowed to retire to the drawing-room soon after the ladies, where I met that indulgence I really stood in need of, and was permitted to take my lounge on a couch without reserve. Mrs. C. no stock.

The gentlemen joined the ladies about ten, after having apparently done especial justice to the claret. We had music, and broke up about twelve o'clock.

June 25th.—In the evening went into the cantonments to dine with our worthy friend and shipmate, Becher. After dinner, sporting, as usual, was the topic, and I matched. Lassuary to run on the 2nd of September (unless I should be ordered to take the field) once round the Bareilly course, carrying 8st. 5lb., against Thornhill's Horatio, carrying 8st. 10lb., for one hundred guineas. Bets on this race immediately followed, to the amount of nearly five hundred guineas before we quitted the table, and were all taken down to avoid misapprehension and mistakes.

June 30th.—Several matches made, and very good sport expected at our Bareilly September meeting. Today I had the pleasure to receive letters and a box of newspapers, with some music, from Yeovil. All the music was exceedingly admired by Mrs. C., and *Just Like Love*, most particularly, as one of the prettiest things ever composed, and no one was more capable of doing it justice than the lady to whom I had the pleasure to present it. She sang it divinely, and it was instantly copied, as I valued the original too much to part with it, even to her.

July 25th.—Handicapped Cockburn's Black Arab and Thornhill's brown horse Horatio to run on the 7th September for 100 guineas. I received the fee for having handicapped them.

July 27th.—Went at daybreak to the course to see the horses take their exercise. It was nearly seven o'clock before they had all gone round, having eleven horses for three boys to ride. The weather very fine and cool.

August 1st.—Some very heavy rain interrupted the training for many days past. The weak state of my health would not admit of my visiting the course, except in a carriage or my *palanquin*. Received a very friendly letter from Wemyss, offering me the loan or use of 15,000 *rupees*, as long as I should require it, but this I declined. Letters today mention the arrival of Lord Cornwallis at Madras from England in March. Received two pairs of shawls from Futty Ghur this morning, price four hundred and fifty *rupees*.

September 4th.—This morning five ponies started for the pony sweepstakes—Hazard, Harping Rou, Fidget, Tooney, and a grey pony mare of Cockburn's; they ran heats two miles, carrying weight for inches. The first heat afforded tolerable sport, between Harping Rou and Cockburn's mare; the latter won it, and the second heat she won easily. The weather extremely unfavourable, and we waited several hours, in the rubbing house, before the rain abated, and the ponies could start.

A large party dined with us this evening; after dinner Lord Lake and the army, with three times three, was drank, this being the anniversary of that ever memorable and glorious day which added lustre to the British arms, by the capture of Ali Ghur. A lottery for the pony race was proposed after dinner and readily filled. A good deal of hard drinking this evening; sickness saved me.

September 7th.—This morning at sunrise the match between Thornhill's Capsicum Colt, four years old, and the Arab horse Filbert (Cockburn's) was run on the straight course, one mile and a quarter, for one hundred guineas. They went off at the top of their speed, and for the first mile, or near it, the colt had the best of it, but age told the latter part of the race, which was, however, uncommonly well contested, and the running remarkably sharp; it was won by the Arab by about two lengths. I won 100 guineas on this race. We returned home, a large party, and breakfasted later than usual. Went afterwards to Cockburn's, where we passed the morning, and another race between the Capsicum Colt and Filbert was talked of. Thornhill rode the former, and Ridge Cockburn's horse. After the race this morning Stevenson's Rockingham Colt, Shairpe's Sir Ralph, and Grey Arab, Cockburn's Collier, and Horatio took their usual exercise. Ridge purchased Filbert of Cockburn for 250 guineas. We thought him a cheap horse.

September 16th.—Today a race was run between Thornhill's Horatio and Shairpe's grey horse Sky Blue; won easily by Sky Blue, which horse also received 70 guineas forfeit of Captain Richards, whose horse was lamed in training and unable to run the match.

September 21st.—Received a letter this morning from Paton, mentioning the arrival of my chestnut horse at Futty Ghur. The *Nabob*, having declined purchasing him at the price of 4,000 *rupees*, determined on sending him to Ridge, to sell him for me at Agra.

October 8th.—Intelligence of Marquis Cornwallis' death reached us this morning; this unpleasant news we heard at Welland's, and it was an event sincerely lamented by all well-wishers of our country. Sir George Barlow expected to succeed to the government.

A Voyage down the Ganges

CHAPTER 27

Journey from Bareilly to Calcutta by River

October 15th.—We sent our baggage on board this morning, and gave orders to our servants to proceed to Mindy Ghaut, and there await our arrival, Becher and myself having determined on going overland to Futty Ghur to pass a day or two with our friends there previous to our quitting the Upper Provinces. Cockburn wrote us an account this morning from Pellibeat of their having killed five tigers. I should have been of this party had my health admitted of it. In the evening Becher and myself drove to poor Cornish's tomb; he was a distant relation of Becher's, who was desirous of seeing that every attention had been paid to the memory of his friend. We dined with Gillman, and had a dark drive to his bungalow.

October 20th.—This morning I drove Mrs. Paton in the *curricle* to the cavalry parade and round the course. In the evening I dined with Mr. Bathurst, where we met a very pleasant little woman, Mrs. Macvitie, married to a great quiz, a lieutenant in the 11th. Met my Etawah friend, Colonel Palmer, this evening, and had a very pleasant chat with him, respecting our proceedings during the siege of Gwalior, in which he bore a conspicuous part. We were sumptuously entertained by Bathurst, a most excellent dinner, with champagne, claret, hock, Madeira, and a most superb dessert.

October 21st.—I was out this morning with Mrs. Paton on

the elephant. We returned about half-past seven o'clock; Major Knox, and Lieutenant Oliver breakfasted at Paton's this morning. Mr. and Mrs. Robinson and a Mrs. Richardson dined with us this evening; the ladies both very pleasant, and we passed a very agreeable day. Mrs. Richardson had very lately returned from England, married to a very old and stingy blade; she strongly expressed her dislike of India, and her anxious wishes to return to Europe, nor could she help exclaiming on the folly of marriage, where the disparity of years were so great as was common in this country (and which, indeed, was precisely her own misfortune).

She seemed to have been well educated, and her manners were very genteel. About eleven I handed this fair lady to her *palanquin*. Wrote to Young, at Cawnpore, requesting him to share my boat with me to Calcutta, to which place, in consequence of his recent promotion and removal to the 34th Regiment, he was bound.

October 23rd.—Dreadful accounts from all quarters of the effects of a fever now raging. Colonel Gunber, Captain Prior, Lieutenant Yates, died in a day or two after being seized, and many others are in a very hazardous state, and in imminent danger, among those of my acquaintance, Major Welsh, Captain Browne, Horse Artillery, and Swinton of the cavalry, great numbers of Europeans dying daily.

October 24th.—This morning Becher and myself went on board his *pinnace*, and sailed immediately for Cawnpore. We got on a sand about six miles from Futty Ghur, owing to the ignorance of the pilot, and were detained several hours in consequence; we were under the necessity of tacking and running several miles to clear the bank on which we struck. At sunset we brought to about twenty miles from Futty Ghur. We were dreadfully annoyed by mosquitoes, so much so that it was impossible to rest, either by day or night, for them. We brought to this evening about sunset, on a very romantic shore.

October 25th.—We were adrift this morning at sunrise, and

at twelve o'clock we arrived at Mindy Ghaut (the mouth of the Rham Gungah), where my boat and Becher's baggage boats were waiting for us. We proceeded immediately on, but owing to the *pinnace* drawing so much water we were frequently aground, and consequently much detained. She struck so violently once that we thought she would have gone over. The tide was uncommonly strong, and she took a woeful heel. Our writing desks were thrown from the table (so came the sheet blotted) and almost all our things completely upset.

October 31st.—This morning we left Cawnpore, and with a favourable wind went rapidly down the river. We carried sail the whole day, and the oars were completely useless. About four in the evening we passed Nudjeif Ghur, where stands the remains of a fine building, erected by General Martini; it appeared to be a *pucka* house of great size and elegant structure. We passed many beautiful views on the banks of the river today, and brought to about thirty-six miles from Cawnpore at sunset. We caught many fish this afternoon, angling from the cabin windows.

November 1st.—We had good angling today, and supplied the servants with fish plenty, after having provided for ourselves. We were many times aground today. A short time before we brought to for the day we descried a *budgerow*, tacking against the stream; a light boat passed us, and told us it belonged to Mr. Mercer, on his way from Mirzapore. Becher immediately sent him an invitation to dine with us. We took a short walk on the river's side this evening, and 1 returned much tired to the boat. Mercer and a black relation of his dined with us, and we sat rather later than our usual hour.

November 2nd.—We cast off our boats this morning at break of day, and I went on board Becher's boat at the usual hour to breakfast. We shot two alligators from the boats this morning, and wounded several. Had good sport angling, and killed more fish than we had occasion for. The weather now daily getting cool, and I found my strength rather returning, though very sparingly indeed. We brought to early, and had a pleasant walk on the river's side; saw some quail, and a brace or two of partridge.

November 3rd.—This morning at nine o'clock we arrived at the Powder Works, five miles above Allahabad. The water between this place and Allahabad, owing to the uncommon rapidity of the stream, is dangerous, and boats, with every precaution, are frequently lost. We found at the Powder Mills a buggy ready to carry us to Mr. Cuthbert's, the collector at Allahabad, and soon after breakfast we left our boats and proceeded in it. I had to drive a troublesome horse, whilst Becher carried the *chattah* (umbrella); the sun very hot, but the *chattah* saved us much.

November 4th.—We received today an invitation from Sir George Barlow, governor-general, to dine with him. I was in hopes of going, but the pain of my head was too violent.

November 5th.—This morning at ten o'clock we left Allahabad, and about eleven cleared the Jumnah. The fort, on the water face, did not appear to me so strong as I expected, and some high ground to the westward of it seemed in a great measure to command it. I am convinced that if the fort of Allahabad belonged to any power but the English, and it was requisite, that we could take it in a week, and perhaps in much less time. We brought to this evening at sunset, near the remains of a very extensive city; the ruins afforded us great entertainment for half an hour before dinner. We saw a great number of peafowls and some grey partridge here.

November 7th.—At noon today we saw Mirzapore, but the wind was unfavourable, and we made but little way. The river today at most parts very narrow. We fired several shots at, and wounded, many alligators. The boats struck the ground several times today, and we were much annoyed by the delay it occasioned. We saw the Chunar Hills this afternoon. I went, and a servant of Becher's with me, in the small boat, to get a shot at some geese. Had a long shot at them and brought down two. Shot also a curlew on the shore.

The views on the banks of the river today uncommonly romantic and grand. A few miles above Mirzapore are some very neat buildings by the natives on a small but very elegant style and scale, and we had views of each from the cabin windows this morning. Observed the people in many places ploughing on the banks of the river, in parts which had been covered by the water, and which appeared a fine rich soil, and likely to be very productive. At three this afternoon we passed the fort of Chunar; to me it appeared a place of much less strength and size than I expected, and, like all the other forts I had seen in this quiet quarter of the country, had a very tame and unwarlike appearance, after those I had visited in the Upper Provinces.

As a hill fort, Chunar Ghur seemed very small; the lowest part of the Rock of Gwalior being at least four times the height of the top of the battlements even of this place. Some small guns were mounted on the north face, and the works regular and handsome. To the westward of the fort, and on the brink of the Ganges, is the burial ground, in which appeared numberless proofs of the pernicious effects of this horrid climate to our poor countrymen. We brought to near the fort; Colonel Grant, commanding, sent us a large supply of oranges and garden stuff, with a very polite note.

About five o'clock Becher and myself got into our *tonjons* and went to look at the cantonments and invalid barracks. We saw a great number of poor fellows (Europeans) who had lost their limbs and been maimed in battle. The last three years had added very considerably to the list of invalids at Chunar, as in the different actions and sieges during that period, very many, of course, had suffered.

The barracks appeared a very clean, comfortable asylum for these poor fellows, and every care seemed to be taken of them. We saw many others, worn out by long service, and the baneful and destructive effects of the climate, whose end appeared to be not very distant. We met Colonel Grant during our peregrination, and saw also a lieutenant of the invalids; he appeared of the very lowest description of European, and was a pretty specimen of what their service must have been like twenty-five years since,, when he was invalided.

November 9th.—Today at break of day we left Chunar, and about seven passed the cantonments of Sultanpore, on the Ganges. banks of the river, not more than three miles from Chunar; it appeared a good spot, and a neat, compact cantonment. The water this morning very slack, and our progress consequently very slow. At eleven o'clock we came in sight of Benares, and the city at the distance of about four miles has a really superb appearance, but as we neared it the high walls next the river obstructed the view, and the city was entirely hid by them. The houses on the bank of the river are uncommonly high, and, like all others in this part of the globe, very shabby and in shocking repair. About twelve o'clock we brought to at the Raje Ghaut, near which was anchored one of the finest, best finished *pinnaces* I ever saw, belonging to the *rajah* of Benares.

November 11th.—At daybreak this morning we left the famed city of Benares, and about nine passed a considerable and extensive work for making indigo, the property of a Mr. Smith; it is remarkable that at this place Mr. Smith, owing to the uncommonly sickly season, lost every servant he had except one *kitmatgar* (footman) and was himself, with his family, at Benares, extremely ill, and had been dangerously so.

November 12th.—At daybreak this morning we moved off; the adverse winds which continued the whole of the forenoon greatly impeded our progress. As we proceeded down the river we observed the proportion of cultivated land daily to increase, and in the Benares district particularly. About three this afternoon a fleet of boats came in sight, and they proved to be employed in carrying the remaining five companies of H.M. 17th Regiment to Cawnpore; there did not appear to be more than four *budgerows*, which induced me to think them short of officers.

In complete *Griffin* style they were blazing away at birds of all kinds on the river. About four we plainly saw the indigo works at Zemineah, at which place I perfectly recollect having had a capital day's shooting as we were marching up the country in 1801. Another part of the fleet, with men of the 17th Regiment, passed us near Zemineah. We caught a great many fine fish today, and made some excellent shots with ball at alligators and large birds on the river.

The weather cool and pleasant on the water, and I discontinued undressing this afternoon for the first day, and dressed only in the evening. The lands appeared all in a highly cultivated state, and the villagers ploughing quite to the water's edge as we passed on. Amused ourselves this afternoon with mixing different kinds of powder country with Europe and trying its strength. We found the best country powder answered very well for ball shooting, with a proportion of Europe thrown among it.

November 13th.—At daybreak this morning: we continued our voyage. The winds were contrary, and we did not come in sight of Gauzipore till eight o'clock. The bungalows and cantonments looked very smart from the river. We dispatched a note to Graham, giving him notice of our approach, and intention to pass the day with him.

During breakfast we received Graham's answer, telling us that *palanquins* were waiting at the *ghaut* (quay) to convey us to his house. About twelve we reached Graham's bungalow, and met with a very hearty reception from them. Mr. Hall and Lieutenant Ralph of the cavalry came in before *tiffin*.

In the evening we got into a buggy and drove round the cantonments; went also to see Lord Cornwallis's tomb. He was buried very near the banks of the river, from which, when finished, his monument will easily be seen. We learnt that His Lordship's coffin was lodged in an arched kind of room, in such a manner as to prevent the earth touching it. It was supposed that this precaution was taken to preserve the coffin, in case his Lordship's friends in Europe should require the body to be sent home. A temporary wall was building around the small tomb at present over His Lordship's grave, and a sentry always posted near it.

We were told that an engineer officer had been ordered up

from the presidency to construct the monument, which it is expected will be one of a most magnificent structure. A subscription opened, which is to extend to Europe, to defray the expense, and which will be immense.

Lieutenant and Mrs. Hall, and Lieutenants Halfield and MacLauclan, of H.M. 17th Foot, dined with us at Graham's this evening, also a Mr. Ryder, the oldest of the Company's civil servants, and one of the greatest oddities I ever met with. After we retired to the drawing-room, Mr. Hall sung us several songs. Off the stage, I thought I never heard so fine a voice, and which he commanded in a most masterly style.

November 14th.—At sunrise this morning I mounted a very nice horse of Inglis's, and went with Graham to see the riding schools and inspect the lines at the station, both of which excelled anything I had ever seen. The stables were elegantly built, and the officers' bungalows all regularly built, at a limited distance in the rear of the lines, the captains and subalterns in one line and field officers in a second, quite close to the river. At Gauzipore they have a very extensive and fine parade, and in its gayest days this must have been a most pleasant station. The situation delightful, and a large society, there being cantonments for four regiments.

We dined today with Mr. Ryder, and had a great deal of fun. Our party consisted of Graham and Mrs. Graham, a Mrs. Lane (whose husband had been dead about three weeks), Miss Gillas, a companion of Mrs. Lane's, Inglis, Becher, and self. Mr. Ryder introduced us to Mrs. Lane as "the widow," and in the course of a few minutes took us into a room at hand and shewed us the bier on which her husband had gone to his long home. It was also that which bore our late revered Governor-General, Lord Cornwallis, to his grave, on which account old Ryder kept it as a rare show.

We had an excellent dinner, and some of the best claret I ever tasted; the old man had seldom been known to give a dinner, and we were resolved to sew him up as completely as we could. After the ladies had withdrawn, the bottle was pushed pretty rapidly, and our host spoke so plainly and loudly that we were necessitated to shut the drawing-room door, and about ten the old fellow reeled away to pay his respects to the ladies, very far gone, and unable to walk without assistance. This was one of the most eccentric characters I had ever met with, and he afforded us no small degree of entertainment. We left him about twelve, fast asleep in his chair; took leave of Graham and Mrs. Graham and Inglis, and walked to our boats; the night remarkably cool.

November 15th.—At daybreak, with a fair wind, we left Gauzipore and made great progress by noon on our way to Buxar. Our boats outsailed those with the baggage considerably; the stream today very strong, and I never recollect to have gone with so much rapidity on the Ganges. We brought to early in order to give the boats astern an opportunity of coming up. At this place it was shocking to see the number of human skulls and skeletons thrown on the banks on the fall of the river. It was a sad proof of the dreadful mortality which had prevailed on this part, as well as most others of the country. We were under the necessity of moving our boats to a spot less, horrid to behold.

We walked inland for a mile before dinner. The weather quite cool and refreshing. By the accounts of the boatmen we sailed nearly fifty miles this day. We had an excellent beef dinner today, a great rarity to me, who had never before, since my arrival in the country been, during the beef season (the cold weather) in a civilized part of the country, but always in that of an enemy, and in camp, where such good fare is not generally known.

November 16th.—I was much shocked at hearing of the death of poor Eamer, as fine a young man as our service or any other could boast of; he was a son of Sir Charles Eamer, and a cornet in the 8th Native Cavalry, to which he was removed from the 3rd. A fine, handsome healthy-looking fellow, but carried off at a very short notice by the destructive climate, in which it was his misfortune (with many others) to be doomed to serve his country. At sunset this evening I went in the cutter to get a shot at some pelican on a sand in the river, and killed one, the longest shot I ever recollect to have made with a ball. We brought to about seven this evening at Chupprah, twenty-two miles from Dinapore.

November 17th.—At daybreak this morning we left Chupprah, and at sunrise we passed a large *pinnace*, in which we learnt by the boats astern was Nuthall. This vexed us much, as we were very desirous of seeing him; but our boats were going with such rapidity, both wind and tide being favourable, that we were nearly three miles from him before we could bring to.

Soon after breakfast it fell calm, and we were under the necessity of taking to our oars. The appearance of the country, and the number of palm and cocoanut trees, told us plainly that we had entered Behar, the huts and buildings of every kind being far different from those of the Upper Provinces. From Becher I learnt that at this place (Chupprah) Mr. Golding made his fortune; he was Collector here, and made his money very rapidly. Mr. Golding, at the age of two and thirty, left India with a fortune of nearly one hundred thousand pounds.

November 18th.—We went on shore this morning, and breakfasted with Mr. Douglas, judge of Patna. We had Major Stuart, commanding the Patna Provincials, and another Scotchman at breakfast. At Patna I expected to have found a Mr. Andrews, famous for taking profiles, which he executed and set very handsomely indeed.

We *tiffed* on board our boats, and dined with Mr. Douglas, the same party we had met at breakfast. We did not break up till past eleven o'clock. At the gate we found Major Stuart in great distress, his servants having taken the horses from the carriage and absented themselves. We left the major in a great rage, to make the best of his hard case, and walked on to our boats.

November 19th.—At seven this morning Becher and myself left our boats to breakfast and pass the day with Mr. Cole, very high in the civil Service. We found the old gentleman in a most princely house, and soon after our arrival we sat down to one of the best breakfasts I ever saw. After breakfast Becher went to visit Mr. Colebrooke, and I to a European shop, one of the best in India, and which afforded everything of the best, but at prices the most extravagant. I gave for one dozen of common cotton stockings seventy *rupees* (English money £8 15s.)

In the evening Becher and myself went to see Mr. Wilton's (the opium agent at Patna) house. It was by far the most stylish place I had seen since I left Calcutta; the finest paintings in India had been collected by Mr. Wilton, and the house was furnished in a most superb way; the dining room exceedingly elegant, and the drawing-room was furnished in a manner which surpassed almost anything I had seen in India. We had some billiard playing before we left the house; the billiard room was a very pleasant one, and the table one of the best I ever saw. Mr. Wilton had gone to Calcutta, but left us an invitation to do as we wished at his house. Mr. Colebrooke and Mr. Chester, of the civil service, met us at Mr. Coles' at dinner.

November 20th.—At daybreak this morning we left Patna. The river continued to widen as we went down, and we quite gave up fishing, as they would only bite near the banks. Shot several ducks and geese from the cutter this morning, and with ball some flamingo, pelican and *syrus*.

November 22nd.—At twelve today we reached Mongheir, saw the hills two hours before. Here we were met at the water's edge by mechanics of all kinds. At Mongheir they made all kinds of furniture equal to any done in the country—couches, tables, chairs, exceedingly neat and very cheap. Becher purchased a great deal of furniture. The fort appeared to have been once a place of considerable strength, but gone entirely to ruin. It was a very extensive place, and the house of the commanding officer stood on an eminence, and was visible many miles before we arrived at the place.

November 23rd.—We went on shore this morning, and walked a short distance. A considerable fleet came in sight about noon today, and in the course of an hour we met them, and found it to be H.M. 53rd Regiment on Ganges. their way to Dinapore. We learnt that the regiment was very unhealthy, at that time having nearly three hundred men in the hospital. Many of the officers, being just from England, were walking on the shore in the heat of the day, by which we concluded that they must have been unacquainted with the nature of this climate, as more experienced men would have reserved their strength till necessity or their duty compelled them to expose themselves.

November 24th.—At seven this morning we got into our *palanquins*, and crossed the island to Mr. Glas's, where we found a very hearty welcome and an excellent breakfast ready for us. After breakfast we went to see Sir Frederick Hamilton and Colonel Toone; with the latter, being a very old friend of mine, I remained the greater part of the day, and on leaving the house Mrs. and Miss Toone loaded my *palanquin* with all kinds of fruits in season, and gave me three pots of fine honey, for which at Boglepore they are remarkable, the neighbouring hills producing great quantities, and of the very best kind.

We dined with Mr. Glas at four o'clock, a very unusual hour in this part of the world, and the first time I had ever dined by the daylight (except in the field, when we dined whenever our duty gave us an opportunity) since my arrival in India. We went across the island to our boats about ten o'clock. This evening my old servant Asseral Khan, who had been left at Patna, came up, having travelled by land nearly one hundred and fifty miles, to overtake the boats.

November 25th.—This morning we left Boglepore at daybreak, and at ten saw the hills at Calgong. At four we brought to at a place near the river, which contained a great deal of various kinds of game and jungle fowls among the rest. We walked for nearly two hours near the banks of the river. Becher shot a fine jungle fowl; they resemble the bantams at home in size and colour, but the flavour very superior; the young ones are delicious, but they are exceedingly shy and difficult to shoot.

November 26th.—We passed the range of hills today between Calgong and Sickly Gully, and a more delightful sight the imagination cannot form, and quite a rarity to us, who, up the country, never scarcely saw a hill or jungle of the kind of those about Calgong. We passed the Gogra Nullah, on the banks of which the Malings and myself had such famous shooting when we went up the country in February, 1801.

About four o'clock we brought to at the village of Sickly Gully, about which are some of the likeliest covers for game I ever saw. The hills here are charming more romantic than can be conceived. We shot some jungle fowl and peacock in our walk from the boats this evening.

In our walk this evening we saw the print of the foot of a rhinoceros, which the villagers told us frequently came out of the hills and did great mischief; a short time before he had killed a man and woman, and the whole neighbourhood was living in dread of him.

November 27th—We left Sickly Gully at daybreak this morning, and about twelve arrived at Rajmehal, where we went on shore and walked over the ruins of a fine building after the style of the natives; it had been a handsome palace, but, except one marble hall, was now quite in ruins. We left Rajmehal about two o'clock, and in the evening came to, quite in the jungle, and within a quarter of a mile of a large *jeel*, on the borders of which, as the sun was setting, we killed four brace of snipe and one and a half brace of painted snipe. We returned later than usual to the boats, had our dinner, and drank our pint of claret each as usual.

November 28th.—At nine this morning we entered the Cossim Bazar River, at the mouth of which we found a great number of country boats sticking on the sands, and it was not without great difficulty that we, by joining our crews, dragged the boats (our own) over. We met a Captain Hicks just arrived from Europe, and a *pinnace* with two ladies, and a Captain Pohlman, bound up the country.

We walked an hour on the shore this afternoon, on the Cossim Bazar Island, once so famous for game, but now entirely ruined by cultivation, and that part which was formerly a jungle was now in a state of fertility equal to any garden. The Cossim Bazar River winds much, and we made but little progress. We hoped to have reached Junglepore in time to have dined with the Honourable Mr. Ramsay, but brought to at sundown five miles from his house.

November 29th.—About eleven this morning we passed the Honourable Mr. Ramsay's house at Junglepore; it appeared a very neat place. He sent us an invitation to stay the day and dine with him, but as Becher was anxious to reach Moorshadabad, we declined going on shore. Mr. Ramsay very kindly sent us bread, butter, fruit, and garden stuff in great abundance. We went on shore this evening, and coming up to the *budgerow* in the small boat, I shot a curlew; it was exactly the bird we have in England, and many of which I had frequently seen at Otterton. We came to this afternoon about four and twenty miles from Moorshadabad.

November 30th.—During the night and the early part of the morning it rained much, and with it we had a great deal of thunder and lightning, which made the air quite cold.

We cast off our boats at daybreak this morning, and, with a fair wind, proceeded on towards Moorshadabad. The Cossim Bazar River winds so exceedingly that we could not make the progress we wished; in one reach the wind was favourable, and in the next quite in our teeth. I went on shore and walked for an hour, and did not find the sun uncomfortably hot; with a *chattah* we shot from the boats some golden plovers and water fowl this morning, and killed some birds with ball as we passed on.

At one o'clock we came in sight of Moorshadabad; the city is one of the most extensive in India, and is situated on each side of the river. About four we were hailed from the shore by some *hircarahs* of Mr. Pattle's, and at a *ghaut* near the *Nabob's* we found a *curricle* waiting to carry us to Mr. Pattle's house. We dressed immediately, and I drove Becher to the house (about five miles from our boats), where we arrived long before dinner.

The house and grounds by moonlight seemed most delightful, and the former one of the most splendid I ever saw—upon an immense scale, and superbly furnished. The dining and drawing rooms were fifty feet long, and built in proportion.

Nothing could exceed the splendour of this place, and at dinner we were regaled with champagne, hock, claret, and Madeira. Mr. and Mrs. Mitford (daughter of Mrs. Pattle) dined here this evening, and we kept much later hours than we had been accustomed to in the Upper Provinces. I was made particularly welcome here not only on account of Becher being a nephew of Mr. Pattle, but a son of the latter having been a shipmate and a great friend of mine.

December 1st.—Instead of seven, we did not get up till nine o'clock this morning. I went round the grounds, which put me more in mind of a gentleman's estate in England than anything I could have expected in India. In the evening Mr. Pattle and Becher went in one *phaeton*, and I had the honour of driving a Miss Fowler (a visitor at Pattle's) in a second *phaeton*, with two of the most beautiful blood-like mares the country afforded.

The roads in the neighbourhood of Moorshadabad are capital, and we did not come in from our drive till after seven o'clock (two hours after the moon got up). We did not dine till eight. Mr. Pattle had been, previous to his coming out the last time to India, in the Directory; at home he lived for many years in a most princely style, and spent an immense fortune. On quitting his Directorship, he returned again to the service to make a second. He has three sons in the civil service, and the fourth came out a cadet when I did.

December 2nd.—At eight this morning I went with Mr. Pattle in the *phaeton* to breakfast with Mr. Oldfield, of the civil service, and Becher drove two beautiful mules after us in a curricle. At Mr. Oldfield's we met Mr. and Mrs. Law; the latter for a long time bore the belle in Calcutta, and was reckoned the prettiest woman in the country; and (my friends *ci-devant* Miss R., and Mrs. C. excepted) she was almost the only handsome woman I had seen for years. Becher returned with Mr. Pattle in the phaeton, and I drove the curricle home after breakfast.

About eleven o'clock Becher and myself went in a chariot to call on Mr. Sturt, judge at Moorshadabad, and brother to Humphry Sturt, who I had often hunted with in Dorsetshire, and after whom I had a number of enquiries made me by Mr. Sturt, who was, himself, a very gentlemanly, pleasant man. We returned about one, and I was persuaded by Mr. Pattle and Becher to write a second letter to Thornhill, advising him of my intention to wait and go down to Calcutta with Becher, which it was not at first my intention to do, but the civility and kindness I met with here induced me to alter my plans, and instead of the fifth we settled it to leave Moorshadabad on the 11th, in the morning.

December 3rd.—At seven this morning we left Mr. Pattle's to breakfast in the cantonments with General Palmer, having been long and intimately acquainted with Colonel Palmer, the General's son. I was very graciously received; after breakfast Mr. Pattle and Becher went to see some friends of theirs, and I played at billiards with a son of the general's and a shipmate in the *Bengal*.

The cantonments at Berhampore exceed in beauty and situation any I had seen in India, not excepting even those at Gauzipore. The barracks are two storeys high, and resemble in front more a superb range of gentlemen's houses, lengthened together than accommodation for soldiers. The officers' quarters, also, of which there are four ranges, are uncommonly spacious and elegantly built; each set contained three excellent rooms, with veranda at either front. The hospital at Berhampore is a very magnificent building, and most wholesomely situated near the banks of the river, on which, indeed, the whole cantonment stands.

At daybreak this morning I mounted a very beautiful Persian horse of Mr. Pattle's, and rode till eight o'clock. We breakfasted at nine, and the day being cloudy and particularly cool, I drove for nearly three hours, after breakfast, in the curricle, and for almost the first time in my life did not find the sun uncomfortably hot.

We *tiffed* at the usual hour, and at six o'clock Mr. Pattle, Becher and self left the house to dine with General Palmer at Berhampore. The two former in a *phaeton* and I alone in the chariot. We had a large party at dinner; the general entertained us splendidly, and about ten we were summoned to the drawing room by the music, and this evening I heard the best singing I ever heard in my life off the stage, for which we were indebted to Mrs. Scott, wife of Captain Scott, of the 3rd; she was particularly plain in her person, but her fine voice, method, and style of singing were really exquisite.

December 5th.—This forenoon I went through Mr. Pattle's stables, in which were no less than seven pairs of carriage horses, besides some of the best bred saddle horses in India. A European coachman, and a very smart fellow, had the direction of the whole, but the grooms under him were very numerous, and everything was kept in a very superior style. Mr. Pattle had, of various descriptions, upwards of one hundred and twenty servants, and everything corresponded in a style of elegance seldom equalled in India even.

December 10th.—At dinner today we had a party of nearly thirty, a very pleasant day. Lots of champagne, claret, hock, port, and Madeira. We went to the drawing room before ten, when the singing and playing commenced. Mrs. Sturt and Mrs. Scott sang several beautiful duets, and Mrs. Droze played some very fine pieces of music. Mrs. Scott's "*No, my Love*," was exceedingly admired, and she certainly sang it most exquisitely. About twelve we went below to supper, and one of the most pleasant parties I ever met broke up early in the morning.

December 11th.—At five we left the house to dine at Mr. Pattle's house in the city of Moorshadabad. We did not arrive till after dark, the distance being full seven miles, and through the city we were obliged to drive slowly, the streets being much crowded with people. Mr. Pattle's house in the town was extremely neat and very handsomely furnished. In the drawing room stood a picture at full length of Lord Wellesley, and a very good likeness. We had a very excellent, snug dinner, but the servants contrived to forget to bring any champagne, at which our hospitable host was much displeased.

After taking each our bottle of claret, we got into our *palanquins* to pay Rajah Davi Sing a visit, and an entertainment was prepared by the *rajah* on our account. He received us at his outer gate, where we went through the ceremony of embracing, etc., etc., after which we were ushered up to an immense room, very handsomely lighted up, and well furnished after the Indian style, with couches, very rich, and some of the finest lustres I ever saw.

As soon as we were seated they commenced offering their presents. We received about £25 each in cash, and a very handsome *hookah* with superb apparatus. The singing commenced about eleven, and after it a kind of pantomime. The singing-girls, which in general have some very pretty women in each set, were not so desirable as might have been expected on such an occasion, and in such a city as Moorshadabad.

We supped at twelve on very excellent fruit, and some good claret was also provided for us, but of it we took but a small quantity. After supper a range of Venetians were thrown open, and a grand display of fireworks were played off in an elegant garden beneath us; they exceeded any I had ever seen, and were the very best that could be procured. The evening finished with a sort of play, and about two we left Rajah Davi Sing's, and got home at half-past.

December 13th.—We breakfasted at eight this morning, and at ten we took our leave of our worthy and hospitable host.

The first seven miles I drove Becher in the *phaeton*, when we got into a buggy, which was laid for the second stage, and the two last stages we performed in our *palanquins*. About four we passed Plassey, and went over the ground on which the ever memorable battle was fought in 1757 by Lord Clive. We arrived at our boats soon after sunset at Agur Diep, where we found our dinner all ready; dressed, and made a sumptuous meal, after which we drank our late host's health in a bumper of claret, and at eleven went to bed.

December 17th.—Arrived this morning at eight o'clock at Barrackpore. Landed, and called on my friend Mrs. Christie; was very happy also in meeting Broughton and Cunynghame, two of my oldest acquaintances. We remained here only for the turn of the tide, and dispatched a boat to Calcutta with a note to Thornhill to advise him of our approach. At four we arrived at the Old Fort Ghaut, and immediately hired a carriage at the moderate price of a gold *mohur* (equal to two guineas). I drove to Thornhill's, and Becher on to his brother's at the cavalry lines. Met with a most friendly reception at Thornhill's, and was congratulated by the whole of the family on my return to Calcutta after the many dangers to which we had been exposed.

CHAPTER 28

Calcutta to Prince of Wales Island (Penang) on Board the *Althea*

December 18th.—Called this morning on the Macan's, and was very much mortified at finding that I was too late to sail in a packet with them. The *Margaret* had been taken up by Government. Colonel Macan took the whole of the accommodation for himself, Major Kelly, Captain Macan, and myself, but in consequence of the packet receiving orders to be in readiness to sail at the shortest notice, and my not having arrived in Calcutta they took on board another officer. The sailing of the packet with the despatches was put off, but the gentleman they had received on board could not be prevailed upon to give up his cabin.

This disappointment induced me to alter my plans, and as there was no prospect of other ships sailing for a considerable length of time, to go directly to China, and if the voyage should prove ineffectual, to proceed on with the China fleet, which I should find at anchor at Canton; but if, on my arrival at China, my health should be perfectly re-established, then to return again to India. This plan was highly approved by Thornhill and his father. I determined on taking my passage on board the *Althea*, a beautiful ship of eight hundred tons burthen.

December 22nd.—This morning I went with MacGregor in his *curricle* to breakfast with the Cumberleges, who had taken a house near the racecourse. We returned by Chowringhie, and I paid a visit to my friend, Mrs. Money (Eliza Ramus, *ci-devant*). Went afterwards to the billiard room, and tiffed with Doveton.

December 25th.—Called this morning on my kind friends, the Elliotts, and afterwards paid a visit to Mr. Davis, the gentleman who so gallantly defended his staircase at Benares, when his house was beset by Vizier Ally Calcutta. and his followers, immediately after their having com- mitted the horrid murder at Mr. Cherry's. They went to Mr. Davis's to perpetrate a similar instance of their cowardice and barbarity there, but Mr. Davis's gallant exertions saved his wife and family, as well as himself, from the cruelty of those wretches. Mrs. Elliott is Mrs. Davis's sister.

Returned by way of Fort William, and went through the Arsenal with Young. I dined today with Mr. Goad, and passed a pleasant evening.

December 29th.—Captain Thornhill informed me this morning of his having secured a passage for me in the *Althea*, but Captain Richardson insisted on taking nothing for my passage. I sent immediately to the wine merchants, and got half a chest of the best English claret, for which I paid 250 *rupees* (£26), and made the captain a present of it. Got all my clothes home from the different tailors today, and was quite prepared for my voyage.

January 1st.—1806. We had a party at Thornhills at dinner today, and about ten we left the house to go to a ball and supper at Lady Anstruther's, the last to be given by her ladyship previous to her departure for England. The evening was very gay☐a great deal of dancing, and at supper we had five long tables, well filled. The party consisted of nearly three hundred persons. I went with Mr. Littledale, a young man of the civil service, in his carriage. We broke up about three in the morning.

January 2nd.—This morning I was summoned on board ship, and accordingly hired a stout boat to carry me down to Saugor Roads, where the *Althea* was lying at anchor. In the evening

Thornhill drove me to take leave of the Elliotts, which I did with rather a heavy heart, and was afterwards set down at Becher's, where I dined. We passed a pleasant evening, and I got home by eleven. Took leave of my kind friend Becher with very sincere regret.

January 3rd.—At ten this morning I left Calcutta, with all my baggage, to go down to the ship. I reached Fulta about nine o'clock, and got a beefsteak and a bottle of claret for my dinner; for the latter they charged me six *rupees* and two for my dinner. The tide serving at one in the morning, I again went on board my boat and sailed for Saugor. Some soldiers from the Custom House at Fulta came on board, and it was with difficulty that I prevailed on them not to detain me, as I had not the necessary papers from the Custom House in Calcutta. I cleared Diamond Harbour before daylight, and about eight brought to for three hours, the tide running so strong that we could make no way against it.

We remained on a point off Saugor Island till eleven, when we got up our anchor and came in sight of the ships at Kedgeree soon after twelve. At two we got into Saugor Roads, and I hailed the first ship I made, which was the *Lord Duncan*, Indiaman, and about a mile astern of her lay the *Althea*, on board of which I arrived about half-past two o'clock, and was very politely received by the officers on board, the chief of whom was Captain Richardson's brother.

January 8th.—At nine this morning the pilot offered to accompany me on shore, and we left the ship in a tow boat. At ten we made the shore, but could not venture to land, on account of the number of tigers on Saugor Island. The pilot pointed out the spot to me on which a son of Sir Hector Munro's was destroyed by one some years ago, when on a shooting excursion from his ship in the roads. We went a long way up one of the most romantic creeks in the world, and as we had our fowling pieces we shot some water fowl, but saw no tigers, nor beasts of any description. The weather was very pleasant, and a fresh breeze carried us on board in an hour.

January 9th.—Soon after breakfast this morning a boat hove in sight to windward, which we concluded was Captain Richardson's. We got on board a tow boat, and drifted down with the tide, till we came within hail, when we found it was Captain Cummings, of the *Albion*; the tide was at this time running so strong that it was with great difficulty we reached the ship, and the men at the oars were nearly exhausted when we got alongside.

Several large ships came in from sea this morning, and the *St. Fiorenzo* (formerly at Weymouth with the King) and *Psyche* frigates, anchored in Kedgeree Roads, having come in from a cruise. At one p.m. a large ship came in, close hauled, with her starboard tacks aboard; she passed us, and tacked close under our stern, and it was one of the prettiest sights I ever saw, as the ship was worked with uncommon dexterity.

January 10th.—At seven this morning Captain Richardson came on board, and we unmoored ship. By the captain we learnt that the *Dedaigneuse* frigate was to accompany us to a certain latitude, at which we were much rejoiced, as the idea of being carried into the Isle of France was not a very pleasant one, and the number of French cruisers now in the Bay would have made our voyage very precarious without a convoy of some kind. The *Althea* mounted twelve guns, short twelve-pounders, but the crew being quite unacquainted with the mode of working them, we could have made but a poor defence against a regular ship of war.

January 11th.—At eight this morning the ships which came in last night passed within hail, and at twelve the *Old Triton* (formerly lost in so disgraceful a manner) came round the south point of Saugor Island. The Ship *Triton* was taken by a pilot schooner and seventeen Frenchmen, early in the last war, to the eternal shame of those on board her.

January 12th.—At daybreak this morning we weighed our

anchor and stood down for the Red Buoy. At four we found that the frigate was the *St. Fiorenzo*, which I remembered to have seen many years since at Weymouth in attendance on His Majesty.

January 14th.—Presented my chest of claret to Captain Richardson this morning. Nothing could exceed his polite *Althea* attention, and everything on board the *Althea* was as comfortable, with as good dinners as could possibly be furnished at sea. With half the Round House, I found myself in somewhat more pleasant accommodation than on board the *Bengal*, where we were heaped in, and pent together in a very comfortless way, as is always the case with the unfortunate cadets on a crowded ship.

January 16th.—Got under weigh at five this morning, with a light but fair breeze. At seven we passed the Gasper Sand, on which many vessels are generally lost in the course of a year. Made a signal (a Jack under the ship's colours) to speak a pilot schooner which stood immediately down for us. Saw the *Albion* astern, working down with royals, and all her studding sails set. At ten we discovered the Red Buoy of the Gasper, bearing south-west, and at noon we had but four and a half fathoms water; the ship drew nearly four fathoms. About two we anchored in five and a half fathoms distant from the Red Buoy of the Gasper about one mile, bearing south-west. *La Forte*, French frigate, taken by Sibyll, used to practice her crew in firing at this buoy.

January 17th.—Lowered the royals on deck this morning; at eight we saw two sail standing down to us, but neither of them had the appearance of the frigate which detained us. At ten two more sail were seen from the masthead, standing down with the wind abeam, and at two o'clock a pilot schooner came alongside and told us the *Dedaigneuse* and *Mornington* were the ships in sight.

Sent our royals aloft, and got the yards across, and all ready to weigh anchor. Gave the pilot charge of a letter to Young in Calcutta, enclosing one for Lord Sidmouth. At one the *Morn-

ington came alongside; we weighed, and Mr. Hammett, the pilot, left us in six fathoms water. At six o'clock the wind came nearly ahead, and we were under some apprehensions that we should not be able to fetch out. At eight the *Dedaigneuse* made a signal to tack; and we worked to windward, which carried us clear of the Saugor Sands. At midnight we were in thirteen fathoms water, under a press of sail, standing out to sea.

February 4th.—We saw Prince of Wales' Island this morning at daybreak, and the breeze continuing fair, we crowded all sail, and at noon were nearly abreast of the southern point of the island. The land had a beautiful appearance as we entered the harbour. The island appeared about eight or nine miles in length, and five or six across. Much wooded, and very hilly. The high land of Queadah on our larboard beam, as we sailed in, had a most majestic appearance; the mainland about three miles distant from us. We saw plainly the pepper plantations on the island at sunset.

About six o'clock it fell calm, and we came to an anchor in eight fathoms water, about one mile astern of the *Rattlesnake* sloop of war, on which Sir Thomas Trowbridge's flag was flying, as commander in-chief of the division of ships on this destination. Saw many ships further up the harbour. A boat from the shore, from the governor, the Honourable Philip Dundas, came on board this evening, just as we anchored.

February 5th.—The tide serving at nine this morning, and the wind veering round, we weighed anchor, and stood farther in, with all sail set. Saw the fort very plainly at ten o'clock. The wind failing us, sent out our jolly boat and *pinnace* to tow the vessel. Prince of Wales' Island appeared very woody, intercepted with plantations of pepper, and had a most romantic appearance from on board. The mainland forms one part of the harbour, and the island from it is not more than three miles distant. Soon after ten we anchored abreast of Fort Cornwallis, in nine fathoms water. The tide running in extremely strong, at the time we let go our anchor, the cable was severely strained in bringing her up.

CHAPTER 29

At Prince of Wales' Island (Penang) Waiting for a Ship

February 6th.—At seven o'clock this morning I went with Captain Richardson on shore in the jolly boat. We walked to Mr. Dickens' house, about half a mile from the beach; was very politely received by Mr. and Mrs. Dickens. Mr. Dickens being the senior judge of the island, and a most respectable character, was much looked up to and admired by the inhabitants.

After breakfast we had a long walk, and Captain Richardson introduced me to Colonel Eales, Captain Drummond, Captain Seton, Captain Ross, and many others of his friends. We were much pleased with Mrs. Drummond, who appeared a very genteel and a very pretty woman. Her husband a thoroughbred Scotchman. The houses or bungalows at Prince of Wales' Island are very small, but neatly constructed, and well furnished. The roads for a drive of nine or ten miles in circumference are good.

Their carriages very small, light, and calculated to the cattle they drive. The tallest horse I saw on the island did not exceed twelve hands. They go at a great rate, and are extremely sure-footed. Most of those ponies are brought from Acheen, in the island of Sumatra, a Malay country, at which we touched for water and provisions on our way to India in 1800. Acheen is not more than six or eight days' sail from Prince of Wales' Island.

After the European custom, we dined today at four o'clock,

and at six Mr. and Mrs. Dickens in one carriage, and Captain Richardson and self in another, left the house, and had a long drive. The roads resembled those of a level country in England; narrow, but very good, with woods running close to the roadside, which made it extremely pleasant and very unusual to an Indian eye. We returned to Mr. Dickens' house about seven o'clock. In our drive we Admiral Sir Thomas Trowbridge, and most of the respectable people on the island. Their carriages are very mean, and after those of Bengal, had quite a shabby appearance, and even the members of the Council did not sport a *curricle*. About eleven o'clock I walked to the beach, and found the boat waiting. Went on board the *Althea*.

February 8th.—As usual I went on shore this morning to breakfast and to pass the day; had many invitations to remain constantly, but preferred sleeping on board. Captain Richardson having brought his curricle on shore, and borrowed of a friend a pair of horses, we left Mr. Dickens' house at five this afternoon, and had a very long drive in the curricle into the country.

The pepper and nutmeg plantations had a very novel and pleasing appearance, and a fine sea breeze made the weather cool and pleasant. There being scarcely such a carriage in the island as a *curricle*, and Captain Richardson's being a very handsome one, we were stared at with astonishment; the horses, though small, were very handsome and fleet, trotting ten miles within the hour with ease. They did not exceed twelve hands, and for Prince of Wales' Island were considered tall horses. We met Admiral Trowbridge in a Prussian carriage (kind of car) with Mr. and Mrs. Grey. Dined today with Captain Drummond.

February 10th.—In consequence of the uncertainty of procuring a passage back from Malacca, and being resolved to return to Europe with the China Fleet, I determined on remaining on the island till their arrival, and at six o'clock this evening, when the *Althea* had got under weigh, I left the ship, having taken my leave of my friend, Captain Richardson, and the officers of the *Althea*, all of whom I left with regret, as they were very pleasant young men.

It blew fresh when I went on shore, and I was completely wet by the sea breaking in. My baggage I had fortunately sent on shore in the morning, or it would have been injured by the salt water. I arrived at Captain Ross's house soon after seven o'clock, and found all my baggage safe.

February 11th.—Went with Captain Ross after breakfast this morning to call on several gentlemen friends of his. Notwithstanding Captain Ross's polite invitation to remain with him, as his house was small, I determined on taking a bungalow for the short time of my stay at Prince of Wales' Island. Sent my servant accordingly to make enquiries. Owing to having been a short time this morning in the sun, I felt its baneful effects, and was quite unwell the whole of the day. Went in the evening to look at a house, and hired it at twenty dollars (equal to £5 10s.) per month.

February 13th.—About an hour before sunset I went to look at the artillery, paraded to fire blank cartridge. Captain Ross and self took a long ride in the direction of the hills in the rear of Georgetown. Dined with Lieutenant Huthwaite, of the Marine Regiment, on duty here; met three officers of the *Phaeton* at dinner, Lieutenants Hawkins, Millwood and another. The sailors took lots of claret, and were quite high before they went on board the frigate.

February 17th.—I seriously began to wish the arrival of the China Fleet to get once clear of the horrid climate. Rode a short distance into the country this evening with Captain Ross. On our way we met with a Dutchman taken prisoner by us at Amboyna, and now holding the appointment of acting ensign in our service.

February 19th.—Breakfasted with Captain Drummond this morning and went after breakfast to be introduced to the Admiral Sir Thomas Trowbridge, whom I found a most gentlemanly, pleasant man. As I was the first officer he had seen from General

Lord Lake's army, he asked a great number of questions, and had all our "battles o'er again." At the admiral's we met Captain Beauchamp Proctor, of the *Dedaigneuse* frigate, and Captain Fothergill, of the *Lancaster* man-of-war. We paid Sir Thomas a long visit.

February 25th.—A very large party this evening at Captain Drummond's, commanding officer of Prince of Wales' Island. Mr. Gray (second in Council), Mrs. Gray, and many of the Scotch invasion, were of the party; met among others a fine young man, Lieutenant La Mesuierer, flag lieutenant to Admiral Trowbridge.

March 1st.—The first paper ever printed on Prince of Wales' Island came out this morning, and a more stupid collection than that which filled it I never saw.

March 2nd.—There was an immense row this evening near Ross's bungalow, it being a Chinese holiday; these people were performing a play in the street, on a stage erected for the purpose. The road was so much crowded that I could not, without much difficulty, get past. Admiral Trowbridge and a number of people were looking on. It appeared to me a very stupid entertainment, and did not even appear sufficiently ridiculous to arrest one's attention.

March 3rd.—A report that the government of this place will be immediately changed, an event which it is supposed will grieve those only who are at the head of it, and whose chief care is said to be to make as much money as possible themselves, and to prevent others doing the same.

March 9th—This morning I went with the judge (Mr. Dickens) to breakfast with Mr. Gray, second in Council; found Mrs. Gray a very pleasant, genteel woman. She was a Miss Bassett, and sister to Lady Essex. We remained with them till about ten, and from thence went to call on the Admiral, Sir Thomas Trowbridge, a great friend of Mr. Dickens. The admiral entertained us with a famous story, which occurred when he was first lieutenant of Sir Edward Hughes' ship in this country, in 1783!

It was noon before we reached our bungalows, and I found myself extremely annoyed by the heat, and which was my principal reason for wishing to visit but little, and to keep to the house, it being very different from Bengal, where *palanquins* are used on such occasions. I saw no such a conveyance on Prince of Wales' Island.

March 11th.—The *Antelope* cruiser came in last night, and brought Europe extracts up to the 15th of September, by which we heard of Admiral Cornwallis' attempt to bring the French fleet, which had got under weigh, to action, and of the gallant manner in which he was seconded by Sir Richard Strachan in the *Caesar*. We learnt also the preparations for a campaign in Europe, and I seriously wished for an opportunity of joining in it, which, if I reach England in good health, I am resolved to effect, if possible. This evening we dined with Captain Keasbury, of the Madras establishment, and there was a great deal of hard drinking, in which I did not join.

March 15th.—This morning I purchased a slave boy of Captain Keasbury to accompany me to England and attend me on board ship. I paid ninety dollars for him (equal to about £25 sterling).

March 16th.—At daybreak this morning I mounted the judge's pony, and rode to a waterfall in the hills. The road to this place was more romantic than any I had ever seen, and the villages through which we rode were really enchanting, but the ascents and descents exceedingly steep, and the paths would barely afford room for a horse to pass in safety, as in many places the precipices on either side were quite terrific, and, on an unsteady, timid horse, very dangerous.

Lieutenant Phillips, of the Madras Infantry, accompanied me, and at the waterfall we dismounted, tied up our horses by the bridle (just as they do in England), and enjoyed a most delightful bathe. The distance of the waterfall from the town (five long miles) is the most unpleasant part of it, as, from the nature of the road, you must necessarily ride slow, and the sun consequently becomes very hot before you reach your quarters. We breakfasted with Lieutenant Huthwaite in the country.

Dined there in the evening, a very gay party, and went home at three in Phillip's buggy. Huthwaite today related a circumstance most honourable and generous of my friend, Captain Ross. They were at sea, passing near Amboyna, and in a stiff breeze, the ship going at seven knots (miles), when a native child, belonging to a servant of Huthwaite's, fell overboard. Ross was standing on the gunwale, and seeing the infant floating past, most generously and humanely dashed overboard, got hold of the child, which he actually supported in the water for upwards of three hours upon a grating which they threw to him. It was that length of time before they could be picked up.

The vessel was going before the wind, and they were obliged to make several tacks, and had frequently lost sight of both Ross and the child before they could get to them; the sea was running high, and they had not a single boat on board that could swim! Fortunately, both were saved, and it is no less singular that the child was soon afterwards drowned in the *Anstruther*, which ship was lost.

March 19th.—The weather cooler today than I had felt it since I came to the island. The China Fleet now daily expected, and I seriously began to prepare for going on board. During breakfast a brace of snipe dropped in Keasbury's Compound within thirty yards of the house. This island swarms with snipe, and of a larger kind than I ever saw elsewhere.

March 21st.—This morning I was informed that the governor had remarked my not calling on him, but as he lived nearly seven miles from the town, and did not bear the character of being a most liberal man, I determined not to put myself out of my way on his account, as I conceived myself to be as independent of the governor as he was of me, nor had I inclination or health to spare, by exposing myself to the climate in paying formal visits, and this was my answer to the person who gave me the information.

March 27th.—Several of the Indiamen came in and anchored in the harbour today, and others were in sight working round the point. The *Cumberland* was among the latter, which made me rather uncomfortable, as I was desirous of finally settling for my passage, as the ships were liable to be ordered off at two hours' notice. I purchased the skins and feathers of five *argus* pheasants today, and prepared them for a voyage to Europe, hoping some day to see them grace some of my lovely friends at home.

March 28th.—This morning came in the *Cumberland*, and Captain Keasbury and myself went to seek Captain Farrer; he was gone to call on the governor and Sir Thomas Trowbridge. We waited two hours, in vain, for him, and Keasbury paid him a second visit, when they agreed for my passage at *drs.* 500. To have sailed from Bengal with the same accommodation (a cabin on the starboard side of the cuddy, the same in which the Miss Wedderburne came out) would have cost 2,000 dollars! I was quite happy and perfectly satisfied with this conclusion to my affairs in India (at least for the time).

March 29th—Keasbury breakfasted with us at Ross's this morning, and afterwards we went, and I was introduced to Captain Farrer, of the *Cumberland*, whose appearance and manners I liked much. The captain gave me to understand that he expected we should not sail before Sunday or Monday. I returned, and sent him the amount of my passage money. Ross asked a large party of officers to meet me at dinner today, but at four o'clock the following note came from Captain Farrer:—

> Dear Sir,—As the Commodore is under weigh, I propose to go on board about five p.m., and, should my cutter not come in time, intend taking a shore boat. I shall be happy with your company.

This note came at the moment I was engaged in correspondence with the government of this place, who affected to give themselves airs because I had not visited them, and on that account hesitated to grant me an order for being received on board, according to the usual forms.

In reply I expressed my astonishment that they were ignorant of the order directing all officers arriving at presidencies or stations to report their arrival to the commanding officer of the forces or town major, and which order, I told them, I had complied with on my arrival at their presidency. I forwarded with this letter a copy of a general order from the establishment under which I served, and desired to know by what authority they detained me.

In answer to this I received a sulky order to be received on board the *Cumberland*. I was much hurried by Captain Farrer's unexpected summons on board, as it was past four when I received it. I immediately mounted my horse and rode to Mr. Dickens's to take my leave of him and Mrs. Dickens, and directly went on board the *Cumberland* with Captain Farrer and his surgeon, Mr. Livestone.

The Indiamen were all getting under weigh as we passed them (the *Cumberland* being the outermost ship), and the Commodore (Captain Fothergill, of H.M. ship *Lancaster*, 64 guns), continued working out and firing signal guns to hurry them in weighing their anchors. The tide was strong against us, and the *Blenheim* fired her evening gun (eight o'clock) before we got on board.

Soon after eight it was to my inexpressible joy that I again put my foot on board ship for Old England, and those only who have been long absent from their friends and native country can conceive what a man's feelings are on such occasions; they cannot be described. I found my cabin a most elegant one, and everything on board had a very delightful appearance.

I had never despaired of the coming of this happy moment, but when I reflected on the many fine fellows I had left, buried in India, and that I had been at all times as liable to the untimely fate that awaited them as themselves, I considered myself a fortunate man in having escaped. I dismissed one of my servants and sent him on shore, keeping only the boy, Delhi, to accompany me during the voyage.

We got under weigh about ten at night, and at twelve the *Henry Addington* was so close alongside, and the wind failing at the same time, that they were obliged to carry out their boats and tow the ship's head round. Commodore firing guns and making signals to ships astern. I did not go to my couch till past twelve o'clock.

CHAPTER 30

On Board the *Cumberland* to St. Helena

At daylight this morning we were about ten miles from the north point of Prince of Wales' Island, and distant from the Quedah shore about five miles. The *Lancaster* (the Commodore) was the only ship ahead of us; she fired a gun, and made signals for ships astern to make more sail about seven o'clock. The sternmost ships were not within four miles of us at this time.

This morning I met at breakfast, and was introduced to, Mr. Seager, chief officer, and Mr. Bethune, second. The following ships in company:—H.M. ship *Lancaster*, 64 guns, Captain Fothergill, giving the convoy; *Wexford*, Captain Clarke; *Henry Addington*, Kirkpatrick; *Bombay Castle*, Hamilton; *Royal George*, Gribble; *Ocean*, Williamson; *Earl Howe*, Murray; *Windham*, Stewart; *Cumberland*, Farrer; *Warley*, Wilson; *Coutts*, Hay; *Exeter*, Meriton; *Hope*, Pendergrass; *Scaleby Castle*.

April 1st.—I went down on the gun deck today, and visited the chief, second and third officers in their cabins. The *Cumberland* one of the finest ships I ever saw. She carried thirty-six eighteen-pounders, short guns on the lower deck, and carronades on the quarter deck.

April 6th.—Light airs, and very sultry. We were in hopes some boats from Sumatra would come off with fruit. (They brought it many miles out to us when we made the land on our way to India). The wind all the morning was on our larboard beam, and, as my cabin was on the starboard side (the same which Miss Wedderburne, sister to the Honourable Mrs. Dundas, occupied on her passage to India when the *Cumberland* came out) it was so close that I could not without difficulty breathe in it.

April 16th.—At noon today, in consequence of a blow from another lad, one of the maintop boys fell out of the top, down on the fife rails. His head was cut in a most shocking manner, and he was carried down apparently lifeless, but recovering his breath, he continued screaming in agonies of pain, and perfectly senseless. Surgeon had no hopes of his recovery. Captain Farrer immediately ordered the boy who struck him to be put in irons.

April 19th.—Worked the gun deck and exercised the great guns. The following are the motions on board ship:—

WORDS OF COMMAND. (AT SEA, ON BOARD THE CUMBERLAND LAT. 1.58 S.)

Take out your tompions; run out your guns; take off your aprons; handle your powder horns; prick your cartridges; prime; bruise your priming; secure powder horns; handle crows and handspikes; point your points; handle your matches; blow your matches; fire; secure the vent; handle your sponges; sponge your guns; load with cartridge; wad your cartridge; ram home; shot your guns; wad your shot; ram home; run out your guns.

Exercising the great guns on board a ship very frequently appeared to me to be of the greatest utility, and a few well-trained men thoroughly acquainted with their quarters, and expert in working the guns, would have infinite advantage over greater numbers less disciplined; and if the China ships were well manned I should conceive them a match for any frigate in the French Service.

May 2nd.—The cool, pleasant wind this way was a perfect balsam to my body and mind, and I felt a glow of spirit to which I had long been a stranger. Some fish were seen about the ship's bows, and I took my station on the sprit sail yard arm with the harpoon for nearly an hour, but saw one fish only.

May 26th.—We had an unfavourable wind during the greater part of this day, and the log did not produce more than sixty miles. It was one of the finest moonlight nights I ever remembered, and it looked well for a pleasant, quiet night when I left the quarter deck at ten o'clock. About midnight the wind freshened, and soon after it came on to blow tremendously. A violent gust of wind came so suddenly that the officer of the watch had barely time to let go the halliards and let fly topgallant sheets to save the topmasts.

The ship laid seemingly half-buried on her side in the sea. I was to leeward, and one of my ports being opened, my hat, which was on one of my trunks, was thrown out of the port and lost overboard. The hat I did not mind, but the bearskin on it was the finest I ever saw, although I had worn it upwards of five years, and on every occasion during the four campaigns I served in India. Captain Farrer insisted on my taking from him an excellent new hat.

May 29th.—At break of day this morning I went up on the quarter deck, from which we could with the greatest difficulty discern the sternmost ships of the fleet. The commodore himself was barely in sight from the masthead, and if a sudden gust of wind or trifling squall had sprung up in the night we must inevitably have been separated from the fleet, and the consequences might have terminated very seriously. The commodore now thought it prudent to heave to for us, which any other officer in his situation would have done last evening. At twelve o'clock we could discern his signal for ships to make sail, and about five in the evening, as we approached the fleet, he made the following signal with the *Cumberland*'s On board pennant flying: "You detain the whole convoy by the your inattention."

Captain Farrer, conscious that no inattention either on his part or on that of his officers, had been the cause of detaining the fleet, was exceedingly vexed at this reprimand, and he had certainly the greatest reason to be so, as from what I saw myself nothing could exceed his anxiety all yesterday, and this morning to get his ship in her station, and if the lives of anyone on board had been depending on it, so far from inattention, greater exertion could not have been made to join the convoy.

June 2nd.—Wind shifted during the night, and came nearly aft. The whole fleet under a press of sails, with a light breeze. At ten a.m. we spoke the *Warley*, Captain Wilson, and from him we learnt the news so anxiously looked for. Captain Wilson informed us that the Cape of Good Hope was in our possession, that Linois, the French admiral, had been captured in his ship, the *Marengo*; that an action had been fought at sea between the English and combined fleets, in which the former were victorious, and that Lord Nelson gloriously fell in the battle.

Were it allowable to lament the loss of a hero who died gloriously fighting the battles of his country, all must be dejected at the death of that great and noble character, who had so often merited and received the applause, and excited the admiration, of a grateful country, by which his memory will forever be held sacred.

June 4th.—About one o'clock the *Bombay Castle* asked the commodore's permission to communicate the intelligence gained from the stranger to the rest of the fleet, which was granted, by signal. The *Bombay Castle* then hoisted the telegraph preparatory flag, and proceeded to telegraph signals to inform us that

> Lord Nelson, with twenty-seven sail of the line, attacked the combined fleets, consisting of thirty sail, off Cadiz in November. One and twenty sail of the enemy were captured in the action, and four ships the following day. The victor (Lord Nelson) was killed. Sir Hume Popham arrived at the Cape on the 1st of January, and it surrendered on the 5th.

> This not only confirmed the intelligence given us a few days

since, but stated to us more particulars. We drank his Majesty's health with cordial good wishes for many returns of the day to him. We had on board the *Cumberland* a French officer, whom the chance of war had thrown into our hands, and it was really affecting to see how much this man seemed to take the misfortunes of his country at heart. He was one of several captured in the Bay of Bengal, and they were distributed through our fleet, and the captains had orders to deliver them over prisoners of war on their arrival in Europe. We ran one hundred and ninety-six miles the last twenty-four hours.

June 6th.—The sea ran mountains high this evening, and constantly deluged the quarterdeck. I was standing in the ship's waist, looking over to windward, when a sea broke completely over me, and I got a complete swilling; all the seamen in the waist at the time were washed down against the booms to leeward. While I am now writing this, it blows as furious a gale as I ever recollect to have witnessed at sea, and the ship going at nine knots with her mainsail furled, the mizzen topsail handed, the foresail and fore and main-topsails close reefed; but it was blowing us towards dear England, and the roaring of the sea and wind, with the ship going at such a rate, was music to our souls.

June 16th.—At seven this morning the commodore made the signal for the fleet to continue its course; he stood directly in for the land, either for the purpose of making it again, or of communicating, if possible, some private signal. At noon the haze cleared away, and we found ourselves just abreast of the tableland at the Cape of Good Hope, and Captain Farrer pointed out to me the land which formed False Bay, and the hill near which Cape Town stands.

June 19th.—Lat. 35-50. The sea was mountains high this morning, and it was almost impossible to walk the deck. It blew so hard a gale that we were under the necessity of lying to, for a considerable time, under storm stay sails. The vessel heeled so much that our leeward cannons were frequently buried in the waves. Owing to the tempestuous night the fleet was a good deal scattered, nor were they all in sight from the masthead.

July 2nd.—We mounted some additional guns this forenoon, and now the *Cumberland*'s complement altogether was fifty-six pieces of cannon, and she was one of the finest merchant ships in the world, and if well manned would be a match for the stoutest frigate in the French Navy. Her quarters for the men at the guns were excellent; more lofty and roomy than on board any vessel of the kind I ever saw. She was the ship that laid alongside of the French admiral's ship, the *Marengo* (eighty guns) on her outward bound passage, and in her turn poured her broadsides into the Frenchman; and it proved a more serious salute, no doubt, than Linois expected.

He sheered off. The *Cumberland* bore part of Commodore Dance's action with Admiral Linois in the *Marengo*, and a squadron of French frigates in the China seas, two years since, so that she had twice bid defiance to this terror of the Indian seas. About ten Captain Farrer came to my cabin windows and told me that land was visible from the deck, and we saw the island very distinctly directly upon our weather bow.

At noon we could distinctly make out the different and most remarkable points of the island.

Two very small detached islands, called Egg Islands, were quite perceptible on the southern extremity, and the Sugar Loaf Hill at the northern point. The breaks in the land along shore, and the craggy beach, which on the eastern face appeared inaccessible, except at Sandy Bay, which is said to be the most vulnerable quarter, and which lies at the eastward most part of St. Helena, afforded really a very romantic and grand spectacle, and the appearance was highly gratifying to me.

At first the island literally appeared a mere speck in the ocean, so very small a place is it in reality. Captain Farrer prepared his despatches and wrote a note to a friend of his to secure lodgings for himself and for me at a comfortable house on the island. In passing close under the Rock and batteries the scene was very grand indeed; the latter on eminences so completely commanded the ships in passing that a shot entering on the quarterdeck would probably pass out at the keel!

On rounding the point on which stands Munden's Battery, the church and village in the valley afford an uncommonly neat and romantic appearance, and what is called the Castle has, from on board, far more the appearance of a barn! About four we anchored in the Roads, and found riding here his Majesty's ship "Adamant" of fifty guns, waiting purposely to give us convoy to dear England. The instant the anchor was gone Captain Farrer and myself dressed and went on shore in the captain's gig.

We went immediately to the castle, and Captain Farrer introduced me to Governor Patten. We remained about half an hour with the governor, and from thence to Mr. Leech's, who gave us very comfortable accommodation. At tea we had Mr. and Mrs. Leech and five daughters, Captain Wilson, of the *Warley* (the same who was cast away in the *Antelope* on the Pelen Islands, and who carried with him Prince Lebar, the king's son, to England, where he unfortunately died island of the smallpox), and several other gentlemen who came also for lodgings at Mr. Leeche's.

Walked a considerable distance up the valley of St. Helena, and by moonlight the stupendous rocks hanging over the houses seemed to threaten them with immediate destruction, and looked really terrific. Returned about nine, and met at supper a very large party. We eat very fine potatoes, and watercresses, which, to people just come off a long voyage, were a great luxury. Mr. Leeche's family seemed exceedingly polite to all their lodgers, and made themselves very pleasant.

CHAPTER 31

Island of St. Helena and Voyage Home

July 3rd.—After dinner Captain Heathcote, of the navy, lately in command of the *Hughes*, of sixty-four guns, Captain Taylor, and myself took a walk to look at the works fronting the harbour, and very near the valley. We were all invalids, Heathcote and Taylor being, like myself, under the necessity of returning to Europe with very shattered constitutions, and much reduced.

July 4th.—After breakfast this morning Heathcote, with Taylor and myself, went to look at the works on Ladder Hill Battery; we were joined by Sir Robert Wilson and Captain Christian (son of Admiral Christian). The Ladder Hill Battery completely flanks the harbour, and consists of full thirty pieces of cannon; among them are several 13-inch mortars. The guns are mostly long twenty-fours. The guns from this battery also have an entire command of the village below, and which might, in the course of an hour, be entirely laid in ashes if an enemy was in possession.

A very strong battery, called High Knowle, overlooks Ladder Hill, from the guns of which you may easily dislodge troops from the latter place. At High Knowle they have storehouses, and reservoirs for water, in case of an attack, and supposing an enemy to be in possession of the lower works and the village, they could not remain, so commanding are the works at High Knowle.

From these batteries you have a perfect view of every part of the decks of all ships that come sufficiently near to gain anchoring ground, and from the direction in which the guns point down a ship would be very easily sunk, and without the possibility of the latter doing any kind of mischief to the batteries, as the At the height is so great that guns from shipping below island of could not be brought to bear on them.

The only landing place on the beach is guarded by very strong batteries of mortars and heavy cannon, exclusive of the support of the works in different parts of the rocks above, and so very lofty is the land at St. Helena that ships must be seen many hours before they could come near enough to effect a landing of troops, and therefore the little island can never have anything to apprehend from a surprise; and in my opinion if liberally supplied with good troops, would be a match for any moderate force. The water underneath the rocks looked quite transparent; although we were at such an immense height, and the depth of water was also very considerable, we could, notwithstanding, distinctly see the bottom of the sea, near the shore.

We did not visit High Knowle this morning; as invalids we were unable to proceed higher up the rock than Ladder Hill. Sir Robert Wilson informed me of poor Carlton's death; he was Lord Dorchester's son, and had he survived would have succeeded to the title. I was long stationed with Carlton, and had experienced much attention from him.

July 6th.—This morning was particularly cool and cloudy. Taylor and myself took the advantage of it, and went to pay a visit to Captain Fothergill on board his ship the *Lancaster*, sixty-four guns. Nothing could exceed the politeness with which we were received on board, and Captain Fothergill accompanied us over every part of the ship. We went on all the decks, and through the different store rooms below.

The *Lancaster* carried long twenty-four pounders on her gun deck and upon the quarter-deck two and thirty pound carronades, and long bow and stern chasers. We left the *Lancaster* about one o'clock, and during our cruise went on board the *Royal*

George and *Windham* Indiamen; called also on board an American ship just come in from Bombay in eighty days, to learn the intelligence from India.

The American had five sick officers on board, returning like ourselves to Europe for their health. Two of the party I recollected to have seen at Bhirtpore with that detachment of the Bombay Army which joined us there. Dined at three o'clock, and after dinner walked to Munden's Battery, which stands in the middle of the Rock, on the opposite flank of the harbour from the High Knowle and Ladder Hill Batteries. The works were in high condition, the strength of Munden's Battery is fourteen guns, thirty-two, and twenty-four pounders, long guns.

At all these posts they have telegraphs, and on the appearance of any ships an alarm is invariably given, both by telegraph signals and by firing a gun for every ship which may heave in sight, to denote the number approaching the island. It was sunset, and the sentinels on board the *Lancaster* and *Adamant* were discharging their pieces before we left Munden's Battery. We were back in time for tea.

July 8th—This evening we had a grand ball and supper at the Castle, given to us by the governor previous to our departure from his little island. We went about ten o'clock. The room was much crowded, and we had a display of all the beauties of St. Helena. I was unable to dance, but was much pleased with the polite attention of some of the islanders. A custom prevails here for which Governor Patten would, I fancy, get terribly hoaxed in any party of England, that of leaving out indiscriminately all the married ladies.

I remarked to some of the young ladies this very extraordinary custom, and wondered that they attended to such invitations. I was told in answer that if their mothers would give them dances at home they would certainly decline visiting the governor on all occasions when the old ladies were excluded. At eleven supper was announced, but those only who had partners were able to succeed in getting a seat, as the Worshipful the Governor had asked more people by half to his ball and supper than could be accommodated either with partners or anything to eat!

July 9th.—At eight this morning the *Adamant* fired a gun, and made the signal to unmoor. We paid off our score (one guinea a day for board and lodgings) and about eleven the commodore got under weigh, when Captain Farrer and myself took his boat and went on board. The anchor was a-weigh before we reached the ship, and we were presently under easy sail, standing out with a fair breeze. The *Warley* and *Coutts* were not out till nearly an hour after the rest of the fleet.

In about a couple of hours we were at least ten miles from the island. I was standing with Captain Farrer on the ship's poop when an alarm was given that a man was overboard, and in looking over the starboard quarter we saw him swimming astern. The ship was in an instant hove to, and the boat lowered down. The vessel was going five knots at the time, but by the noble exertions of the gallant fellows in the boat they got hold of him just as he was sinking, and brought him on board; although every endeavour to recover him was ineffectual, he never breathed again.

July 12th.—A pleasant trade wind all this day, and in the afternoon it freshened and we went seven and eight knots. Every day now told, and most anxiously did we look forward to the result of the next month's sailing. My mind was much relieved this evening, and I felt quite happy in seeing that one of the English papers mentioned my father in December last, nine months later than any accounts I had received by letter, my last before I left Bengal being dated March, 1805.

July 17th.—Lat. 2.30 S. We had no hopes of clearing the Southern Hemisphere today, as the wind continued very light all the day. The opinion of the officers on board our vessel that the commodore was steering too much to the westward to make a good course of it. The *Coutts*, carrying the senior captain of the Indiamen, made a signal to ask if he should alter his course a point to starboard, which was not answered in any manner by Captain Styles, from which it was concluded that he was in dudgeon at their asking the question, which, in fact, was nothing more nor less than telling him (Captain Styles) that he was steering a wrong course. Thousands of flying fish about the ship this evening.

July 24th.—Lat. 5.31 N. At six this morning the commodore made signal to communicate by the telegraph, and then informed us that the sail spoken to yesterday gave him information of a French line of battleship, and two frigates being very near us, and cautioned all commanders to be prepared. About ten the commodore gave the signal to clear ship for action, and we immediately commenced clearing the guns on the quarter and gun decks. All the water on the latter was hoisted up and stowed away in the waist, so that our men had excellent quarters at the guns. We were all day prepared for battle, as from the commodore's motions and signals there appeared little doubt but that the enemy was near us. We had hands all day on the royal yards looking out.

July 3rd.—Lat. 12.17. All clear for action, but no enemy yet had made his appearance. At seven this morning the wind, which had all the night been variable and light, freshened considerably, and it was judged from the quarter from whence it came that it was the commencement of the North-East Trades, and, as it proved so, we considered ourselves extremely fortunate in bringing the South-East Trades so near it.

Afternoon it came somewhat more favourable, and no one doubted its being a confirmed trade.

It was a beautiful moonlight night, and I did not quit the deck till a late hour, and then so much engaged were my thoughts with the prospect of speedily meeting my worthy friends in Old England that I could not go to rest.

Lat. 14.40. The breeze continued all night, with squalls and some rain at times. The ship heeled considerably, and I was under the necessity of lashing my chair to my couch to be able to sit at my table to read. About eleven, whilst I was standing with Farrer on the poop, the *Exeter* fired a gun and made the signal for a strange sail in the north-east. We conceived it to be one of the squadron of French, which we lately heard was cruising in these seas. Got all ready for battle, and the *Adamant* hauled out of the line, tacked, and made sail towards the stranger.

We kept a good look out from the mast head, but no other ships heaving in sight, and the stranger standing directly down for our fleet, it was judged to be either an English ship or an American.

July 31st.—Lat. 16.23 N. This evening we had a very severe squall, and it came on so suddenly that there was scarcely a ship in the fleet that escaped its ravages. Our foretopsail, mizzen topsail, and foretopmast staysail were torn in pieces by the gale, and the ship laid almost upon her beam ends. A young lad, nephew of Captain Farrer's, who had never been at sea till he came on board us at Saint Helena, was so terribly alarmed that islands. I was really apprehensive that he would have fainted.

Farrer was employed on the quarter deck giving his orders, and attending to the duties of the ship, and I took the lad into my cabin and kept him there till the gale abated.

At seven it cleared up a little, and the rain, which had been very violent, abated. The *Wexford* and *Addington* got so close to the *Adamant* that she fired into or over them, as it is a very wise precaution taken by men-of-war to prevent any ships whatever approaching them after dark. (Lat. 16.23 N.) I was walking the quarterdeck, and saw plainly the flashes of the *Adamant's* musketry, and at first supposed it to have been something more serious, but as no cannons were fired I hardly thought it could be an enemy. Farrer, who was on the poop deck, explained it.

(Lat. 18.43 N.) I purchased today of one of the officers of the ship a piece of china crape for gowns, and for which I paid him £8. In Europe it costs nearly double that sum, and my getting it was a great favour.

August 7th.—The wind considerably fallen off during the night, it still continued to blow from the right quarter, and had the appearance of a Trade, though very light in comparison to what we had latterly experienced.

The people this morning employed in overhauling the cables, which had something the appearance of our approach to land, and we hoped that another fortnight would, if not set us on shore, carry us very near to Albion's white cliffs.

August 8th.—Lat. 31-15 N. This morning it was nearly calm, and we had some difficulty in keeping the vessel's head in the right direction. The third officer of the *Coutts* (a Mr. Hamilton) came on board us, and we learnt that the French squadron, which was the cause of our clearing ship for battle, had been seen by the American, which gave us information of them, the evening only before we spoke of her; she sailed two days in company with them, and understood they were cruising purposely to intercept us, and had we been a few hours only sooner, they must have fallen in with us, and much bloodshed would, in all probability, have been the result. The French squadron consisted of a line of battleship and two very stout frigates. Our Commodore carried fifty guns only, so that much assistance would have been expected and required from us, and we were prepared to do our best.

August 20th.—Lat. 41.20. The breeze continued very favourable, and the *Adamant* made the signal to steer north-east, as we had by this time got well to the westward of the Azores or Western Island. By Captain Clarke, of *Wexford*, who with a Mr. Walters, his passenger, came on board us last evening, we learnt that one of the strange ships lately spoken with gave information that an English squadron was cruising off the Cape de Verd Islands, in quest, we imagined, of the French squadron we heard of near the Line, and which Captain Clarke informed us was supposed to be the fleet said to have sailed under the orders of Jerome Buonaparte.

August 26th.—Lat. 49.2 N. The gale continued fair for us, and rather increased than otherwise. The sea literally ran mountains this morning, and constantly broke over us. Our quarterdeck was most completely drenched, and we found it a very wet berth, and left it for the poop. By calculation today at noon we were not more than three hundred and sixty miles from Cape Clear in Ireland, and about five hundred from the Lizard. Yesterday and today we ran by the log good four hundred miles. At one o'clock the *Wexford* came very close alongside, and we sheered over to port to keep clear of her.

August 29th.—We had constant hard blowing weather ever since the 26th, the first part from the north-west, and thence it shifted to south-west. The sea ran mountains high, and was constantly beating over us. On the 27th at daybreak the *Hope* made a signal for seeing a strange sail, bearing north-east. At eight she passed close under our stern, and we saw plainly that she was an English frigate. She shewed the *Adamant* her number, sheered up under her lee, spoke her, and continued her course to the southward. The frigate appeared to mount forty-four guns, had thirteen ports of a side, mounted twelve guns on her quarter-deck, and four on her forecastle. This evening we were by our reckoning nearly abreast of the Scilly Islands, our course east and by south.

August 30th.—All hands eagerly looking out for the land of Old England; the morning was extremely hazy and accompanied with very heavy squalls and hard rain.

At eleven the *Bombay Castle* had her signal flying for seeing the land, but with all our eyes we could not discover it. At one p.m. Captain Farrer sent to me and from the poop pointed out to me the Lizard bearing north-north-east, and it was with joy indescribable that I once more beheld my native country, a happiness not to be expressed or imagined by those who never left it.

Most fervently did I pray for the weather to clear up, to give them a sight of us from the shore, that boats may come off, as my desire was to land on the Western Coast, and to go home before I went to London.

ALSO FROM LEONAUR
AVAILABLE IN SOFTCOVER OR HARDCOVER WITH DUST JACKET

A JOURNAL OF THE SECOND SIKH WAR by *Daniel A. Sandford*—The Experiences of an Ensign of the 2nd Bengal European Regiment During the Campaign in the Punjab, India, 1848-49.

LAKE'S CAMPAIGNS IN INDIA by *Hugh Pearse*—The Second Anglo Maratha War, 1803-1807. Often neglected by historians and students alike, Lake's Indian campaign was fought against a resourceful and ruthless enemy-almost always superior in numbers to his own forces.

BRITAIN IN AFGHANISTAN 1: THE FIRST AFGHAN WAR 1839-42 by *Archibald Forbes*—Following over a century of the gradual assumption of sovereignty of the Indian Sub-Continent, the British Empire, in the form of the Honourable East India Company, supported by troops of the new Queen Victoria's army, found itself inevitably at the natural boundaries that surround Afghanistan. There it set in motion a series of disastrous events-the first of which was to march into the country at all.

BRITAIN IN AFGHANISTAN 2: THE SECOND AFGHAN WAR 1878-80 by *Archibald Forbes*—This the history of the Second Afghan War-another episode of British military history typified by savagery, massacre, siege and battles.

UP AMONG THE PANDIES by *Vivian Dering Majendie*—An outstanding account of the campaign for the fall of Lucknow. This is a vital book of war as fought by the British Army of the mid-nineteenth century, but in truth it is also an essential book of war that will enthral.

BLOW THE BUGLE, DRAW THE SWORD by *W. H. G. Kingston*—The Wars, Campaigns, Regiments and Soldiers of the British & Indian Armies During the Victorian Era, 1839-1898.

INDIAN MUTINY 150th ANNIVERSARY: A LEONAUR ORIGINAL

MUTINY: 1857 by *James Humphries*—It is now 150 years since the 'Indian Mutiny' burst like an engulfing flame on the British soldiers, their families and the civilians of the Empire in North East India. The Bengal Native army arose in violent rebellion, and the once peaceful countryside became a battleground as Native sepoys and elements of the Indian population massacred their British masters and defeated them in open battle. As the tide turned, a vengeful army of British and loyal Indian troops repressed the insurgency with a savagery that knew no mercy. It was a time of fear and slaughter. James Humphries has drawn together the voices of those dreadful days for this commemorative book.

AVAILABLE ONLINE AT
www.leonaur.com
AND OTHER GOOD BOOK STORES

ALSO FROM LEONAUR
AVAILABLE IN SOFTCOVER OR HARDCOVER WITH DUST JACKET

WAR BEYOND THE DRAGON PAGODA by *J. J. Snodgrass*—A Personal Narrative of the First Anglo-Burmese War 1824 - 1826.

ALL FOR A SHILLING A DAY by *Donald F. Featherstone*—The story of H.M. 16th, the Queen's Lancers During the first Sikh War 1845-1846.

AT THEM WITH THE BAYONET by *Donald F. Featherstone*—The first Anglo-Sikh War 1845-1846.

A LEONAUR ORIGINAL

THE HERO OF ALIWAL by *James Humphries*—The days when young Harry Smith wore the green jacket of the 95th-Wellington's famous riflemen-campaigning in Spain against Napoleon's French with his beautiful young bride Juana have long gone. Now, Sir Harry Smith is in his fifties approaching the end of a long career. His position in the Cape colony ends with an appointment as Deputy Adjutant-General to the army in India. There he joins the staff of Sir Hugh Gough to experience an Indian battlefield in the Gwalior War of 1843 as the power of the Marathas is finally crushed. Smith has little time for his superior's 'bull at a gate' style of battlefield tactics, but independent command is denied him. Little does he realise that the greatest opportunity of his military life is close at hand.

THE GURKHA WAR by *H. T. Prinsep*—The Anglo-Nepalese Conflict in North East India 1814-1816.

SOUND ADVANCE! by *Joseph Anderson*—Experiences of an officer of HM 50th regiment in Australia, Burma & the Gwalior war.

THE CAMPAIGN OF THE INDUS by *Thomas Holdsworth*—Experiences of a British Officer of the 2nd (Queen's Royal) Regiment in the Campaign to Place Shah Shuja on the Throne of Afghanistan 1838 - 1840.

WITH THE MADRAS EUROPEAN REGIMENT IN BURMA by *John Butler*—The Experiences of an Officer of the Honourable East India Company's Army During the First Anglo-Burmese War 1824 - 1826.

BESIEGED IN LUCKNOW by *Martin Richard Gubbins*—The Experiences of the Defender of 'Gubbins Post' before & during the sige of the residency at Lucknow, Indian Mutiny, 1857.

THE STORY OF THE GUIDES by *G.J. Younghusband*—The Exploits of the famous Indian Army Regiment from the northwest frontier 1847 - 1900.

AVAILABLE ONLINE AT **www.leonaur.com**
AND OTHER GOOD BOOK STORES

www.ingramcontent.com/pod-product-compliance
Lightning Source LLC
Chambersburg PA
CBHW031307150426
43191CB00005B/106